世界上最美丽的英文合集

精读+详解

主 编 樊 玲 常 波
副主编 张 静 沈庆丰 项 群 李雅婷

中山大學出版社
·广州·

版权所有 翻印必究

图书在版编目（CIP）数据

世界上最美丽的英文合集：精读+详解/樊玲，常波主编 .—广州：中山大学出版社，2016.2

ISBN 978-7-306-05240-7

Ⅰ.①世… Ⅱ.①樊… ②常… Ⅲ.①英语—自学参考资料 Ⅳ.①H31

中国版本图书馆 CIP 数据核字（2015）第 056998 号

SHIJIESHANG ZUIMEILI DE YINGWEI HEJI：JINGDU + XIANGJIE

出版人：徐 劲
责任编辑：刘学谦
封面设计：小鸟设计工作室
责任校对：林彩云
责任技编：何雅涛
出版发行：中山大学出版社
电　　话：编辑部 020-84111996，84113349，84111997，84110779
　　　　　发行部 020-84111998，84111981，84111160
地　　址：广州市新港西路135号
邮　　编：510275　传　真：020-84036565
网　　址：http://www.zsup.com.cn　E-mail：zdcbs@mail.sysu.edu.cn
印 刷 者：广东省农垦总局印刷厂
规　　格：889mm×1194mm　1/16　24.25 印张　620 千字
版次印次：2016 年 2 月第 1 版　2017 年 5 月第 2 次印刷
印　　数：3001～5000 册　定　价：29.80 元

如发现本书因印装质量影响阅读，请与出版社发行部联系调换

前言

　　编一部英汉对照的英语美文是一项具有挑战性的工作。只读译文的话，很难欣赏到原文的精妙之处。反之，倘若没有相当的文字基础和文学素养，只读原文，难免似懂非懂，一知半解。读者可以先从原文入手，后读译文以便加深理解，一来可以提高读原著的能力，二来对于学习翻译也很有帮助。这样原文和译文就能相得益彰，对于读者大有裨益。

　　本书的内容和范例如下：

　　一、全书共选编85篇英文美文，分8章。第一章哲理美文，第二章人间有情，第三章人与自然，第四章热门话题，第五章世界名人，第六章灵魂思索，第七章生活艺术，第八章成功凯歌。在内容和题材上，采取精选和博采相结合的办法。体例主要由作者简介、节选原文、原文翻译、文化点滴、写作特点、品味鉴赏和美文感悟组成。

　　二、作者简介主要介绍作家的教育背景、生平事略及主要的创作活动或其在文学史上的影响，并列举其代表作。

　　三、原文绝大多数是独立成篇的。个别文章由于篇幅过长，在基本不损害全篇整体性的前提下，采用节录的办法。

　　四、每篇译文后附一篇品味鉴赏，仅为编者个人的读后感而已，旨在配合译文和注释，帮助读者进一步领会原文。

　　本书面向在校英语专业及非英语专业的学生以及广大英语爱好者。由于编写时间仓促，难免有错误和疏漏之处，所以殷切企盼年轻的莘莘学子和英语界同行们提出宝贵的修改意见和建议，以便本书在修订再版时，可以和编者共同完成一部比较完善的对照文选。

　　本书的音频可以通过封面上的二维码读取，或从出版社网站 (http:www.zsup.com.cn) 下载。

编　者

Chapter 1 哲理美文

1. Life Grows in the Soil of Time
   生命在时间的土壤里成长 ………………………………… 2

2. Walk Clean Around the Hill
   横看成岭侧成峰 …………………………………………… 5

3. I Do a Lot of Office Fishing
   办公室的垂钓者 …………………………………………… 9

4. Discovery in a Thunderstorm
   雷雨中的醒悟 ……………………………………………… 13

5. Fixing up the Run-down Places
   修补破损之处 ……………………………………………… 17

6. I Live Four Lives at a Time
   我的四种生活 ……………………………………………… 21

7. What Makes Me Feel Big
   什么使我胸怀宽广 ………………………………………… 25

8. What Are People Good For?
   人们行善是为了什么？…………………………………… 29

9. Three O' Cat Is Still a Game
   没有我世界照常运转 ……………………………………… 33

10. The World a Reflex of Mental States
    世界源于你的思想 ………………………………………… 37

Chapter 2 人间有情

11. I Will Greet This Day with Love in My Heart
    我要用全身心的爱来迎接今天 ……………………………………… 44

12. A Boy and His Father Become Partners
    父子伙伴情 ……………………………………………………………… 47

13. Not Being Grateful Without Missing
    失去后才懂得珍惜 ……………………………………………………… 50

14. The Value of Friendship
    友谊的价值 ……………………………………………………………… 53

15. I Forgive You
    宽恕 ……………………………………………………………………… 56

16. Wherever You Are
    情暖今生 ………………………………………………………………… 60

17. Please Let Me Have a Little World
    给我一个小小的世界 …………………………………………………… 64

18. Saving a Neighbor's Life
    拯救邻居的生命 ………………………………………………………… 67

19. Letter to His Son
    给儿子的一封信 ………………………………………………………… 71

20. Keeping the Passion of Love Alive
    保持爱的热情 …………………………………………………………… 74

Chapter 3 人与自然

21. Spell of the Rising Moon
    醉人月光 ………………………………………………………………… 78

22. Rural Life in England
    英国的乡村生活 ………………………………………………………… 83

23. Nature and Man in One

　　天人合一 ·· 87

24. Under the Power of Nature

　　在自然威力之下 ·································· 91

25. The Windmill

　　风车 ··· 95

26. Population and Natural Resources

　　人口与自然资源 ·································· 100

27. Significance of Wildlife Protection

　　保护野生生物意义重大 ··························· 104

28. An Afternoon Walk in October

　　十月的下午散步 ·································· 107

29. July

　　七月 ··· 111

30. The Ant-lion

　　蚁狮 ··· 114

Chapter 4 热门话题

31. Low-carbon Cities

　　低碳城市 ··· 118

32. Buying Accommodation

　　购房 ··· 121

33. A Global Economy

　　全球化经济 ······································ 124

34. New Product Development

　　新产品的开发 ···································· 128

35. Happiness Index

　　幸福指数 ··· 133

36. Life-styles of the 21st Century

21世纪的生活方式 ……………………………………………… 138

37. Human Seeks Alien

寻找外星人 ……………………………………………………… 142

38. Home Wreckers

家园正遭破坏 …………………………………………………… 146

39. The "Xiao Yue Yue" Incident as a Source of Complete Despair and a Glimpse of Hope

"小悦悦"事件：彻底的绝望和希望的一瞥 ………………… 151

Chapter 5 世界名人

40. Magic Mama—J. K. Rowling

魔法妈妈——J. K. 罗琳 ……………………………………… 156

41. 10 Lessons Learned from Facebook Founder Mark Zuckerberg

从"脸书"创始人马克·扎克伯格那里学到的10课 ………… 161

42. Starbucks: 19,555 Stores in 58 Countries and Still Growing

星巴克：58个国家的19,555家店面并且还在增长 …………… 167

43. Warren Edward Buffett

沃伦·爱德华·巴菲特 ………………………………………… 172

44. Duty, Honor, Country

责任、荣誉和国家 ……………………………………………… 178

45. Getting to Know Steven Allen Spielberg

认识斯蒂文·阿兰·斯皮尔伯格 ……………………………… 184

46. Nicholas Sparks and His Dear John

尼古拉斯·斯帕克斯和他的《分手信》 ……………………… 189

47. Whitney Elizabeth Houston Remembered

铭记惠特妮·伊丽莎白·休斯顿 ……………………………… 194

48. Oprah Winfrey—Talk Show Queen

奥普拉·温弗瑞——脱口秀女王 ……………………………… 200

49. Andrew Carnegie — the King of Steel

安德鲁·卡内基——钢铁大王 ………………………………… 205

Chapter 6 灵魂思索

50. Expressing One's Individuality
    个性的表现 ································ 212

51. What You See Is the Real You
    你所见到的就是真正的你 ················ 217

52. Have You Seen the Tree?
    你见过那棵树吗? ·························· 222

53. On Doors
    论门 ·· 226

54. The Essay and the Essayist
    散文和散文家 ······························· 230

55. Compting in a Flat World
    无国界竞争 ································· 234

56. A Retrospect
    回首往事 ····································· 239

57. The Goodness of Life
    生命的美好 ································· 244

58. The Grief
    悲怆 ·· 248

59. The "Present"
    今天是一份馈赠 ··························· 253

60. If
    假如 ·· 256

61 My Time and Space
    时空于我 ····································· 260

62. If I Were a Boy again
    假如我又回到了童年 ······················ 264

63. The Death of Moth
    飞蛾之死 ····································· 267

64. Human Happiness Is Sensuous
    快乐是一种感觉 ··························· 273

5

生活艺术

65. A Treatise on Good Manners and Good Breeding
    论礼貌与教养 ·················· 278

66. Change Your Bad Habits to Good
    改掉坏毛病，养成好习惯 ·················· 282

67. Take Your Home into Your Own Hands
    亲手布置自己的家 ·················· 288

68. The Art of Living Simply
    平淡生活的艺术 ·················· 292

69. How Should One Read a Book?
    书应该怎么读？ ·················· 299

70. How to Grow Old?
    如何慢慢变老？ ·················· 303

71. The Two Roads
    两条路 ·················· 307

72. The Lesson of a Tree
    一棵树的启示 ·················· 310

73. The Joys of Writing
    写作的乐趣 ·················· 313

74. Dream Big
    远大理想 ·················· 319

75. Are We Having Fun Yet?
    我们快乐吗？ ·················· 323

成功凯歌

76. Be an Expert in Your Field
    成为本领域的专家 ·················· 328

77. The Challenge to Succeed
   通往成功的挑战 …………………………………………… 332

78. Secrets to Be Ten Great Geniuses
   伟大天才的秘密 …………………………………………… 337

79. The Greatest Salesman in the World
   世界上最伟大的推销员 …………………………………… 343

80. The Strenuous Life
   勤奋的生活 ………………………………………………… 347

81. ELDORADO
   黄金国 ……………………………………………………… 351

82. A Ball to Go Around
   滚球 ………………………………………………………… 356

83. Contemplation on Success
   如何心想事成之苦思冥想篇 ……………………………… 359

84. Self-surpassing
   自我超越 …………………………………………………… 363

85. Five Forms of Wealth
   财富的五个表现形式 ……………………………………… 369

Chapter 1

哲理美文

人生只有3天,昨天是回忆,今天是人生的中心,只有抓紧今天,才能在明天生活得更美好。人生一世,草木一秋。短暂人生,百般滋味,余味绵长……包含着许多痛苦,才有闪亮的年华、光辉的业绩。珍惜生命吧,享受人生的成功与失败、欢乐与痛苦,这都是我们每个人人生中最闪亮的经历,是永恒的回忆。

没有短暂，没有开始与结束，没有生与死，时间也就不复存在。永恒是毫无意义的停滞，它意味着时间永远没有结束，也永远没有开始，绝对令人乏味。

Life Grows in the Soil of Time
生命在时间的土壤里成长

作者简介：

托马斯·曼（Thomas Mann，1875—1955），德国作家。1875 年生于德国北部吕贝克的一个望族。1924 年长篇小说《魔山》的发表，使其誉满全球。20 世纪 30 年代初，托马斯·曼预感到法西斯的威胁，发表了中篇佳作《马里奥与魔术师》（1930），对法西斯在意大利制造的恐怖气氛做了生动的描述。因《布登勃洛克一家》获诺贝尔文学奖。

What I believe, what I value most, is **transitoriness**[1].

But is not transitoriness—the **perishableness**[2] of life—something very sad? No! It is the very soul of existence. It imparts value, dignity, interest to life. Transitoriness creates time—and "time is the essence." Potentially at least, time is the supreme, most useful gift.

Time is related to—yes, identical with—everything creative and active, every process toward a higher goal.

Without transitoriness, without beginning or end, birth or death, there is no time, either. Timelessness—in the sense of time never ending, never beginning—is a **stagnant**[3] nothing. It is absolutely uninteresting.

Life is possessed by tremendous **tenacity**[4]. Even so its presence remains conditional, and as

---

注释
1. **transitoriness** ['trænzɪtərɪnɪs] *n.* 短暂，暂时
2. **perishableness** ['perɪʃəblnɪs] *n.* 腐败性；易朽性
3. **stagnant** ['stæɡnənt] *adj.* 停滞的；不景气的；污浊的；迟钝的

it had a beginning, so it will have an end. I believe that life, just for this reason, is exceedingly enhanced in value, in charm.

One of the most important characteristics distinguishing man from all other forms of nature is his knowledge of transitoriness, of beginning and end, and therefore of the gift of time.

In man transitory life attains its peak of animation, of soul power, so to speak. This does not mean man alone would have a soul. Soul quality pervades all beings. But man's soul is most awake in his knowledge of the **interchangeability**5 of the term "existence" and "transitoriness".

To man time is given like a piece of land, as it were, entrusted to him for faithful tilling; a space in which to strive incessantly, achieve self-realization, more onward and upward. Yes, with the aid of time, man becomes capable of wresting the immortal from the mortal.

Deep down, I believe—and deem such belief natural to every human soul—that in the universe prime significance must be attributed to this earth of ours. Deep down I believe that creation of the universe out of nothingness and of life out of **inorganic**6 state ultimately aimed at the creation of man. I believe that man is meant as a great experiment whose possible failure of man's own guilt would be **paramount**7 to the failure of creation itself.

Whether this belief be true or not, man would be well advised if he behaved as though it were.

原文翻译

短暂是我的信仰，也是我最珍视的东西。

然而短暂，如生命的消逝，不是非常悲哀的事情吗？不！这正是生命存在的精髓。它赋予了生命价值、尊严和情趣。短暂创造了时间——而"时间正是其本质"。至少，时间是至高的，是最有用的礼物。

时间与所有富有创造力和活力的事物，及每一个达到更高目标的进步息息相关——是的，它甚至等同于这一切。

没有短暂，没有开始与结束，没有生与死，时间也就不复存在。永恒是毫无意义的停滞，它意味着时间永远没有结束，也永远没有开始，绝对令人乏味。

生命顽强无比。即便如此，它的存在也依赖于一定的条件，正如它有始亦有终。也因此，我坚信，生命的价值与魅力将会不断地增长。

人同自然界其他事物之间最重要的区别之一就是，人懂得短暂、始与终，所以也了解时间是一种恩赐。

可以这么说，在人身上，短暂的生命达到了其活力与精神力量的巅峰。这并不是说只有人拥有灵魂，万物皆有灵性。但是对于"存在"与"短暂"的可互换性，只有人的大脑才能最清楚地意识到。

对于人类来说，时间就如赐予的一片土地，等待他去辛勤耕种；是一个让他不断奋斗进取，实现自我价值，不断前进向上的空间。是的，在时间的帮助下，人可以从有限的生命中获得永恒。

在内心深处，我相信宇宙中最为重要的当属我们的地球，并认为这样的信念存在于每一个人的心中。从内心深处，我相信混沌中宇宙的创造，无机中生命的萌芽，最终都是为了创造人类。我相信人类本身便是一项伟大的实验，它可能会因人类自身的罪恶而失败，但这也成为创造本身最主要的失败。

无论这个信仰是否真实，人类如果能依此行事，将会获得更为有益的忠告。

注释

4. **tenacity** [tɪ'næsɪtɪ] *n.* 韧性；固执；不屈不挠；黏性
5. **interchangeability** [ˌɪntəˌtʃeɪndʒə'bɪlɪtɪ] *n.* [数] 可交换性，可交替性
6. **inorganic** [ɪnɔː'gænɪk] *adj.* [无化] 无机的；无生物的
7. **paramount** ['pærəmaʊnt] *adj.* 最重要的，主要的；至高无上的

文化点滴

self-realization："自我实现"是美国管理学家、心理学家马斯洛（Abraham Maslow）提出的。所谓自我实现，指的是人都需要发挥自己的潜力，表现自己的才能，只有人的潜力充分发挥出来，人的才能充分表现出来，人才会感到最大的满足。人们除了上述的社会需求之外，还有一种想充分运用自己的各种能力，发挥自身潜力的欲望。

写作特点

本文第二段最后一句"Potentially at least, time is the supreme, most useful gift."使用了隐喻的修辞手法，把时间比作至高的、最有用的礼物。以此物隐喻彼物，将某一事物以另一个与其相似的事物来表达，是一种含蓄的比喻，即隐喻，暗示有比较，但又不充分说出这种比较。如：the key to the mystery（即解开奥秘的方法就像开门的钥匙一样）；the light of knowledge（知识之光）；to have a stone face（表情呆板）；等等。隐喻不用比喻词，但可以用 be 动词或者只用逗号、破折号将本体和喻体连起来。

下面我们来看几个例子：The green plant is a kind of food factory.

绿色植物是一种食物工厂。（把绿色植物说成一种食物工厂。）

The next day he had a very red face.

第二天他非常尴尬。（脸红暗指不好意思。）

Sons are the anchors of a mother's life.

儿子们是母亲生活中的依靠。（把儿子比喻成给人安全感的依靠。）

品味鉴赏

索尔仁尼琴曾经说过："生命最长久的并不是活得时间最多的人。"只要我们好好把握时间，让生活活得有意义、有价值，我们的生命就会长久，我们不要轻易地就放弃生命。生命是美丽的，生命的价值与珍贵是自己认识的问题，生命只给予人一次，人也只能在世上活一次，我们不要让自己的人生碌碌无为。我们在有限的时间里，可以做很多助人为乐的事情。

只要我们珍爱生命，我们就可以得到我们想要的东西。只要我们不荒废自己的生命，这样的生命对我们来说就是有意义的。这样的生命也是长久的。

在我们有限的生活里，我们有很多的不如意，但这也算我们在生命里的一个挫折吧，挫折只会教导我们，不会让我们在朦胧的生命里迷失方向。我们要从乐观的角度去看每一个问题。挫折与痛苦只会引导我们走向光明之路。

美文感悟

从不同角度看待事物,你就能更轻松地抓住生活的精髓;而当你仅从一个角度片面地观察世界时,就很可能会变得愤世嫉俗。

Walk Clean Around the Hill
横看成岭侧成峰

作者简介:

达里尔·F. 柴纳克(Darry Francis Zanuck, 1902—1979),美国作家、制片商、演员及导演,是好莱坞历史上从事电影事业最长的人士之一,曾获得三次奥斯卡奖。

Now that I can look back across the years from the so-called **vantage**[1] point of experience in two World Wars, travel throughout a large part of the world, and contact with many of the outstanding personalities of our time, it gives me a great deal of real **reassurance**[2] each day to know that way down deep I learned some fundamental values when I was a boy in a small town in Nebraska.

I have found one thing to be so very true—the virtues I learned as a boy are still fundamental virtues. My point of view has changed, of course over the years, and so has that of my friends, but so much of all this change of viewpoint is like a small boy **gazing at**[3] a hill on the plains of Nebraska. The hill remains the same. The small boy only sees it from another angle as he grows up.

注释
1. **vantage** ['væntɪdʒ] n. 优势、有利地位
2. **reassurance** [ˌriːəˈʃʊərəns] n. 使安心;再保证
3. **gaze at** 凝视;瞄;注目;盯
4. **in existence** 存在

I have always tried to walk completely around every hill I have found **in existence**[4] since, so that I could get a view from every angle. This, I think, reveals the difference between honesty and **cynicism**[5]. When you see the hill from every angle, you have a much better chance at keeping life in focus. When you only see it from one angle you run the very great danger of becoming **cynical**[6].

Two of the fundamental virtues that have been such a great comfort to me in my life, from the days of my boyhood in Wahoo, Nebraska, until now are loyalty and charity. There are other fundamentals I learned as a boy, but principally loyalty and charity.

Loyalty is not only just a term—it has been a way of life for me. I mean not only loyalty to my friends and family, but to the honest values on which our country was founded. And to me, this **guidepost**[7] of loyalty of necessity means loyalty to one's own self.

When I was growing up, I **rebelled against**[8] so many things, and fought against so many of the basic ideas of life—but I found after so much rebellion and walking completely around that hill on the Nebraska plains, in my mind's eye, that these virtues had not been tested over the centuries **in vain**[9].

Charity is another rule that has been of great comfort to me in so many trying situations. Charity is something you must learn. I have been very lucky in life because I have been in a position to give charity, and one should never expect any other reward from charity that the satisfaction it gives.

In taking part in any charity you must give from your heart. Any other type of giving is a terrible cheat on life itself.

Charity and loyalty are two things that have touched my life very deeply. They have been a source of tremendous satisfaction to me every day I have lived. This rule of loyalty has caused me to check back on the course of my activities **at the close of**[10] each day, to be sure I haven't **knowingly**[11] hurt anyone in my day's activities.

I have tried to repair any hurts I have caused before the day's end. This undoubtedly is very selfish of me because I have learned that this rechecking of each day gives me a good night's sleep.

In walking around the hill on the plain each day of my life, the virtues I see—whether I am in London, Paris, Rome, Cairo, New York, Hollywood or Wahoo, Nebraska—are always the same.

I am grateful for those old-fashioned virtues that I learned as a boy in Nebraska. And I hope I will have enough **humility**[12] always to be thankful I was born in a country that gave me this chance at life.

注释

5. **cynicism** ['sɪnɪ,sɪzəm] *n.* 讥笑，讥讽的言辞；愤世嫉俗；玩世不恭

6. **cynical** ['sɪnɪkəl] *adj.* 怀疑的；愤世嫉俗的；冷嘲的；见利忘义的

7. **guidepost** ['gaɪdpəʊst] *n.* 路标，路牌；指路牌

8. **rebel against** 反抗；反叛

原文翻译

我经历了两次世界大战，环游了世界大部分的地方，接触过很多当代的名人。如今，回想起这些丰富的阅历，我深感欣慰，因为它们肯定了我儿时在内布拉斯加州一个小镇上学到的那些基本价值观。

我发现有一点极为正确——儿时学到的很多美德在今天依然重要。岁月流逝，我和朋友们的想法与观点自然都有所变化，然而这不过是个人看待事物的方式改变了。就好比一个小男孩站在内布拉斯加平原上看山，山没有变，只是随着男孩的长大，他看山的角度发生了变化。

从此，为了从不同的角度看山，我总会试着围绕发现的每一座山走上整一圈。我认为，这就是诚实正直之人与愤世嫉俗者之间的区别。从不同角度看待事物，你就能更轻松地抓住生活的精髓；而当你仅从一个角度片面地观察世界时，就很可能会变得愤世嫉俗。

从我在内布拉斯加州瓦胡镇的童年时代起，直到今天，忠诚与仁爱这两种最基本的美德始终为我的生活带来莫大的慰藉。孩提时，我还学到了其他的一些基本准则，但最重要的还是这两条。

在我看来，忠诚不只是一个简单的词，而是一种生活方式。我所指的并不只是忠于家庭与朋友，还要忠于我们建国的基础，即诚实正直的价值观。我认为，忠诚这一必需的原则也意味着对我们内在自我的忠诚。

成长过程中，我曾几度叛逆，与生活中的很多基本观念背道而驰。但是，多次叛逆后，我想象着自己围绕内布拉斯加平原的那座山走了整整一圈，终于明白这些美德的确经得起时间的考验。

在逆境中给予我莫大安慰的另一个原则是仁爱。这是我们必须学习的美德。生活中的我很幸运，因为我能够乐善好施。行善者不应祈求回报，因为我们从行善中所得到的满足感便是最好的报答。

行善，必须真心诚意。否则，任何形式的给予皆是对生命本身极大的欺骗。

仁爱与忠诚深深感动着我的生命，为我生活的每一天带来极大的满足。每天临睡前，忠诚这一原则都会提醒我反省自己一天的行为，确保当日的所作所为没有为他人带来任何故意的伤害。

每天临睡前，我都会努力为自己对他人造成的伤害予以弥补。这无疑是种自私的行为，因为只有这样，每夜我才不会辗转难眠。

横看成岭侧成峰，人生亦是如此。无论是在伦敦、巴黎、罗马、开罗、纽约、好莱坞还是内布拉斯加的瓦胡镇，我所看到的美德始终不变。

感谢儿时在内布拉斯加学到的那些传统美德。我希望，我能永远对我所出生的这个国家满怀谦恭、心存感激，因为它给予了我生存的机会。

文化点滴

Nebraska：内布拉斯加州是美国中西部的一个州，位于高平原中心，北接南达科他州，南邻堪萨斯州，西接怀俄明州，东隔密苏里河与艾奥瓦州相望，西南与科罗拉多州接壤。居民大部分聚居在密苏里河和普拉特河附近。内布拉斯加州的名称来自美国原住民中的欧图族（Oto），意为"平顺之水（Flat water）"。该州是农业领先的州之一。内布拉斯加州目前致力于发展科学农业技术，企图将大草原里某些地方改变成大型牧场或农场。该州的大部分历史都是由农耕者和垦荒者创造的。

注释

9. **in vain** 白费地；徒劳无益地；无效果的；无用的；机警地
10. **at the close of** 在……结束时
11. **knowingly** ['nəʊɪŋli] adv. 会意地；故意地；狡黠地；
12. **humility** [hjuːˈmɪlɪti] n. 谦逊，谦恭，谦让的行为；谦虚谨慎

写作特点

　　本文使用了重复的修辞手法，重复了关键词 virtue, charity 和 loyalty。重复法作为一种修辞手段，在不同层次、不同场合的交际中屡见不鲜，其目的是达到某种修辞效果，抑或使描写更为生动、诙谐，使音韵更为悦耳、和谐，从美学的角度增添感染力。

　　同一个词在短语或句子中反复出现，起强调和加强语气的作用。这种重复的修辞手法在各种语言各种场合中都被广泛使用，它在英语中占有不可忽视的作用。

　　例如：China! Go, go, go!

　　中国队加油!

　　Government of the people, by the people, for the people shall not perish from the earth.

　　民有，民治，民享的政府永世长存。

品味鉴赏

　　忠诚，这个世界上最美好的字眼之一。自从人类诞生起，它就深深地扎根在我们每个人心底。它没有一条法律的界定，却无处不在；它没有成文的约定，评判的标准又那么清晰。从国家到政党，从社会关系到宗教信仰，从来没有人质疑过它存在的原因，因而是那么容易得到和失去。就像在爱情里，忠诚就像金钱，只有在你没有的时候，你才体会到它曾经在你身边。忠诚这个东西，无关乎对方，无关乎什么关系，它只是你心里最宝贵的东西，最想珍惜、最想呵护的东西。

　　用仁爱去滋养心灵，智慧、勇敢、忠诚等美德就会彰显出来。缺少仁爱的滋养，"智会荡""勇会乱""直会绞""刚会狂"……追问人类的美德：智慧、勇敢、忠诚、尊重等等，它们都植根于仁爱的滋养。用仁爱滋养，人的心灵会显明美德；缺少仁爱的滋养，人的心灵会蔓生恶德。

美文感悟

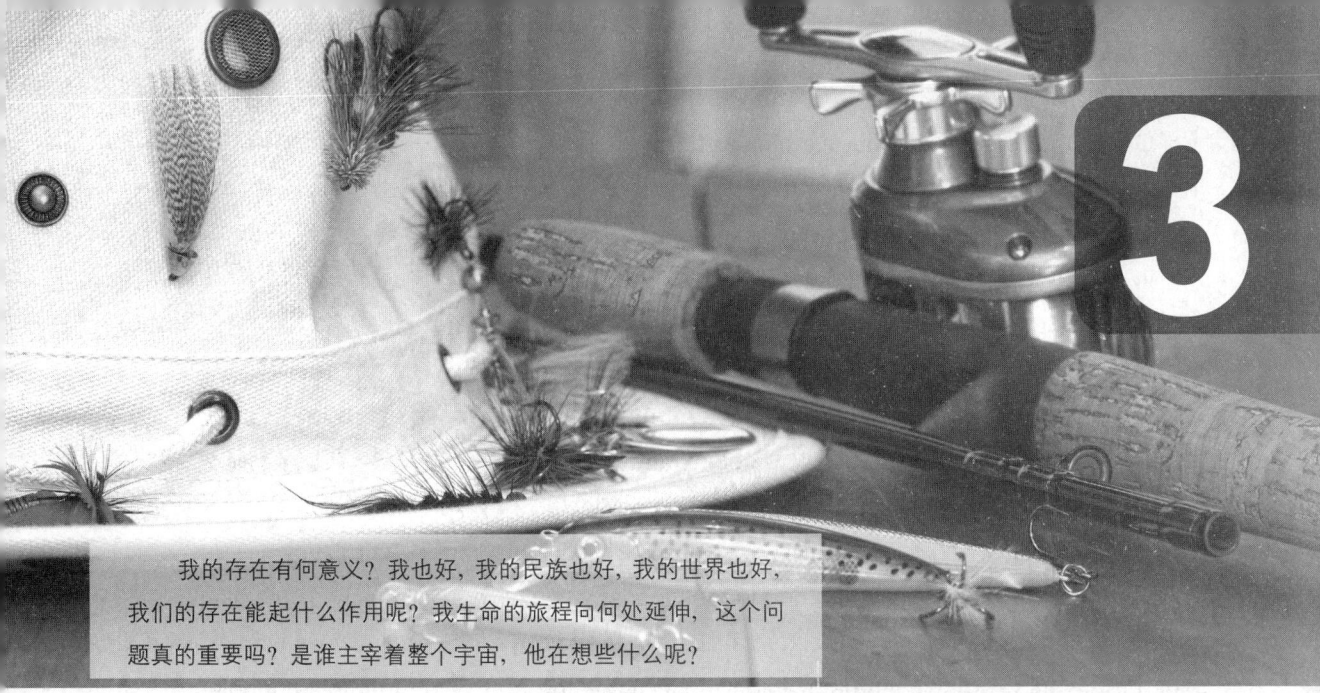

我的存在有何意义？我也好，我的民族也好，我的世界也好，我们的存在能起什么作用呢？我生命的旅程向何处延伸，这个问题真的重要吗？是谁主宰着整个宇宙，他在想些什么呢？

I Do a Lot of Office Fishing
办公室的垂钓者

作者简介：

理查德·萨蒙（Richard Samon），艺术家兼作家。

Some years ago, I started to look at the stars through high-powered **binoculars**[1] and began reading books written by astronomers for people like me. I became an entranced stargazer for a while.

The men who have learned as much as we know about the universe point out that the sun is an insignificant, moderately hot star in a **nebula**[2] where it is fixed. The Milky Way, which I have always wanted to spell "w-h-e-y," is composed of our brothers and sisters, and we are all moving around a central **hub**[3]. And the hub is moving toward some place, I don't know where. My brothers and sisters are numbered in billions of billions, and our galaxy itself is one of many, many…how many, I don't know.

注释
1. **binocular** [baɪˈnɒkjʊlə] n. [常用复数] 双筒望远镜；双目显微镜
2. **nebula** [ˈnebjələ] n. 星云；星云状的星系
3. **hub** [hʌb] n. 轮轴；中心，焦点
4. **offspring** [ˈɒfsprɪŋ] n. 后代，子孙；产物，结果；（动物的）崽；幼苗

Our sun is so small and our earth, its **offspring**⁴, is so tiny that when I think of the **magnitude**⁵, I think of what O.Henry described as a "Statue of What's the Use."

What difference does it make that I exist? What possible influence can I make, or my nation make, or a world make?

Where am I going on this ride and does it make any sense? Who's the boss and what's He got in mind?

That's what I got to thinking…it's all too big, too inevitable, too uncontrollable, and if I think about it with my eyes closed, it's a pretty **pessimistic**⁶ picture.

Then one day I saw a hunting dog in the woods, an English setter flecked with black. His tail tangled with dock burs. This is a common occurrence to guys like me. I always want to stop and pull out the burs. But this time, out of nowhere, came the realization that this bounding, healthy dog was performing an important job: the job of transporting seeds that were constructed for the very purpose of **hitchhiking**⁷. The fluff of milkweed sails on the wind to start a new colony miles from its original parent. This dog and its tangle of dock burs are all part of a plan. And so am I.

I believe the plan on this small, lonely earth is to make the best of it—a policy that is becoming increasingly more difficult as the number of human beings increases.

When I came to New York many years ago, I found that in big cities people live faster and decide things quicker than country folk. They have to, in order to survive in the struggle for existence.

Several times a week I slug it out with city dwellers for a place in the subway. They seem a bad lot. But when I pass a city dweller on a trout stream I find he's just like other people. He'll speak to me with interest, even warmth. He will ask me how many trout I've taken, what fly was successful. And I break down and tell him, and point out that perhaps the black gnat he's using is too large.

I have tried to make the best of it by doing a lot of office fishing, some front porch fishing, and some quiet mulling about the magnificent things such as dock burs and remote stars. What's more, I have found it fun; fun that has brought me a lot of happiness, a lot of contentment, and a lot of peace.

原文翻译

几年前我开始用高倍望远镜观察星空，按自己的想法解释天文学家撰写的天文学入门读物。很快我就迷上了观星。

迄今为止，人类对宇宙的探索表明太阳不过是星云中极为普通的一颗燃烧着的恒星。银河（我总想称其为"星河"）里有许多颗地球的姊妹星球，大家都围绕着同一个轴心旋转，而这个轴心又在向某个我不知道的地方移动。地球是银河系里亿万星球中的一颗，而银河系不过是许多星系中的一个。宇宙中到底有多少星系，我也说不清。

注释

5. magnitude ['mæɡnɪtjuːd] n. 巨大，广大；重大，重要；量级；（地震）级数
6. pessimistic [ˌpesɪ'mɪstɪk] adj. 悲观的，厌世的；悲观主义的
7. hitchhike ['hɪtʃ,haɪk] v. 搭乘；＜美口＞作搭便车式的旅行

太阳在宇宙中是那么微小，太阳的孩子地球则更是微不足道，以至于我一想到地球的分量，就想起欧·亨利说过的那句话——"无用的化身"。

我的存在有何意义？我也好，我的民族也好，我的世界也好，我们的存在能起什么作用呢？

我生命的旅程向何处延伸，这个问题真的重要吗？是谁主宰着整个宇宙，他在想些什么呢？

这是我得思考的问题……一切都那样浩渺无边、无法避免、无法掌控。当我闭上双眼思考这一切时，脑海里便浮现出一幅令人相当悲观的画面。

有一天，我在小树林里看见一只长着黑色斑点的英国种塞特猎犬，尾巴上缠着几根酸模芒刺。这种情况像我这样的人在森林里经常碰到，每次我都会停下来把刺拔掉。可这一次，不知道为什么，我突然意识到这只活蹦乱跳的猎狗身负着一个重要的使命：那就是把芒刺播撒到某个地方，这和司机让陌生人搭个便车是同一道理。芳草花凭借风力离开故土，飘向自己新的家园；而这几根芒刺靠的就是这只猎犬的尾巴。一切在冥冥中自有安排，我也是如此。

我相信微小而孤寂的地球应妥善处理自己的一切——这一原则随着人口增加而越来越难实现。

多年前我初到纽约之时，发现大都市里的生活和办事节奏远比小镇上要快。人们必须如此，方可在激烈的竞争中生存。

我一个星期要挤好几次地铁，满眼所见尽是面目可憎的都市人。但当我在溪边钓鳟鱼碰到一个城里人时，会发现他和其他人并无两样。他会饶有兴致、甚至十分热情地与我聊天，询问我的战果，或是请教关于鱼饵的问题。我也会停下来，提醒他那块黑蠓鱼饵可能得掰小点儿。

就这样，我努力妥善处理一切，在办公室和自家院子里都像在溪边垂钓时一样，多与同事或邻里交流，并常常静下心来体味世间伟大的万物，诸如那几根芒刺，又或是遥远的星辰。这样做乐趣无穷，且让我幸福，让我满足，让我能求得内心的宁静。

文化点滴

O. Henry：欧·亨利（1862—1910）是其笔名，原名为威廉·西德尼·波特（William Sydney Porter）。美国著名批判现实主义作家，世界三大短篇小说大师之一。曾被评论界誉为曼哈顿桂冠散文作家和美国现代短篇小说之父。他的作品构思新颖，语言诙谐，结局常常出人意料。代表作有小说集《白菜与国王》《四百万》《命运之路》等。其中一些名篇，如《爱的牺牲》《警察与赞美诗》《带家具出租的房间》《麦琪的礼物》《最后一片藤叶》等使他获得了世界声誉。

写作特点

本文在第四段和第五段采用了修辞疑问句的写作手法。

What difference does it make that I exist? What possible influence can I make, or my nation make, or a world make?

Where am I going on this ride and does it make any sense? Who's the boss and what's He got in mind?

修辞疑问句作为一种间接言语行为在人际交往中起着极为重要的作用，讲话者借助疑问这一形式表达了他对事件强烈的肯定或否定的态度，因此修辞疑问句实际上是强调的陈述，并且同时引起读者或听者的思考与反思。

更多的例子如下：Why should you listen to him?

你没有必要听他的。

What is this to you?

你甭管，这事与你无关。

Who knows?

天晓得。

Who does not know?

此事尽人皆知。

品味鉴赏

人的一生看似漫长，实则稍纵即逝；但每个人都是自己人生命运的编剧、导演和主角，每个人都有权利将自己的一生演绎得精彩绝伦，因为人的旅程时刻处于"零公里"处，只有时刻追求充实的生活，自己的精神境界才会绽放出绚丽的色彩……

有人说，每个人的生活追求不同，这话有一定道理；追求虽然不同，但需要时时刻刻保持一种平常的心态，如果不能很好地保持平常心态，总是事事看不惯，整天怨天尤人，甭说事业有成，连身心健康也难以保证。著名科学家霍金在微软电脑领域可谓收获颇丰。在他的一次学术报告会上，有人问他："卢伽病已将你永远地固定在轮椅上，你不认为自己命运让你失去太多了吗？"面对突兀而尖锐的提问，霍金先生微笑着从容不迫地用手指击打着键盘说："我的手指还能活动，我的大脑还能思维，我有终身追求的理想，有我爱和爱我的亲人和朋友，对了，我还有一颗感恩的心……"

常言说得好，人生道路坎坷多于平坦，而面对繁杂的生活环境，只有时刻珍惜生活中那如意的十分之一二，你的心境才会得到平衡，才会在无意中享受人生的快乐。

朋友，学会在生活中寻找快乐吧！因为自我寻找快乐也是一种修养、一种心态、一种境界……

美文感悟

暴风雨不会永不停息，任何不适也并非难以容忍。只要勇敢地面对困难，失望而不沮丧，成功而不骄傲，那我们的人生之战便取得了一半的胜利。

Discovery in a Thunderstorm
雷雨中的醒悟

作者简介：

内尔松·格卢克博士（Dr. Nelson Glueck, 1900 —1971）美国犹太法学博士、学者及考古学家。内尔松·格卢克博士从1947年直至去世一直担任希伯来联合学院院长。在《圣经》考古方面进行了开拓性的研究工作，发现了1500多处古代遗址。

Many years ago I was on a bicycle trip through some **exceedingly**[1] picturesque countryside. Suddenly, dark clouds piled up overhead and rain began to fall, but strange to relate, several hundred yards ahead of me the sun shone brilliantly. Pedaling, however, as rapidly as I could, I found it impossible to get into the clear. The clouds with their rain kept advancing faster than I could race forward. I continued this unequal contest for an exhausting half hour, before realizing that I could not win my way to the bright area ahead of me.

Then it **dawned upon**[2] me that I was wasting my strength in unimportant hurry, while paying no attention whatsoever to the landscape for the sake of which I was making the trip. The storm

---

注释
1. **exceedingly** [ɪkˈsiːdɪŋlɪ] *adv.* 非常，极其，特别，十分；极大地；过分地；极度地，极端
2. **dawn upon** 顿悟
3. **entrancing** [ɪnˈtrɑːnsɪŋ] *adj.* 使人神魂颠倒的，使人入神的
4. **turn to account** 利用

could not last forever and the discomfort was not unendurable. Indeed, there was much to look at which might otherwise have escaped me. As I gazed about with sharpened appreciation, I saw colors and lines and contours that would have appeared differently under brilliant light. The rain mists which now crowned the wooded hills and the fresh clearness of the different greens were **entrancing**[3]. My annoyance at the rain was gone and my eagerness to escape it vanished.

It had provided me with a new view and helped me understand that the sources of beauty and satisfaction may be found close at hand within the range of one's own sensibilities.

It made me think, then and later, about other matters to which this incident was related. It helped me realize that there is no sense in my attempting ever to flee from circumstances and conditions which cannot be avoided but which I might bravely meet and frequently mend and often **turn to** good **account**[4]. I know that half the battle is won if I can face trouble with courage, disappointment with spirit, and triumph with humility. It has become ever clearer to me that danger is far from disaster, that defeat may be the forerunner of final victory, and that, in the last analysis, all achievement is perilously fragile unless based on enduring principles of moral conduct.

I have learned that trying to find a carefree world somewhere far off involves me in an endless chase in the course of which the opportunity for happiness and the happiness of attainment are all too I often lost in the chase itself. It has become apparent to me that I cannot wipe out the pains of existence by denying them, blaming them largely or completely on others, or running away from them.

The elements of weakness which mark every person cannot **absolve** me **from**[5] the burdens and blessings of responsibility for myself and to others. I can magnify but never lessen my problems by ignoring, evading or exercising them. I believe that my **perplexities**[6] and difficulties can be considerably resolved, if not completely overcome, by my own attitudes and actions. I am convinced that there can be no guarantee of my happiness except that I help evoke and enhance it by the work of my hands and the dictates of my heart and the direction of my striving. I believe that deep faith in God is necessary to keep me and hold mankind uncowed and confident under the **vagaries**[7] and ordeals of mortal experience, and particularly so in this period of revolutionary storm and travail. If my values receive their sanction and strength from relationship to divine law and acceptance of its ethical imperatives, then nothing can really harm me. "The Lord is my shepherd; I shall not want."

注释

5. absolve ... from... 解除，赦免，宽恕 absolve sb. from sin 赦免某人的罪
6. perplexity [pə'pleksɪtɪ] n. 困惑；混乱；复杂；困难
7. vagary ['veɪɡərɪ] n. 奇想，奇特行为；异想天开；怪异多变

原文翻译

多年前，我曾骑着自行车从一片风景如画的郊野中穿过。突然，乌云密布，大雨滂沱，然而令人惊奇的是，在前方几百码的地方却是阳光灿烂。我蹬着车使劲往前冲，却发现怎么也到不了那片阳光普照之地。乌云夹着大雨比我冲得还快。半小时后，精疲力竭的我停止了这场不公平的抗争，意识到自己根本无法到达那片晴朗的天地。

顿时，我豁然开朗，我在毫不重要的事情上疲于奔波，却不曾欣赏途中的景致，忘记了自己旅行的目的。暴风雨不会永不停息，任何不适也并非难以容忍。的确，我差点错过了途中许多美好的景致。我满怀感激地凝望着眼前的景色，此刻所见的色彩、线条和轮廓比起在阳光下别有一番风味。树木繁茂的山上，烟雨朦胧；别样的绿树清新明朗，令人神迷。大雨带给我的烦恼顿时消散，想要逃离的欲望也不复存在。相反，它带给我一种全新的视觉景观，让我懂得美与满足就源自于我们身边，只要细心发现便能唾手可得。

这次经历从此也引导着我去思考相关的事物。它让我明白，对于无法避免的环境与条件，企图逃避毫无意义，但我可以勇敢面对它们，并常常对其进行修整与改善。我知道，只要勇敢地面对困难、失望而不沮丧，成功而不骄傲，那我们的人生之战便取得了一半的胜利。我也更清楚地意识到，危险远非灾难，而失败也许就是最终胜利的先行者。因此，归根结底，一切成就如果不经受道德准则的考验，就会脆弱不堪，危机重重。

我已经明白，当自己无休止地追寻，试图在遥远之地寻找一个无忧无虑的世界时，也常常会在追寻中错过获得幸福与成就的机会。显然，拒绝承认生存的痛苦，将它们多数或全部归咎于他人，或者逃避，都无法将它消除。

每个人都有不足之处，但我为自己与他人排忧解难和祈求祝福的责任并不能因此免除。我可以将问题放大，却绝不会为缩小问题而忽视、逃避或求助神灵。我相信，通过自己的态度与行为就可解决我的疑惑与难题，即使无法全部克服。我确信，要想使幸福有所保障，接受心灵的指引，就必须靠自己的双手，朝着目标努力奋斗，去创造并积累幸福。我相信，若想在人世间的变幻莫测与严酷考验中，特别是当今革命风暴的艰难时刻，保持无所畏惧与信心十足，就必须对上帝保持虔诚的信仰。如果我的价值观能从其与神律的联系和伦理要求的承诺中获得支持与力量，那任何事物都无法给我造成真正的伤害。"耶和华是我的牧者，我将一无所求。"

文化点滴

"The Lord is my shepherd; I shall not want.": shepherd 意为牧羊人，《圣经》中说，人类是迷失的羔羊，所以在基督教中，神就叫 shepherd。最有名的一句话是：The Lord is my shepherd; I shall not want. 耶和华是我的牧者，我必不至于缺乏（来自《圣经·旧约》）。耶稣这样说：I am the good shepherd. The good shepherd lays down his life for the sheep. 我是好牧人，好牧人为羊舍命。现在教会里服侍人也可以描述他们是 shepherd，寓意为"带领众信徒跟随神"。

写作特点

本文第三段中"I know that half the battle is won if I can face trouble with courage, disappointment with spirit, and triumph with humility."使用了排比的修辞手法。

排比用结构相同或相似、语气一致的词语或句段，以表达相关的内容。

排比的句式匀称，音韵铿锵，一气贯下，其作用在于加强语势，提高表达效果。排比用于叙事，可使语意畅达，层次清楚；用于抒情，能收到节奏和谐、感情奔放的效果。

Their powers of conversation were considerable. They could describe an entertainment with accuracy, relate an anecdote with humour, and laugh at their acquaintance with spirit.

她们的健谈本领真是吓人，描述起宴会来纤毫入微，说起故事来风趣横溢，讥笑起一个朋友来也是有声有色。

By their wit, sense, and eloquence together, they generally contrive to govern their husbands.

她们把风趣、道理和流利的口才一齐用起来，通常可以控制自己的丈夫。

品味鉴赏

人生需要面对的事情太多太多，面对自己，面对亲人，面对工作，面对形形色色的人。人本身就是那么复杂的自热界的产物，我们最难面对的也便是人类自身。怎么办呢？我们是勇于面对还是选择逃避？

相信每个人的心中都会有答案——那就是勇于面对它，与其害怕而不敢去面对倒不如去勇于挑战它，因为挫折是一块试金石，它会很好地让你得到历练，让你发出属于你自己的"光芒"，畏畏缩缩是解决不了问题的，迎头解决才能让你站在人生的更高舞台上。

遇到各种问题，记住，应该多想想如何去解决，而不是怎么逃避。

相信自己！让自己学会去面对各色人，各种事！在磨炼中成长！在挫折中锻炼！在挑战中提高！

美文感悟

_____
_____
_____
_____
_____
_____

事实上,上帝和时间会解决很多问题。上帝眷顾着我们,他让我们懂得世界上善的力量总大于恶的力量,只要我们追随着善,就一定会从我们努力成就的事业中获得更多的快乐和幸福。

Fixing up the Run-down Places
修补破损之处

作者简介:

大卫·达拉斯·琼斯博士(DR.David Dalas Jones),取得卫斯理公会教徒大学、哥伦比亚大学以及霍华德学院的学位,现为美国北卡罗来纳州格林斯博罗市贝内特学院的校长。

Every life **coheres**[1] around certain fundamental core ideas whether we realize it or not. If I were asked to state the ideas around which my life and my life's work have been built, it would seem that they were very simple ideas. An old professor of mine used to say that "effort counts." "The surest thing in the world," he would say, "next to death is that effort counts." This I believe with all my heart. We seldom realize the sense of glow, the sense of growing self-esteem, the sense of achievement, which can come from doing a job well. Just working at a thing with enthusiasm and with a belief that the job may be accomplished, however uncertain the outcome, lends **zest**[2] to life.

注释
1. **cohere** [kəʊ'hɪə] *vi.* 黏合;联合;结合;(指看法、推理等)前后一致
2. **zest** [zest] *n.* 兴趣,热情,风味,滋味,风趣 *v.* 给……调味
3. **run down** 撞倒;走下坡路;诽谤;(使)虚弱
4. **from the outset** 从……开始
5. **integrity** [ɪn'tegrɪtɪ] *n.* 正直,诚实;完整

If I were to start life again, I think I would do just what I have done in the past—this past having been done by mere chance. I would start at some task which very much needed to be done. I would start in a place which was **run down**³ and I would believe with all my heart that if the thing needed to be done and if effort were put into it, results would come for human good.

Too, **from the outset**⁴, my wife and I have had the feeling that no matter what else we did in life, we had to devote our best thinking and our best living to our children. Now that they are all grown, we have sincere satisfaction in the fact that trying to do a job and trying to earn a living did not take away from us this urgency to be and do so that our children could have a feeling of the importance of **integrity**⁵, honesty and straightforwardness in life. It seems to me far too often this is overlooked. We people in public life do the jobs we have to do and fail to save our own children. This second thing is important—doing the task you have to do but beginning at home to bring peace, love, happiness and contentment to those whom God has given you.

The third idea, around which I have tried to live and work, is that there is an overshadowing **Providence**⁶ that cares for one. **Ofttimes**⁷ struggles are too intense, too "eager **beaverish**⁸" when, as a matter of fact, time and God can solve many problems. Never in my life have I gotten away from the idea that God cares and that He provides that the forces of good in the world are greater than the forces of evil and that if we will lend ourselves to those forces, **in the long run**⁹ we have greater joy and happiness in the thing which we try to achieve. This I learned from my mother as a boy. Although she was ill and although we were poor—as poor as people can be—I do not now recall a moment of discouragement in her presence. There was always an overpowering belief that God was in His heaven and that, as Joe Louis said, "God is on our side."

These things I believe with all my heart.

原文翻译

无论我们能否认识到这点，每个人的人生都与某种基础的核心思想密切相连的。倘若有人问我，我的生命与工作基于何种观念？我觉得它们非常简单。"一分耕耘，一分收获。"这是我的一位老教授过去常说的话。他说："除了死亡之外，世界上最确切的事就是'一分耕耘，一分收获'。"我对此深信不疑。我们很少能意识到工作带给我们的乐趣，对我们自尊心的培养，以及给予我们的成就感。只要带着热情去做一件事情，

注释
6. **Providence** ['prɒvɪdəns] n. 深谋远虑；天意，上帝，神的眷顾
7. **ofttimes** ['ɒft,taɪmz] adv. 时常
8. **beaverish** ['biːvə,rɪʃ] adj. （beaver 的变形）工作勤奋的人，埋头苦干的人，兢兢业业的人
9. **in the long run** 从长远来看，终究；一来二去；归根到底

并坚信一定可以完成，无论最终会有怎样的结果，它都会为我们的生活带来激情。

如果再给我一次生命，我想我仍会做过去所做的事——虽然过去所做的一切纯属偶然。我会从急需去做的事情做起，从破损之处做起；我会由衷地相信，只要是必须做的事，只要付出努力，就一定会获得对人类有益的结果。

并且，我和妻子从一开始就认为，无论生活中还有任何什么别的事等待我们去做，我们都必须全身心为孩子们提供最好的生活。如今，他们都已长大成人。我们感到无比满足，我们为生计奔波，努力工作，但都不曾忽略孩子，这样孩子们才能真正明白生活中正直、诚实和坦率的重要性。而我觉得，人们通常都忽略了这些。为了在社会中生存，人们不得不去工作，于是忽略了自己的孩子。然而，后者更为重要——做你必须做的事，但先要把和平、爱心、幸福和满足感带给家中的那些上帝恩赐予你的孩子们。

上天始终眷顾着我，这是维系我的生活与工作的第三个观念。有时，我们会过于积极，过于"急功近利"，而事实上，上帝和时间会解决很多问题。上帝眷顾着我们，他让我们懂得世界上善的力量总大于恶的力量，只要我们追随着善，就一定会从我们努力成就的事业中获得更多的快乐与幸福，这正是我在一生中都不曾背离的一种观念。它们是我儿时从母亲那里学到的。虽然母亲染病在身，虽然我们的生活一贫如洗，但是在我的记忆中，母亲从未有过一刻的气馁。她始终坚信，正如乔·路易斯所说："上帝与我们同在。"上帝就在天堂。

对于这些观念，我是由衷地相信的。

文化点滴

约瑟夫·路易斯·巴罗（Joseph Louis Barrow, 1914—1981），小名乔·路易斯（Joe Louis），外号称"褐色轰炸机"，是一位职业重量级拳击手，被认为是历史上最伟大的重量级拳击手之一，出生在美国斐特，并长期居住在底特律。乔·路易斯维持拳王头衔超过 11 年，并成功卫冕头衔 25 次之多；参加过 27 次重量级冠军战，仍是史上最高纪录并受到许多美国人的喜爱与欢迎。他曾于 1951 年访问台湾，并击败当时台湾最有名的拳王张罗普。

写作特点

本文第四段 "Never in my life have I gotten away from the idea that God cares and that He provides that the forces of good in the world are greater than the forces of evil and that if we will lend ourselves to those forces, in the long run we have greater joy and happiness in the thing which we try to achieve." 使用了倒装的修辞手法。

倒装是故意颠倒句子中正常的或自然的词语顺序。

倒装的作用在于能加强语势，突出重点，协调音节，错综句法。

Afer a brief interval, forth came good Mr. Hooper also, in the rear of his flock.

过了片刻，胡波牧师随着教民也走出来了。

Most true is it that "beauty is in the eye of the gazer."

"情人眼里出西施"，说得对极了。

修补破损之处

品味鉴赏

　　上天对每个人都是公正的，不会因出身的高低贵贱而漠视耕耘者的辛劳，只有那些不畏艰险、风雨无阻、辛苦劳作的人，才有可能到达理想的顶点。天底下没有免费的午餐，天上也不会掉下馅饼来。人生在世，想要有所收获就一定得付出辛劳，正所谓"一分耕耘，一分收获"。

　　古人常云"吃得苦上苦，方为人上人"。想要出人头地、想要实现自己的人生目标，不付出努力是不可能的。正所谓"梅花香自苦寒来，利剑锋从磨砺出"。世间万事都是这样的一个道理：有付出才有收获。能够享受付出的人生，就是能够获得较大成功的人生，也是能够获得更多幸福的人生。

美文感悟

_____
_____
_____
_____
_____
_____
_____

> 我的尝试和成败得失熔铸成一个坚定的信念——绝非仅我一人试图理解与尊重他人。我相信合作与相互关爱正是人类的本性。

I Live Four Lives at a Time
我的四种生活

作者简介：

艾丽斯·汤普森（Alice Thompson）是《十七岁》杂志的发行人及总编，她是美国国家级杂志发行人中第一位、也是唯一的一位女性。

I live a life of four dimensions—a wife, a mother, a worker, an individual in society. Diversified roles, yes; but they are well knit by two major forces: an attempt to discover, understand, and accept other human beings; and a belief in my responsibility toward others. The first began in my childhood when my father and I acted out Shakespeare.

He refused to let me merely parrot Hamlet's **brooding**[1] **soliloquy**[2], Lady Macbeth's sleepwalking scene, or Cardinal Woolsey's self-analysis. He made a fascinating game of helping me understand the motivations behind the poetic words.

In college, a professor further sparked this passionate curiosity about the essence of

---

注释

1. **brooding** ['bruːdɪŋ] adj. 郁闷的；沉思的；徘徊不去的
2. **soliloquy** [sə'lɪləkwiː] n. 自言自语；（戏剧中的）独白
3. **transmute** [trænsˈmjuːt] vt. 使变形，使变质，把……变成……
4. **quota** ['kwəʊtə] n.（正式限定的）定量，定额；配额；指标
5. **anguished** ['æŋɡwɪʃt] adj. 极其痛苦的

others and, by his example, **transmuted**[3] it into a deep concern, a sense of responsibility that sprang not from stern Calvinistic principles, but from an awareness of all I received—and must repay with gladness.

I believe this acceptance, this tenderness one has for others, is impossible without an acceptance of self. Just when or where I learned that the full **quota**[4] of human weakness and strength was the common property of each of us, I don't know. But somewhere in my late twenties, I grew able to admit my own drives—and, rid of the **anguished**[5] necessity of re-costuming them, I was free to face them, and recognize that they were neither unique nor uncontrollable.

The rich and happy life I lead every day brings new witness to the **validity**[6] of my own philosophy, for me. Certainly it works in marriage. Any real marriage is a constant understanding and acceptance, **coupled with**[7] mutual responsibility for one another's happiness. Each day I go out strengthened by the knowledge that I am loved and love.

In the mother-child relationship, those same two forces apply. Words are useless to describe my efforts to know my own children. But my great debt to them for their understanding of me is one I have often failed to repay. How can I overvalue a youngster with the thoughtfulness, the imagination to always phone when a late arrival might cause worry? To always know how to reassure. How can I repay the one who dashed into adulthood far too young but has carried all of its burden with a firm, joyous spirit?

My job itself is a reaffirmation of that by which I live. Very early in my working life, I was a small **cog**[8] in a big firm. Emerging from a tiny job, I found a strange frightening world. Superficially, everyone was friendly. But beneath the surface were raging suspicion, distrust; the hand ever ready to **ward off**[9]—or deliver—the knife in the back. For years I thought I was in a world of monstrous people. Then I began to know the company's president. What he had been I have no way of knowing. But at seventy, he was suspicious, distrusting, sure that no one was telling him the truth. He had developed a technique of pitting all of us against each other. Able to see the distortion he caused, I youthfully declared that if I every ran a business, it would be on the reverse principle.

For the last two years, I have had that opportunity, and had the joy of watching people—widely different people, too—learn to understand each other, accept each other, feel mutually responsible.

My trials and errors have really synthesized into one great belief, which is that I am not alone

注释

6. **validity** [vəˈlɪdɪti] n. 有效，合法性；效力；正确，正当；正确性

7. **couple with** 与……连接在一起

8. **cog** [kɒg] n. 钝齿；雄榫

9. **ward off** 避开，挡住

in my desire to reach my fellow man. I believe the human race is inherently cooperative and concerned about its brother.

原文翻译

　　我在生活中有着四重身份——既为人妻，又为人母，既有自己的事业，又是社会的一分子。是的，角色不同，但配合得很好，因为它们都受两种主要力量的支配：一是努力观察、理解和接受他人，二是对他人尽职尽责。第一种努力早在孩童时代我和父亲一起"出演"莎剧时就开始了。

　　无论是哈姆雷特深沉的独白、麦克白夫人的梦呓，还是伍思里主教的自我剖析，父亲都不让我机械地背诵，而是通过有趣的游戏帮我揣摩诗句中隐含的角色内心活动。

　　在大学时代，一位教授的言传身教进一步引发了我理解他人本质的热忱与好奇，从他身上，我学到了如何将这种热忱与好奇转化为对他人深切的关爱和对他人应负的责任。这种责任心绝非源自卡尔文教派严格的教义，而是源自对我所获得一切的欣然回报。

　　我相信人若不能接受自己，便不可能接受和善待他人。不知从何时何地开始，我意识到每个人都有优点和缺点。在我快满30岁的时候，我学会了承认内心的冲动，而非痛苦地将其掩饰，我泰然自若地应付它们，因为它们乃人之共性，只需善于驾驭。

　　我想我的人生哲学是正确的——我度过的充实而快乐的每一天便是明证。我的人生哲学也适用于婚姻生活，因为真正幸福的婚姻都建立在夫妻之间彼此不断理解和相互接受的基础之上，双方应尽职尽责，让对方幸福。每天我外出工作，知道我的爱得到了回报，便浑身有了力量。

　　这两种力量在母子关系之间也发挥了效用。我为了解孩子们所做出的努力远非文字所能形容，而孩子们对我的理解更让我无以为报。是怎样的想象力、心灵相通和体贴，让一个孩子在母亲迟迟未归时总是打电话确认她的行踪与安危？他用稚嫩的双肩快乐而坚定地担起成人的责任，我要怎样做才能报答这位早熟懂事的孩子？！

　　我的人生信条在工作中也得到了印证。从业之初，我只是一家大公司的无名小卒。我从低微的职位慢慢晋升，发现公司是个十分古怪而可怕的世界。每个人表面上和和气气，暗中却相互猜忌，人人自危，既怕自己背后射来暗箭，又想伺机捅人一刀。几年下来，我觉得公司里每个人都是魔鬼，后来才发现这一切都是总裁一手造成的。他从前为人如何我无从得知，但年已七旬的他满腹狐疑，不相信任何人，觉得所有人都在欺骗他，便运用手段挑起员工之间的争斗。明白了他何以使人心扭曲，年轻的我暗下决心：他年我若自行创业，一定运用完全相反的原则。

　　两年前我终于有机会自立门户，有了观察人的工作。我看到各种不同的人如何学会相互理解和接受，对彼此尽责。

　　我的尝试和成败得失熔铸成一个坚定的信念——绝非仅我一人试图理解与尊重他人。我相信合作与相互关爱正是人类的本性。

文化点滴

　　威廉·莎士比亚（William Shakespeare，1564—1616年，华人社会亦常尊称其为莎翁）是英国文学史上最杰出的戏剧家，也是西方文艺史上最杰出的作家之一，全世界最卓越的文学家之一。

写作特点

　　本文结构安排清晰、缜密，使用了总—分—总的写作技巧。作者开篇阐述了自己所过的四种生活：妻子、母亲、工作者及社会中的一分子，四个角色能很好地配合，因为它们都受两种主要力量的支配：一是努力观察、理解和接受他人，二是对他人尽职尽责；然后在后面的篇章里依次分别详述了这两种主要的力量在作者所过的这四种不同生活中是如何发挥作用的，以及作者从中得到的不同体会和感悟；最后在文章的末尾进行总结，得出结论：合作与相互关爱正是人类的本性。

品味鉴赏

　　我们的生活就是"理解万岁"的时代，无论你是给别人打工还是自己单干，都会遇到多方面的压力与不快，当我们还处在不满之情与无谓的抱怨之时，请停下我们的脚步，静下心来，冷静地想想"换位思考，理解他人"这句话的真正含义，并非只是口头上说说这样简单。为了自己美好的未来和成功的事业而多一分理解与宽容吧！

　　理解与宽容是一种良好的心态，就是用一颗悲天悯人的爱心，平静地接受所遇到的困难与烦恼，宽容别人的人其心胸像天空一样广阔透明。有一颗宽广的心，才能容下天地万物；有一颗平静的心，才能鉴别人性中的弱点，洞察人内心的波谲云诡，才能具有清浊并蓄、化浊为清的能力。

　　理解与宽容是最美丽的一种情感，他们懂得站在别人的角度去看问题，把别人的感受当作自己的去感同身受，首先替别人着想，容忍别人和自己不同的地方，容忍别人的缺点和过失，不追究、不计较自己的利害得失，试着帮助对方改正缺点和过失，慢慢地趋向完美。

　　　　理解与宽容是对亲人的理解、对爱人的体谅、对朋友的忍让，是一种高尚的情操！胸宽的人，会以宽容的态度包容他人的错误，甚至不注重个人的得失，它能够寻求化解矛盾冲突的办法，把自己变得豁然开朗，并且自己也能够得到别人的理解与宽容。

美文感悟

> 并非所有坚定的真理都是美好的,但"美即是真"。所有伟大的艺术都追求这样的目标,即美融合爱,也被爱所融合。它无处不在,唾手可得。

What Makes Me Feel Big
什么使我胸怀宽广

作者简介:

J. 弗兰克·多比(J.Frank Dobie, 1888-1964),美国以西南部历史及民俗的著作著称的历史学家,著作有《一个灌丛地区的骑马牧人》《郊狼之声》和《长角牛》。

"My mind is big when I look at you and talk to you," Chief Eagle of the Pawnees said to George Bird Grinnell when, after years of absence, that noble writer appeared at his friend's **tepee**[1].

It is very difficult in drawing up a **credo**[2] to be severely honest about one's self, to avoid all traditional cant. We actually believe in what we value most. Outside of the realms of **carnality**[3] and property, which men appearing in public generally pretend not to notice, I believe in and draw nourishment from whatever makes me feel big.

I believe in a Supreme Power, unknowable and impersonal, whose handiwork the soul-

注释	1. **tepee** ['ti:pi:] n.(兽皮或树皮制的)圆锥帐篷	4. **firmament** ['fɜ:məmənt] n. 天空,苍穹
	2. **credo** ['kri:dəʊ] n. 信经,信条	5. **credulity** [krɪ'dju:lɪtɪ] n. 轻信,易受骗
	3. **carnality** [kɑː'nælɪtɪ] n. 淫荡	6. **budge** [bʌdʒ] vt.&vi.(使)稍微移动;(使)改变主意

enlarging **firmament**[4] declares. However, I believe in questionings, doubtings, searchings, skepticism, and I discredit **credulity**[5] or blind faith. The progress of man is based on disbelief of the commonly accepted. The noblest minds and natures of human history have thought and sung, lived and died, trying to **budge**[6] the **status quo**[7] towards a larger and fuller status.

I am sustained by a belief in evolution—the increasing purpose of life in which the rational is, with geological slowness, evolving out of the irrational. To believe that goodness and wisdom and righteousness, in Garden of Eden perfection, lie somewhere far ahead instead of farther and farther behind, gives me hope and somewhat explains existence. This is a long view. I do not pretend that it is a view always present in me. It does raise me when I have it, however.

I feel no resentment so strongly as that against forces which make men and women afraid to speak out forthrightly. The noblest satisfaction I have is in witnessing the up movement of suppressed individuals and people. I make no pretense to having rid myself of all prejudices, but at times when I have discovered myself freed from certain prejudices, I have felt rare **exhilaration**[8].

For me, the beautiful resides in the physical, but it is spiritual. I have never heard a sermon as spiritual in either phrase or fact as, "Waters on a starry night are beautiful and free." No **hymn**[9] lifts my heart higher than the morning call of the bobwhite or the long fluting cry of sandhill cranes out of the sky at dusk. I have never smelled incense in a church as refining to the spirit as a spring breeze laden with aroma from a field of bluebonnets.

Not all hard truths are beautiful, but beauty is truth. It incorporates love and is incorporated by love. It is the goal of all great art. Its presence everywhere makes it free to all. It is not so abstract as justice, but beauty and intellectual freedom and justice, all incorporating truth and goodness, are constant **sustainers**[10] to my mind and spirit.

原文翻译

在离开朋友波尼族印第安人首领雄鹰的兽皮帐篷几年后，作家乔治·伯德·格林又回到那里。这位首领对他高尚的朋友说："凝视着你，与你交谈，让我感到心胸宽广。"

我们很难为自己拟出一个既能严格遵守又能避免传统教条的信念。事实上，我们最为珍视的东西便是我们的信仰。除了人们在公共场合总会假装视而不见的俗念与财产之外，所有能让我胸怀宽广的都是我的信仰、

注释

（使）让步；（立场等）动摇

7. status quo [ˈsteɪtəsˈkwəʊ] n. 现状

8. exhilaration [ɪɡˌzɪləˈreɪʃən] n. 愉快的心情，高兴；

9. hymn [hɪm] n. 赞美诗；圣歌 vt. 唱赞歌；赞美

10. sustainer [səsˈteɪnə] n. 支持者，维持者，主动动机；主级发动机

它们是我力量的源泉。

我相信有一种至高无上且无法控制的未知力量,它的创造,宣告了灵魂拥有无限伸展的空间。然而,我也相信询问、质疑、探索与怀疑,但拒绝轻信或盲从的信仰。人类的进步是基于对普遍接受的质疑。人类历史上,拥有最高尚思想的人们曾经思考过、歌唱过、生活过,最终离去,他们也曾努力扩展并充实现状。

我始终相信进化论,即生活目的在不断增加,而其中从非理性到理性的进化时间就像地质变化一样漫长。我相信,伊甸园中完美的善良、智慧与正义就在遥远的前方,给予我希望,并或多或少地解释了生存的意义。这是一个长远的观点。我不会假装认为,自己始终拥有这样的观点。然而,当我拥有它时,我的灵魂的确得到了升华。

使人不敢坦诚言论的势力,是我最为憎恨的。当看到受压迫的个人与民族奋起反抗时,我便会心生敬慕,感到满足。我并不伪称自己已经摒弃了所有的偏见,但有时当我发现自己摆脱了某些偏见时,我就会狂喜不已。

我认为,美虽然存在于肉体,但却属于精神。我从未听说过,有哪句布道词能从言辞或事实上表现出这样的精神美:"夜晚繁星点点,湖水自由荡漾。"北美鸠清晨的鸣唱或黄昏时天空中沙丘鹤笛鸣般的长吟,是任何赞美诗都无法媲美的。柔和的春风中弥漫着田野间矢车菊的芳香,让我的灵魂也更加高尚,这是教堂中任何焚香都无法比拟的。

并非所有坚定的真理都是美好的,但"美即是真"。所有伟大的艺术都追求这样的目标,即美融合爱,也被爱所融合。它无处不在,唾手可得。它不像正义那样抽象,但美、心智的自由及正义,都与真与善融合,这便是我思想与精神的永恒支柱。

文化点滴

Pawnees:(北美)波尼族印第安人。

George Bird Grinnell:乔治·伯德·格林(1849—1938),美国人类学家、历史学家、自然主义者及作家。

写作特点

本文在第四段中的"To believe that goodness and wisdom and righteousness, in Garden of Eden perfection, lie somewhere far ahead instead of farther and farther behind, gives me hope and somewhat explains existence."使用了对照的修辞手法,ahead 和 behind 形成对比。

对照把两种对立的事物或者同一事物的两个不同方面放在一起,互相比较。

运用对照,或使对立事物的矛盾鲜明突出,揭示本质,给人深刻启示;或使事物对立的两个方面互相映衬,相得益彰,给人深刻印象。

To be prepared for war is one of the most effectual means of preserving peace.

准备战争是维护和平的一种最有效的方法。

Let us never negotiate out of fear, but let us never fear to negotiate.

让我们永不因畏惧而谈判,但让我们永不要畏惧谈判。

品味鉴赏

"美即是真,真即是美"中的"真"指的是现实,即被保存下来的能够获得永恒的现实;"美"指的是基于现实但又超越现实的永恒之美。在这种意义上,"美"就是"真","真"即是"美",是同一个概念的两个不同侧面。"真"强调现实和永恒,现实因而永恒,"美"强调的魅力,是使现实的瞬间成为永恒。本身不能凭空创造美,但可以保存"美",使在现实中不能永久的美得以永恒。

美文感悟

我们可以选择面对生活的方式。当我们选择正直、坚韧、尊严与同情时,任何不幸的威胁都无法影响到我们。

What Are People Good For?
人们行善是为了什么?

作者简介:

艾娜·科琳娜·布朗(Irak.Brown, 1896—1984),教师,出生在美国德克萨斯州,著有《美国黑人故事》《民主制度下的种族关系》及《理解他国文化》。

One's beliefs are revealed not so much in words or in formal creeds as in the assumptions on which one habitually acts and in the basic values by which all choices are tested.

The cornerstone of my own value system was laid in childhood with parents who believed that personal integrity came first. They never asked, "What will people think?" The question was, "What will you think of yourself, if you do this or fail to do that?" Thus, living up to one's own conception of one's self became a basic value, and the question, "What will people think," took a **subordinate**[1] place.

A second basic value, in some ways an extension of the first, I owe to an old college

注释
1. **subordinate** [sə'bɔːdɪnɪt] *adj.* 级别或职位较低的;下级的;次要的;附属的
2. **fortitude** ['fɔːtɪˌtjuːd] *n.* 坚韧,刚毅;刚毅精神
3. **transcend** [træn'send] *vt.* 超越,超出……的限度;优

professor, who had suffered more than his share of grief and trouble. Over and over he said to us, "The one thing that really matters is to be bigger than the things that can happen to you. Nothing that can happen to you is half so important that the way in which you end it."

Gradually I realized that here was the basis of the only really security and peace of mind that a human being can have. Nobody can be sure  when disaster, disappointment, injustice, or humiliation, may come to him through no fault of his own. Nor can one be guaranteed against one's own mistakes and failures. But the way we meet life is ours to choose. And when integrity, **fortitude**[2], dignity, and compassion are our choice, the things that can happen to us lose their power over us.

The acceptance of these two basic values led to a third. If what one is and how one meets life are of first importance, one is not impressed by another's money, status, or power, nor does one judge people by their race, color, or social position. This opens up a whole new world of relationships, for when friendships are based on qualities of mind and character, one can have friends among old and young, rich and poor, famous and unknown, educated and unlettered, and among people of all races and all nations.

Given these three basic values, a fourth became inevitable. It is one's duty and obligation to help create a social order in which persons are more important than things, ideas more precious than gadgets, and in which individuals are judged on the basis of personal worth. Moreover, for this judgment to be fair, human beings must have an opportunity for the fullest development of which they are capable. One is thus led to work for a world of freedom and justice through those social agencies and institutions which make it possible for people everywhere to realize their highest potentialities.

Perhaps all this adds up to a belief in what has been called the human use of human beings. We are set off from the rest of the animal world by our capacity consciously to **transcend**[3] our physical needs and desires. Men must concern themselves with food and with other physical needs, and they must protect themselves and their own from bodily harm, but these activities are not exclusively human. Many animals concern themselves with these things. When we worship, pray, or feel compassion, when we enjoy a painting, a sunset or a **sonata**[4], when we think and reason, pursue ideas, seek truth, or read a book, when we protect the weak and helpless, when we honor the noble and cherish the good, when we cooperate with our fellow men to build a better world, our behavior is worthy of our status as human beings.

注释　于或胜过……

4. sonata [sə'nɑːtə] n. <音> 奏鸣曲

Chapter 1 哲理美文

原文翻译

人类的信仰并非全是通过言辞或形式的教条，以及对一个人行为习惯的设想或其做出选择所依据的价值观所体现出来的。

孩提时，父母的教诲正是我个人基本价值观的来源，他们相信人格是一切之首。他们从不问："人们会怎么想？"而是问："如果你做这件事而不做那件，你会怎么想？"因此，按自己的意愿生活便成为最基本的价值观，而"人们会怎么想？"这个问题则退居二线。

从某种程度上来说，第二条基础价值观就是对第一条的延伸，这是我从一位大学老教授那里了解到的。他所遭受的不幸与痛苦比常人要多得多。他不止一次地告诉我们："你要比发生在你身上的苦难更为强大；面对不幸的态度比你所遭受的不幸更为重要。这一点很重要。"

慢慢地，我了解到，这正是人类拥有真正安全感与平和心态的基础。即使自己并无任何过错，也没人确切地知道，灾难、失望、不公或羞辱何时会降临到自己的头上，而且也没人敢保证自己不会犯错、不会失败。但是，我们可以选择面对生活的方式。当我们选择正直、坚韧、尊严与同情时，任何不幸的威胁都无法影响到我们。

当你接受了前两条基本的价值观，也就能够接受这第三条。如果一个人坚持自我以及自己的生活方式，那他就不会为他人的金钱、地位与权利所动，也不会以人们的种族、肤色或社会地位来评价他们。全新的人际关系世界就此开启了。因为，当友谊基于思想与人品时，老人与青年、富人与穷人、名人与普通人、受过良好教育的人、目不识丁者，以及不同种族、不同民族的人们都能够成为你的朋友。

有了上面三条基本的价值观，第四条自然就无法避免。它是一个人协助创造社会秩序的责任与义务。在这个社会秩序中，人比物重要，思想比精巧的器具重要，个人的价值是以人的基本原则为基础的。此外，为保证这个评判的公正，人类必须有机会全面发展自身的能力。于是，社会组织与机构便致力于使世界各地的人们认识到他们最大的潜能，并引导人们为创造一个自由公平的世界而工作。

也许，所有这一切加起来就形成了一种信仰，那就是人类如何实现自我价值。我们人类之所以优于动物，是因为人拥有自觉控制自身需求与欲望的能力。人类必须考虑食物与自身的需求，必须保护自身与亲人不受伤害，但是这些行为并不只限于人类。很多动物都拥有这方面的本能。当我们膜拜、祈祷或感动时，当我们欣赏画作、夕阳或奏鸣曲时，当我们思考推理、追随灵感、寻求真相或阅读一本书时，当我们保护弱者与无助的人时，当我们尊敬高尚的人、心怀行善的愿望时，当我们为建设更美好的世界与他人合作时，我们的行为才使我们无愧于"人类"这个称呼。

写作特点

本文最后一段的末尾使用了排比的修辞手法："When we worship, pray, or feel compassion, when we enjoy a painting, a sunset or a sonata, when we think and reason, pursue ideas, seek truth, or read a book, when we protect the weak and helpless, when we honor the noble and cherish the good, when we cooperate with our fellow men to build a better world, our behavior is worthy of our status as human beings."起到了加强语势的作用。

She was taken with his good looks, his well-cut clothes, his voice, his gaiety.

她完全为他的堂堂仪表、裁剪精美的衣服、说话的声音以及他那欢快的性格所陶醉。

品味鉴赏

人世间最宝贵的是什么？雨果说得好：善良。"善良是历史中稀有的珍珠，善良的人几乎优于伟大的人。"美国作家马克·吐温称善良是一种世界通用的语言，它可以使盲人"看到"、使聋子"听到"。善良的心，像真金一样闪光，像甘露一样纯洁、晶莹。善良的心胸是博大、宽宏的，能包容宇宙万物，造福于人类苍生。行善而不求回报的人经常能够得到意料之外的回馈，这是因果循环的自然规律。善良之人经常造福于他人，实质上也是造福于自己。"帮助别人，就是帮助自己。"这句话绝不只是简单的因果报应，而是做人的根本。

让善良与生命同在，对于人来讲是莫大的福分。生命中有了善良，人生才能经常充满喜悦；生命中有了善良，人生才能幸福常在；生命中有了善良，灵魂才能不断得到升华。善良是生命中的黄金，善良是人性中最为宝贵的生命之光。珍惜善良，呵护善良，用善良铸造一个民族的魂魄，让善良举托一个民族的辉煌。

美文感悟

当我有能力做一件事，有人也希望我做时，我就必须去做。不为人所需是人生中最大的悲剧。只要你有能力并愿意为人们做一些事，人们就会需要你。你肯定能够做到，那就不要推辞。

Three O' Cat Is Still a Game
没有我世界照常运转

作者简介：

莉莲·比诺·麦丘（Lillian Bueno Mccue, 1902—1993），生于美国纽约，研究领域为19世纪英国文学，写过多部著名的长篇小说，若干篇短篇小说和12部戏剧。

What do I believe? What laws do I live by? There are so many answers—work, beauty, truth, love—and I hope I do live by them.

But in everyday things I live by the light of a supplementary set of laws. I'd better call them **rules of thumb**[1]. Rules of thumb aren't very grand, but they do make the wheels go round.

My father and mother sent me to good schools, but the finest thing they did for my education was to have seven children. I was the oldest, and my brothers and sisters were my best teachers.

I learned first to **pull my own weight**[2] in the boat. Kids making a **bob-sled**[3] have no use for

---

注释　1. **rule of thumb** 凭感觉的方法；单凭经验的方法；经验法则；拇指规则　　2. **pull one's own weight** 努力做好分内的工作　　3. **bob-sled** n. 长橇

the **loafer**[4] who wants a free ride. Neither has the world. I learned to make the bed I slept in, and wash the glass I used, and mend what I broke, and **mop up**[5] where I spilled. And if I was too lazy or too **dainty**[6] or too busy, and left it for someone else, somebody else soon taught me different.

Then, the same way, I learned that anger is a waste. It hurts nobody but me. A fit of the sullens got short shrift in our house. It wasn't pulling my weight in the boat. It was spoiling sport. And among seven children it got me nowhere. It might reduce four o'cat to three o'cat, but the game went on just the same, and where was I? Out of it. Better go in and join the group around the piano and forget my grievance. Better still, next time don't **fling down**[7] my bat in a **tantrum**[8]; keep my temper, and stay in the game.

Here's a rule thumb that's important, and the older I get, the more important I think it is. When I can do something, and somebody wants me to do it, I have to do it. The great tragedy of life is not to be needed. As long as you are able and willing to do things for people, you will be needed. Of course you are able; and if so, you can't say no. My mother is seventy-seven. In seventy-seven years she has never said no. Today she is so much in demand by thirteen grandchildren and countless neighbors that her presence is eagerly contended for. When I want to see her I have to pretend emergency.

Then there's the rule of curiosity. Your body would die if you stopped feeling hunger and thirst, and your mind will die if you lose your curiosity. This I learned from my father. My father was a naturalist. He could see the beetle under the bark, and draw it forth unharmed for us to **squint at**[9] through the magnifying glass. He sampled the taste of thirty-three different caterpillars. Fired by his example, once, my sister ate an ant. In case you are wondering, caterpillars taste like the green leaves they eat, and ants taste of lemon. I personally haven't tasted any **entomological**[10] specimens lately, but I am still rejoicing in the limitless curiosity that draws me to books and people and places. I hope I never lose it. It would be like pulling down the blind.

Finally, there is the rule of happiness. Happiness is a habit. I was taught to cultivate it. A big stomach-ache, or a big heart-ache, can interrupt happiness, but neither can destroy it unless I permit. My mother simply wouldn't have unhappy faces **moping about**[11] the place. If it was stomach-ache, she does it. If it was heart-ache, she administered love and understanding and lots of interesting things to do, and soon the sun came out again. Even the heartbreaks that can't really be mended, even those seem to **yield to**[12] the habit of finding happiness in doing things, in love and in the memory of love. I hope I never lose that habit either. It would be like putting out the light.

注释

4. **loafer** ['ləʊfə] n. 虚度光阴者；游手好闲者；无业游民；平底便鞋

5. **mop up** 做扫尾工作；擦；抹；痛击

6. **dainty** ['deɪntɪ] adj. 精致的；娇俏的；（指人）品位高雅的；难以取悦的

7. **fling down** 挑战；把……扔下；罢工；使迅速卧倒

So I learned to live, by the great laws, and these little rules of thumb. I wouldn't take a million dollars for any one of them, or a million times that for the years at home that taught them to me.

原文翻译

什么是我所信仰的？什么是我生活的准则？答案很多，比如工作、美丽、真理、爱心，但愿我能以它们为准则。

然而，生活中的我还履行着另外一套附加的法则，即经验法则。这一法则虽然简单，但却能使事情顺利地进行下去。

父母把我送到一所很好的学校学习，但养育了7个孩子，才是他们为我的教育做得最好的事。我是家中长女，而弟弟妹妹就是我最好的老师。

我最先学会了身为长女的责任。对一个想搭顺风车的流浪者来说，会做雪橇的孩子毫无用处。对这些孩子而言，世界也是如此。我学会了睡觉前自己铺床，洗自己用过的杯子，修补自己弄坏的东西，用拖布拖干自己溅到地上的水。如果我过于懒惰、挑剔或忙碌，而让别人来做这些事，马上就会有人教我不能这么做。

于是，我同样也明白了生气于事无补。除了我自己，它伤害不了任何人。在我们家里，闷闷不乐是不会有人搭理你的。尽管不是我的责任，但却会让人觉得扫兴。何况在7个孩子中间生闷气对我并没有好处。没有我，"四只小猫"的游戏变成"三只小猫"，一样可以玩得很好。而我呢？只能被排除在外了。最好的办法就是，忘掉自己的委屈，加入他们，和大家一起围着钢琴玩。还有，最好下次不要再乱发脾气；控制好自己的情绪，继续玩游戏。

此外，还有一条经验法则同样重要。随着慢慢长大，我也越来越认识到它的重要性。当我有能力做一件事，有人也希望我做时，我就必须去做。不为人所需是人生中最大的悲剧。只要你有能力并愿意为人们做一些事，人们就会需要你。你肯定能够做到，那就不要推辞。我的母亲已经77岁了。但77年来她从未说过"不"字。如今，她的13个孙儿和无数的邻居依然很需要她，希望她能在身边。因此当我想见她时，不得不假装有紧急的事情。

除此之外，还有好奇法则。当你感觉不到饥饿和干渴时，你的身体就停止运转了；如果你失去了好奇心，那你的思想就不再工作了。这是父亲传授给我的。他是一位博物学家。他能看到树皮下的甲虫，并把它毫发无伤地捉下来，放在放大镜下让我们看。他尝过33种不同毛虫的味道。有一次，在父亲的示范与鼓励下，妹妹吃了一只蚂蚁。假如你对它们的味道感到好奇，我会告诉你，毛虫的味道就像它们所吃的树叶，而蚂蚁的味道像柠檬。我个人最近并未品尝任何昆虫的标本，但我仍欣喜于自己无限的好奇心，它促使我博览群书、乐于与人交往和四处旅行。我希望永远拥有好奇心。没有它，就仿佛放下了窗帘，让我无法欣赏到窗外的美景。

最后，还有幸福法则。幸福是一种习惯。我学会了去养成这种习惯。剧烈的胃痛与心痛都会阻碍幸福，但没有我的允许，它们绝对无法破坏幸福。母亲不愿意看到家中有人闷闷不乐。如果有人胃痛，母亲会给他吃药；如果是心痛，她会给予爱和理解，并做很多有趣的事让他忘记痛苦，重新展露笑颜。即使心碎了，无法再修补，即使有人习惯在工作、爱与爱的回忆中寻找幸福，我也希望我永远不会将这一习惯丢弃。拥有它，就仿佛点亮了生命的明灯。

因此，我学会了生活，并遵循着伟大的定律与这些琐碎的经验法则。即使给我100万美元，也换不去它们中的任何一个；或者即使给我无尽的时间，也无法交换那些让我懂得这些法则的家中岁月。

注释

8. tantrum ['tæntrəm] n. 突然发怒；〈口〉发脾气
9. squint at 斜眼看
10. entomological [ˌentəˈmɒlədʒɪkəl] adj. 昆虫学的
11. mope about <贬>忧郁地闲荡
12. yield to 让步于；使自己受到……的支配（使）陷入；接替

写作特点

本文第四段的"I learned first to pull my own weight in the boat."使用了隐喻的修辞手法，用"boat"来暗喻作者应该承担的责任。

隐喻在两类不同的事物（本体和喻体）之间含蓄地比较，以表明相同关系的比喻。

隐喻不用喻词联结本体和喻体，有时甚至本体和喻体词都不出现，直接由喻体代替本体。

Life's but a walking shadow.

人生不过是一个行走的影子。

The ship spread its wings to the breeze.

那条船迎风展翅。

品味鉴赏

好奇心对一个人来说非常重要，因为它会成为一个人积极的动力，会对周围的事物产生浓厚的兴趣，会去专心研究自己感兴趣的内容。因为专心会喜爱，喜爱会在人的心里产生一种积极的意识，这种意识是人努力的动力。因为作为个人而言，他心里明白自己的目标及努力的方向，他会努力弥补自身的不足，并以积极的态度对待新的知识，不会停下学习的脚步，学习成为一个人的乐趣，如一日三餐一样平常，他明白学习是为自己。

好奇心使一个人充满了活力，这活力给自己的生命增添了许多色彩，从而更加热爱自己的生命，会珍惜自己的时间，合理利用每分每秒，让生命更加有意义。好奇心对一个人来说是不能缺少的。人人都知道学无止境的意义，而好奇心是人学习的动力。让我们更加健康快乐地生活，也是一件很美的事情。

美文感悟

一个人懦弱还是英勇，愚蠢还是聪明，烦躁还是平静，内心决定了他的精神状态，而与外界没有丝毫关联。环境对你的影响取决于你对环境的克制程度。

The World a Reflex of Mental States
世界源于你的思想

作者简介：

詹姆斯·艾伦（James Allen，1864-1912）被誉为 20 世纪人文科学领域的神秘者。1864 年出生于英国莱斯特。《做你想做的人》是詹姆斯·埃伦最重要的作品之一，它奠定了整个西方成功学的基础，极大地影响了包括戴尔·卡耐基和拿破仑·希尔等在内的成功学大师。《做你想做的人》与卡耐基《人性的弱点》、希尔《积极心态的力量》并列为世界三大励志经典，被誉为"人类文坛上最闪亮的钻石之一"。

What you are, so is your world. Everything in the universe is resolved into your own inward experience. It matters little what is without, for it is all a reflection of your own state of consciousness.

It matters everything what you are within, for everything without will be mirrored and colored accordingly.

All that you positively know is contained in your own experience; all that you ever will know must pass through the gateway of experience, and so become part of yourself.

Your own thoughts, desires, and aspirations comprise your world, and, to you, all that there is

---

注释
1. **mar** [mɑː] *vt.* 毁坏，损坏；弄糟；糟蹋；玷污
2. **sordid** [ˈsɔːdɪd] *adj.* 肮脏的；污秽的；卑鄙的；邋遢的
3. **despondent** [dɪˈspɒndənt] *adj.* 沮丧的，泄气的；
4. **debilitating** [dɪˈbɪlɪteɪtɪŋ] *adj.* 使衰弱的

in the universe of beauty and joy and bliss, or of ugliness and sorrow and pain, is contained within yourself.

By your own thoughts you make or **mar**[1] your life, your world, your universe. As you build within by the power of thought, so will your outward life and circumstances shape themselves accordingly.

Whatsoever you harbor in the inmost chambers of your heart will, sooner or later by the inevitable law of reaction, shape itself in your outward life.

The soul that is impure, **sordid**[2] and selfish is gravitating with unerring precision toward misfortune and catastrophe; the soul that is pure, unselfish, and noble is gravitating with equal precision toward happiness and prosperity.

Every soul attracts its own, and nothing can possibly come to it that does not belong to it. To realize this is to recognize the universality of Divine Law.

The incidents of every human life, which both make and mar, are drawn to it by the quality and power of its own inner thought-life. Every soul is a complex combination of gathered experiences and thoughts, and the body is but an improvised vehicle for its manifestation.

What, therefore, your thoughts are, that is your real self; and the world around, both animate and inanimate, wears the aspect with which your thoughts clothe it.

"All that we are is the result of what we have thought. It is founded on our thoughts; it is made up of our thoughts." Thus said Buddha, and it therefore follows that if a man is happy, it is because he dwells in happy thoughts; if miserable, because he dwells in **despondent**[3] and **debilitating**[4] thoughts.

Whether one be fearful or fearless, foolish or wise, troubled or **serene**[5], within that soul lies the cause of its own state or states, and never without. And now I seem to hear a chorus of voices exclaim, "But do you really mean to say that outward circumstances do not affect our minds?" I do not say that, but I say this, and know it to be an infallible truth, that circumstances can only affect you in so far as you allow them to do so.

You are swayed by circumstances because you have not a right understanding of the nature, use, and power of thought.

You believe (and upon this little word belief hang all our sorrows and joys) that outward things have the power to make or mar your life; by so doing you submit to those outward things, confess that you are their slave, and they your unconditional master; by so doing, you invest them with a power which they do not, of themselves, possess, and you succumb, in reality, not to the mere circumstances, but to the gloom or gladness, the fear or hope, the strength or weakness, which your thought-sphere has thrown around them.

注释
5. serene [sɪ'riːn] *adj.* 平静的；安详的；清澈的；晴朗的 侈的
6. grumble at 抱怨
8. pulsating [pʌl'seɪtɪŋ] *adj.* 脉动的；脉冲的；搏动的
7. superfluous [suː'pɜːfluəs] *adj.* 多余的；不必要的；奢

I knew two men who, at an early age, lost the hard-earned savings of years. One was very deeply troubled, and gave way to chagrin, worry, and despondency.

The other, on reading in his morning paper that the bank in which his money was deposited had hopelessly failed, and that he had lost all, quietly and firmly remarked, "Well, it's gone, and trouble and worry won't bring it back, but hard work will."

He went to work with renewed vigor, and rapidly became prosperous, while the former man, continuing to mourn the loss of his money, and to **grumble at**[6] his "bad luck", remained the sport and tool of adverse circumstances, in reality of his own weak and slavish thoughts.

The loss of money was a curse to the one because he clothed the event with dark and dreary thoughts; it was a blessing to the other, because he threw around it thoughts of strength, of hope, and renewed endeavor.

If circumstances had the power to bless or harm, they would bless and harm all men alike, but the fact that the same circumstances will be alike good and bad to different souls proves that the good or bad is not in the circumstance, but only in the mind of him that encounters it.

When you begin to realize this you will begin to control your thoughts, to regulate and discipline your mind, and to rebuild the inward temple of your soul, eliminating all useless and **superfluous**[7] material, and incorporating into your being thoughts alone of joy and serenity, of strength and life, of compassion and love, of beauty and immortality; and as you do this you will become joyful and serene, strong and healthy, compassionate and loving, and beautiful with the beauty of immortality.

To the many, the ocean is but a dreary expanse of water on which ships sail and are sometimes wrecked; to the soul of the musician it is a living thing, and he hears, in all its changing moods, divine harmonies.

Where the ordinary mind sees disaster and confusion, the mind of the philosopher sees the most perfect sequence of cause and effect, and where the materialist sees nothing but endless death, the mystic sees **pulsating**[8] and eternal life.

原文翻译

你的内心世界如何决定着你生活的好坏。宇宙中的一切事物都源于你的内心体验。外界的影响微乎其微，因为这完全是你内心意识的一种反映。

你的思想影响着所有错综复杂的关系，因为外界的事物会如实、具体地反映着你的内心世界。

同样的道理，你所掌握的知识都是从以前的经历中得来。你每一点知识的积累，一定要经历时间的验证，最终才造就了如今的你。

你的世界是由你自己的思想、愿望和热情塑造的，对你来说，这个世界是环境优美，到处欢声笑语、祝福不断，还是丑陋破旧，周围唉声叹气、痛苦不堪。这些早已印刻在你的思想中了。

你可以用自己的思想改变或毁灭你的生活，你的世界，甚至你的宇宙。正是因为你用自己的思想塑造了自我，你周围的生活与环境也会相应地变化。

在无法阻挡自然规律下，无论如何，你的内心深处都要坚持梦想，那么总有一天你会美梦成真。

动机不纯、肮脏、自私的灵魂一直与不幸和灾难藕断丝连，而真诚、无私、高贵的灵魂则与幸福和美好息息相关。

每个人的灵魂都是与众不同的，没有什么其他的灵魂能够与之为伍。

创造也好，毁灭也罢，个人内心世界的品质和力量决定了人生所经历的每一件事情。每个人的灵魂都是个人的经验积累与思想的复杂结合体。我们的身体仅仅为实现思想而时刻准备着的工具而已。

所以你心中的所思所想，才是一个真实的自我。无论是一片欣欣向荣，还是郁郁寡欢，你周围的世界都是穿着你思想的外衣。

一个人胆怯还是英勇，愚蠢还是聪明，烦躁还是平静，内心决定了他的精神状态，与外界没有丝毫关系。现在我似乎听见很多人提出异议："可是，你真的是想说外部的环境不会影响你的内心世界吗？"我绝对没有这个意思，我所强调的是客观存在的真理，环境对你的影响取决于你对环境的控制程度。

你的心情由于环境的变化而摇摆不定，那是因为你没有正确地理解思想的本性、用途和力量。

你相信周围的环境拥有成就或毁坏你生活的力量（这简单的词汇决定了你的快乐与悲伤），那样的话，你便会屈服于环境的支配；那样的话，你便会承认自己是环境的奴隶，你成了绝对服从的人；那样的话，你便赋予了环境原本不属于它的权利。实际上，你不仅屈从了环境，更重要的是放弃了自己思想的出发点，放弃了选择悲伤或快乐、恐惧或希望、优点或弱点。

我有两个朋友，一把年纪时失去了含辛茹苦多年而积攒的储蓄。面对这样的困境，其中一个人从此一蹶不振，并陷入了无尽的愤懑、担忧与失望之中。

而另一个人在读早报时，才发现存钱的那家银行倒闭了，自己将分文皆无。他只是镇定而坚定地说道："既然已经没了，烦恼与忧愁也不会将损失挽回来，还是继续努力工作挽回损失吧！"

精神焕发的他再次全身心地投入到工作中去，不久以后便又成了有钱人。而前者还在为失去的钱而悲痛不已，并不停地抱怨自己的坏运气。他依然迷失在艰难的处境里，而这都是自己软弱而卑微的思想造成的。

对前者来说，失去全部金钱意味着最恶毒的诅咒，因为他会用阴暗、悲观的情绪去对待这件事情；不过，对后者而言，失去了全部金钱却无异于一种恩赐，因为他从中学到了坚强，拥有了希望与重新焕发的力量。

假如环境拥有足够的力量去祝福或摧毁我们的生活，那么它应该一视同仁。然而现实生活中，相同的境遇却产生了两种截然相反的思想——积极的思想和消极的思想。由此可见，在遇到某种境遇后，一个人心境好坏不在于环境，而仅仅在于人们内心不同的反映。

当你认识到这个道理，你就可以掌握自己的思想，调节并训练自己的思想。最终重塑灵魂的宫殿，彻底驱除所有华而不实、没有价值的思想，并让快乐与平静、生命与活力、爱心和怜悯围绕在你的身边。

在大多数人看来，广阔无垠的大海不过是既可以让船只航行，又可以让其颠覆而已。然而在音乐家的眼中，大海却是活生生的，他可以倾听大海变化多端的情绪，还有一种美妙和谐的韵律。

普通人只看得到灾难与不幸，而哲人头脑中却预见了理想的因果关系；相同的道理，实物主义者的眼中除了无尽的死亡，别无他物，神秘主义者却能体会到永恒跳动的生命。

品味鉴赏

一个人的处境是苦是乐，其实是自己的主观意志所决定的。有人安于某种生活，有人不能。因此，能安于自己目前处境的不妨就如此生活下去，不能的只好另找出路。

苦乐全凭自己判断，这和客观环境并不一定有直接关系，正如一个不爱珠宝的，即使置身在极其重视虚荣的环境，也无伤他的自尊。拥有万卷书的穷书生，并不想去和百万富翁交换钻石或股票。乐于田园生活的人，也并不艳羡任何学者的荣誉头衔或高官厚禄。

Chapter 1 哲理美文

美文感悟

Chapter 2

人间有情

爱情、亲情、友情是人类永恒的话题,这三者始终伴随着我们的一生。

我赞美敌人，敌人于是成为朋友；我鼓励朋友，朋友于是成为手足。我要常想理由赞美别人，绝不搬弄是非，道人长短。想要批评人时，咬住舌头，想要赞美人时，高声表达。

I Will Greet This Day with Love in My Heart
我要用全身心的爱来迎接今天

作者简介：

奥格·曼狄诺（Auger Mandinuo，1924—1996）是当今世界撰写自我帮助方面书籍最流行最有灵感的作家。他著有14部书，销量超过3000万册，被译成18种语言。成千上万的来自生活中各行各业的人们，都盛赞奥格·曼狄诺改变了他们的生活，他们从他的书中得到了神奇的力量。他的书充满智慧、灵感和爱心。他的著作包括：《世界上最伟大的奇迹》《世界上最伟大的推销员》《世界上最伟大的成功》等。

    I will greet this day with love in my heart. For this is the greatest secret of success in all **ventures**[1]. Muscle can split a shield and even destroy life but only the unseen power of love can open the hearts of men. I will make love my greatest weapon and none can defend against its force.

    And how will I do this? **Henceforth**[2] will I look on all things with love and I will be born again. I will love the sun for it warms my bones; yet I will love the rain for it cleanses my spirit. I will love the light for it shows me the way; yet I will love the darkness for it shows me the stars. I will welcome happiness for it enlarges my heart; yet I will endure sadness for it opens my soul. I will **acknowledge**[3] rewards for they are my due; yet I will welcome obstacles for they are my

---

注释
1. **venture** ['ventʃə] n. 企业；风险；冒险
2. **henceforth** ['hensfɔːθ] adv. 今后；从此以后
3. **acknowledge** [əkˈnɒlɪdʒ] vt. 承认；答谢
4. **applaud** [əˈplɔːd] vi. 喝彩；鼓掌欢迎

challenge.

And how will I speak? I will laud my enemies and they will become friends; I will encourage my friends and they will become brothers. Always will I dig for reasons to **applaud**[4]; never will I scratch for excuses to gossip. When I am tempted to criticize I will bite on my tongue; when I am moved to praise I will shout from the roofs.

Is it not so that birds, the wind, the sea and all nature speak with the music of praise for their creator? Cannot I speak with the same music to his children? Henceforth will I remember this secret and it will change my life.

And how will I act? I will love all manner of men for each has qualities to be admired even though they are hidden. With love I will tear down the wall of suspicion and hate which they have built round their hearts and in its place will I build bridges so that my love may enter their souls.

I will love the ambitious for they can inspire me! I will love the failures for they can teach me. I will love the kings for they are but human; I will love the meek for they are divine. I will love the rich for they are yet lonely.

I will love the poor for they are so many. I will love the young for the faith they hold; I will love the old for the wisdom they share. I will love the beautiful for their eyes of sadness; I will love the ugly for their souls of peace.

But how will I react to the actions of others? With love, for just as love is my weapon to open the hearts of men, and love is also my shield to **repulse**[5] the arrows of hate and the spears of anger. Adversity and discouragement will beat against my new shield and become as the softest of rains.

And how will I confront each whom I meet? In only one way—In silence and to myself I will address him and say "I Love You". Though spoken in silence these words will shine in my eyes, unwrinkled my brow, bring a smile to my lips, and echo in my voice; and his heart will be opened.

原文翻译

我要用全身心的爱来迎接今天。因为，这是一切成功的最大秘密。强力能够劈开一块盾牌，甚至毁灭生命，但是只有爱才具有无与伦比的力量，使人们敞开心扉。在掌握了爱的艺术之前，我只算商场上的无名小卒。我要让爱成为我最大的武器，没有人能抵挡它的威力。

我该怎样做呢？从今往后，我对一切都要满怀爱心，这样才能获得新生。我爱太阳，它温暖我的身体；我爱雨水，它洗净我的灵魂；我爱光明，它为我指引道路；我也爱黑夜，它让我看到星辰。我迎接快乐，它使我心胸开阔；我忍受悲伤，它升华我的灵魂；我接受报酬，因为我为此付出汗水；我不怕困难，因为它们给我挑战。

注释　**5. repulse** [rɪˈpʌls] *vt.* 拒绝；驱逐；憎恶

我该怎样说呢？我赞美敌人，敌人于是成为朋友；我鼓励朋友，朋友于是成为手足。我要常想理由赞美别人，绝不搬弄是非，道人长短。想要批评人时，咬住舌头；想要赞美人时，高声表达。

飞鸟，清风，海浪，自然界的万物不都在用美妙动听的歌声赞美造物主吗？我也要用同样的歌声赞美她的儿女。从今往后，我要记住这个秘密，它将改变我的生活。

我该怎样行动呢？我要爱每个人的言谈举止，因为人人都有值得钦佩的性格，虽然有时不易察觉。我要用爱摧毁困住人们心灵的高墙，那充满怀疑与仇恨的高墙。我要铺就一座通向人们心灵的桥梁。

我爱雄心勃勃的人，他们给我灵感。我爱失败的人，他们给我教训。我爱王侯将相，因为他们也是凡人。我爱谦恭之人，因为他们非凡。我爱富人，因为他们孤独。

我爱穷人，因为穷人太多了。我爱少年，因为他们真诚。我爱长者，因为他们有智慧。我爱美丽的人，因为他们眼中流露着凄迷。我爱丑陋的人，因为他们有颗宁静的心。

我该怎样回应他人的行为呢？用爱心。爱是我打开人们心扉的钥匙，也是我抵挡仇恨之箭与愤怒之矛的盾牌。在我用爱铸成的盾牌面前，挫折变得如春雨般温和。

我该怎样面对遇到的每一个人呢？只有一种办法，我要在心里默默地为他祝福。这无言的爱会闪现在我的眼神里，流露在我的眉宇间，让我嘴角挂上微笑，在我的声音里响起共鸣，他的心扉才会向我敞开。

写作特点

本文第二段、第六段和第七段用到了排比的修辞手法，使其行文非常工整有气势。

品味鉴赏

我们要用全身心的爱来迎接今天，迎接未来。因为我们是为了希望而活着，为了有意义、有价值的人生而奋斗，我们的思想应该如同这灿烂的阳光一样明媚，我们的生命应该如同这翠绿的树木一样充满活力，我们的心灵应该如同路边的鲜花一样美丽。

爱身边的每一个人，包括朋友也包括敌人，因为心里充满爱，敌人也将变为朋友。最主要的是我们要爱自己。只有这样，我们才会认真检查我们的思想、精神、头脑和灵魂。

美文感悟

父爱是严肃、刚强而且博大精深的。父爱同母爱一样伟大，只是父亲表达爱的方式不同而已。

A Boy and His Father Become Partners
父子伙伴情

作者简介：

拉尔夫·穆迪（Ralph Muddy，1898—1982），美国作家，著有17部小说及自传，大部分情节或背景都涉及美国西部。

I like all kinds of chocolate. Best of all, though, I like bitter baking chocolate. Mother had bought a bar of it, and **somehow**[1] I couldn't stop thinking about it.

I was helping father on the **winnower**[2]. It was right then I got the idea. I could **whack**[3] a chunk off the end of that bar of chocolate. Mother would be sure miss it, but before she had any idea who had done it, I could confess I'd taken it. Probably I would not even get a spanking.

I waited until mother was out feeding the chickens. Then I told father I thought I'd go in for a drink of water. I got the bar down but I heard mother coming just when I had the knife ready to whack. So I slipped the chocolate into the front of my shirt and left quickly. Before I went back

注释
1. **somehow** ['sʌmhaʊ] *adv.* 以某种方法；莫名其妙地
2. **winnower** ['wɪnʊəə] *n.* 风车，扬谷器
3. **whack** [wæk] *vt.* 重击；猛击
4. **corral** [kəˈrɑːl] *n.* 畜栏

to help father, I went to the barn and hid the chocolate there.

I told myself that I hadn't really stolen the whole bar of chocolate, because I meant to take only a little piece. If I put back the whole bar, I wouldn't have done anything wrong at all.

I nearly decided to put it all back. But just thinking so much about chocolate made my tongue almost taste the smooth bitterness of it. I got thinking that if I slice about half an inch of the end with a sharp knife mother might never notice it.

I was nearly out to where the cows were when I remembered what father had said once—some of the family money was mine because I had helped to earn it. Why wouldn't it be all right to figure the bar of chocolate had been bought with my own money? That seemed to fix everything.

That night I couldn't sleep. At last I got up, slipped out into the yard, and took the ax from the chopping block. Then I went into the barn and got the chocolate. I took it outside and laid it on the lower rail of the **corral**[4] fence. The moon gave enough light for me to see what I was doing.

Just as I was starting cut, father said, "Son!"

I couldn't think of a thing to say. I grabbed up the bar of chocolate and hid it next to my chest before I turned around. Father picked me up by the shoulder straps of my overalls and took me over to the woodpile. I didn't know anybody could spank as hard as he did!

Then he stood me on my feet and asked if I thought I had deserved it. He said it wasn't so much that I'd taken the chocolate, but that I'd tried to hide it from him.

"Son," he said, "I know you help to earn the family money. We might say the chocolate was yours in the first place. You could have had it if you'd asked for it, but I won't have you being sneaky about things. Now, do you want to keep your money separate from mine—or are we partners?"

I never knew till then how much I wanted my money to go in with Father's. When I went to sleep my hand was still hurting from where he squeezed it when we shook hands.

原文翻译

我喜欢各种各样的巧克力，不过我最喜欢那种做糕点用的无糖巧克力。妈妈买了一块这种巧克力，我不知怎么总在不停地打它的主意。

我在帮爸爸扬谷，这时我突然有了个主意，我可以从那块巧克力的一头敲下一块来。妈妈肯定会发现丢了巧克力，但在她意识到这件事是谁干的之前，我可以先承认是我偷吃的，也许连屁股也不会挨打。

我一直等到妈妈出去喂鸡，然后我对爸爸说我要回屋去喝口水。我拿到那块巧克力，但正当我准备用刀切的时候，我听见妈妈进屋的声音，所以就悄悄把巧克力塞进我衬衫的硬衬胸中，赶紧溜出房间。在我回去帮爸爸干活之前，我走进谷仓把巧克力藏在那里。

我对自己说，我并不真的要偷整块巧克力，我只想弄那么一小块。如果我把整块巧克力放回去的话，那我就根本没干过什么错事了。

我几乎已经决定把它完整无损地放回去了。但是，我对巧克力的向往使我的舌头似乎尝到它那绝妙的味道。我一再想，假如我用快刀从它的一头切下半英寸，妈妈或许不会注意到它的。

我快走进牛群的时候，突然记起了爸爸曾经有一次讲过的话——家里的钱有我一份，因为我已帮着家里挣钱了。为什么不可以说这块巧克力是用我自己的钱买来的呢？看来一切都说得过去。

那天晚上，我怎么也睡不着。最后，我翻身下床，悄悄溜到院子里，从劈柴墩上抓起一把斧头，然后我进入谷仓把巧克力拿了出来。我把它拿到外面，搁在牛厩篱笆的下面横栏上。月光足以使我看得清要干的事。

就在我动手要切巧克力时，爸爸叫道："孩子！"

我不知道说什么好，转身之前我抓起这块巧克力，把它藏进胸前的衬衫里。爸爸抓住我工装服上的背带，把我拎到柴堆那里。我不晓得还有谁打屁股像他打得那样狠！

然后他叫我站直，问我这是不是我应得的惩罚。他说我拿走巧克力不算什么，但不该瞒着他。

"孩子，"他说，"我清楚你帮家里挣了钱，可以说巧克力本来就是你的。要是你坦率地要它，你本可以得到它的，但我不允许你做事偷偷摸摸的。现在你是想把你的钱和我的分开呢，还是与我结成伙伴呢？"

直到这时，我才知道我是多么想把我的钱和爸爸的合在一起。我去睡觉时，我的那只手——我们握手时父亲曾用力握过的地方——还在痛呢。

品味鉴赏

如果说，母亲给予的爱是温柔乡，那么父爱就是避风港，父亲的情感也许表达得没有母爱细腻，但同样包含着深情款款，教会我如何面对人生道路上的种种境遇。父亲的爱总是无言的，严肃的，在当时往往无法细诉。然而，它让你在往后成长的日子里越体会越觉得幸福，满满的一辈子难忘。父亲的爱是一缕阳光，让我们的心灵即使在严寒的冬天也感受得到温暖；父亲的爱是一泓清泉，让我们即使在情感受挫时即使蒙上岁月的风尘依然纯洁明净。父爱，是我们人生旅途中的一盏明灯，在我们迷路时，照亮我们的行程。

美文感悟

千万别在错过月亮的时候哭泣,那么,你连星星也错过了。也千万别在失去后才懂得珍惜,让我们从现在起,好好珍惜眼前的一切,不要等到失去后才后悔,才懂得珍惜啊!

Not Being Grateful Without Missing
失去后才懂得珍惜

All of us have read thrilling stories in which the hero had only a limited and specified time to live. Sometimes it was as long as a year; sometimes as short as twenty-four hours, but always we were interested in discovering just how the doomed man chose to spend his last days or his last hours. I speak, of course, of free men who have a choice, not condemned criminals whose sphere of activities is strictly **delimited**[1].

Such stories set up thinking, wondering what we should do under similar circumstances. What associations should we crowd into those last hours as mortal beings? What happiness should we find in reviewing the past, what regrets?

Sometimes I have thought it would be an excellent rule to live each day as if we should die tomorrow. Such an attitude would emphasize sharply the values of life. We should live each day with gentleness, vigor, and keenness of appreciation which are often lost when time stretches

注释
1. **delimited** [dɪˈlɪmɪtɪd] *adj.* 划定界限的;被限定了的
2. **panorama** [ˌpænəˈrɑːmə] *n.* 全景,全貌;全景画;概论
3. **chasten** [ˈtʃeɪsn] *vt.* 惩罚;磨炼;抑制
4. **listless** [ˈlɪstlɪs] *adj.* 倦怠的;无精打采的;百无聊赖的

before us in the constant **panorama**[2] of more days and months and years to come. There are those, of course, who would adopt the epicurean motto of "Eat, drink, and be merry", most people would be **chastened**[3] by the certainty of impending death.

Most of us take life for granted. We know that one day we must die, but usually we picture that day as far in the future, when we are in buoyant health, death is all but unimaginable. We seldom think of it. The days stretch out in an endless vista. So we go about our petty task, hardly aware of our **listless**[4] attitude towards life.

The same **lethargy**[5], I am afraid, characterizes the use of our faculties and senses. Only the deaf appreciate hearing, only the blind realize the manifold blessings that lie in sight. Particularly does this observation apply to those who have lost sight and hearing in adult life. But those who have never suffered impairment of sight or hearing seldom make the fullest use of these blessed faculties. Their eyes and ears take in all sights and sound hazily, without concentration, and with little appreciation. It is the same old story of not being grateful without missing.

原文翻译

我们都读过一些令人兴奋激动的故事，故事的主人公只能再活一段很有限的时光。有时长达一年，有时却短至 24 小时。但是，在探究这个将要离世的人选择怎样度过他最后岁月的问题上，我们都充满兴趣。当然，我说的是有选择权利的自由人，而不是死刑犯。死刑犯的活动范围是受严格限制的。

这样的故事使我们思索，如果我们自己处在相似的情况下，应该做什么？临死之时，什么样的事情、体验、关系该被放入最后的时光中呢？回忆往昔，什么使我们快乐开心？什么又使我们悔恨抱憾呢？

有时，我常这样想，每天活得要像明天即将死去一样，这或许是一个非常好的规则。这样的态度可以鲜明地强调生命的价值。我们应该活得优雅从容、朝气蓬勃、观察敏锐，而这些将会日复一日、月复一月、年复一年慢慢丢失。当然，也有一些人一生只是"吃、喝、享受"；然而，大多数人在得知死亡的确存在时都会有所收敛。

我们大多数人认为活着是理所当然的。我们知道总有一天要面对死亡，但总认为那一天还在遥远的将来。当我们身强体健时，死亡好像是不可想象的，我们很少考虑它，日子多得好像没有尽头。因此，我们一味忙于琐事，却没意识到这种对待生活的态度太盲目。

我担心同样的冷漠也存在于我们对自己所有官能和意识的使用上。只有聋子感激欣赏听力，只有瞎子体会得到看见事物的乐趣。这种研究特别适合那些在成年时丧失了视力与听力的人。而那些从未体会过丧失视力和听力之苦的人们，很少能充分使用这些美好的官能。他们心不在下焉，也不太感兴趣，用眼睛和耳朵模

注释   5. lethargy ['leθədʒɪ] n. 昏睡；死气沉沉；嗜睡（症）

糊地看着和听着周围的一切。正如人们不知道珍惜自己拥有的，直到失去了才明白它的价值一样，人们只有在病的时候，才意识到健康的好处。

品味鉴赏

  生命是一个过程，可悲的是它不可以重来，可喜的是它也不可能重来。生命中很悲哀的事就是当你遇到一个对你来说意味很多的人，但你，只是在未来才发现，而这时你已无力回天。人，往往就是这样，得到的东西不懂得珍惜，失去后才知道它的珍贵。于是，漫漫人生，有多少人这样喟叹：覆水难收，后悔莫及。阳光雨露，鸟语花香，对每一个人都公平给予；欢乐喜悦，烦恼忧伤，却属于个别人私有。生命总是美丽的，不是苦恼太多，只是我们不懂生活；不是幸福太少，只是我们不懂把握。曾经有不少人问我同样的一个问题：为什么人总等到失去后才懂得珍惜？

  人总是在失去后才懂得珍惜！有许多人不懂得珍惜身边的一切，总是在失去后才会后悔。人的一生会遇到许多人，她／他也许是你生命中的一段插曲。拥有不该拥有的，拥有是一种失落，失去是一种收获。世界好大，值得珍惜，为什么感情的砝码就只加在一个人的天平上？没有错误的感情，而是在感情中你有没有爱对人，是在感情中你有没有珍惜过。拥有一段美好的旋律也够了，不是所有的人都可以拥有的，要会珍惜，就算只剩下回忆。当你真正地失去以后，才后悔，才遗憾，原来已经失去了那么多。但世上没有后悔药，走过的路，做过的事情，只能留作自己的回忆。也许会很伤感，很难过。但是一切已经注定，努力去挽回她／他，挽回这段感情。如果当自己无能为力了，那就洒脱地放开手，学会放弃。

美文感悟

亲密而相互信任的朋友彼此坦诚相待，他们觉得安心，不会被戏弄或嘲笑，他们的彼此信任令人尊敬，背信弃义会使友谊迅速而痛苦地终结。友谊会日渐深厚，其纽带也会随之更加坚固。密切的关系丰富了人们的生活。使友谊茁壮成长的一些要素是诚信、朴实、慎重和某些共同兴趣。

The Value of Friendship
友谊的价值

Friendship is both a source of pleasure and a component of good health. People who have close friends naturally enjoy their company. Of equal importance are the concrete emotional benefits they derive. When something sensational happens to us, sharing the happiness of the occasion with friends intensifies our joy. Conversely, in times of trouble and tension, when our spirits are low, unburdening our worries and fears to compassionate friends alleviates the stress. Moreover, we may even get some practical suggestions for solving a particular problem.

Adolescence[1] and old age are the two stages in our lives when the need for friendship is crucial. In the former stage, teems are plagued by uncertainty and mixed feelings. In the latter stage, older people are upset by feelings of uselessness and insignificance. In both instances, friends can make a dramatic difference. With close friends in their lives, people develop courage and positive attitudes. Teenagers have the moral support to assert their individuality; the elderly approach their advanced years with optimism and an interest in life. These positive outlooks are vital to cope successfully with the crises inherent in these two stages of live.

Throughout life, we rely on small groups of people for love, admiration, respect, moral

注释
1. **adolescence** [ædə'lesns] n. 青春期
2. **gravitate** ['ɡrævɪteɪt] vi. 受引力作用；被吸引
3. **candidly** ['kændɪdlɪ] adv. 坦白地；率直地
4. **thriving** ['θraɪvɪŋ] adj. 繁荣的；旺盛的

友谊的价值

support, and help. Almost everyone has a "network" of friends: co-workers, neighbors, and schoolmates. While both men and women have such friends, evidence is accumulating that indicates men rarely make close friends. Men are sociable and frequently have numerous business acquaintances, golf buddies, and so on. However, friendship does not merely involve a sharing of activities; it is a sharing of self on a very personal level. Customarily, men have shied away from close relationship in which they confide in others. By bottling up their emotions, men deprive themselves of a health outlet for their negative feelings.

People choose some friends because they are fun to be with; they "Make things happen". Likewise, common interests appear to be a significant factor in selecting friends. Families with children, for instance, tend to **gravitate**[2] toward families with children. It is normal to be friend people who have similar life styles, and organizations such as Parents without Partners have appeared on the scene as a natural out growth of this tendency. These groups provide an opportunity to socialize, make new acquaintances and friends, obtain helpful advice in adapting smoothly to a new lifestyle. Other groups focus on specific interest such as camping or politics. It is perfectly acceptable to select friends for special qualities as there is a balanced giving and taking that is mutually satisfying.

Vary close and trusted friends share confidences **candidly**[3]. They feel secure that they will not be ridiculed or derided, and their confidences will be honored. Betraying a trust is a very quick and painful way to terminate a friendship.

As friendships solidify, ties strengthen. Intimate relationships enrich people's lives. Some components of a **thriving**[4] friendship are honesty, naturalness, thoughtfulness, and some common interests.

Circumstances and people are constantly changing. Some friendship last "forever"; others do not. Nevertheless, friendship is an essential ingredient in the making of a heartful, rewarding life.

原文翻译

友谊既是快乐之源泉，又是健康之要素。有知己的人总是很自然地享受到朋友们的陪伴。而他们所得到的情感益处和这种陪伴同样重要。如果有好事发生，和朋友们分享会使这份快乐变得更多，当烦恼和压力使我们的情绪低落时，把我们的担忧和害怕给好朋友分担将会帮我们减轻压力。而且我们甚至可以从朋友那里得到解决某个具体问题的切实可行的建议。

青少年时期和老年时期是人一生中对友谊最依赖的两个年龄阶段。在前一个阶段，青少年总是被不确定和杂乱的思绪困扰着。而在后一个阶段，老年人总是因为自己的无用而倍感心烦。在两个例子中，朋友会起到很重要的作用。有了知己，人们就会有勇气和积极的人生态度。青少年有了维护独立的精神支持，而老年人的生活就会充满乐观和对生活的兴趣。在这两个生命阶段中，要想成功化解出现的危机，一种乐观的态度是至关重要的。

整整一生，我们都依附于一些小群体给我们的爱、赞赏、尊重、精神支持和帮助。几乎人人都有一个"友情网"：同事、邻居、同学。尽管男人和女人都有一些这样的朋友，但种种迹象表明，男人很少有知己。他们善于交际，经常有很多生意上的伙伴、高尔夫球友等等。但是，友谊不仅仅是共同参加一些活动，也有分享纯私人范围内的东西的时候。通常，男人羞于向他人倾诉，因而远离了亲密的友谊。由于抑制自己的感情，他们消极的情绪因得不到释放而有损健康。

人们选择一些朋友，是因为觉得他们很有趣，他们"生机勃勃"。同样，共同的兴趣似乎也是择友的重要因素。比如说，有孩子的家庭易于彼此吸引，有相似生活方式的人也很正常地成为朋友。"离异父母协会"这一组织的出现，也是这种趋势的必然结果。这些组织提供了一个交际、结识新朋友的机会，同时为更好地适应新生活提供了很有帮助的建议。另外一些组织因一些特殊的兴趣和爱好而聚集，如野营或政治。选择有特性的人做朋友，只要付出与得到平衡，使双方满意就好。

亲密而相互信任的朋友彼此坦诚相待，他们觉得安心，不会被戏弄或嘲笑，他们的彼此信任令人尊敬，背信弃义会使友谊迅速而痛苦地终结。

友谊会日渐深厚，其纽带也会随之更加坚固。密切的关系丰富了人们的生活。使友谊茁壮成长的一些要素是诚信、朴实、慎重和某些共同兴趣。

环境和人在不断地变化中。有些友谊能持续到"永远"，有点却不能。不管怎样，友谊都是健康有益的人生不可或缺的一部分。

品味鉴赏

有人说："A friend is someone who knows the song in your heart, and can sing it back to you when you have forgotten the words." 古今中外有很多文人墨客不惜笔墨来歌颂友谊的美丽，但本文独辟蹊径，不但提到友谊会使人快乐，而且认为友谊能使生活更健康。友谊的价值何在？答案：友谊无价！

美文感悟

让愤怒不再萦绕心头,让伤害远离自己的心田,以一颗平和的心面对曾经,继续好好生活。

I Forgive You
宽恕

Let go of bitterness marriage isn't the only relationship that needs forgiveness. It's required with our children, friends, workmates, neighbors and even strangers. In fact, no human relationship can survive without the oxygen of forgiveness. It's not an optional nicety for people who are into that kind of thing; it's a universal necessity for relationships and for your own health and **sanity**[1].

Some of us may think that we've been hurt too deeply, or too often, to forgive. But ironically, it's those of us who've been most hurt that really need to forgive, for one simple reason: like cancer, bitterness can destroy its host. Unless it's swiftly rooted out, it takes hold and grows, crippling and eventually even killing those who insist on **clinging** determinedly **to**[2] it.

For the truth is that unless we can forgive, we can never recover. Our wounds will continue to **fester**[3] and never heal. As the ancient Chinese proverb puts it, "Whoever seeks revenge should dig two graves."

Taking the first step for some people forgiveness feels impossible because they have no idea how to go about it. The first and most important thing you need to accept is that the act of forgiveness is not going to easy. In fact, it will probably be the hardest thing most of us ever have to do.

It seems totally unfair that we should have to forgive when we're the ones who have been

注释
1. **sanity** ['sænətɪ] n. 明智;头脑清楚;精神健全
2. **cling to...** 坚持;依靠;依附
3. **fester** ['festə] vi. 溃烂;化脓
4. **crux** [krʌks] n. 关键;难题;十字架形

hurt. And that's the **crux**[4] of forgiveness.

The saying "Forgive and forget" may roll off the tongue, but it's as shallow as it is short. For one thing, it's downright impossible. For another, it misses the whole point of forgiveness. The things we most need forgive in life are the things we can't forget. Rather than sweeping them under the carpet, we need to draw a line under them, deliberately choosing not to count them against the person who did them, and moving on.

That's why, sometimes, the initial act of forgiveness may seem relatively easy, but dealing with the emotions that follow every time you see that person, or speak to them or just think about them, can be harder to deal with. True forgiveness is not a not-off act, it's a constant emotional confrontation.

And the longer you wait to forgive someone, the harder it becomes. Time really doesn't heal, it just gives the bitterness and resentment longer to eat away at you from inside. If you wait for the "right time" you may never do it.

A question you should ask yourself before you begin to tackle the art of forgiveness is this: How many of us are ever completely innocent in any given situation?

Some years ago, my wife, Cornelia, and I bought a piece of cheap, flatpacked, pine **veneered**[5] furniture. For the first few months, it fooled everyone it was smart, functional and impressive, and we felt it fitted our home perfectly. But as time rolled by, the veneer slowly began to peel at the edges. It didn't create the same impression any more, but at least it was being honest! The fact is that. Like it or not, behind our smart veneer, we're all just chipboard. So before we become other people's judge and jury, we'd be wise to take a long, hard look at ourselves in the mirror. And the more we see ourselves, warts and all, the more we'll want to and be able to forgive others for their flews, and the more we forgive, the more we'll know true contentment.

Would you rather be right or happy? Forgiving others can get a satisfying reaction. I've found that saying sorry to my kids has not only healed broken relationships but has helped defuse the situation, making it easier for my kids to ask for forgiveness themselves. So if you think you're right and can't find it in yourself to forgive, ask yourself this question: Would you rather be right or happy?

One of the hardest things about forgiveness is making that first move especially when you haven't spoken to the person who hurt you for a while. But remember they'll probably be happy to hear from you. They might even be impressed that you've done what they've wanted to do for years. But keep in mind you're doing this for you just as much as them, so don't be upset if they

注释 5. veneer [vɪ'nɪə] vt. 虚饰；给镶以饰片

don't react as you hoped.

Of course, some people don't believe they've done anything wrong, or don't care, so telling them you forgive them would only frustrate them and you. But that doesn't mean you can't find forgiveness in your heart. In fact, that's what true forgiveness is letting go of your anger and hurt, becoming at peace with what happened and moving on.

The more you nurture your resentment, the more unhappy you'll become. Unless you learn to develop the "lost art" of forgiving, you'll always remain a victim, not just of people who've done you wrong, but also of your own emotions.

Forgiving puts you in control. However tough it is, the alternative is far worse. The phrase "Forgive us our sins, though we refuse to forgive those who sin against us" doesn't exist in the Bible. And there's a reason for that.

原文翻译

　　宽恕不仅在婚姻中需要，在与子女、朋友、同事、邻居，甚至陌生人的相处中也同样需要。事实上，缺少宽恕，人际关系就无法持续。宽恕他人不是可有可无的善举，而是维系良性人际关系、促进身心健康的必要因素。

　　有些人认为，自己屡屡受创，对伤害自己的人很难宽恕。然而，正是这些受伤至深的人，更急需要宽恕。这似乎看起来有些矛盾，但其实很简单，就像癌症能夺人生命一样，仇恨也会给人致命的打击。如果不尽快根除，它就会滋生蔓延，最终使那些执迷于仇恨的人命丧黄泉。

　　如果满怀仇恨，心中的伤口就会逐渐溃烂，无法愈合。中国有句谚语说得好，"复仇者终会自掘坟墓"。

　　对于有些人来说，因为不知如何原谅他人，迈出第一步似乎举步维艰。那么，首要的是必须承认宽恕之举并非易事。事实上，对于大多数人来说，这是极为艰难的事。

　　受了伤，还要原谅他人，这似乎很不公平。但这是施以宽恕的关键所在。

　　人们可能会随口说"我原谅你，就让它过去吧"，但说来容易做来难。一方面，这显然是不可能的，另一方面，这不是真正意义上的谅解。生活中，久久不能释怀的就是最需谅解的事。人们不应该回避，而要牢记，并有意识地不要把错误归咎于当事人，然后继续自己的生活。

　　因而，宽恕之举最初看似简单，后来却甚为艰难。无论在相见、攀谈或是回忆中，都需要压抑情绪。真正的宽恕是持续的情绪斗争，而不是一次性的举动。

　　时间越长，就越难以原谅别人。其实，时间并不能抚平伤痛，只会增强仇恨，使你愤懑满怀。如果伺机报复，那永远无法宽恕他人。

　　宽恕他人之前，我们首先要扪心自问：有多少人没有受过伤害呢？

　　数年前，我和妻子科妮莉亚买了一套价格实惠的家具，扁平型、松木镶面的。起初的几个月里，我们都觉得它美观、实用又招人喜欢，认为它是最合适的家居用品。但日子久了，边脚地方松木镶面的皮开始脱落，不再美观了，但还能用。事实上，不管我们喜欢与否，那漂亮的镶面下只是刨花板。因此，在对他人做出评判前，应首先在镜子里审视一下自己。发觉自身的缺陷，就能原谅别人的过错，也就能体会施以宽恕所带来的满足感。

　　选择真理还是快乐？宽恕他人会产生满足感。我发现向自己的孩子道歉不仅修复了我们破裂的关系，也帮助缓和了紧张的局面，使孩子们更容易请求我的原谅。坚信自己是对的，就难有宽恕之心，那么试着扪心自问：选择真理还是快乐？

　　施以宽恕，第一步恐怕是最难的——特别是许久不再和伤害者讲话。但千万别忘了，他们或许很希望与你交谈，甚至会深受感动，这些或许是他们想做而未做的事。切记：这样做既利己又利人，即使他们没有表现出你预期的反应,也不要过于懊丧。

　　当然,有些人并没有意识到自己所犯之错,对这些事也没放在心上。假如告诉他们你宽恕了他,那只会让双方备感失望。即使不说出原谅之意,并不意味着不会原谅。其实,这才是宽恕之真正意义:让恼怒不再萦绕心头,让伤害远离自己心田,以一颗平和的心面对曾经,继续好好生活。

　　心中淤积越多仇恨,就越苦恼。除非学会"忘记的艺术",否则就永远是伤痕累累。不仅伤害的人会如此,自己情感上也会有莫大的负重。

　　宽恕他人让自己更加理性。当然,这个过程是艰难的,但"绝不原谅"所付出的代价却极为巨大。"请宽恕我们吧——我们曾拒绝宽恕曾经伤害过我们的人。"这句话虽未被写入《圣经》,却是很有道理的。

品味鉴赏

　　宽容是一种修养,是一种境界,是一种美德。宽容是原谅可容之言、饶恕可容之事、包涵可容之人。

　　宽容,最重要的是容人,它是容言、容事之根本。人,也有高低之分,学人之长,是宽容修养的基础,所以,做起来也比较容易。但是,容人之短,尤其是容持不同观点的人的缺点,则需要较大的胆识。所以,要用真诚的心来观察他人的长处,容纳他人的不足,善于发现、培养、发挥他人的长处,求同存异,共同发展,互惠互利,才能成就事业,拥有更多的成功。

　　所以,宽容是人之博大、人之崇高、人之快慰的优良品德。在这世界构建的新的文明中,愿更多的朋友,能拥有一颗宽容之心,宽厚待人,宽厚至语,宽厚做事。宽容于己不会失去什么,反而可以收获快乐,收获成功,会给人间增添多一些的欢乐和温情。

　　学会宽容别人。因此我的心胸变得宽阔了。因为宽容之于爱,正如和风之于春日,阳光之于冬天。它是人类灵魂里美丽的风景。有了博大的胸怀和宽容一切的心灵,宽容自然会散发出浓浓的醇香。宽容能使我活得轻松,使我的生活更加快乐。

美文感悟

有时候，一句赞美的话可以改变一个人的一生，就像本文的小主人公因为一个老太太的一句称赞的话而享受到了母亲般的关怀，使他无论身在何处，都会感激这位老太太曾经给予他的幸福。

Wherever You Are
情暖今生

作者简介：

罗杰·迪恩·凯瑟

作者从小就被送到孤儿院，所以对生活感受良多。现主要从事短篇小说写作和短小影视片的制作。

When the school bell rang, I headed out the back door and down Spring Park Road. It was not easy for a ten-year-old, runaway boy to walk the streets of Jacksonville, Florida. I travelled for what seemed to be miles before I crossed over the Main Street Bridge. I walked, as fast as I could, through the downtown area hunting for something to eat.

I made my way down to Bay Street and stopped and stood in the doorway of the bus station. I watched as the dirty looking **bums**[1] drank from their brown paper bags and argued with one another.

"Sonny! Can you go into that store across the street and cash in these here glass bottles for me? I'll buy you a candy," said the old woman.

注释
1. bum [bʌm] n. 流浪汉
2. stomp [stɒmp] v. 跺脚
3. retarded [rɪˈtɑːdəd] adj. 智力迟钝的；智力发育迟缓的
4. remainder [rɪˈmeɪndə] n. 剩余物；其他人员；差数

"Sure. I can do that for you for nothing," I told her.

I loaded the bottles into the store a few at a time. Her large wooden type wagon cart was filled to the top with all varieties of soda bottles.

I cashed in the bottles and I walked back out of the store to give her the money.

"Can you count the money out for me, Sonny?" she asked me.

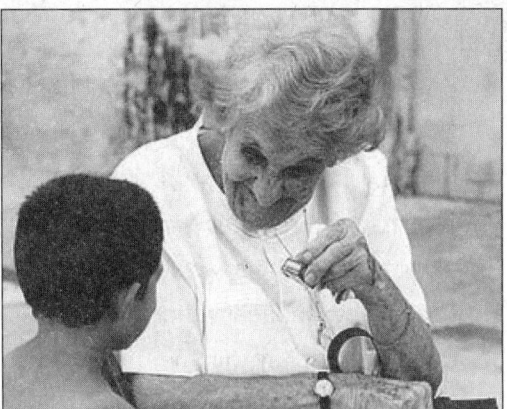

"Can't you count?" I questioned.

"It's not that, Sonny. I just can't see very well," she told me.

As I stood there counting out money in her hand, two large boys walked up and began pulling on her coattail. One of the boys was trying to grab the money from our hands while the other boy pulled her backwards. I immediately closed my hands and I fell to the ground trying to catch the coins which had fallen.

"OUCH!" I yelled out as one of the boys **stomped**[2] on my hand, pinning it to the ground.

"Boy, you sure stink lady," said one of the boys.

"You boys go on now. Leave us alone!" she yelled out at the two.

"Shut up you **retarded**[3] old bag!" yelled the young man as he started across the street with his friend.

I got back down on my knees and I picked up what money had been left on the ground. Again, I recounted the money and I placed it in her hands.

"You sure counts awful good for being little like you are. And you can count fast too." she said, as she laughed.

"Are you retarded too, like me?" I asked the old woman.

"You ain't retarded boy. You as smart as a whip. Look how fast you can count. And you're real cute too." she replied.

"You really think so?" I said, with a big smile on my face, and my eyes open wide.

For the **remainder**[4] of the day, I walked around and talked with the old woman. I stayed as close to her as possible, all the while hoping that she would once again say something nice about me.

Throughout the years, I have often thought about the old woman, especially when I drive through a large city and see someone pushing a shopping cart down the street.

I could count on one hand the times that any grown adult ever gave me a **compliment**[5] or made me feel proud of myself. The few times that it did happen, I soaked up the experience like a sponge soaking up water.

I can remember exactly what she looked like and exactly how she smelled. I can remember her legs being fat at the ankles and the many veins in her legs were dark and broken. Her lips were rough and cracked and her hands were scarred and she had many sores about her hands

注释　5. compliment ['kɒmplɪmənt] n. 恭维；敬意

and wrists.

But what I remember most about her was her kind smile.

Not the kind of look that one has when they actually smile—it was a look that she must have been born with—a constant smile which stayed on her face even when she was resting on the bus stop bench. I remember we parted company late in the afternoon on the day we met. I stood for a while, watching her as she disappeared into the evening.

I never saw her again after that.

But that was okay with me.

Even if it was only for a moment, she gave me what I needed from a "mother"—the thought that I might not be retarded, that I was handsome, and best of all, that I was "smart as a whip".

Those few words turned into feelings and they followed me for the next 50 years of my life.

This year, the Mother's Day flowers are for you. Wherever you are.

原文翻译

　　下课铃一响，我就冲出后门，沿着斯普林公园路而下。对于一个10岁的逃学孩子而言，走在佛罗里达杰克逊维尔的大街上并不是件悠闲的事。我走了漫长的一段路，才穿过缅街桥。我尽量加快脚步，准备穿过市区去找些东西吃。

　　走到海湾路，我停下来站在公共汽车站门口。我看到脏兮兮的流浪汉喝着牛皮纸袋里的东西，互相吵闹着。

　　"小家伙，你能到对面的店里帮我把瓶子换成钱吗？我给你买糖吃。"一位老妇人说。

　　"好的，不过我什么都不要。"我对她说。

　　我每次只能拿几个瓶子去商店。她那木质的大手推车里堆满了各种各样的汽水瓶。

　　我走进商店把瓶子换成现金，然后出来交给她。

　　"小家伙，你能帮我数数这些钱吗？"她问我。

　　"您不会数吗？"我问道。

　　她告诉我："不是，小家伙，我的眼神不太好。"

　　正当我站在那里数她手里的钱的时候，两个大男孩走过来拉扯她一角。其中一个往后拽她，另一个要抢钱。我立刻握紧手里的钱，正当我试图抓住掉下的硬币时，一下子摔倒在地。

　　一个男孩一脚将我的手踩在地上，我痛得哎哟大叫起来。

　　"臭小子，臭老太婆！"一个男孩骂道。

　　"你们又胡闹，快滚开！"她向那两个男孩大喊道。

　　他们正准备过马路时，其中一个嚷道："闭嘴！你这个弱智迟钝的老家伙！"

　　我跪下来捡起掉到地上的钱，又数了一遍，交给了老太太。

　　她笑着说："你年纪这么小，就数得这么好，这么快。"

　　"您像我一样反应迟钝吗？"我问她。

　　"孩子，你一点儿也不迟钝。你很聪明。看你数得多快呀！而且你真的很可爱。"她回答道。

　　"您真的这么觉得吗？"我说着，睁大了眼睛，灿烂地笑了。

　　我和老太太边走边聊，度过了那天余下的时光。我尽可能地靠近她，期待着她能再说一些赞美我的话。

　　许多年过去了，我仍会常常想起那位老妇人，特别是当我开车穿过大城市，看到街边有人推着购物小车时。

　　大人们的称赞让我有自豪感的时候少之又少。我用一只手就可以数完，当出现这种罕有的时刻时，我总会尽情享受那份愉悦，就像一块海绵尽情吸饱水一样。

　　我依然清楚地记得老妇人的长相和她身上的味道，还记得她那粗胖的脚踝，以及腿上曲张的深色血管。她的嘴唇粗糙干裂，满手疤痕，双手及手腕也有多处伤口。

但我对她的记忆最深的还是她那和蔼的微笑。

但那并不是一个人微笑时才会有的表情，而是与生俱来的，她时刻面带笑容，甚至在公共汽车站的长凳上休息时都保持着这种微笑的表情。那天黄昏分别时的情景，我依然记忆犹新。我站了许久，望着她消失在夜色中。

从此，我再未见过她。

但我并没有感到失落。

尽管那段时光很短暂，但她给予我的却是母亲般的关怀，让我知道我并不愚钝，而且长得帅气，最重要的是，我也是个聪明的孩子。

这简短的几句话已经转变了我对自己的看法，并在之后的 50 年间一直萦绕着我。

无论您身在何处，今年的母亲节，我都要将一束鲜花献给您。

文化点滴

1. Jacksonville, Florida：杰克逊维尔，美国佛罗里达州东北部港口城市。

2. as smart as a whip：用来比喻人的聪明灵活。老练的车把式把鞭子挥舞得活了似的。他手上的鞭子非常灵巧敏捷，能百发百中打死叮牲口的马蝇却不伤牲口一根毫毛。这也许就是 as smart as a whip 这个习惯用语的出典。

品味鉴赏

现实生活中，我们时常会听到别人的赞美，也曾赞美过别人。赞美是一种心情，是一种品德，是一种境界；被赞美是一种快乐，是一种幸福。赞美是人际关系的润滑剂，它可以使人际关系和谐，缩短人们之间的心理距离，增强彼此的亲近感，可以启发人们去寻找心中尚未开垦出的美，激起人们保持乐观向上、积极进取的人生态度；赞美是一种慰藉，它像一股清爽甘洌的泉水，使人们干涸的心灵得到润泽；赞美是一缕阳光，它将拨开生活的阴霾，给人们心灵以光明；赞美是一种能源，它将给人生旅途的跋涉者以取之不尽、用之不竭的力量。我们应该适时地给别人奉上真诚的赞美，也应该学会理智地对待赞美。让赞美这朵美丽的鲜花时刻温暖人们的心房，也希望人们不要在赞美这朵鲜花的芬芳中迷醉自己。多赞美别人，不用花钱，就能使人快乐，何乐而不为呢？

美文感悟

夜空中，如果只有孤寂的月亮，而没有群星闪耀，会是一片沉闷，了无生气。为何不让闪耀的月光和璀璨的群星交相辉映呢？

Please Let Me Have a Little World
给我一个小小的世界

Please, my dear, be so generous as to let me have a little world of my own. If you find me scrawling on a piece of paper, please don't peep over my shoulders. It may be that I'm **venting**[1] some **pent-up**[2] feelings, long denied expression, or trying to compose a little poem not yet **presentable**[3] for a time being, or attempting to sketch out something visualized from my childhood memories which glows in my mind like a rainbow. When I am in such a mood, please leave me along and let me write as the pen dictates. Don't disturb me, my dear, when I get nostalgic over some old photos or letters which bring tears to my eyes or smiles on my lips, for those were things that had happened to me before I met you, the joys and sorrows, partings and reunions that taste like green olive or glitter like scattered pearls. They are my cherished memories which, ready as I am to share with you, I would like to indulge in by myself for a while.

I hope you won't mind when I go without you for a nice chat with a close friend of mine. You are my bosom friend, but you cannot take the place of other friends any more than they can

---

注释
1. **vent** [vent] *v.* 表达；发泄
2. **pent-up** ['pent'ʌp] *adj.* 被压抑的；被抑制的
3. **presentable** [prɪ'zentəbəl] *adj.* 拿得出的；像样的
4. **solitary** ['sɒlɪtəri] *adj.* 独自的，独立的；隐居的

do yours. I need their care, encouragement and sobering criticism just as I do yours. A starless sky with a **solitary**[4] moon would be dull and cheerless, why not let there be a moonlit night **resplendent**[5] with twinkling stars.

I may occasionally want to make a tour of faraway places. Please don't hold me back when I start picking for it. You are the center of my life, but certainly not the whole of it. I yearn to see the mysteries and wonders of the world miles away beyond the mountains; So let me have a chance to explore my "Alice's Wonderland" as a "lone ranger". Some time later when I come back to you with exotic experiences and fresh insights, I'm sure you will look at me in a new light.

My dear, so long as you let me have such a little, little world, I'll be very much **indebted**[6] to you.

原文翻译

　　亲爱的丈夫，请大度地给我一个小小的世界。当你发现我在纸上胡涂乱写的时候，请不要在我身后窥视。我或许在发泄某种压抑在心中长期未诉说的情绪，或是在设法构思一首暂时还羞于见人的小诗，或是在试图勾勒某件依然在我脑际像彩虹般闪着光彩的童年往事。或是处于这样的心境时，请别管我，请让我信笔驰骋。当我对着昔日的照片和书信沉思、垂泪或微笑，怀旧之情油然而生的时候，我亲爱的，请不要打扰我。因为那些照片和书信记录着我遇到你之前所经历的一些事儿——那些悲欢离合如同青色的橄榄一样酸涩，像散落的珍珠闪闪发光。这些是珍藏于我心中的回忆，尽管我愿意和你共同分享，但我还是想独自沉浸于这些往事中，品味一番，细数一阵。

　　当我一个人出去同我的一位挚友聊天时，希望你不要介意。你是我的知己，但你不能代替我的其他朋友，正像我需要你这么做一样。没有星星点缀而只有月亮高悬的夜空多么清寂，请让我拥有一个群星闪耀、月光皎洁、交相辉映的美好夜空吧！

　　我也许偶尔想去远处旅游一番。当我开始打包装箱整装待发时，请不要阻挡我。你是我生活的世界的中心，但并不是我的整个世界。我渴望看看群山之外遥远世界的神奇奇观，请让我有机会作为"独行侠"去探索我的"爱丽丝仙境"。过些时候，当我带着奇异的经历和新的领悟力满载而归时，我相信你一定会对我刮目相看。

　　亲爱的丈夫，如果你能给我这样一个小小的世界，我会对你充满深深的感激。

注释　**5. resplendent** [rɪ'splendənt] *adj.* 华丽灿烂的、辉煌的；光芒万丈的　　**6. indebted** [ɪn'detɪd] *adj.* 感激的；受惠的；负债的

文化点滴

Alice's Wonderland

《爱丽丝梦游仙境》是英国作家查尔斯·路德维希·道奇森以笔名路易斯·卡罗尔于 1865 年出版的儿童文学作品。故事叙述一个名叫爱丽丝的女孩从兔子洞进入一处神奇国度，遇到许多会讲话的生物以及像人一般活动的纸牌，最后发现原来是一场梦。本书出版之后即广受欢迎，儿童和成人都喜爱这部作品，并且反复再版至今。该书至今已有超过 50 种语言的译本，上百种不同版本，以及许多戏剧、电影等改编作品。在英文中，本书通常被简称为 *Alice in Wonderland*，并适用于大部分的改编作品。

品味鉴赏

婚姻是把两个没有血缘关系的人紧密地联系在一起并共同生活。步入婚姻，不但要彼此关爱体贴，牵手一生，而且要彼此忠诚、信任、尊重、理解和宽容。

既然决定选择对方共度一生，就应该彼此忠诚、相互信任，给予对方充分的尊重，允许对方保留相对的隐私和独立的空间，让对方更轻松愉快地工作和生活，自己也可以分享一份愉快。始终相信，婚内男女，只要心中有爱，就不会忘记回家的路和家中的另一半。夫妻之间能够彼此尊重隐私，给予相对的自由空间，是个人修养、风度的体现，更是一种睿智、文明的体现。愿围城中的男女将这些美好的东西发扬光大，在各自的婚姻中演绎出更多的精彩。

美文感悟

Saving a Neighbor's Life
拯救邻居的生命

远亲不如近邻，邻里情令人感动。本文作者的邻居冒着生命危险将其从熊熊烈火中拯救出来，拥有如此善良、勇敢的邻居是他的庆幸。

There was no way he was going to listen to his neighbor scream and die in the burning house, so he told the 911 dispatcher he was going in.

Lightning flashed through the darkness over Donald Lubeck's bedroom **skylight**[1]. Before the 80-year-old retired international aid worker could count "one thousand one," he was shaken by a blast of thunder. It was 11 p.m. The storm had moved directly over his two-story wood home in the rural town of Belchertown, Massachusetts. Then he heard the smoke alarm beeping. Lubeck **padded down**[2] the stairs barefoot to investigate; he opened the door to the basement, and flames exploded out.

The sudden gust from the doorway instantaneously created an **inferno**[3] from a smoldering fire, most likely caused by lightning, in the basement fuse box. His face and hair singed, Lubeck fled back upstairs to call 911 from his bedroom. "I felt safe because the room had a separate outdoor stairway," he explains. "I was counting on that."

注释
1. **skylight** ['skaɪˌlaɪt] *n.* 天窗
2. **pad down** 轻轻走过
3. **inferno** [ɪnˈfɜːnəʊ] *n.* 地狱；阴间；可怕的东西
4. **run into** 驱车造访

But the phone didn't work, and when Lubeck tried to go down the exterior stairway, he was stopped by a wall of flames. "I started panicking," he says.

Lubeck realized he was trapped. His daughter and young granddaughters, who lived with him, were away for the night. No one will even know I'm home, he thought. His house was three miles off the main road and so well hidden by pines that Lubeck knew calling for help would be fruitless.

"I could hear the fire moving through the house—boom, crash, bang, boom—and you know it's coming for you," Lubeck says. "The thing that got me was to die alone. Not to say goodbye to someone."

Up a hill about a third of a mile away lived Lubeck's closest neighbors, Jeremie Wentworth and his wife. Wentworth had been lying down listening to crickets chirping when it occurred to him that the sound was more like a smoke detector. He jumped out of bed, grabbed a cordless phone and a flashlight, and headed down the hillside toward the noise. That's when he saw the roiling mountain of black smoke.

He dialed 911, then called out, "Is anyone there?" as he approached the house. Wentworth knew that Lubeck lived in the house, and the two men were friendly.

Then he heard, "Help me! I'm trapped!" coming from the balcony off Lubeck's bedroom. On the phone, the 911 dispatcher warned Wentworth not to enter the house. "But there was no way I was going to listen to Don scream and die in that fire," he says. "I told the dispatcher, 'I'm sorry, but I'm going in.'"

Inside the house, windows shattered all around him. "I was yelling, 'Don, where are you?' Then I had to run outside to catch my breath."

After one more attempt inside the house, he gave up and circled around back. The wind parted the black smoke just enough for him to glimpse Lubeck on the second-floor balcony. But there was no way to get to him. "I shined the flashlight into the woods next to an old shed and noticed a ladder," says Wentworth. He dragged it over to the balcony and pulled Lubeck down just as the second floor of the house collapsed.

Within the year, Lubeck and his family built a new two-story wood house at the site of the fire. Wentworth and Lubeck don't **run into**[4] each other regularly, but Lubeck now knows that if he ever needs help, Wentworth will be there.

Lubeck still **chokes up**[5] when he tells the story. "I was alone," he says. "Then I heard the most beautiful sound in my life. It was Jeremie."

注释　5. choke up 因感情冲动说不出话来

原文翻译

听着他的邻居在着火的房子里惨叫,将被活活烧死,对他是不可能的,所以他告诉911调度员,他要进到失火的房子里去。

闪电在黑暗中闪过唐纳德·吕贝克的卧室天窗。在这位80岁的退休国际援助工作者数到"一千一"之前,他被爆炸的雷声吓了一跳。此时是晚上11点。风暴直接袭击了位于马萨诸塞州的乡村小镇柏赤镇他的两层木屋,然后,他听到烟雾报警器的蜂鸣声。吕贝克赤着脚一步步走下楼去查看个究竟,他打开通往地下室的门,火焰爆炸似的扑面而来。

从门口突然吹来的一阵风瞬间引燃了地下室保险丝盒里闷烧的火焰,像地狱之火般可怕,很有可能是由闪电引起的。他的脸和头发被烧焦,吕贝克逃回到他楼上的卧室,拨打911。他解释道:"因为房间里有独立的室外楼梯,我当时感到很安全,我就靠它了。"

但电话不好使。当吕贝克试着从外部楼梯下去时,一堵火墙阻挡了他的去路。他说:"我开始恐慌"。

吕贝克意识到他被困住了。和他住在一起的女儿和孙女们今晚不回来。他想甚至都没有人会知道我在家。他的房子在主干道三英里外,隐藏在松树林里,吕贝克知道大声呼救是徒劳的。

"我能听到火舌在逐渐吞噬着我的房子——隆隆,嘭嘭,咔咔作响——吕贝克说:"你能感觉到它正在向你逼近。让我精神崩溃的是我将孤独地死去,没机会向任何人说再见。"

大约1/3英里远的一座小山上住着距离吕贝克最近的邻居热雷米·温特沃斯和他的妻子。温特沃斯躺在床上,听着蟋蟀的鸣叫,这时他听到了好像是烟雾探测器的叫声。他立刻跳下床,抓起一个无绳电话和一把手电筒,循着声音从山坡上走下去。这时候,他看到了冒着滚滚黑烟的山。

他拨通了911,他一边朝房子走去一边大声喊道"有人吗?"。温特沃斯知道吕贝克住在那所房子里,两人很要好。

随后,他听到"救救我!我被困住了!"。声音来自吕贝克卧室外的阳台。在电话中,911调度员警告温特沃斯不要进到房子里面。他说:"听着唐在着火的房子里惨叫,将被活活烧死,对我来说是不可能的。我告诉911调度员,我要进到失火的房子里去了"。

屋内,窗户碎了一地。"我大声喊道:'唐,你在哪里?'随后,我不得不跑到外面去吸气。"

再次尝试进到屋子里,他放弃了,然后绕到房子后面。风把黑色的烟雾吹开了,足以让他瞥见二楼阳台上的吕贝克。但是没有办法去救他。温特沃斯说道:"我拿着手电筒向老棚子旁边的树林里照去,发现了一个梯子。"他把梯子拖到阳台上,把吕贝克救了下来,随后二楼的房子瞬间倒塌。

在这一年内,吕贝克和他的家人在火灾现场建起了一个新的两层木屋。温特沃斯和吕贝克彼此不会定期地拜访对方,但吕贝克现在知道,如果他需要帮助,温特沃斯会随叫随到。

每当吕贝克讲起这个故事的时候仍然会哽咽。他说:"我当时独自一人在家,然后我听到了我生命中最美丽的声音,那就是热雷米的声音。"

品味鉴赏

何其幸，吕贝克能拥有如此热心而勇敢的邻居！人常说"远亲不如近邻"，"远水不解近渴"。这充分说明了邻居的重要性，邻里之间和睦相处，是我们明智的选择。

邻里之间相处得好，你帮助我，我帮助你，互敬互爱，不计得失。闲暇时谈天说地，有事时互帮互助，不是一家人，胜似一家人。邻里关系是一种十分重要的人际关系。俗话说："行要好伴，住要好邻。""隔邻居，不隔心。"处理好邻里关系，做到互敬、互信、互助、互让，和睦相处，不仅有利于各自的工作、学习和生活，使大家过得愉快，有利于各家的生活幸福，而且也有利于社会的安定团结。

邻里情给我们送来爱心，这份爱心就像黑夜里的一盏明灯，为我们指引前进的方向；邻里情让我们拥有友谊，这份友谊犹如汩汩而过的清泉，甘甜隽永润泽我们的心田；邻里情为我们注入活力，这份活力胜似一剂灵丹妙药，瞬间驱走平日的烦闷和疲惫；邻里情给予我们温暖，这份温暖仿佛一缕冬日明媚阳光，抚慰着冰冷的心房；邻里情令我们充满希望，这份希望仿佛沙漠里的一片绿洲，让黄沙漫天的困顿旅途豁然开朗。

美文感悟

_____

_____

_____

_____

_____

父亲通过书信的形式对即将走向社会的儿子提出谆谆教导。该教导情真意切,感人至深。

Letter to His Son
给儿子的一封信

Dear boy,

The art of pleasing is a very necessary one to possess, but a very difficult one to acquire. It can hardly be reduced to rules; and your own good sense and observation will teach you more of it than I can. "Do as you would be done by," is the surest method that I know of pleasing. Observe carefully what pleases you in others, and probably the same things in you will please others. If you are pleased with the **complaisance**[1] and attention of others to your humors, your tastes, or your weaknesses, depend upon it, the same complaisance and attention on your part to theirs will equally please them. Take the tone of the company that you are in, and do not pretend to give it; be serious, gay, or even **trifling**[2], as you find the present humor of the company; this is an attention due from every individual to the majority. Do not tell stories in company; there is nothing more tedious and disagreeable; if **by chance**[3] you know a very short story, and exceedingly applicable to the present subject of conversation, tell it in as few words as possible; and even then, **throw out**[4] that you do not love to tell stories, but that the shortness of it tempted you.

Of all things banish the **egotism**[5] out of your conversation, and never think of entertaining people with your own personal concerns or private affairs; though they are interesting to you, they are tedious and **impertinent**[6] to everybody else; besides that, one cannot keep one's own private affairs too secret. Whatever you think your own excellencies may be, do not affectedly display them in company;

注释
1. **complaisance** [kəmˈpleɪsəns] *n.* 讨好,殷勤
2. **trifling** [ˈtraɪflɪŋ] *adj.* 微不足道的;轻浮的
3. **by chance** 偶然地,意外地;无意之中;碰巧;偏巧
4. **throw out** 拒绝,否决;提出(暗示、建议等)

nor labor, as many people do, to give that turn to the conversation, which may supply you with an opportunity of exhibiting them. If they are real, they will **infallibly**[7] be discovered, without your pointing them out yourself, and with much more advantage. Never maintain an argument with heat and clamor, though you think or know yourself to be in the right; but give your opinion modestly and coolly, which is the only way to convince; and, if that does not do, try to change the conversation, by saying, with good humor; "We shall hardly convince one another; nor is it necessary that we should, so let us talk of something else."

Remember that there is a local propriety to be observed in all companies; and that what is extremely proper in one company may be, and often is, highly improper in another. The jokes, the **bon mots**[8], the little adventures, which may do very well in one company, will seem flat and tedious, when related in another. The particular characters, the habit, the cant of one company may give merit to a word, or a gesture, which would have none at all if deprived of those accidental circumstances. Here people very commonly err; and fond of something that has entertained them in one company, and in certain circumstances, repeat it with emphasis in another, where it is either insipid, or, it may be, offensive, by being ill timed or misplaced. Nay, they often do it with this silly **preamble**[9]: "I will tell you an excellent thing," or, "I will tell you the best thing in the world." This raises expectations, which, when absolutely disappointed, make the relator of this excellent thing look, very deservedly, like a fool.

If you would particularly gain the affection and friendship of particular people, whether men or women, endeavor to find out their predominant excellency, if they have one, and their prevailing weakness, which everybody has; and do justice to the one, and something more than justice to the other. Men have various objects in which they may excel, or at least would be thought to excel; and though they love to hear justice done to them, where they know that they excel, yet they are most and best flattered upon those points where they wish to excel, and yet are doubtful whether they do or not.

原文翻译

亲爱的孩子：

惹人喜欢要有必要的条件，但又是一门不易学到的艺术，很难将其归纳成规则。你自己良好的判断力与观察力将使你领悟比我教授给你的还要多的东西。"己所不欲勿施于人"，据我所知，这是取信于人的最可靠的办法。细心留意别人怎样做让你愉快，那么很可能你做同样的事也会使别人愉悦。如果别人对你的性情、兴趣甚至弱点甚为关心，让你满心欢喜，请相信，你对别人施以同样的热情和关照，也一定会使他们高兴。与人为伴来往时，需顺应其中的氛围，勿矫揉造作，发现同伴的幽默之处，就诚然开怀一乐甚至调笑一番，

注释

5. **egotism** [ˈiːgətɪzəm] n. 自我中心，自尊自大
6. **impertinent** [ɪmˈpɜːtnənt] adj. 无礼的；莽撞的；不切题的
7. **infallibly** [ɪnˈfælɪblɪ] adv. 绝对无误地
8. **bon mot** 名言
9. **preamble** [ˈpriːˌæmbəl] n. 序；绪言；前言

这是每个人对群体应具备的态度。在人前不要说瞎话，没有比这更让人讨厌和不悦的事了。如果你恰好有一则很简短而又相当切题的故事，可用最简洁明了的语言叙述一番。即使如此，也要表示出你并不擅长讲述，而仅是因为它实在太简短才使你情不自禁地这样做。

在交谈中，首先要摈弃以自我为中心的癖好，绝不要试图让别人对自己的私事或者自己关注的事产生兴趣。尽管这些事对你来说兴趣盎然，但对于别人却味同嚼蜡，不得要领。再者，个人的私事也不可能永远隐秘。无论你自以为有什么好处，切忌在人前自爱自怜地展示，也不要像许多人那样，挖空心思地引导谈话，以伺机自我表现一番。如果你确实有长处，必会被人发现，不必自己点出，何况这样做最好。当与人有是非之争时，绝不要激动地大喊大叫，即使你自以为正确或者知道自己是正确的，也要善加控制，冷静地说出自己的意见，这是说服人的唯一方法。但如果这样仍不奏效，就试着变个话题，高高兴兴地说："我们谁也说服不了谁，而且也不是非得说服对方不可，我们讨论别的吧。"

要记住，与人交往时要尊重习俗的礼仪。在这一群人中恰如其分的话语，对另一群人而言却不适宜。与某些人适宜的幽默、妙语甚至小小的出格行为，换个地方会显得平淡自然，或令人苦恼。说一个词儿或者打一个手势，在某群人中即暗示着某种性格、习惯和隐语，而一旦离开那种特定的氛围，就会毫无意义。人们常常在这一点上犯过失。他们喜欢把在某群人、某种环境中的得意言行随意搬到别的地方使用，而此时却风趣尽失，或不合时宜，或张冠李戴而唐突无聊。是的，他们常用这样笨拙的开场白："告诉你一件很棒的事！"或者"我要告诉你世上最绝妙的……"，希望这些话能勾起对方的期待，但结果是彻底的绝望，使得说这些话的人看起来像个十足的傻子。

如果你获得别人的好感和情感，无论是男人或女人，要特别留意去发现他们可能具备的长处，以及他们明显的不足之处。人人都会有缺陷，但要公正而善意地对待别人的这个或那个不足。人们还会有许多过人之处，或者至少具有可以称作优异的地方。尽管人们喜欢听到对其自知的优点的赞美，但他们最感兴趣的乃是对自己渴望具备且尚不自信的长处的赞许。

品味鉴赏

总有一个人，默默地将我们支撑；总有一份爱，让人心灵震颤。这个人就是父亲，这份爱就是父爱。

父爱中蕴藏着的是太阳的光泽，是莽莽苍苍山林的气息。无需语言，甚至无需何种方式——父爱，只默默生成，慢慢积淀，静静流淌……

父爱如伞，为我们遮风挡雨；父爱如雨，为我们濯洗心灵；父爱如路，伴我们走向人生旅途……

恐惧时，父爱是一块踏脚的石；黑暗时，父爱是一盏照明的灯；枯竭时，父爱是一湾生命之水；努力时，父爱是精神上的支柱；成功时，父爱是鼓励与警钟……父爱——人间美好而难得的感情！

父爱是一种精神，它让我们泪流满面；父爱是一种力量，它让我们信心倍增；父爱更是一种人格，它教导我们信步风雨人生！

美文感悟

年轻人的爱好似火焰,很美丽,往往非常火热而猛烈,但是只有忽隐忽现的光线。年长的、有自律的爱好似煤炭,充分燃烧,难以抑制。

Keeping the Passion of Love Alive
保持爱的热情

作者简介：

芭芭拉·安吉利斯（Barbara De Angelis，1951—），美国关系咨询师、演讲家及作家、电视名人、关系及个人成长顾问。

Young love is a flame; very pretty, often very hot and fierce, but still only light and flickering. The love of the older and disciplined heart is as coals, deep burning, **unquenchable**[1].

——Henry Ward Beecher, American clergyman

Imagine that you've decided to build a fire, perhaps while you're camping, or at home in your fireplace. You carefully choose the logs, the **kindling**[2], and after lighting a match to start the fire, you watch over it until you're sure the fire is burning strongly and steadily. Then you sit back and enjoy the comforting warmth, the delightful play of the flames, the magical light. You don't need to be as **vigilant**[3] about keeping the fire blazing, since it has enough fuel for now. But at some point, when you notice it's getting a little colder, or the light is growing dim, you realize that the fire needs your attention again. And so you rouse yourself from whatever you've been doing and

注释
1. **unquenchable** [ʌnˈkwentʃəbl] *adj.* 难抑制的，不能消灭的
2. **kindling** [ˈkɪndlɪŋ] *n.* 引火柴
3. **vigilant** [ˈvɪdʒələnt] *adj.* 警惕的，警觉的；警戒的；机警
4. **ember** [ˈembə] *n.* 余烬，余火

add more wood, or adjust the position of the logs so that, once more, the flames can rise high.

Even if you've neglected the fire for a while, even if it appears to have died out, you see that the **embers**[4] still radiate a deep, orange glow that can only be created by hours of extreme heat. The embers are deceptive, and they contain great power within their quiet light. Although by themselves they produce no flames, they can **ignite**[5] a newly added piece of wood in seconds, suddenly rekindling the full force of the fire, transforming the dormant coals into a roaring blaze.

We can learn a lot about the passion between two lovers by thinking about what we intuitively know about building and maintaining a fire. When you first meet someone and fall in love, you carefully court and seduce him or her, adding the right amount of intimacy, the perfect amount of commitment until the fire of passion **flares up**[6] between your hearts and your bodies. For a while, this blaze burns brightly on its own and you grow accustomed to the joy it brings into your life. How lucky we are, you tell yourself, to have such a passionate relationship!

But one day, you realize there is less light, less heat between you and your mate, and that, in fact, it's been that way for some time. You don't feel the same intense degree of physical attraction, the same desire to unite, the same stimulation you once felt with each other. The passion is gone, you may conclude. I guess I've fallen out of love. This relationship is over.

How many people ask themselves, at this critical point in a love affair, if the fire of passion has died down simply because no one has been tending it, because no one has added the fuel necessary to keep it burning? How many people walk away from the smoking embers of their marriage, certain that the fire has died out, without noticing that the coals of love still contain enough heat to reignite into flames, if only they are given a chance?

Respect the fire of passion, the fire of love. Understand that to stay alive, it needs to be honored, to be cared for, to be tended as diligently as you would tend a fire you had built in the wilderness to help keep you warm and safe from harm. Feed the fire of your love with kindness, communication, appreciation and gratitude, and it will always blaze strong and brightly for you.

原文翻译

年轻人的爱好似火焰，很漂亮，往往非常火热而猛烈，但是只有忽隐忽现的光线。年长的、有自律的爱好似煤炭，充分燃烧，难以抑制。

——美国牧师亨利·华德·比彻

注释
5. **ignite** [ɪgˈnaɪt] vt. 点燃；使燃烧；使激动
6. **flare up** 突然爆发；勃然大怒；突然燃烧起来

保持爱的热情

试想一下，也许当你露营的时候，或者在家里的壁炉里，你决定生一堆火。你仔细选择原木和火种，点燃火柴开始引火，你注视着它，直到火熊熊地燃烧起来。然后你坐下来，享受火苗带来的温暖的舒适感，火苗愉悦地跳动着，发出神奇的光。有足够的木头让火一直烧下去，所以你无需一直照看火苗。但在某些时候，当你觉得变得有点冷，或光线越来越暗的时候，你就应该照看一下火了。你放下手头正在做的事，去添些木材，或挪动一下原木的位置，这样火焰再次燃烧起来。

即使你有一段时间没照看火苗，即使它似乎已经熄灭了，你仍然能看到余烬焕发出深邃的橘红色的光芒，这种光芒只能是长达几个小时的高温产生的。余烬是有欺骗性的，在它们平静的光芒下隐藏着巨大的能量。虽然余烬本身不产生火焰，但它们可以在几秒钟内点燃新加的一块木头，使其顿时剧烈燃烧起来，休眠的煤炭转化成熊熊燃烧的火焰。

通过直观地了解到生火和让火持续燃烧下去的道理，我们从中可以学到很多关于两个恋人之间的激情的问题。当你对某人一见钟情的时候，你会小心翼翼地向他／她献殷勤，诱惑他／她，加入适度的亲密行为，许下完美的承诺，直到你们的心灵和你们的肉体都燃烧起火一般的激情。一段时间后，这火焰自己耀眼地燃烧起来，你习惯了它给你的生活带来的欢乐。你告诉你自己我们是多么幸运，拥有这样一种充满激情的关系！

但是有一天，你意识到你和你的伴侣之间的光和热量越来越少了，其实上，这种状态已经持续了一段时间了。你感到你们之间不像以前那样彼此的身体强烈地互相吸引，渴望结合，激情也逐渐消退了。你可能会得出结论，你们之间没有激情了。我想我已经不再爱他／她了。这段关系结束了。

有多少人问自己，在这段恋情的关键点上，激情之火的燃尽，是不是只是因为没有人照料它，是不是因为没有人继续添加燃料？有多少人从他们婚姻的冒着烟的余烬走开，确信火已经完全熄灭了，但是他们没有注意到，如果给余烬一个机会，爱的煤炭仍然有足够的热量来重新燃起火焰呢？

尊重激情之火，尊重爱情之火。明白了这一点并保持爱的激情，它需要得到尊重、照顾，就像你呵护在荒野里生的一堆火一样，细心地照顾它，以便帮助你保持温暖以及安全，不受伤害。用友善、沟通、赞赏和感恩滋养你的爱情之火，它会永远为你而熊熊燃烧。

写作特点

文中将爱及激情比喻成火焰，给读者一个非常传神而生动的形象，同时也更容易让读者理解作者所要表达的思想。

品味鉴赏

爱就要相互欣赏、相互理解、相互包容、相互支持，坦诚以待，有情有义，彼此交心包容又没有排他性，这样的爱才是你一生中最大的资产！

只要真心，真诚，一朵玫瑰和 99 朵玫瑰是等价的。所以，真正能天长地久的爱情，还是像白开水一样的爱情。但不是说白开水式的爱情就一味地平静，它们也有激情的时候，毕竟水在成为白开水之前也有沸腾的过程。但更多是平静，也只有白开水才能真正地"解渴"，才能真正地滋润爱情永恒的心田。

美文感悟

Chapter

人与自然

本章节选了 **10** 位名家的 **10** 篇散文、小说、童话故事等，体现了他们的写作风格，展现了他们的写作技巧。从这些作品中，我们可以看到笔者对肮脏、畸形的现实社会所进行的淋漓尽致、疾恶如仇的讽刺和挖苦，对传统、腐朽的世俗习气的无情鞭挞和猛烈抨击，也可以读到作者对美的向往和所作的引人入胜的描绘；甚至还可以捕捉到某些寓意深刻但又难以捉摸的纤细的思绪。当然，有些"奇篇怪章"使人不大好懂，这或多或少地反映了资本主义社会不可解脱的种种矛盾在作家和一部分知识分子中所引起的精神危机以及病态心理。

Spell of the Rising Moon
醉人月光

浪漫诗仙李白平生最喜爱的便是月亮。"床前明月光""举杯邀明月"……

他连最后的辞世也是那么诗情画意,传说是醉酒的他天真地想捞起水中的月亮,最终抱着月亮的倒影离开了……

作者简介:

彼得·斯坦哈特,美国自然主义作家、艺术家,曾连续12年担任美国《奥杜邦杂志》(*Audubon Magazine*)的编辑和专栏作家。该杂志是美国国内影响力极大的群众性环保组织——奥杜邦协会出版发行的一份杂志,该协会致力于促进鸟类学研究。彼得·斯坦哈特的文章多次出现在《纽约时报》(*the New York Times*)和《洛杉矶时报》(*the Los Angeles Times*)等多家报刊上。他还曾两次入围美国国家杂志奖(*National Magazine Award*)。他的散文优美清新,给人以美的享受。至今,他已出版了多部书籍,其中有 *The Company of Wolves*, *Undressed Art: Why We Draw* 等。目前他居住在美国加利福尼亚州西部的帕拉托(Palo Alto)市,在写作的同时还从事绘画创作。

There is a hill near my home that I often climb at night. The noise of the city is a far-off murmur. In the **hush**[1] of dark I share the cheerfulness of crickets and the confidence of owls. But it is the drama of the moonrise that I come to see. For that restores in me a quiet and clarity that the city spends too freely.

From this hill I have watched many moons rise. Each one had its own mood. There have

---

注释
1. **hush** [hʌʃ] *a.* 安静,宁静
2. **smudge** [smʌdʒ] *vt.* 弄脏,使冒浓烟,使模糊,用浓烟
3. **unerring** [ʌnˈɜːrɪŋ] *a.* 准确无误的,无偏差的,一贯正确的,可靠的

been broad, confident harvest moons in autumn; shy, misty moons in spring; lonely, white moons in winter, rising into the utter silence of an ink-black sky; and smoke **smudged**2, orange moons over the dry fields of summer. Each, like fine music, excited my heart and calmed my soul.

Moon gazing is an ancient art. To prehistoric hunters the moon overhead was as **unerring**3 as a heartbeat. They knew that every 29 days it became full-bellied and brilliant, then sickened and died, and then was reborn once again. They knew that the **waxing**4 moon appeared larger and higher overhead after each succeeding sunset. They knew that the **waning**5 moon rose later each night, until it vanished in the sunrise. To have understood the moon's patterns from experience must have been a profound thing.

But we, who live indoors have lost contact with the moon. The glare of street lights and the dust of pollution veil the night sky. Though men have walked on the moon, it grows less familiar. Few of us can say what time the moon will rise tonight.

Still, it tugs at our minds. If we unexpectedly encounter the full moon, huge and yellow over the horizon, we can't help but stare back in awe at its commanding presence. And the moon has gifts to **bestow**6 upon those who watch.

I learned about its gifts one July evening in the mountains. My car had mysteriously **stalled**7, and I was **stranded**8 and alone. The sun had set, and I was watching what seemed to be the bright-orange glow of a forest fire beyond a ridge to the east. Suddenly, the ridge itself seemed to burst into flames. Then, the rising moon, huge, red and **grotesquely**9 misshapen by the dust and sweat of the summer air, **loomed**10 up out of the woods.

Distorted by the hot breath of earth, the moon seemed somewhat ill-tempered and imperfect. At a nearby farmhouse, dogs barked nervously, as if this strange light had wakened evil spirits in the weeds.

But as the moon lifted off the ridge, it gathered firmness and authority. Its complexion changed from red, to orange, to gold, to impassive yellow. It seemed to draw light out of the darkening earth, for as it rose, the hills and valleys below grew dimmer. By the time the moon stood clear of the horizon—full-chested, round and the color of ivory—the valleys were deep shadows in the landscape. The dogs reassured that this was the familiar moon, stopped barking. And all at once I felt a confidence and joy close to laughter.

The drama took an hour. Moonrise is slow and **serried**11 with **subtleties**12. To watch it, we must slip into an older, more patient sense of time. To watch the moon move **inexorably**13 higher is to find an unusual stillness within ourselves. Our imaginations become aware of the vast distances of space, the immensity of the earth, and the huge improbability of our own existence. We feel small but privileged.

Moonlight shows us none of life's harder edges. Hillsides seem silken and silvery, the oceans

注释
4. wax [wæks] vt. 给……打蜡，给……上蜡；渐渐变大
5. wane [weɪn] vi. 衰落；（月）亏，缺；结束；变暗淡
6. bestow [bɪ'stəʊ] vt. 赠给，授予；放置，安置，贮藏
7. stall [stɔl] vt. 搪塞，暂缓，搁置，停顿
8. strand [strænd] vt. 使滞留，使搁浅，使陷于困境
9. grotesquely [grəʊ'teskli] ad. 奇异地，荒诞地

still and blue in its light. In moonlight we become less calculating, more drawn to our feelings.

And odd things happen in such moments. On that July night, I watched the moon for an hour or two, and then I got back into the car, turned the key in the **ignition**[14] and heard the engine start, just as mysteriously as it had stalled a few hours earlier. I drove down from the mountains with the moon on my shoulder and peace in my heart.

I often return to watch the rising moon. I feel drawn to it, especially when events crowd ease and clarity of vision into a small corner of my life. This happens often in the fall. In such moments I go to my hill and wait the hunter's moon, enormous and gold over the horizon, filling the night with vision.

An owl **swoops**[15] from the ridge top, noiseless but bright as flame. A cricket shrills in the grass. I think of poets and musicians. Of Beethoven's *Moonlight Sonata* and of Shakespeare, whose Lorenzo declaims in *The Merchant of Venice*, "How sweet the moonlight sleeps upon this bank!/ Here will we sit and let sounds of music/ Creep in our ears." I wonder if their verse and music, like the music of crickets are in some way voices of the moon. With such thoughts my **citified**[16] confusions melt into the quiet of the night.

Lovers and poets find deeper meaning at night, when we are all apt to pose deeper questions—about our origins and destinies. We indulge in riddles rather than in the impersonal geometries that govern the day-lit world. We become philosophers and mystics.

At moonrise, as we slow our minds to the pace of the heavens enchantment steals over us. We open the **vents**[17] of feeling, and exercise parts of our minds that reason locks away by day. We hear, across the distances murmurs of ancient hunters and see **anew**[18] the visions of poets and lovers of long ago.

原文翻译

我家附近有座小山，我常在晚间爬上山去。此时，城市的喧嚣成了遥远的低语。在这黑夜的静谧中，我尽情地分享蟋蟀的欢乐和猫头鹰的私语。不过，我上山是来看月出的，因为这可以让我的内心重新得到被城市肆意挥霍的宁静与清新。

在这座山上，我欣赏过许多次月亮升起的景象。每一次，月亮的脾性都有所不同。秋天，满月如轮，充满自信；春天，月色迷蒙，月儿羞答答的；冬天，银白色的月亮挂在墨黑的、悄无声息的夜空中，显得那样孤寂；夏天，橘黄色的月亮似被烟尘笼罩，俯瞰干燥的田野。每一种月景，都像美妙的音乐，使我心灵震撼，灵魂平静。

观月是一门古老的艺术。在远古的猎人眼里，天空中月亮变化的规律如同心跳一样准确无误。他们知道每29天，月亮就会变得饱满明亮，然后萎缩、消失，然后又再次复活。他们知道，月盈期间，每经一次日落，头顶的月亮会显得更高更大；他们还知道，月亏期间，月亮每晚的升起时间都会推迟，直到消失在日出里。他们竟能从经验中了解到月亮的变化规律，真可谓意义深远。

但我们这些深居室内的人，已与月亮失去了联系。耀眼的街灯、污浊的烟尘掩盖了夜空。虽然人类已在月球上行走过，但月亮对于我们却更加陌生了。很少有人能说出今晚月亮会何时升起。

但无论怎样，月亮依然牵动我们的心灵。如果我们偶然遇见一轮黄灿灿的硕大的满月高高挂在空中，我们都会禁不住满怀敬畏凝望她那高贵的仪容。而月亮也会向那些注视她的人赐予厚礼。

注释
10. **loom** [luːm] *vi.* 隐约地出现，赫然耸现；迫在眉睫
11. **serry** ['serɪ] *v.* 拥挤，密集；使（军队行列等）靠拢，使排紧
12. **subtlety** ['sʌtltɪ] *n.* 精妙，巧妙，敏锐，敏感，狡猾，阴险；细微的差别
13. **inexorably** [ɪn'eksərəbəlɪ] *ad.* 无情地，冷酷地

我得到她的厚礼是在山间7月的一个夜晚。我的车突然无缘无故地熄了火,我孤身一人被困在山中,束手无策。太阳已经西沉,我看见东边山脊处涌出一团橘黄色的明光,好像森林起火一般。突然,山脊自己也似乎迸射出火焰。一会儿,一轮又大又红的月亮从树林里钻了出来,夏天空气中弥漫的灰尘与湿气令它扭曲变形,显得异常怪异。

大地灼热的气息扭曲了它,它变得有些暴躁,不再完美。附近一间农舍的狗紧张地狂吠起来,似乎这团奇怪的光亮叫醒了野草丛中邪恶的幽灵。

然而,当月亮缓缓从山脊处升起,它浑身聚集了坚定与威严。它的面孔也由红色变成了橘红,又变成金色,最后变成沉静的黄色。它似乎吸收了渐渐转暗的大地的光亮,因为随着它的升起,下面的丘陵、山谷变得愈来愈暗淡朦胧。等到皓月当空,满月如盘,闪耀着象牙般乳白的清辉,山谷便成了风景中一片片幽深的阴影。那些狗确信了那团光原来是它们熟悉的月亮,也安定下来,停止了吠叫。霎时间,我也觉得信心倍增,心情舒畅,几乎笑了出来。

这奇特的景观持续了一个小时。月出是缓慢的,充满着一个个微妙的变化。观看月出,我们必须重拾过去那种对时间的耐心。观看月亮不可阻挡地升上空中,会让我们的内心找到不寻常的安宁,我们的想象力能让我们看到宇宙的辽阔和大地的广袤,能让我们忘掉自己的存在。我们感到自身的渺小但又深感大自然的厚待。

月色下,我们看不到生活坚硬的棱角。山坡在月光下如同笼上了柔和的轻纱,一片银白;大海在月光下静谧而碧蓝;我们在月光下也不再像白日那般精于算计,而是更加沉醉在自己的情感中。

这种时候总会发生奇特的事情。在那个7月的夜晚,我欣赏了一两个小时的月景后,回到车里,转动钥匙点火,听到发动机居然响了起来,就像几个小时前它熄火时那样神秘而突然。我身披月光,内心平静,驱车下山回家。

我经常回到山上看月出。我沉醉其中,尤其是当接踵而来的事情使我身心疲惫、判断失准的时候。这种情况经常发生在秋天。这时我就登上那座小山,等待猎人的月亮出现,等着那金黄巨大的圆月跃出地平线,为黑夜带来光明。

一只猫头鹰从山顶俯冲下来,悄无声息地如一道火焰闪过。一只蟋蟀在草丛中长鸣。我想起了诗人和音乐家,想起了贝多芬的《月光奏鸣曲》,以及莎士比亚笔下《威尼斯商人》中洛伦佐的话:"月光沉睡在这岸边多么甜美!/我们坐在这里,让音乐之声/潜入我们的耳内。"我不知道他们的诗句和乐曲,以及蟋蟀的歌声,是否都可算作月亮的微语。想到这些,我那被喧嚣的城市扰乱了的心融化在夜的幽静之中。

我们都倾向于问一些关于生命的起源和命运的深刻问题,恋人和诗人往往在夜里能找到生活更深刻的意义。在夜里,我们沉溺于难解的谜团中,而不是那些统治着白天世界的无关个人的几何学理论。在夜里,我们都成了哲学家和神秘主义者。

月出之时,当我们放慢自己的思想,让它跟天国的节奏同步,一种心醉神迷的感觉会流遍全身。我们会打开情感的窗口,会让白天被理智锁住的那部分思绪尽情奔涌。我们能穿越时空,听见远古猎人的低语,再次看到很久以前的诗人与恋人眼中的景象。

文化点滴

Beethoven

路德维希·凡·贝多芬(Ludwig van Beethoven,1770—1827),德国作曲家、钢琴家、指挥家。维也纳古典乐派代表人物之一。他一共创作了9首编号交响曲、35首钢琴奏鸣曲(其中后32首带有编号)、10部小提琴奏鸣曲、16首弦乐四重奏、1部歌剧、2部弥撒、1部清唱剧与3部康塔塔,另外还有大量室内乐、艺术歌曲与舞曲。这些作品对音乐发展有着深远影响,因此被尊称为乐圣。

注释	14. ignition [ɪɡˈnɪʃən] n. 发火装置,着火,燃烧,点火,点燃	16. citify [ˈsɪtɪfaɪ] vt. 使都市化
		17. vent [vent] n. (感情等的)发泄,吐露;孔,口,通风孔
	15. swoop [swuːp] vi. (鹰)俯冲,猛冲,突然扑向	18. anew [əˈnjuː] ad. 再,重新

Moonlight Sonata

《月光奏鸣曲》，是贝多芬最为出名的代表作之一，又称《第十四钢琴奏鸣曲》，创作于1801年。

Shakespeare

莎士比亚（1564—1616），英国剧作家、诗人。他的戏剧作品被认为是英语文学作品中最伟大的戏剧，其中包括历史剧，如《理查德二世》，喜剧，如《皆大欢喜》，悲剧，如《哈梅雷特》等。此外，他还写了154首十四行诗。

The Merchant of Venice

《威尼斯商人》，莎士比亚的一部著名喜剧。它是莎士比亚早期的重要作品，大约创作于1596至1597年间。该剧本的主题是歌颂仁爱、友谊和爱情，同时也反映了资本主义早期商业资产阶级与高利贷者之间的矛盾，表现了作者对资产阶级社会中金钱、法律和宗教等问题的人文主义思想。这部剧作的一个重要文学成就，就是塑造了夏洛克这一唯利是图、冷酷无情的高利贷者的典型形象。

写作特点

这是一篇散文。英语散文，尤其关注其形式在英国语言中的地位，情形更是如此。散文的"松散"无疑给文学史家带来更多的困难。他需要仔细分析对比散文有别于其他文学形式同时又重叠其他形式的特点；梳理导致散文产生的特别因素，比较它们与其他文学形式产生的因素之间有何不同；追踪散文流变的脉络，不同类型散文的产生与发展，各个类型之间的相互关系，以及因此而给散文带来的丰富与圆满。本文中一些句子语言优美而又意味深长，比如："Each, like fine music, excited my heart and calmed my soul."（每一次月出，就像美妙的音乐一样，激动我的心弦，然后又抚慰我的心灵。）"每一次月出"如同"美妙的音乐"一样能够净化人的心灵。句子用了一个形象的比喻，写出了"每一次月出"的美妙所在和作者对它的独特感受。

品味鉴赏

生活就像品茶，会随着时间的推移，越来越浓。读一篇优美的散文，如品一杯香茗，馨香绕怀，久久不忘。在人类的生命中，会经历很多事物，有些可以逐渐被时光带走而淡忘，有些却历久弥新永生不忘。把这些生命中的馨香记录下来的文字，时时品读，如咀嚼生命的芬芳，每一次都会有新的感动与体悟。本文语体优美，话语优雅，把这些语言记录下来，不仅是对英语能力的锻炼，对知识面的扩展，对自身写作、文学鉴赏能力的提高，也是对性情的一种陶冶，对人生观的一种有益影响。

美文感悟

外国人若欲对英国人的特性有一个正确认识，切不可将视野局限于都市。他须深入乡间，逗留于大小村庄；游览城堡、别墅、农房、村舍；漫步园林，沿树篱和青葱小道缓缓而行；流连于乡村教堂，参加教区节庆、定期集市等乡村节日，并与身份、习惯和性格各异者交往。

Rural Life in England
英国的乡村生活

作者简介：

华盛顿·欧文（Washington Irving，1783—1859），美国作家、短篇小说家、散文家、诗人、游记作家、传记作家和专栏作者，在文学史上素有"美国短篇小说之父"的美称。本书所选主要是短篇小说和散文两大部分，都是欧文脍炙人口的优秀作品。短篇小说如《瑞普·凡·温克尔》《睡谷的传说》《鬼新郎》《大块头先生》《闹鬼的屋子》等，新鲜有趣，引人入胜；散文如《伦敦寻幽》《英国的乡村生活》《乡村葬礼》等，娓娓道来，耐人寻味。

Nothing can be more **imposing**¹ than the **magnificence**² of English park **scenery**³. Vast lawns that extend like sheets of vivid green, with here and there **clumps**⁴ of **gigantic**⁵ trees, heaping up rich piles of **foliage**⁶: the solemn pomp of groves and woodland glades, with the deer trooping in silent herds across them; the hare, bounding away to **covert**⁷; or the **pheasant**⁸, suddenly bursting upon the wing: the brook, taught to wind in natural meanderings or expand into a glassy lake: the **sequestered**⁹ pool, reflecting the quivering trees, with the yellow leaf sleeping on its bosom, and the trout roaming fearlessly about its limpid waters; while some rustic temple

注释
1. imposing [ɪmˈpəʊzɪŋ] a. 印象深刻的，壮观的，威风的
2. magnificence [mæɡˈnɪfɪsns] n. 华丽，富丽堂皇
3. scenery [ˈsiːnəri] n. 风景，景色；舞台布景；风景画；舞台面
4. clump [klʌmp] n. 丛；笨重的脚步声；土块
5. gigantic [dʒaɪˈɡæntɪk] a. 巨大的，庞大的，巨人似的
6. foliage [ˈfəʊlɪɪdʒ] n. 植物的叶子（总称），叶子及梗和枝

or **sylvan**[10] statue, grown green and **dank**[11] with age, gives an air of classic **sanctity**[12] to the **seclusion**[13].

These are but a few of the features of park scenery; but what most delights me, is the creative talent with which the English decorate the **unostentatious**[14] abodes of middle life. The rudest habitation, the most unpromising and scanty portion of land, in the hands of an Englishman of taste, becomes a little paradise.

The sterile spot grows into loveliness under his (an Englishman) hands, and yet the operations of art which produce the effect are scarcely to be perceived. The cherishing and training of some trees; the cautious pruning of others; the nice distribution of flowers and plants of tender and graceful foliage; the introduction of a green slope of velvet turf; the partial opening to a peep of blue distance, or silver gleam of water: all these are managed with a delicate tact, a **pervading**[15] yet quiet assiduity, like the magic touchings with which a painter finishes up a favorite picture.

The residence of people of fortune and refinement in the country has diffused a degree of taste and elegance in rural economy that descends to the lowest class. The very laborer, with his thatched cottage and narrow slip of ground, attends to their embellishment. The trim hedge, the grass, plot before the door, the little flower, bed bordered with snug box, the **woodbine**[16] trained up against the wall, and hanging its blossoms about the lattice, the pot of flowers in the window, the holly, providently planted about the house, to cheat winter of its dreariness, and to throw in a **semblance**[17] of green summer to cheer the fireside: all these bespeak the influence of taste, flowing down from high sources, and pervading the lowest levels of the public mind. If ever Love, as poets sing, delights to visit a cottage, it must be the cottage of an English peasant.

原文翻译

英国园林景致的艳丽确实天下无双。那里真的是处处芳草连天，翠茵匝地，其间巨树蓊郁，浓荫翳日；在那林薮与空旷处，不时可以瞥见结队漫游的鹿群，四处窜匿的野兔与扑簌而起的山鸡；一湾清溪，蜿蜒迂回，极具天然曲折之美，时而又汇潴为一带晶莹的湖面；远处幽潭一泓，林木倒映其中，随风摇漾，把水面的黄叶轻轻送入梦乡，而水下的鳟鱼，往来迅猛，正腾跃于澄澈的素波之间；周围的一些破败的庙宇雕像，虽然粗鄙简陋，霉苔累累，却也给这幽僻之地平添了某种古拙之美。

注释
7. **covert** ['kʌvət] n. 遮蔽处，树丛
8. **pheasant** ['fezənt] n. 雉，野鸡，野鸡肉
9. **sequester** [sɪ'kwestə] vt. 使隔绝，使隔离
10. **sylvan** ['sɪlvən] a. 森林的，林木的；乡村的
11. **dank** [dæŋk] a. 阴湿的，阴冷的
12. **sanctity** ['sæŋktɪtɪ] n. 圣洁，神圣，不可侵犯

这只是公园景观特色的一小部分；但最让我欣赏的是，英国人装饰他们朴实无华的中产阶级生活的创造性才智。最粗鲁的生活习惯，最没有希望的小小的一部分土地，但用英国人的品位来说，却成了一个小小的天堂。

这一方贫瘠的土地在英国人的手下却成了可爱之地，但艺术所创造出来的效果很少被发现。对一些树木的保护和培育，给另外一些树木精心地修剪，花儿散布周围，以及植物的柔嫩而优雅的落叶，绿色斜坡上天鹅绒似的草皮，半掩得仅能瞥见的远处蓝银交映的水光：所有这些都是精心设计的，一份默默而又无处不在的耕耘，就像一位画家完成了他心爱的画时那种充满魔力的触摸。

豪门雅士之居所，弥漫着英格兰乡村优雅之清趣，此类情调虽为阳春白雪，亦可惠及下里巴人。劳其力者，虽居茅庐陋室，耕方寸薄地，亦知修身饰居。宅前树篱齐整，绿草茵茵，花圃精巧，四周黄杨密植；忍冬缘墙而上，其花绽放，星星点点，缀于窗棂；窗台饰有盆花，居所四周植有冬青，聊以消解寒冬之孤寂。室内炉火熊熊，虽非夏日，宅前院后绿意浓浓，亦使居者倍感惬意。凡此种种，皆孕高雅之情趣，自绅士名流，至草根百姓，泽被万民。诗云：爱神若降临尘世，必至英格兰农夫之茅庐。

文化点滴

thatched cottage

茅草屋，听起来很一般，贫穷落后的标志。正当世界上很多地方在破旧立新，将一切旧的东西甚至还不太旧的东西推倒重来的时候，代表贫穷落后的茅草屋在英国却成了国宝。英国各地有很多这种茅草屋，大多都有百年以上的历史，每一个茅草屋都有说不尽的故事。正是由于其独特的历史文化特点，它们基本上都被列为受到国家保护的英国历史文化遗产。

这些茅草屋和其他现代建筑一样可以正常住人，正常在房屋市场上买卖交易。但是，即使你是合法房主，也不可以随便改变它们，它们的外观是一定要保持原样的，内部或许可以稍加变动，但必须经过专门部门的批准，没有他们的批准，你什么都不可以动。

这些茅草屋的价格都不菲，维护费用更不低。它们都年代久远，总会有些地方需要维护修缮。由于草顶易燃，茅草屋的保险费用都很高，保险公司都会收取昂贵的保险金。近年来，由于受到全球气候的影响，茅草的产量迅速减少，翻修屋顶的费用因而成倍增长。

英国人似乎特别喜欢古老的东西，这点和其他很多国家正相反，从他们的服饰到他们乘坐的车子，处处显得老式。再回头想想茅草屋，或许是人家好日子过到了一定的程度，真正理解了什么是生活了吧。

paradise

天堂是天理通透灵魂至上纯净的圣界。每一个人都掌管着天堂。地狱是天理混淆灵魂龌龊不堪的俗世。每一个人也都掌管着地狱。

当人通晓事理，真正读透生命、心醒自觉的时候，精神升华到超然的境界，在开启智慧的一瞬间，便拥有了天堂。当我们迷茫困惑，被世俗蒙蔽窒碍住心灵的时候，我们自然就生活在地狱。

上帝赋予了我们足够的超凡入圣的智慧，可我们一直没有耕播起精神的乐土，始终在世俗中纠缠、在地狱里挣扎。

注释
13. **seclusion** [sɪˈkluːʒən] *n.* 隔绝，隔离，隐居
14. **unostentatious** [ˌʌnˌɒstenˈteɪʃəs] *a.* 不夸耀的，不傲慢的，不虚饰的，朴素的
15. **pervade** [pəˈveɪd] *vt.* 遍及，弥漫，渗透，充满
16. **woodbine** [ˈwʊdbaɪn] *n.* 忍冬属植物
17. **semblance** [ˈsembləns] *n.* 外表，外观；类似；假装；副本，拷贝

写作特点

本文是一篇典型的"华盛顿·欧文"式的散文。欧文散文的最大特点是幽默、诙谐，不拘泥于形式。欧文运用了通俗的文体，在自己18世纪的从容自若、幽默、诙谐及英国式的活泼里加进了当时流行的英国浪漫主义的怀旧之情。

例如，本文的最后一段。外国人对于英国的民族性，如欲认识正确，其观察范围切不可限于大都市。他必须走入农村，在大村小村住一个时期：古堡、别墅、田舍、茅屋他都应该去看一看。

欧文来自荒蛮的、未开化的新大陆，他对英国充满了感情，他的祖辈在那里源远流长，他的胸间洋溢着异国异代的情怀。他对英国的热爱流露于字里行间。

品味鉴赏

欧文是散文大师，是美国文学奠基人之一。他的文笔优雅自然，清新精致，时常流露出温和的幽默。《英国的乡村生活》这篇文章在描写现实生活的细节中巧妙地体现了欧文的幽默与幻想。它的浪漫气息给本文增添了不少风采和魅力。本文的缺点在于书卷气较重，有时流露出感伤的情绪。但是，欧文本身是一位乐观的幽默家，他没有某些文人那种玩世不恭的态度。他对人类充满信心，即使在缅怀古人、凭吊陈迹的时候，也没有悲观失望的情调。

美文感悟

Nature and Man in One
天人合一

"天人合一"的思想观念最早是由庄子阐述,后被汉代思想家、阴阳家董仲舒发展为天人合一的哲学思想体系,并由此构建了中华传统文化的主体。

作者简介:

拉尔夫·沃尔多·爱默生(Ralph Waldo Emerson,1803—1882),生于波士顿。美国思想家、文学家、诗人。爱默生是确立美国文化精神的代表人物。美国前总统林肯称他为"美国的孔子""美国文明之父"。他的生命几乎横贯19世纪的美国,他出生时候的美国热闹却混沌,一些人意识到它代表着某种新力量的崛起,却无人能够清晰地表达出来。

To speak truly, few adult persons can see nature. Most persons do not see the sun. At least they have a very **superficial**[1] seeing. The sun **illuminates**[2] only the eye of the man, but shines into the eye and heart of the child. The lover of nature is he whose inward and outward senses are still truly adjusted to each other, who has retained the spirit of **infancy**[3] even into the era of manhood. His intercourse with heaven and earth becomes part of his daily food. In the presence of nature, a wild delight runs through the man, in spite of real sorrows. Nature says, he is my creature, and **maugre**[4] all his **impertinent**[5] griefs, he shall be glad with me. Not the sun or the

注释
1. **superficial** [ˌsjuːpəˈfɪʃəl] *a.* 表面(上)的,肤浅的,缺乏深度的,一知半解的
2. **illuminate** [ɪˈljuːmɪneɪt] *vt.* 照亮,照明;阐明,说明;装饰,使灿烂

summer alone, but every hour and season yields its tribute of delight; for every hour and change corresponds to and authorizes a different state of mind, from breathless noon to grimmest midnight. Nature is a setting that fits equally well a comic or a mourning piece. In good health, the air is **cordial**[6] of incredible virtue. Crossing a bare common, in snow puddles, at twilight, under a clouded sky, without having in my thoughts any

occurrence of special good fortune, I have enjoyed a perfect **exhilaration**[7]. Almost I fear to think how glad I am.

In the woods too, a man casts off his years, as the snake his **slough**[8], and at what period so ever of life, is always a child. In the woods, is **perpetual**[9] youth. Within these plantations of God, a decorum and sanctity reign, a perennial festival is dressed, and the guest sees not now he should tire of them in a thousand years. In the woods, we return to reason and faith. There I feel that nothing can befall me in life, —no disgrace, no calamity, which nature cannot repair. Standing on the bare ground,— my head bathed by the blithe air, and uplifted into infinite space,—all mean egotism vanishes. I become a transparent eye ball. I am nothing. I see all. The currents of the universal being circulate through me; I am part of the particle of God. The name of the nearest friend sounds then foreign accidental. To be brothers, to be acquaintances,— master or servant, is then a trifle and disturbance. I am the lover of uncontained and immortal beauty. In the wilderness, I find something more dear and **connate**[10] than in streets or villages. In the tranquil landscape, and especially in the distant line of the horizon, man beholds somewhat as beautiful as his own nature.

原文翻译

坦白地说，很少有成年人能够看得见自然。大部分人看不到太阳，至少他们只能看到很表面的东西。因为成年人只用眼睛来观察，而小孩则同时用眼睛和心灵去感受。真正热爱自然的人是这样的，他能够迅速调整，将内心的感受和外来的刺激统一起来，虽然到了成人年龄，仍然拥有一颗孩子的心境。与天地的交流，已经成为他每日不可或缺的精神食粮。面对自然，即使有真正的痛苦，他仍能够沐浴在狂喜之中。大自然说，他是我的孩子，尽管有再多莫名的痛苦，他和我在一起终究会快乐。不仅仅太阳和夏天，每个时辰、每个季节都会让人愉悦，因为从气喘吁吁的中午到冷峻寂静的午夜，每个时辰、每个变化都会造就和主宰完全不同的心境。自然是个大舞台，可以上演喜剧，也可以上演悲剧。在身心健朗的日子，空气就如同一杯醇美的令

注释
3. **infancy** ['ɪnfənsiː] *n.* 婴儿期，幼年时代，初期，摇篮时代
4. **maugre** ['mɔːɡə] *prep.* 不管
5. **impertinent** [ɪm'pɜːtnənt] *a.* 无礼的，莽撞的，不切题的，不中肯的

人难以置信的甘酒。在黄昏时，穿过一片空地，走在雪地里，头顶云雾缭绕，脑子中没有任何发财的意念，完全沉浸在极度的欢愉之中。我几乎不敢去想我有多么快乐。

在森林中，一个人完全可以像蛇蜕皮一样摆脱他的年龄的羁绊，不管到了什么岁数，都可以犹如稚子。在森林中，青春可以永久存在。这是上帝的种植园，里面充满礼仪和神圣，终年装扮一新，客人在这里，住上一千年也不会生厌。在森林中，我们重返理性和信念。在那里，我觉得没有厄运会降临，没有屈辱，也没有自然不能修复的灾难。站在林中空地，我的思绪沐浴在清风之中，宛若飘入无限太空，所有卑劣的傲慢张狂顷刻间不复存在。我变成了一个透明的眼球。没人可以看到我，但我可以看到万物。我穿过世界万物轮回的激流，成为上帝之粒的一部分。最亲密朋友的名字似乎成了不相关的事情，兄弟或熟人，主人或奴仆，都成了微不足道和徒增烦恼的琐事。广袤和不朽之美成为我的至爱。在野外，我发现了比在街道或乡村中更珍贵和纯粹的事物。在宁静的风景中，究其是在遥远的地平线上，人们可以看到和他们天性一样美的东西。

文化点滴

Nature and Man in One

"天人合一"思想，是中华民族五千年来的思想核心与精神实质。它首先指出了人与自然的辩证统一关系；其次表明了人类生生不息，则天、希天、求天、同天的完美主义和进取精神，体现了中华民族的世界观、价值观的思维模式的全面性和自新性。合，就是互相理解，结成友谊。西方人总是企图以高度发展的科学技术征服自然掠夺自然；而东方先哲却告诫我们，人类只是天地万物中的一个部分，人与自然是息息相通的一体。

God

神或至高之物，认为是宇宙万物的创造者和主宰者。《圣经》的思想虽然是公元前七八世纪的产物，但在当时多神教的社会中也称得上"极具想象力"。我们不能否认，"创造上帝的上帝"这种说法所带有的形而上学的色彩使得"唯一上帝"论的发展成为必然。

写作特点

本文的写作，令人感到亲切，富有一种奇异的带有强烈个人色彩的声音。这篇散文在端庄凝重的说教之中每每流溢出特有的富有魅力的睿智、幽默感和文学、哲思的深度来。本文言词文本雄辩有力而辉煌，语调变幻莫测，显示出作者深奥的文学技巧。

注释
6. **cordial** [ˈkɔːdjəl] *a.* 热诚的，诚恳的，兴奋的
7. **exhilaration** [ɪɡˌzɪləˈreɪʃən] *n.* 愉快的心情，高兴
8. **slough** [slu:] *n.* 蜕下的皮（或壳）；泥坑，泥沼，绝境
9. **perpetual** [pəˈpetʃuəl] *a.* 永久的，不断的，无期限的；四季开花的
10. **connate** [ˈkɒneɪt] *a.* 天生的，先天的；同族的

品味鉴赏

　　爱默生是超验主义的倡导者。19世纪的美国被一些历史学家认为是独特的美国文化诞生和成长的时期，是继政治独立之后美国精神、文化从欧洲大陆的母体断乳而真正独立的时期。正是在这样的特殊时代，以爱默生和梭罗等代表的超验主义思潮"横空出世"，成为美国人的精神独立宣言。《天人合一》这篇文章是爱默生超验主义的代表作之一，它综合了美国的个人主义、实用主义和民主精神，摆脱了欧洲的影响，创造出了具有美国性格的独特文化。文章推崇人的能力，对人的本质精神大力颂扬，是自由和民主的精神，为美国的本土文化奠定了根基，推动了美国思想文化的空前繁荣，促进了美国文化和美国精神的独立。

美文感悟

哥特小说，属于英语文学派别，是西方通俗文学中惊险神秘小说的一种。他可以说是恐怖电影的鼻祖，更重要的是，他使我们今天习惯地将哥特式与黑暗、恐怖联系在一起。哥特小说元素包括恐怖、神秘、超自然、厄运、死亡、颓废、住着幽灵的老房子、癫狂、家族诅咒等。

Under the Power of Nature
在自然的威力之下

作者简介：

埃德加·爱伦·坡（Edgar Allan Poe，1809—1849），19 世纪美国诗人、小说家和文学评论家。

During the whole of a dull, dark, and soundless day in the autumn of the year, when the clouds hung up pressively low in the heavens, I had been passing alone, on horseback, through a singularly **dreary**[1] tract of country; and at length found myself, as the shades of the evening

---

注释

1. **dreary** ['drɪərɪ] *a.* 沉寂的，阴沉的，令人厌烦的，枯燥的
2. **melancholy** ['melənkəlɪ] *n.* 忧郁，悲哀，愁思，闷闷不乐
3. **glimpse** [glɪmps] *n.* 一瞥，一看
4. **insufferable** [ɪnˈsʌfərəbl] *a.* 难以忍受的，令人不能容忍的
5. **sedge** [sedʒ] *n.* 莎草
6. **reveler** ['revlə] *n.* 摆设酒宴者，饮酒狂欢者

drew on, within view of the **melancholy**² House of Usher. I knew not how it was—but, with the first **glimpse**³ of the building, a sense of **insufferable**⁴ gloom pervaded my spirit. I say insufferable; for the feeling was unrelieved by any of that half-pleasurable, because poetic, sentiment with which the mind usually receives even the sternest natural images of the desolate or terrible, I looked upon the scene before me—

upon the mere house, and the simple landscape features of the domain, upon the bleak walls, upon the vacant eye-like windows, upon a few randy **sedges**⁵, and upon a few white trunks of decayed trees—with an utter depression of soul which I can compare to no earthly sensation more properly than to the afterdream of the **reveler**⁶ upon opium; the bitter lapse into everyday life, the **hideous**⁷ dropping off of the veil. There was an **iciness**⁸, a sinking, a sickening of the heart, an **unredeemed**⁹ **torture**¹⁰ into ought of the **sublime**¹¹. What was it I paused to think what was it that so unnerved me in the **contemplation**¹² of the House of Usher? It was a mystery all **insoluble**¹³; nor could I **grapple**¹⁴ with the shadowy fancies that crowded upon me as I **pondered**¹⁵. I was forded to fall back upon the unsatisfactory conclusion, that while, beyond doubt, there are combinations of very simple natural objects which have the power of thus affecting us, still the analysis of this power lies among considerations beyond our depth.

原文翻译

那年秋天，一个阴沉、昏暗、岑寂的日子，乌云低垂，厚重地笼罩着大地。整整一天，我孤零零地骑着马，驰过乡间一片无比萧索的旷野。暮色四合之际，令人忧伤的厄榭府终于遥遥在望。我也说不清是怎么回事，一瞥见那座建筑，心灵就充满难以忍受的忧伤。我说难以忍受，那是因为即使人们看到最最严峻、荒凉或可怕的自然景象时，头脑里通常还有某种由景象的富有诗意所产生的几分快感，但此情此景却丝毫引不起此种感情。我看着眼前的情景——宅第本身，房子周围单调的景象，光秃秃的墙壁，空空的、眼睛窟窿似的窗户，几丛杂乱的菅茅，几株灰白的枯树——心情十分沮丧，同人世间任何心情相比，把它比作过足鸦片烟瘾的人，从梦幻中醒来，回到现实生活里的痛苦心情，最为适当了。心中一凉，只觉得往下沉，难受极了。还有一种不可驱除的凄凉之感，无论作何设想也不能激起我的兴致。那么，究竟是什么——我停下来考虑——究竟是什么使我在凝望厄谢尔宅第时如此心烦意乱呢？这是个破解不了的谜。沉思间，模糊的幻想涌满心头，却又无从捉摸。我只得退而求其次，自圆其说罢了——简单的自然景物凑在一起，确实有左右人情绪的力量，但要剖析这种感染力，即便费尽心机，也是无迹可寻。

注释

7. **hideous** [ˈhɪdɪəs] *a.* 令人惊骇的，极其丑陋的，可怕的，丑恶的，讨厌的

8. **iciness** [ˈaɪsɪnɪs] *n.* 冰冷的性质，冰冷

9. **unredeemed** [ˌʌnrɪˈdiːmd] *a.* 尚未实现的，未履行的，未得救的

10. **torture** [ˈtɔːtʃə] *n.* 拷问，折磨，痛苦

文化点滴

opium

鸦片，又叫阿片，俗称大烟，源于罂粟植物蒴果，其所含主要生物碱是吗啡。鸦片因产地不同，呈黑色或褐色；有氨味或陈旧尿味，味苦，气味强烈。生鸦片经烧煮和发酵，可制成精制鸦片，呈棕色或金黄色，吸食时散发香甜气味。鸦片最初是作为药用，目前在药物中仍有应用，如阿片粉、阿片片、复方桔梗散、托氏散、阿橘片等，主要用于镇咳、止泻等。

sedge

莎草，是一种单子叶植物，多年生草本，很少一年生。从表面上看来，它就像是杂草一般。高15～95cm。茎直立，三棱形；根状茎匍匐延长，部分膨大呈纹外向形，有时数个相连。叶丛生于茎基部，叶鞘闭合包于茎上；叶片线形，长20～60cm，先端尖，全缘，具平行脉，主脉于背面隆起。花序复穗状，3～6个在茎顶排成伞状，每个花序具3～10个小穗，线形，长1～3cm，宽约1.5mm；颖2列，紧密排列，卵形至长圆形，长约3mm，膜质两侧紫红色有数脉。基部有叶片状的总苞2～4片，与花序等长或过之；每颖着生1花，雄蕊3；柱头3，丝状。小坚果长圆状倒卵形，三棱状。花期5～8月，果期7～11月。

写作特点

爱伦·坡是比较早的神秘主义和哥特小说的先驱，其显著元素包括恐怖、神秘、超自然、厄运、死亡、颓废，不过其风格特征上又有明显的唯美主义倾向，他的小说准确地说应是——心理式哥特小说。其小说内容怪异离奇，充满恐怖气氛，所用的语言文字又甚是优美华丽。

他一向主张"为艺术而艺术"（Art for Art's Sake）。他的艺术主张几乎贯穿于他的所有作品中，包括诗歌、短篇小说和论文。在这些作品中，他声称"一切艺术的目的是娱乐，不是真理"。他认为："在诗歌中只有创造美——超凡绝尘的美才是引起乐趣的正当途径。音乐是诗歌不可缺少的成分，对诗人力求表现超凡绝尘的美尤其重要。而在故事写作方面，艺术家就不妨力图制造惊险、恐怖和强烈情感的效果。而且每篇作品都应该收到一种效果。"

他把滑稽提高到怪诞，把害怕发展到恐惧，把机智扩大成嘲弄，把奇特变化为怪异和神秘。

注释

11. **sublime** [sə'blaɪm] *a.* 庄严的，雄伟的，令人赞叹的 *n.* 庄严，崇高，至高无上，顶点
12. **contemplation** [kɒntəm'pleɪʃən] *n.* 注视，凝视；沉思；意图
13. **insoluble** [ɪn'sɒljəbəl] *a.* 不能解决的，不溶的
14. **grapple** ['græpəl] *vi.* 抓住，格斗
15. **ponder** ['pɒndə] *vi.* 仔细考虑，沉思

品味鉴赏

爱伦·坡是美国19世纪杰出的诗人、小说家与文艺评论家,一生作品颇丰,涉猎广泛,被誉为多才多艺的侦探小说鼻祖、恐怖小说大师。在世时长期担任报刊编辑工作。其作品是在任何时代都具有"独一无二"的风格。语言和形式精致、优美,内容多样。其小说风格怪异离奇,充满恐怖气氛。受到过爱伦·坡影响的主要人物有:柯南·道尔、波德莱尔、斯特芳·马拉美、儒勒·凡尔纳、罗伯特·路易斯·斯蒂文森、希区柯克、蒂姆·伯顿等。

爱伦·坡最著名的文艺理论是"效果论"。坡力图在自己的作品中先确立某种效果,再为追求这种效果而思考创作。他在《怪异故事集》序中称"自己的作品绝大部分都是深思熟虑的苦心经营"。

他一生写了六七十篇短篇小说,虽然只写了四五篇推理小说,但是举世公认为推理小说的鼻祖。代表作《毛格街血案》《玛丽·罗热疑案》《窃信案》和《金甲虫》都被奉为这类小说的先河,对后世起了很大影响。他在前三篇小说中塑造的业余侦探杜宾的形象,可以说是柯南道尔笔下的福尔摩斯的前辈。

本文被认为是爱伦·坡最著名的散文作品,是美国哥特文学的杰作。本文体现了坡的作品情感基调,特别是恐惧、厄运和内疚的感觉。事实上,在坡的许多故事中,他都借用了哥特式的传统。本文也被批评为过于公式化:重复的主题,如疾病、疯狂和复活。

美文感悟

安徒生童话具有独特的艺术风格,即诗意的美和喜剧性的幽默。前者为主导风格,多体现在歌颂性的童话中,后者多体现在讽刺性的童话中。

The Windmill
风车

作者简介:

汉斯·克里斯蒂安·安徒生(Heinz Christian Andersen,1805—1875),丹麦作家、诗人,他以其童话故事而世界闻名。他最著名的童话故事有《小锡兵》、《冰雪女王》、《拇指姑娘》、《卖火柴的小女孩》、《丑小鸭》和《红鞋》等。安徒生生前曾得到皇家的致敬,并被高度赞扬为给全欧洲的一代孩子带来了欢乐。他的作品已经被译为150多种语言,成千上万册童话书在全球陆续发行出版。他的童话故事还激发了大量电影、舞台剧、芭蕾舞剧以及电影动画的制作。

A windmill stood upon the hill, proud to look at, and it was proud too. "I am not proud at all," it said, "but I am very much **enlightened**[1] without and within. I have sun and moon for my outward use, and for inward use too; and into the **bargain**[2] I have stearine candles, train oil and lamps, and tallow candles. I may well say that I'm enlightened. I'm a thinking being, and so well constructed that it's quite delightful. I have a good windpipe in my chest, and I have four wings that are placed outside my head, just beneath my hat. The birds have only two wings, and

注释
1. enlighten [ɪnˈlaɪtən] *vt.* 启发,启蒙,开导,教导　　便宜货
2. bargain [ˈbɑːɡɪn] *n.* 契约,协定,交易;特价商品,　　3. gallery [ˈɡæləri] *n.* 画廊;走廊

are obliged to carry them on their backs. I am a Dutchman by birth, that may be seen by my figure— a flying Dutchman. They are considered supernatural beings, I know, and yet I am quite natural. I have a **gallery**³ round my chest, and house-room beneath it; that's where my thoughts dwell. My strongest thought, who rules and **reigns**⁴, is called by others 'The Man in the Mill.' He knows what he wants, and is lord over the

meal and the bran; but he has his companion, too, and she calls herself 'Mother.' She is the very heart of me. She does not run about stupidly and awkwardly, for she knows what she wants, she knows what she can do, she's as soft as a **zephyr**⁵ and as strong as a storm; she knows how to begin a thing carefully, and to have her own way. She is my soft temper, and the father is my hard one. They are two, and yet one; they each call the other 'My half.'

"These two have some little boys, young thoughts, that can grow. The little ones keep everything in order. When, lately, in my wisdom, I let the father and the boys examine my throat and the hole in my chest, to see what was going on there,—for something in me was out of order.

"The little ones made a **tremendous**⁶ noise. The youngest jumped up into my hat, and shouted so there that it tickled me. The little thoughts may grow— I know that very well; and out in the world thoughts come too, and not only of my kind, for as far as I can see, I cannot **discern**⁷ anything like myself; but the wingless houses, whose throats make no noise, have thoughts too, and these come to my thoughts, and make love to them, as it is called. It's wonderful enough— yes, there are many wonderful things.

"Something has come over me, or into me,— something has changed in the mill-work. It seems as if the one half, the father, had altered, and had received a better temper and a more **affectionate**⁸ helpmate— so young and good, and yet the same, only more gentle and good through the course of time. What was bitter has passed away, and the whole is much more comfortable.

"The days go on, and the days come nearer and nearer to clearness and to joy; and then a day will come when it will be over with me; but not over altogether. I must be pulled down that I may be built up again; I shall cease, but yet shall live on. To become quite a different being, and yet remain the same! That's difficult for me to understand, however enlightened I may be with sun, moon, stearine, train oil, and tallow. My old wood-work and my old brick-work will rise again from the dust!

注释

4. **reign** [reɪn] *n.* 君主的统治，君主统治时期，任期，当政期 惊人的，极好的
5. **zephyr** ['zefə] *n.* 和风，微风
7. **discern** [dɪ'sɜːn] *vt.* 看出，理解，了解，识别，辨别
6. **tremendous** [trɪ'mendəs] *a.* 极大的，巨大的，可怕的，
8. **affectionate** [ə'fekʃənɪt] *a.* 深情的，挚爱的，慈爱的，

"I will hope that I may keep my old thoughts, the father in the mill, and the mother, great ones and little ones—he family; for I call them all, great and little, the company of thoughts, because I must, and cannot refrain from it. And I must also remain 'myself,' with my throat in my chest, my wings on my head, the gallery round my body; else I should not know myself, nor could the others know me, and say, 'There's the mill on the hill, proud to look at, and yet not proud at all.'"

That is what the mill said. Indeed, it said much more, but that is the most important part.

And the days came, and the days went, and yesterday was the last day.

Then the mill caught fire. The flames rose up high, and beat out and in, and bit at the beams and **planks**[9], and ate them up. The mill fell, and nothing remained of it but a heap of ashes. The smoke drove across the scene of the **conflagration**[10], and the wind carried it away.

Whatever had been alive in the mill remained, and what had been gained by it has nothing to do with this story. The miller's family—one soul, many thoughts, and yet only one-built a new, a splendid mill, which answered its purpose. It was quite like the old one, and people said, "Why, **yonder**[11] is the mill on the hill, proud to look at!" But this mill was better arranged, more according to the time than the last, so that progress might be made. The old beams had become worm—eaten and **spongy**[12]—they lay in dust and ashes. The body of the mill did not rise out of the dust as they had believed it would do. They had taken it literally, and all things are not to be taken literally.

原文翻译

　　山上有一个风车。它的样子很骄傲，它自己也真的感到很骄傲。"我一点也不骄傲！"它说："不过我的里里外外都很明亮。太阳和月亮照在我的外面，也照着我的里面，我还有用鲸油烛和牛油烛混合做成的蜡烛。因此我敢说我现在是又明亮又聪明。我还是一个有思想的人；我的构造很好，一看就叫人感到愉快。在我的怀里有一块很好的磨石；我的翅膀有四个，比鸟儿的翅膀还多两个，而且鸟的翅膀只生在背上，而我的翅膀恰恰在我的帽子底下。'我生出来就是一个荷兰人'；这点可以从我的形状看得出来——'一个飞行的荷兰人'。我知道，大家把这种人叫作'超自然'的东西，但是我却很自然。我的肚皮上围着一圈走廊，下面有一个住室——我的'思想'就藏在这里面。别的'思想'把我一个最强大的主导'思想'叫作'磨坊人'。他知道他的要求是什么，他管理面粉和麸子。他也有一个伴侣，名叫'妈妈'。她是我真正的心。她并不傻里傻气地乱跑，因为她知道自己要什么，知道自己能做什么。她像微风一样温和，像暴风雨一样强烈。她知道怎样以她的方式应付事情。她是我的温柔的一面，而'爸爸'却是我的坚强的一面。他们是两个人，但也可以说是一个人。他们彼此称为'我的老伴'。

　　"这两个人还有几个小孩子——小'思想'，这些'小思想'也能长大成人。这些小家伙总是做得井井有条。

注释	有感情的	11. yonder ['jɒndə] ad. 在那边，在远处
	9. plank [plæŋk] n. （厚）木板；支持物；政纲条目	12. spongy ['spʌndʒɪ] a. 海绵似的，柔软吸水的，富有弹性的
	10. conflagration [ˌkɒnfləˈgreɪʃən] n. 大火（灾）	

最近我曾经严肃地叫'爸爸'和孩子们把我的喉咙和怀里的磨石检查一下。我希望知道这两件东西到底出了什么毛病，因为我的内部现在是有毛病了。

"这些小家伙闹出可怕的声音来。最小的那几个钻到我的帽子里乱叫，弄得我怪不舒服。小'思想'可以长大起来，这一点我知道得清清楚楚。外面也有别的'思想'来访，不过他们不是属于我这个家族，因为据我看来，他们跟我没有共同之点。那么没有翅膀的屋子——你听不见他们磨石的声音——也有些'思想'。他们来看我的'思想'并且跟我的'思想'谈起所谓恋爱来。这真是奇妙；的确，奇妙的事也真多。

"我的身上——或者身子里——最近起了某种变化：磨石的活动有些异样。我似乎觉得'爸爸'换了一个'老伴'：他似乎得到一个脾气更温和、更热情的配偶——非常年轻和温柔。但人还是原来的人，只不过时间使她变得更可爱、更温柔罢了。不愉快的事情都没有了，一切都非常愉快。

"日子过去了，新的日子又到来了。时间一天一天地接近光明和快乐，直到最后我的一切完了为止——但不是绝对地完了。我将被拆掉，好使我又能够变成一个新的、更好的风车。我将死亡，但是我将继续活下去！我将变成另一个东西，但同时又没有变！这一点我却难得理解，不管我是被太阳、月亮、混合烛、兽烛和蜡烛照得怎样明亮，我的旧木料和砖土将会再次从地上立起来。

"我希望我仍能保持住我的老'思想'们：磨坊里的爸爸、妈妈、大孩和小孩——整个的家庭。我把他们大大小小都叫作'思想的家属'，因为我没有他们是不成的。但是我也要保留住我自己——保留住我胸腔里的磨石，我头上的翅膀，我肚皮上的走廊，否则我就不会认识我自己，别人也不会认识我，同时会说：'山上有一个磨坊，看起来倒是蛮了不起，但是也没有什么了不起。'"

这是磨坊说的话。事实上，它说得比这还多，不过这是最重要的一部分罢了。

日子来，日子去，而昨天是最后的一天。

这个磨坊着了火。火焰升得很高。它向外面燎，也向里面燎。它舔着大梁和木板。结果这些东西就全被吃光了。磨坊倒下来了，它只剩下一堆火灰。燃过的地方还在冒着烟，但是风把它吹走了。

磨坊里曾经活着过的东西，现在仍然活着，并没有因为这件意外事件而被毁掉。事实上它还因为这个意外事件而得到许多好处。磨坊主的一家——一个灵魂，许多"思想"，但仍然只是一个思想——又新建了一个新的、漂亮的磨坊。这个新的跟那个旧的没有任何区别，同样有用。人们说："山上有一个磨坊，看起来很像个样儿！"不过这个磨坊的设备更好，比前一个更现代化，因为事情终归是进步的。那些旧的木料都被虫蛀了，潮湿了。它们现在变成了尘土。它起初想象的完全相反，磨坊的躯体并没有重新站起来。这是因为它太相信字面上的意义了，而人们是不应该从字面上看一切事情的意义的。

文化点滴

flying Dutchman

飞翔的荷兰人，又译作漂泊的荷兰人、彷徨的荷兰人、飞行的荷兰人等，是传说中一艘永远无法返乡的幽灵船，注定在海上漂泊航行。飞翔的荷兰人通常在远距离被发现，有时还散发着幽灵般的光芒。据说如果有其他船只向她打招呼，她的船员会试图托人向陆地上或早已死去的人捎信。在海上传说中，与这艘幽灵船相遇，在航海者看来是毁灭的征兆。飞翔的荷兰人用来形容受诅的荷兰人永远漂泊在海上，四处航行，却始终无法靠岸的悲惨宿命。

super nature

超自然现象，可以理解为超越自然科学常规和可知性范围的一种极端现象。或者说，超越了当代自然科学知识的极限而被认为不可能产生或无法解释的现象。超自然通常指超自然力量或者超自然现象，即在自然界无法见到同时无法用通常手段证实的力量或现象。一旦超自然能够被证实，则它就不再是超自然了。超自然超出科学的范畴，因为科学的研究对象必须是可证实的测量以及通过同行评审。超自然一般同宗教信仰和形而上学紧密联系，有时跟超常现象一词同义。

写作特点

本文诗意浓重，优雅，浪漫，多情善感，充满古典诗意美。这正是安徒生魅力的所在，安徒生把诗溶入他所要描写的东西中，使人产生一种仿佛置身其中，并不自觉地感受到他童话所散发的幸福的感觉。这样的写法是安徒生性情的一个表现，同时也吻合儿童的心理，并能给予他们以正确的审美引导。安徒生的童话主要是讲给读者听的，他在"听"字上大下功夫。他独创了一种童话体裁，完全是老奶奶讲故事的口吻，但又打破了传统童话的"从前有个国王"之类的俗套，而采取一种与读者亲密无间的谈心的形式。安徒生的想象力特别丰富，形象思维能力很强。凡是他的想象力所接触的事物都有了生命，都发出光辉。他能细察各种生物和无生物的灵魂，给他们以独特的容貌和语言，使他们像人类一样生活着、劳动着，像人类一样有爱情，也有痛苦。

品味鉴赏

《风车》的描写很有生气，它是有生命的、活的。本文摒除世俗的一切规则，口气完全是天真的、单纯的。文章描写地方特有的景象，让人极易联想到它本身的描写来表现童话所处的社会环境，自然、不繁冗。本文用特定存在的地方影射童话背景，使描写不会显得大而无当，会很充实，让人更容易接受。安徒生把他去过的地方的特点总结起来，作典型的描写，既增长了读者的知识，又充实了他的故事。我们写文章亦需如此，源于生活，高于生活。

美文感悟

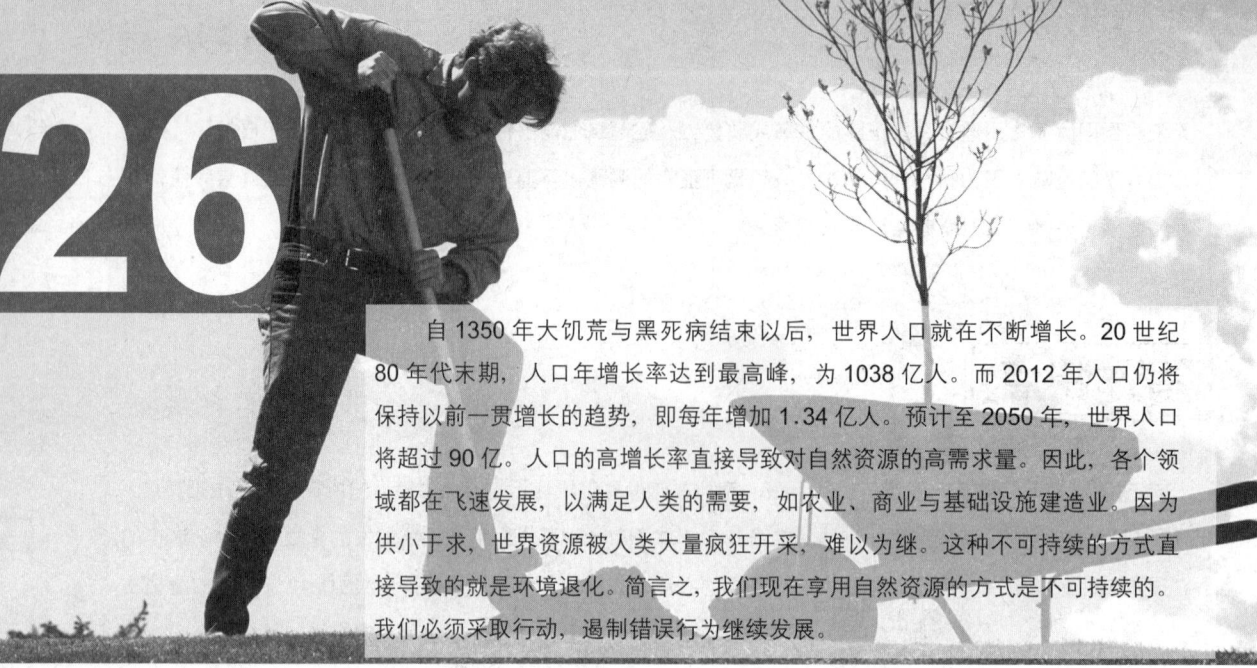

自1350年大饥荒与黑死病结束以后,世界人口就在不断增长。20世纪80年代末期,人口年增长率达到最高峰,为1038亿人。而2012年人口仍将保持以前一贯增长的趋势,即每年增加1.34亿人。预计至2050年,世界人口将超过90亿。人口的高增长率直接导致对自然资源的高需求量。因此,各个领域都在飞速发展,以满足人类的需要,如农业、商业与基础设施建造业。因为供小于求,世界资源被人类大量疯狂开采,难以为继。这种不可持续的方式直接导致的就是环境退化。简言之,我们现在享用自然资源的方式是不可持续的。我们必须采取行动,遏制错误行为继续发展。

Population and Natural Resources
人口与自然资源

Populations increase and decrease relatively not only to one another, but also to natural resources. In most parts of the world, the relation between population and resources is already unfavorable and will probably become even more unfavorable in the future. This growing poverty in the midst of growing poverty **constitutes**[1] a **permanent**[2] menace not only to peace but also to **democratic**[3] **institutions**[4] and personal liberty. For overpopulation is not **compatible**[5] with freedom. An unfavorable relationship between numbers and resources tends to make the earning of a living almost intolerably difficult. Labor is more abundant than goods, and the individual is compelled to work long hours for little pay. No surplus of **accumulated**[6] purchasing power stands between him and the **tyrannies**[7] of unfriendly nature or of the equally unfriendly wielders of political and economic power. Democracy is, among other things, the ability to say "no" to the boss. But a man cannot say "no" to the boss, unless he is sure of being able to eat when the boss's favor has been withdrawn. And he cannot be certain of his next meal unless he owns

注释
1. **constitute** [ˈkɒnstɪtjuːt] vt. 构成,组成
2. **permanent** [ˈpɜːmənənt] a. 永恒的,永久的
3. **democratic** [ˌdeməˈkrætɪk] a. 民众的,民主的
4. **institution** [ˌɪnstɪˈtjuːʃən] n. 设立,制度,事业单位

the means of producing enough wealth for his family to live on, or has been able to accumulate a surplus out of past wages, or has a chance of moving to virgin **territories**[8], where he can make a fresh start. In an overcrowded country, very few people own enough to make them financially independent; very few are in a position to accumulate purchasing power; and there is no free land. Moreover, in any country where

population presses hard upon natural resources, the general economic situation is apt to be so **precarious**[9] that government control of capital and labor, production and consumption, becomes inevitable. It is no accident that the twentieth century should be the century of highly centralized governments and totalitarian dictatorships; it had to be so for the simple reason that the twentieth century is the century of **planetary**[10] overcrowding.

原文翻译

　　各国人口的增长与减少不单彼此相关，而且与自然资源也有关联。在世界上大部分地方，人口和资源的关系已经非常不利而且在将来会变得更加不利。不断扩大的贫穷不仅对和平构成永久的威胁，也对民主制度和个人自由形成威胁。因为人口过剩与自由是不相容的，人口与资源的不利关系会导致谋生成为难以忍受的困难。劳动力比商品更加丰富，个人被强迫工作很长时间而只得到很少的工资。在他与不友善的自然肆虐或者同样不友善的政治和权力支配者的暴虐之间，是没有任何积累起来的剩余购买力可言的。民主，除了其他特点，就是向老板说"不"的能力。但是，一个人不能对老板说"不"，除非在他的老板撤销了对他的恩惠之后他仍然能有饭吃。而且，除非他拥有生产足够养家糊口的财富的生产资料，或者能从他以前的工资中攒下一定的余钱，或者有机会迁徙到未开垦的地区，在那里他可以重新开始大有作为，否则，他不能肯定他的下一顿饭是否有着落。在一个人口过多的国家里，很少有人拥有足够的财富使其在经济上独立；能够积累购买力的人也极少；并且没有空闲的土地。而且，在任何国家里，人口对自然资源施压过大的话，总的经济形势会非常不稳定，以致政府对资本和劳力、生产和消费的控制就不可避免了。20 世纪是高度中央集权政府和极权主义独裁的世纪，这并不是偶然的，道理很简单，20 世纪是地球上人口过分拥挤的世纪。

注释
5. **compatible** [kəmˈpætəbl] *a.* 协调的，相融的
6. **accumulate** [əˈkjuːmjuleɪt] *vt.* 积累
7. **tyranny** [ˈtɪrəni] *n.* 暴虐，残暴
8. **territory** [ˈterɪtəri] *n.* 领土，领域
9. **precarious** [prɪˈkeərɪəs] *a.* 不稳定的
10. **planetary** [ˈplænɪˌteri] *a.* 行星的；俗世的，现世的

文化点滴

populations

历史发展表明，人口增长模式是由原始型转向传统型，继而向现代型逐步过渡。一个国家或地区人口增长模式的转变与社会经济发展、传统文化观念和相关的人口政策等密切相关。

世界上不同国家和地区的人口增长模式都在发生着变化。由于不同国家、地区的工业化进程和社会经济发展差异的扩大，世界人口增长模式的地区差异也随之扩大。尤其在第二次世界大战以后，世界人口增长模式的地区差异更加明显。

20 世纪 50 年代后，发达国家的人口出生率不断降低，到 70 年代中期，以欧洲和北美为代表的发达地区的人口自然增长率平均不足 1%，人口增长模式已进入现代型。目前，一些发达国家的人口自然增长率很低，甚至呈现负增长。大多数发展中国家的人口死亡率已降至与发达国家相当的水平，但是人口的出生率仍然较高，人口增长模式还没有完成从传统型向现代型的转变。由于发展中国家的人口占世界人口的绝大多数，所以，总体看来，世界人口增长模式仍处于由传统型转向现代型的过渡阶段。

中国是世界上人口最多的国家，人口增长模式能否顺利实现转变，对世界人口增长模式的转变起着举足轻重的作用。20 世纪 70 年代以来，中国由于大力开展计划生育工作，目前已基本实现了人口增长模式从传统型向现代型的转变。

一个地区人口的自然增长，是由出生率和死亡率共同决定的。回顾历史，世界人口数量变化的总趋势是不断增长的，但是不同的历史时期，人口数量增长的特点不同。自然增长率大于 0，表示人口增加。

出生率是一年内出生婴儿数占总人数的比率，死亡率是一年内死亡的人数占总人数的比率。

人口的数量自有记录以来，在 18 世纪以前，人口增长得十分缓慢；18 世纪以后，特别是 20 世纪以来，世界人口的增长速度才大大加快。

natural resources

凡是自然物质经过人类的发现，被输入生产过程，或直接进入消耗过程，变成有用途的，或能给人以舒适感，从而产生有价值的东西。自然环境中与人类社会发展有关的、能被利用来产生使用价值并影响劳动生产率的自然诸要素，通常称为自然资源。自然资源可分为有形自然资源（如土地、水体、动植物、矿产等）和无形自然资源（如光资源、热资源等）。自然资源具有可用性、整体性、变化性、空间分布不均匀性和区域性等特点，是人类生存和发展的物质基础和社会物质财富的源泉，是可持续发展的重要依据之一。自然资源包括生物资源、农业资源、森林资源、国土资源、矿产资源、海洋资源、气候气象、水资源等。

写作特点

本文具有深刻的教育意义，体现出了通俗易懂的特点，举例子是本文主要的写作方法之一。

例 如：Democracy is, among other things, the ability to say "no" to the boss. But a man cannot say "no" to the boss, unless he is sure of being able to eat when the boss's favor has been withdrawn. And he cannot be certain of his next meal unless he owns the means of producing enough wealth for his family to live on, or has been able to accumulate a surplus out of past wages, or has a chance of moving to virgin territories, where he can make a fresh start. 这段话举例清晰浅显。把复杂的道理简单化正是举例子写作方法的特点，通过举例法，本文更加贴近生活实际，更有说服力。

品味鉴赏

我国是世界上最大的发展中国家，人口基数大是我国的基本国情，且资源相对短缺，关系着人类基本生存的淡水、耕地、森林、草地人均占有量分别只有世界人均水平的28.1%、32.3%、14.3%和32.3%。加之高负荷的人口因素，造成土地过度被垦殖，森林资源锐减，水土流失严重，生态环境恶化，自然灾害频繁。未来人们面临着生存和发展的双重压力。

我们要正确处理两个关系：

一是正确处理人口与资源环境相适应的关系；

二是正确处理开发与保护并重的关系。

解决好人口、资源和环境与社会经济的协调发展，并形成良性循环的运行机制，我国要全面实施可持续发展战略的根本保障，这也是保持我国可持续发展的首要问题。

美文感悟

随着经济社会的迅速发展,野生动植物资源受到了前所未有的威胁,许多野生动植物资源急剧减少甚至消失。人类要保护生物链条,保护生态平衡。

Significance of Wildlife Protection
保护野生生物意义重大

With rapid **extinction**[1] of many wild species, more and more people come to realize the great significance of wildlife protection.

We have to understand the problem, in a new light that we protect ourselves by protecting wildlife. On the one hand, any species of wildlife, as a critical joint of the **ecological**[2] chain, helps to establish the ecological balance. If one species becomes extinct, it will disappear forever. What is more, it will inevitably result in the extinction of a chain of wildlife and the **disruption**[3] of the ecological balance. Unpredictable disasters may occur. On the other hand, with the development of modern science and technology, man is just beginning to learn about wildlife. For example, if wild rubber trees

注释
1. extinction [ɪkˈstɪŋkʃən] n. 灭绝,绝种
2. ecological [ˌiːkəˈlɒdʒɪkəl] a. 生态的,生态学的
3. disruption [dɪsˈrʌpʃn] n. 分裂,瓦解
4. preserve [prɪˈzɜːv] v. 保护,维持,保存

had been extinct two centuries ago, there would be no auto industry today. Moreover wildlife **preserves**[4] unknown genetic codes, which may turn out to be a vital importance and free human beings from fatal diseases and natural disasters in the future.

It is **imperative**[5] for us to protect wildlife right now before it is too late, because man has already polluted the environment seriously and threaten the existence of many wild species. Let's take action to protect wildlife. Learning to live in **harmony**[6] with all wildlife is part of modern civilization.

原文翻译

随着许多野生物种的迅速灭绝，越来越多的人开始意识到保护野生生物的重要性。

我们必须从新的角度来理解这个问题：通过保护野生生物来实现自我保护。一方面，任何野生生物物种都是生物链的关键一环，都帮助建立生态平衡。如果一个物种消亡了，那它就永远地消失了。并且，这将不可避免地导致一连串的野生物种消亡并打破生态平衡，不可预知的灾难就将出现。另一方面，随着现代科学和技术的发展，人类正开始了解野生生物。比如，如果野生橡胶树在两个世纪前灭绝了，就不会有今天的汽车工业。而且，野生生物保存了一些未知的基因密码，这些也许会被证明极其重要，可能在未来把人类从致命的疾病和自然灾害中解脱出来。

现在我们必须保护野生生物，这是刻不容缓的事情，否则就太晚了。因为人类已经严重地污染了环境并且威胁到许多野生生物的存在。让我们行动起来，保护野生生物。学会和野生生物和谐共存是现代文明的一部分。

文化点滴

wildlife protection

野生动物是大自然的产物，自然界是由许多复杂的生态系统构成的。有一种植物消失了，以这种植物为食的昆虫就会消失。某种昆虫没有了，捕食这种昆虫的鸟类将会饿死；鸟类的死亡又会对其他动物产生影响。所以，大规模野生动物毁灭会引起一系列连锁反应，产生严重后果。

ecological balance

生态平衡是指在一定时间内生态系统中的生物和环境之间、生物各个种群之间，通过能量流动、物质循环和信息传递，使它们相互之间达到高度适应、协调和统一的状态。也就是说，当生态系统处于平衡状态时，系统内各组成成分之间保持一定的比例关系，能量、物质的输入与输出在较长时间内趋于相等，结构和功能处于相对稳定状态，在受到外来干扰时，能通过自我调节恢复到初始的稳定状态。在生态系统内部，生产者、消费者、分解者和非生物环境之间，在一定时间内保持能量与物质输入、输出动态的相对稳定状态。

注释
5. imperative [ɪmˈperətɪv] *a.* 紧急的，必要的，命令的
6. harmony [ˈhɑːmənɪ] *n.* 协调，调和，和谐

写作特点

　　本文采取了递进式的写法，文章各层次之间层层深入，引出保护野生生物意义重大。作者使用了四个表示递进关系的短语：On one hand, What is more, On the other hand, Moreover. 这些短语的使用，体现了文章层次感鲜明，步步深入，使读者更加容易理解文章的中心思想。

品味鉴赏

　　所谓生态平衡，首先是生物数量上的相对平衡，因此，为了保持生态系统的稳定，必须保持各生物物种的相对数量。人类居于能量金字塔的最顶端，按理个体数量不应该很大。然而，世界人口还在快速增长，使得地球生态系统面临崩溃的危险。人类又是最典型的杂食动物，几乎能从每一个营养级中摄取食物，因此，食物链与人类休戚相关。如果食物链受污染，那么就要危及人类的生存，这就是各国关注农药及化学污染的重要原因。大自然是一个完整的生物链，人和动物的和谐相处会使我们所生活的环境更加美好，保持生态平衡是我们义不容辞的责任。

美文感悟

威廉·黑尔·怀特的这篇文章笔法老到，韵味空灵，具有惊人的魅力。

An Afternoon Walk in October
十月的下午散步

作者简介：

威廉·黑尔·怀特（William Hale White，1831—1913），英国小说家、评论家。长期用"马克·拉瑟福德"的笔名发表作品。有《马克·拉瑟福德自传》和小说《坦纳巷的革命》等作品。

It was a day by itself, coming after a fortnight's storm and rain. The sun did not shine clearly, but it spread through the clouds a tender, diffused light, crossed by level cloud-bars, which stretched to a great length, quite **parallel**[1]. The tints in the sky were wonderful, very **conceivable**[2] shade of blue-grey, which contrived to modulate into the golden brilliance in which the sun was veiled. I went out in the afternoon. It was too early in the year for a heavy fall of leaves, but nevertheless the garden was covered. They were washed to the sides of the roads, and lay heaped up over the road-gratings, masses of **gorgeous**[3] harmonies in red, brown, and yellow. The chestnuts and acorns dropped in showers, and the patter on the **gravel**[4] was a little weird. The chestnut husks split wide open when they came to the ground, revealing the polished

注释
1. **parallel** ['pærəlel] *a.* 平行的，相同的，类似的
2. **conceivable** [kən'siːvəbl] *a.* 可想到的，可相信的，可想象的，可能的
3. **gorgeous** ['gɔːdʒəs] *a.* 华丽的，艳丽的，极好的，称心的

brown of the shy fruit.

The **lavish**[5], **drenching**[6] downpour in **extravagant**[7] excess had been glorious. I went down to the bridge to look at the floods. The valley was a great lake, reaching to the big trees in the fields which had not yet lost the fire in their branches. The river-channel could be discerned only by the boiling of the current. It had risen above the crown of the main stone arch, and swirled and **plunged**[8] underneath it. A furious backwater, repulsed from the smaller arch, aided the **tumult**[9]. The wind had gone and there was perfect silence, save for the **agitation**[10] of the stream, but a few steps upwards the gentle tinkle of the little runnels could be heard in their deeply-cut, dark, and narrow channels. In a few minutes they were caught up, **rejoicing**[11], in the embrace of the deep river which would carry them with it to the sea. They were safe now from being lost in the earth.

I went a little further up the hill: a flock of about fifty sheep were crossing from a field on one side of the road to another directly opposite. They were packed close together, and their backs were an **undulating**[12] continuous surface. The shepherd was pursuing a stray sheep, and they stood still for a minute in the middle of the road. A farmer came up in his gig and was held back. He used impatient language. Oh farmer! Which is of more importance to the heavenly power—that you should not be stopped, or that the sheep should **loiter**[13] and go into that field at their own pace? All sheep, by the way, look sad. Perhaps they are dimly aware of their **destiny**[14].

原文翻译

接连两个星期的狂风暴雨之后，天终于放晴了。阳光还不是十分明亮，穿过水平的条状云朵，抛洒出一片柔和的光芒。那水平的云朵横贯长空，好似一条条平行线。天空呈现出奇异的色彩，每一种可以想象得到的蓝灰色，都在努力变成灿烂的金光，给太阳蒙上面纱。这天下午我信步出门。还不到一年中落叶纷飞的季节，花园却已被枯叶覆盖。它们被雨水冲到路边，堆积在阴沟格栅上，红色的、褐色的、黄色的，一堆堆、一丛丛，既绚丽多彩，又和谐悦目。栗子和橡子雨点般纷纷坠下，嗒嗒地拍打在鹅卵石上，给人一种神秘感。栗子的外壳撞击在地面上时完全绽裂开来，露出油光光羞答答的褐色果肉。

倾盆暴雨过后留下了一幅壮观的景象。我走到桥上，观看桥下的洪水。此时山谷已成一片湖泽，一直延

注释
4. **gravel** ['grævl] n. 沙砾；鹅卵石
5. **lavish** ['lævɪʃ] a. 过分慷慨的，非常浪费的，过分丰富的，浪费的，放肆的
6. **drenching** ['drentʃɪŋ] n. 湿透
7. **extravagant** [ɪks'trævɪɡənt] a. 过度的，过分的，奢侈的，
8. **plunge** [plʌndʒ] n. 投入，陷入；游泳，跳水
9. **tumult** ['tuː,mʌlt] n. 吵闹，喧哗，激动的吵闹声

伸到田野中的大树，大树的枝干上还残留着天火留下的痕迹。河道在翻腾的水流中隐约可见。水流已升至石桥主洞的顶部，在那里翻滚咆哮。遇到小些的石洞返回的湍急回流，让流水更加汹涌澎湃。风已停息，除了水流的翻腾躁动声，四处一片静寂谧。但朝着细流的方向稍走几步，就可以听到细流在幽深、黑暗、狭窄的水道中汩汩的声音。过不了几分钟，这些细流就欢快地流向深深的河流，这些流水把它们带向海洋。现在，它们安全了，再也不用担心会消失在泥土里。

我继续朝山上走了一段路：只见一群绵羊，大约 50 多头，正从路边一块田野穿过大路，走向正对面的另一块田野。它们紧紧地挤在一起，背部构成一片绵延起伏的平面。牧羊人去追赶一头离群的羊，羊群一时停在了大路中间。一个农夫这时架着一辆双轮马车走过来，被挡住了去路。他不耐烦地使用了粗暴的语言。啊，农夫！对于万能的上帝，哪件事情更加重要呢——你不应该被挡住去路，还是羊群应该以它们自己的速度慢悠悠地走向对面那块田野？顺便说一句，羊群里的每一头羊，都是满脸的悲哀神色。也许，它们已经隐隐约约知道自己的命运。

文化点滴

acorn

橡子是栎树的果实，形似蚕茧，故又称栗茧。橡子外表硬壳，棕红色，内仁如花生仁，淀粉含量达 60% 左右；既可食，又可作纺织工业浆纱用的原料。橡子是号称比水稻、小麦"资格"还要老的粮食。人们食用橡子的历史至少可以追溯到公元前 600 多年。在过去漫长的岁月中，橡子一直是许多山区人民的主要食物。每百斤橡仁可酿 55 度的白酒 40 斤左右。鄂东山区都有橡子，可供采摘。

gig

轻便双轮马车是马拉的车子，或载人，或运货。它的历史极为久远，几乎与人类的文明一样漫长。一直到 19 世纪，马车仍然是城市交通十分重要的交通工具。人们喜欢马车的优雅和诗意，喜欢乘坐马车从容地穿过乡村大道或古旧的城区街巷去访问朋友。随着火车和汽车的出现，车轮转动的速度越来越快。至此，马车的黄金时代宣告结束。

注释
10. **agitation** [ˌædʒɪˈteɪʃən] *n.* 搅动，搅拌；激动，煽动，鼓动
11. **rejoice** [rɪˈdʒɔɪs] *vi.* 高兴，欢庆
12. **undulate** [ˈʌndʒəˌleɪt] *vi.* 起伏，波动，呈波浪形；震动
13. **loiter** [ˈlɔɪtə] *vi.* 走走停停，闲逛，游荡，磨蹭
14. **destiny** [ˈdestɪnɪ] *n.* 命运，天命，天数

写作特点

本文是一篇描写景物的散文，运用了大量的拟人（personification）修辞手法。例如：

1) …revealing the polished brown of the shy fruit.

2) It had risen above the crown of the main stone arch, and swirled and plunged underneath it.

3) All sheep, by the way, look sad. Perhaps they are dimly aware of their destiny.

Personification is a figure of speech in which the *n.*, *v.*, *adj.*, and *adv.* which are originally used to describe a man are now used instead to describe other living things, inanimate objects, and abstract concept, thus attributing the characteristics of humans to them. Personification reflects the way we understand the outside world and also is the result of our creative imagination.

品味鉴赏

金秋十月的一个晴朗的下午，清新、优雅，还有几分忧郁的气息。雨停、风住，流水潺潺，水道、河流、海洋、喧闹欢快，而这背后是难得的宁谧世界。世界上有羊群、有农夫，世界是美丽的、安宁的、理想化的，而现实，使人心中渐渐产生一丝哀愁。

美文感悟

> 四季更迭的自然之美,可以越过悠远的年代,在任何时候都能够捕捉住人的视线。诗人优美的文字及其中对季节变换、人生从激情绚烂转至平淡宁静的沉思,读起来让人不禁反复咀嚼,细细品尝依然回味无穷。

July
七月

作者简介:

艾丽丝·梅内尔(Alice Meynell,1847—1922),英国著名女诗人、散文家及随笔作家,著有散文集《生活的色彩》(*Color of Life*)。

One has the leisure of July for perceiving all the differences of the green of leaves. It is no longer a difference in degrees of **maturity**[1], for all the trees have darkened to their final tone, and stand in their differences of character and not of mere date. Almost all the green is grave, not sad and not dull. It has a darkened and a daily color, in **majestic**[2] but not obvious harmony with dark grey skies, and might look, to inconstant eyes, as prosaic after spring as eleven o'clock looks after the dawn.

Gravity[3] is the world—not solemnity as towards evening, nor menace as at night. The daylight trees of July are signs of common beauty, common freshness, and a mystery familiar and **abiding**[4]

注释:
1. **maturity** [mə'tjuərɪtɪ] *n.* 成熟;完备
2. **majestic** [mə'dʒestɪk] *a.* 宏伟的,壮丽的,庄重的
3. **gravity** ['grævɪtɪ] *n.* 重力,万有引力,地心引力;重要性,严重性;严肃,庄重

as night and day. In childhood we all have a more **exalted**[5] sense of dawn and summer sunrise than we ever fully retain or quite recover; and also a far higher sensibility for April and April evenings—a heartache for them, which in riper years is gradually and **irretrievably**[6] **consoled**[7].

The poetry of mere day and of late summer becomes perceptive to mature eyes that have long ceased to be **sated**[8], have taken leave of **weariness**[9], and cannot now find anything in nature too familiar; eyes which have, indeed, lost sight of the further awe of midsummer day break, and no longer see so much of the past in April twilight as they saw when they had no past; but which look freshly at the dailiness of green summer, of early afternoon, of every sky of any form that comes to pass, and of the darkened **elms**[10].

原文翻译

　　七月间，人们有余暇观察树叶绿翠的千差万别。这不再是成熟上的差异，因为所有的树木，或转苍翠，或呈墨绿，色调均已固着定格，从而展现出来的，并非时节上的不同，而是各自品格上的差异。几乎各种绿色，品味凝重，既不流于悒郁，也不失之沉闷，它具有一种深沉、日常的色泽，与灰暗的苍穹浑然一体，构成庄重却非一眼可见的和谐，故而在游览扫掠的目光看来，可能会有阳春繁景过后的平淡之感。一如黎明之后 11 点的光景。

　　凝重，乃是最贴切的字眼——不是时近黄昏的阴沉，亦非黑夜之中的森然。七月白昼的葱郁树木，体现出普通的美，常见的清新，是一种如同黑夜白昼般惯常而又永恒不变的不解之谜。童年时代，我们看到黎明和夏天日出盛景，会油然生出一股日后无法充分保留、也难以完全恢复的奋激狂喜；同时，对四月和四月的日暮黄昏，还产生一种陶然忘情的欣赏共鸣——一种为之怦然心动的神驰向往，进入壮年之后，又无可挽回地逐渐淡化平息。

　　只有阅历丰富的慧眼，才能感受到白昼本身的夏末时令固有的诗意——这双慧眼已久未获满足矣，同时也摆脱了厌倦感，此刻发现在自然界，即使最常见的景物也另有一番情趣；诚然，面对仲夏红日的喷薄欲出，已不再萌发敬畏之情；凝望四月的苍茫暮色，也不会比一无阅历的童年，引发更多的联想，然而，对司空见惯的日常景象——树木葱茏的盛夏，日过中天的午后，来而复去、变幻不定的每一片云天，还有幽暗的榆树——反倒会投以新的目光。

文化点滴

mature eyes

　　一般为佛教语。五眼之一，指二乘的智慧之目，亦泛指能照见实相的智慧。慧眼又称灵眼，其来源于印度教湿婆神的巨大慧眼，可以洞察凡间一切。

注释　**4. abiding** [ə'baɪdɪŋ] *a.* 持久的，永久的，不变的，由来已久的
5. exalt [ɪg'zɔːlt] *vt.* 提高，提升；赞扬；使得意；加强
6. irretrievably [ˌɪrɪ'triːvəbli] *ad.* 不能挽回地，不能补救地

midsummer

如果一年时间均匀分成四个阶段，春夏秋冬，那么夏就是正午太阳最直射我们头顶的前和后一共那1/4年，如果把夏分成三个均匀的段，那么孟夏、仲夏、季夏就是这三个段按时间先后的名称，所以仲夏就是盛夏。盛夏，就是最夏天的意思。

写作特点

本文是一篇描写散文（descriptive essay），它是作家对外部世界精彩的个性化描写，它往往不仅仅是单纯的写景文字，更融注了作者的个人情怀，情景交融，物我合一。例如：

1) It has a darkened and a daily color, in majestic but not obvious harmony with dark grey skies, and might look, to inconstant eyes, as prosaic after spring as eleven o'clock looks after the dawn.

2) The poetry of mere day and of late summer becomes perceptive to mature eyes that have long ceased to be sated, have taken leave of weariness, and cannot now find anything in nature too familiar…

这些精彩的语句无不反映了作者的真情实感。以物触感，也是描写散文的精髓所在。

品味鉴赏

英国女诗人艾丽丝·梅内尔这段关于夏日的描绘虽然写于100多年前，然而，四季更迭的自然之美，可以越过悠远的年代，在任何时候都能够捕捉住人的视线。诗人优美的文字及其中对季节变换，人生从激情绚烂转至平淡宁静的沉思，读起来让人不禁反复咀嚼，细细品尝依然回味无穷。

美文感悟

___

___

___

___

___

注释

7. console [kən'səul] *vt.* 安慰，慰问

8. sate [seɪt] *vt.* 使满足，使厌腻

9. weariness ['wɪərɪnɪs] *n.* 疲倦，困乏，消沉，厌倦

10. elm [elm] *n.* 榆树

> 生活是一座迷宫，我们还没有学会行走，就已经迷失了方向。
> ——西里尔·康诺利

The Ant-lion
蚁狮

作者简介：

西里尔·康诺利（Cyril Connolly，1903—1974），散文家、批评家。文学生涯开始于报章写作，曾任《观察家》杂志编辑。1939年与人创办文学杂志《地平线》并主持笔政，在20世纪40年代颇有影响。他唯一的长篇小说《岩池》笔调讽刺夸张，描写一位英国青年的堕落过程。自传性质的《不平静的坟墓》别具一格，美国评论家埃德蒙·威尔逊称之为"战时英国出版的优秀之作"。另有散文集《十年文选》、《受谴责的游乐场所》等多种。

The Maures are my favorite mountains, a range of old rounded mammalian **granite**[1] which rise three thousand feet above the coast of Provence. In summer they are covered by dark forests of **cork**[2] and pine, with paler **interludes**[3] on the northern slopes of bright splay-trunked chestnut, and an undergrowth of **arbutus**[4] **and bracken**[5]. There is always water in the Maures, and the mountains are green throughout the summer, never baked like limestone, or like the Southern Alps a **slagheap**[6] of **gritty**[7] oyster-shell. They swim in a golden light in which the

注释
1. **granite** ['grænɪt] n. 花岗岩，花岗石
2. **cork** [kɔːk] n. 软木；软木塞
3. **interlude** ['ɪntəˌluːd] n. 插曲；穿插；幕间节目
4. **arbutus** [ɑːˈbjuːtəs] n. 野草莓树；藤地莓

radiant ebony green of their vegetation stands out against the sky, a region hardly inhabited, yet friendly as those dazzling landscapes of Claude and Poussin, in which shepherds and sailors from antique ships meander under incongruous elms. Harmonies of light and color, drip of water over **fern**[8]; they inculcate in those who stay long in the Midi, and whose brains are addled by **iodine**[9], a habit of moralizing, a **brooding**[10] about causes. What makes men divide up into nations and go to war? Why do they live in cities? And what is the true relationship between Nature and Man?

原文翻译

　　莫尔山岭是我恋恋不舍的群山，一片古老圆形的哺乳动物般的花岗岩，兀立于普罗旺斯海岸之上，高达3000英尺。夏日为一碧如黛的森森软木和松木所覆盖，北面山坡间以叠翠渐渐舒朗的树干较差的栗树。莫尔山岭清流常在，夏季自始至终绿色满山，不像灰岩似的受到烘烤，也不像南阿尔卑斯山那样，犹如一堆含沙牡蛎壳的熔渣。群山沐浴在一片金闪闪的日光中，在天空的映衬下，满山的草木润泽墨绿，分外夺目，这一带人烟罕至，然而在克劳德和普桑那些艳丽照人的风景画中，却似曾相识，画中的牧童和古舟上登岸的渔夫，在颇不协调的榆树下徜徉。光与色的和谐效果，羊齿植物上的滴水，它们濡染着久居米迪的那些人，由于碘酒的作用，他们的头脑变得糊里糊涂的，养成了道德说教的习惯，对来龙去脉苦思冥想。是什么致使世人分割为邦国而又彼此交战？世人为何在城市里生活？自然与人类之间的真正关系又是什么？

文化点滴

Provence

　　普罗旺斯是罗马帝国的一个行省，英文简称PACA，现为法国东南部的一个地区，毗邻地中海，和意大利接壤。从阿尔卑斯山经里昂南流的隆河，在普罗旺斯附近分为两大支流，然后注入地中海。普罗旺斯是世界闻名的薰衣草故乡、旅游胜地。

　　如果有人说普罗旺斯是彻底的浪漫，大概也不过分，因为这里除了很久流传的浪漫爱情传奇，还有因《马赛曲》而闻名的马赛，因《基督山伯爵》而为众人皆知的依夫岛，还有儒雅的大学城艾克斯和阿维尼翁，回味久远的中世纪山庄，街边舒适的小咖啡馆，等等，令人沉醉。

Alps

　　阿尔卑斯山脉是欧洲中南部大山脉，覆盖了意大利北部边界、法国东南部，以及瑞士、列支敦士登、奥地利、

注释
5. **bracken** [ˈbrækən] n. 欧洲蕨；凤尾草
6. **slagheap** [slæɡˈhiːp] n. 矿渣堆
7. **gritty** [ˈɡrɪti] a. 多沙的，含沙的；勇敢的，坚毅的，坚定的
8. **fern** [fɜːn] n. 羊齿植物，蕨类植物
9. **iodine** [ˈaɪədaɪn] n. 碘
10. **brooding** [ˈbruːdɪŋ] n. 孵卵 a. 郁闷的；沉思的；徘徊不去的

德国南部及斯洛文尼亚。该山系自北非阿特拉斯延伸，穿过南欧和南亚，直到喜马拉雅山脉，从亚热带地中海海岸法国的尼斯附近向北延伸至日内瓦湖，然后再向东北伸展至多瑙河上的维也纳。欧洲许多大河都发源于此，水力资源丰富，为旅游、度假、疗养胜地。

写作特点

由微见著历来为中外行文的一大妙诀，也是本文最为显著的一个特色。作者着眼于细微之物，思绪如丝如缕，文章寄托了思古之幽情，蕴含着历史文化的丰富内容，同时也不乏一针见血的时事评论。诗人威廉·布莱克的名句"一粒尘沙看世界"，佛典《华严》中的"毛孔藏刹海，芥子包须弥"之说，值得认真参悟，对于深刻领会本文内涵颇有启迪。

品味鉴赏

山水之乐固然足以游目驰怀，怡情养性；尺幅之图固然足以包罗万象。但是作者之意并不在于峰峦丹青之间。尽管描写了山光水色和画家名作，纵观全文不难看出，它既非爱恋光景的小品，亦非品藻翰墨的画论。

从历史背景的角度来看，文章发表于 1939 年，时值战争风云席卷欧陆之际，其中蕴含的警世意味当可起到振聋发聩的作用。胸有丘壑故能挥洒自如，文含理趣故能启发深思。天然情致与哲理沉思相映成趣，从而令人心神一爽，浮想联翩。

美文感悟

Chapter 4

热门话题

本章选取了9篇有关社会热点话题的文章,包括当下人们关心的诸多社会问题和现象。通过阅读这些文章,读者意识到如今的社会生活中环保、经济、可持续发展、道德等问题的重要性。读者可从这些文章中发掘出社会的核心价值和做人道德至上的品质。

Low-carbon Cities
低碳城市

> **背景介绍：**
>
> 低碳城市是指以低碳经济为发展模式及方向、市民以低碳生活为理念和行为特征、政府公务管理层以低碳社会为建设标本和蓝图的城市。

China is serious about going green.

The National Development and Reform Commission of China has asked five provinces and eight cities to go low-carbon. They are the first select group for a pilot project.

The provinces and cities are required to present their low-carbon development strategies and green policies and build low-carbon and energy-efficient industries as soon as possible. They are also requested to offer **statistics**[1] on their greenhouse gas **emissions**[2] and encourage their residents to live a green life.

For Liaoning province, one of China's heavy industrial bases and part of the pilot program, there is a long hard journey ahead. But the low-carbon pilot program is significant as it offers role

---

注释

1. **statistics** [stəˈtɪstɪks] *n.* 统计，统计学，统计法，统计资料；统计数字
2. **emission** [ɪˈmɪʃən] *n.* 排放，辐射；排放物，散发物
3. **formulate** [ˈfɔːmjuleɪt] *vt.* 构想出，规划；确切地阐述；

models for the rest of the nation to go green.

Perhaps even more important is the collection and building up of data on greenhouse gas emissions, which will present policy makers with a true and clear picture for **formulating**³ and **implementing**⁴ the right policies for the future.

Gross domestic product continues to be a significant economic indicator. For years, in the fervor to pursue GDP growth, we have seen suburban **cropland**⁵ **devastated**⁶ by factories and settlements, and air and water polluted by heavy industry and human misconduct.

We have managed to unleash double-digit growth in our GDP, which is **envied**⁷ by many, yet we have paid a high environmental price for it.

The pilot program compels the local governments to pursue a development outlook that is environmentally friendly, socially **conscious**⁸ and beneficial to all.

原文翻译

中国的环保形势很严峻。

中华人民共和国国家发展和改革委员会（简称国家发改委）让五省八市实施低碳。它们是第一批选出来做这个实验性项目的。

这些省市被要求提出它们的低碳发展战略和环保政策，并且尽快建立低碳、高效能的工业。它们还被要求提供温室气体排放的数据并鼓励居民过绿色生活。

对于辽宁省，中国的重工业基地之一，该实验性计划的一部分，有很长很艰难的路要走。但是这个低碳试验计划是很有意义的，因为它为中国其他地区绿化提供了榜样。

可能更重要的是收集和建立温室气体排放的数据，这将为施政者展现真实而清晰的图画，来为未来规划和实施正确的政策。

国内生产总值不断成为一个重要的经济指标。多年以来，狂热地追求 GDP 的增长，我们看到乡下的农田被工厂和移民所毁坏、重工业造成的空气和水污染以及人类对环境的胡作非为。

我们已经实现国内生产总值呈两位数增长，这使得很多国家都很嫉妒，然而我们却在环境上付出了高昂的代价。

这个试验性的计划迫使地方政府推行一种善待环境、具有社会意识、对人人都有利的发展观。

注释

3. 用公式表示
4. **implement** ['ɪmplɪmənt] vt. 实施，执行； 使生效，实现
5. **cropland** ['krɒplænd] n. 农田，耕地
6. **devastate** ['devəsteɪt] vt. 破坏； 毁灭； 蹂躏； 使荒废
7. **envy** ['envi] vt. 嫉妒，妒忌； 羡慕
8. **conscious** ['kɒnʃəs] a. 有意识的、神志清醒的

文化点滴

The National Development and Reform Commission of China

中华人民共和国国家发展和改革委员会（简称国家发改委），作为国务院的职能机构，是综合研究拟订经济和社会发展政策、进行总量平衡、指导总体经济体制改革的宏观调控部门。国家发改委的前身是国家计划委员会，成立于1952年。原国家计划委员会于1998年更名为国家发展计划委员会，又于2003年将原国务院体改办和国家经贸委部分职能并入，改组为国家发展和改革委员会，简称国家发改委。

Gross Domestic Product

国内生产总值（Gross Domestic Product，简称GDP），是指在一定时期内（一个季度或一年），一个国家或地区的经济中所生产出的全部最终产品和劳务的价值，常被公认为衡量国家经济状况的最佳指标。它不但可反映一个国家的经济表现，还可以反映一国的国力与财富。

写作特点

本文的写作特点是 Problem-Response 的写法。首先提出问题：China is serious about going green。然后着重陈述各方面的 Response。这样的写作模式，主题鲜明，探讨深入，把问题和各方面的反响呈现出来，使读者对于这个话题有全方位的认识。

品味鉴赏

从我们国家情况来看，环境保护对经济增长发挥了很大的促进作用。比如，我国刚刚对汽车尾气进行控制的时候，有的企业大叫"如果再控制汽车尾气排放，我们的汽车厂就要倒闭了"。但是，国家的立场没有动摇，坚持采用了欧洲的一号标准、二号标准、三号标准。虽然标准强化了，但是我们国家的汽车工业却真正发展起来了，现在不仅仅在国内销售，还有出口。从这个角度来看，到底环境保护对经济是起了促进作用还是阻碍作用呢？答案是显而易见的。

美文感悟

Buying Accommodation
购房

背景介绍：

购房，是指向房地产商或者其他开发单位购买商品住房，或者向其他房产业主购买二手住房。购房一般通过广告获取房子的详细信息，然后经过比较后决定购买。获取房产信息的渠道有户外广告、报纸广告、网络广告、朋友介绍等。

Along with the development of the market economy in China, many people have bought or are going to buy **accommodation**[1] for themselves. Before buying accommodation, you have to consider the following points.

When buying a flat or house, it's important to know exactly how much money you can spend. The **mortgage**[2] department of a local bank can help you figure out how much you can spend on a flat or house. This is based on your monthly income and expenses. When you buy accommodation, you must pay part of the total cost right away. This is known as the down payment. Down payments are at least 10 percent of the price of the house. A bank (or other

注释
1. **accommodation** [ə,kɒmə'deɪʃən] n. 住处；适应；便利；和解
2. **mortgage** ['mɔːgɪdʒ] n. 抵押
3. **loan** [ləʊn] n. 借款，贷款

购房

lender) lends you the rest of the money by making payments directly to the seller. You must repay the **loan**³ plus interest over a set period of time. The more money you put down, the smaller your loan or mortgage payments will be.

Once you know exactly how much money you can spend, it's time to choose a location. Some locations are more expensive than others; therefore, it's important to choose a neighborhood that's within your **budget**⁴. If you rely on public **transportation**⁵, a train or bus should be within walking distance. If you have children, you may want your accommodation to be near their school or school bus route. In addition, you may want to be in walking distance of a **grocery**⁶ store, bank, church, park, playground, or library.

Finally, it's also important to decide how much space you need or how little you'll settle for. Generally the larger the accommodation is, the more it will cost. Your family's needs will, of course, determine its size—how many bedrooms you'll need, and whether or not you'll need a big yard.

原文翻译

随着中国市场经济的发展，许多人已经或打算为自己买房。买房之前，你必须考虑以下几点。

买房子的时候，确切地知道你能花多少钱是很重要的。本地银行的贷款部根据你每月的收入和支出可以帮你算出你买房的支付能力，这以你的月收入和开销为基本。买房时，你必须立即付一部分房费，称为首付。首付款额至少是房子价格的10%。银行（或其他贷方）通过向卖房者直接付款的方式借给你余下的欠款。你必须在规定的时期内付清借款和利息。你自己付款越多，你的借款额就越少。

你一旦确定了自己的购房消费能力之后，就该选择房址了。某些房址昂贵很多。因此，在你的预算之内选择一个邻近地区是很重要的。如果你依靠公共交通，那么在步行距离内应当有火车或公共汽车。如果你有孩子，你也许希望住房靠近孩子的学校或校车路线。此外，你也许还希望附近有杂货店、银行、教堂、公园、游乐园或者图书馆。

最后，决定你需要多少住房面积也是很重要的。一般说来，房子越大，价格越高。家庭的需要当然决定了房子的大小——你需要多少间卧室，需不需要一个大院子。

注释
4. budget ['bʌdʒɪt] n. 预算（对于未来可能收支之估计） 6. grocery ['ɡrəʊsərɪ] n. 食品杂货店；食品杂货业
5. transportation [ˌtrænspɔː'teɪʃən] n. 运送，运输

文化点滴

buying accommodation

购房，是指向房地产商或者其他开发单位购买商品住房，或者向其他房产业主购买二手住房。购房前一般通过广告获取房子的详细信息，然后经过比较后决定购买。获取房产信息的渠道有户外广告、报纸广告、网络广告、朋友介绍等。

market economy

市场经济（又称为自由市场经济或自由企业经济）是一种经济体系，在这种体系下产品和服务的生产及销售完全由自由市场的自由价格机制所引导，而不是像计划经济一般由国家所引导。在市场经济里，并没有一个中央协调的体制来指引其运作，但是在理论上，市场将会透过产品和服务的供给和需求产生复杂的相互作用，进而达成自我组织的效果。市场经济的支持者通常主张，人们所追求的私利其实是一个社会最好的利益。

写作特点

本文采取顺叙的写作手法，按照事件的先后顺序来叙述事情，这就跟事情发生发展的实际情况相一致，所以易于把文章写得条理清楚，脉络分明。本文剪裁得当，重点突出，层次鲜明，叙事很多但并不是简单的罗列，也不是单纯的平铺直叙。顺叙的写法最忌讳像一本流水账，使人读了索然无味。

品味鉴赏

买房子前首先要估算下自己的经济实力（比如购买几室的、总价多少，或者贷款买房首付多少，等等），接下来选择自己意向的片区。有时间最好多到附近去溜达溜达，看看周边环境、交通等等。买房子是大事，切不可操之过急；特别是对于普通的工薪阶层来说，一套房子很有可能就是一辈子的积蓄！

美文感悟

A Global Economy
全球化经济

背景介绍：

全球化经济是指世界经济活动超越国界，通过对外贸易、资本流动、技术转移、提供服务、相互依存、相互联系而形成的全球范围的有机经济整体（简单地说也就是世界经济日益成为紧密联系的一个整体）。经济全球化是当代世界经济的重要特征之一，也是世界经济发展的重要趋势。

Today's economy is global. We live in an era in which information, goods and capital speed around the globe, every hour of every day. Whether we like it or not, all of our fortunes are tied together. We are truly **interdependent**[1].

America supports international trade because we believe fundamentally that trade will enrich those nations who embrace its discipline. The great promise of trade is its potential to promote mutual **prosperity**[2] and to strengthen the bonds between **sovereign**[3] nations.

The U.S. and China both demonstrate the potential of trade to improve the lives of our people. You know better than I the great achievements of the Chinese economy over the past

注释
1. interdependent [ˌɪntədɪˈpendənt] a. 互相依赖的，互相依存的
2. prosperity [prɒsˈperɪtɪ] n. 繁荣；兴旺，昌盛；成功
3. sovereign [ˈsɒvrɪn] n. 君主；最高统治者；独立国

two decades. In 1977, the sum total of Chinese imports and exports was less than $15 billion, putting China's share of world trade at 0.6 percent. The most populous country in the world, China ranked a distant 30th among exporting nations. By 1993 China's exports and imports totaled nearly $200 billion. China had become the world's tenth largest exporter.

Since 1978, when China began opening its economy to increased foreign investment and trade, **aggregate**[4] output has more than doubled. The strongest growth has occurred in the coastal areas near Hong Kong and opposite Taiwan, where foreign investment and modern production methods have spurred production of both domestic and export goods. Per capita GNP has grown at an average rate of 7.6% from 1980 to 1992.

The numbers are interesting, but how has this affected the people of China? In the last decade, telephone connections rose more than 60%. Electrical production more than doubled to 621 million kilowatt hours. In short China has improved the economic well-being of its people.

The people of the United States also have experienced the benefits of world trade. Since World War II, the U. S. has been the world's largest economy and, in most years, the world's largest exporter.

But the importance of trade in our economy has exploded in the past three decades. In 1970, the value of two way trade was equal to just 13% of the U.S. economy. Last year, that figure, at 28%, was more than twice as high. In just the last seven years, jobs supported by U.S. exports (goods and services) have risen by 4 million, to a total of 11 million. That's almost one out of ten American jobs. Last year U.S. trade **equalized**[5] $1.8 trillion dollars.

Nor is the importance of trade likely to **diminish**[6] for either China or the United States. China will continue to depend upon **lucrative**[7] export markets to earn the foreign exchange it needs to develop and grow. At the same time, China's imports will supply the much needed machinery and technology to fuel its continued development.

For the United States, new commercial opportunities will grow most rapidly in the emerging markets. We estimate that three quarters of new export opportunities over the next 20 years — that's an **incredible**[8] $ 1.9 trillion in potential exports — will come in the emerging markets of Asia and Latin America. This means jobs for American workers and a higher standard of living for the American people.

注释

4. **aggregate** ['ægrɪgɪt] *a.* 总数的，总计的
5. **equalize** ['i:kwəlaɪz] *vt.* 使相等；补偿；使均衡；打成平局
6. **diminish** [dɪ'mɪnɪʃ] *vt.* （使）减少，缩小，减弱……的权势
7. **lucrative** ['lju:krətɪv] *a.* 获利多的，赚钱的；合算的
8. **incredible** [ɪn'kredəbl] *a.* 不可思议的；惊人的；难以置信的；未必可能的

原文翻译

当今的经济是全球性的。我们生活在这样一个时代：信息、货物和资金每时每刻都在全球流动。不管我们是否喜欢，我们的命运紧密相连。我们绝对是相互依靠的。

美国支持国际贸易，因为我们从根本上相信，贸易会使那些遵守贸易准则的国家富裕起来。贸易的前景十分光明，因为贸易具有促进相互繁荣并加强主权国家之间联系的潜在力量。

美中两国都显示一种能提高两国人民生活水平的贸易潜力。你们比我更了解中国经济在过去20年中所取得的伟大成就。1977年，中国进出口总额还不到150亿美元，仅占世界贸易总额的0.6%，世界上人口最多的国家中国在出口国家中排名靠后到了第30位。1993年到来之际，中国进出口总额接近2000亿美元。中国成为世界上第十大出口国。

自从1978年以来，中国经济开始为日益增加的外国投资和贸易敞开大门，总产量翻了一倍多。最强劲的增长出现在靠近香港和台湾对面的沿海地区。在那些地区，外国投资和现代生产手段的使用促进了国内货物和出口货物的生产。从1980年至1992年，人均国民生产总值平均增长率为7.6%。

看看数字是很有趣的，然而它又是怎样影响中国人民的呢？在过去10年中，电话用户增加了60%多；电力生产增加了一倍多，达到6.21亿千瓦时。总之，中国提高了人民的生活水平。

美国人民也有得益于国际贸易的经历。自从第二次世界大战以来，美国一直是世界上最大的经济强国，而且很多年以来，美国又是世界上最大的出口国。

但在过去30年中，贸易在我国经济中的重要性大大地增加了。1970年，双边贸易总值仅占整个美国经济的13%。去年是28%，比1970年增加了一倍还多。仅仅在过去的7年中，美国的出口（货物和服务）创造的就业机会增加了400万个，总数上升到1100万个。这个数字就占美国就业总数的1/10。去年，美国贸易总数达到了1.8万亿美元。

无论是中国还是美国，都不会减少贸易的重要性。中国会继续依靠获利的出口市场来赚取外汇，以发展和增长自己的经济。同时，中国的进口货物将提供促进中国继续发展所需要的机械和技术。

对于美国来说，在不断涌现的市场上，新的贸易机会将以最快的速度增加。我们估计，在未来的20年中，新的出口中的3/4的机会，即数量可观的1.9万亿美元的潜在出口额，将来自亚洲和拉丁美洲不断出现的新兴市场。这意味着美国工人的就业机会和美国人民生活水平的提高。

文化点滴

International Trade

"国际贸易"这一说法着眼于"贸易在全球国家之间开展"；"对外贸易"（Foreign Trade 或 External Trade）着眼于开展贸易的一国。因此，"国际贸易"（International Trade）与"对外贸易"（Foreign Trade 或 External Trade）并无本质上的区别，只是着眼点不同而已。

国际贸易是在一定的历史条件下产生和发展起来的。形成国际贸易的基本条件有两个：

一是社会生产力的发展；

二是国家的形成。

社会生产力的发展产生出用于交换的剩余商品，这些剩余商品在国与国之间交换，就产生了国际贸易。

GNP

国民生产总值（Gross National Product，简称GNP），是一国所拥有的生产要素所生产的最终产品价值，是一个国民概念。与国内生产总值（GDP）不同，国内生产总值是在一国范围内生产的最终产品的价值，是一个地域概念。具体来讲，国民生产总值中有一部分是本国拥有的生产要素在国外生产的最终产品价值。GNP 是与所谓的国民原则联系在一起的。

写作特点

本文列举了许多数字，主要集中在第三、五、七段。例如："In 1977, the sum total of Chinese imports and exports was less than $15 billion, putting China's share of world trade at 0.6 percent." "Electrical production more than doubled to 621 million kilowatt hours." "Last year, that figure, at 28%, was more than twice as high. In just the last seven years, jobs supported by U.S. exports (goods and services) have risen by 4 million, to a total of 11 million." 等等，列举数字既简明扼要，又准确具体，一目了然，能给读者留下清晰印象。

品味鉴赏

经济全球化的过程早已开始，尤其是 20 世纪 80 年代以后，特别是进入 90 年代，世界经济全球化的进程大大加快了。经济全球化，有利于资源和生产要素在全球的合理配置，有利于资本和产品在全球流动，有利于科技在全球的扩张，有利于促进不发达地区经济的发展，是人类发展进步的表现，是世界经济发展的必然结果。但经济全球化对每个国家来说，都是一柄双刃剑，既是机遇，也是挑战。特别是对经济实力薄弱和科学技术比较落后的发展中国家，面对全球性的激烈竞争，所遇到的风险、挑战将更加严峻。目前，经济全球化过程中急需解决的问题是建立公平合理的新的经济秩序，以保证竞争的公平性和有效性。

进入 21 世纪以来，经济全球化与跨国公司的深入发展，既给世界贸易带来了重大的推动力，同时也给各国经贸带来了诸多不确定因素，使其出现许多新的特点和新的矛盾。为此，研究和了解这一问题有着一定的现实意义。

美文感悟

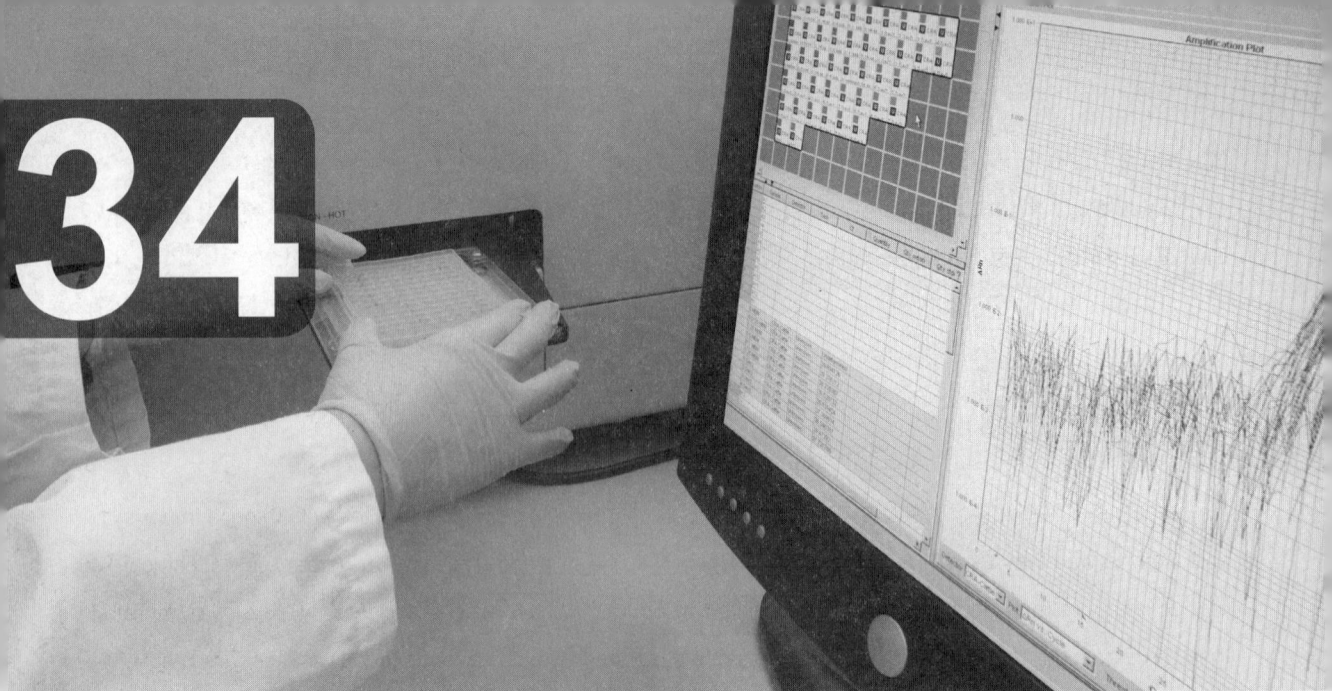

34

New Product Development
新产品的开发

背景介绍：

新产品开发，是指从研究选择适应市场需要的产品开始，到产品设计、工艺制造设计，直到投入正常生产的一系列决策过程。从广义而言，新产品开发既包括新产品的研制，也包括原有老产品的改进与换代。新产品开发是企业研究与开发的重点内容，也是企业生存和发展的战略核心之一。

The average cost of developing and introducing a major new product has jumped to well over $100 million. To make things worse, many of these costly new products fail. So companies are now pursuing new product strategies that are less costly and risky than developing completely new brands. Here we describe three new product strategies: acquiring new brands, developing "me-too" products, and reviving old brands.

Acquiring New Brands

Instead of building its own new products from the ground up, a company can buy another company and its established brands. The mid-1980s saw a dramatic **flurry**[1] of one big company

注释
1. **flurry** ['flʌrɪ] *n.* 阵风；阵雨；小雪；突然的紧张慌乱；激动不安
2. **acquisition** [ˌækwɪ'zɪʃən] *n.* 获得，取得，习得；获得物
3. **tricky** ['trɪkɪ] *a.* 棘手的；微妙的；狡猾的，诡计多端的

gobbling another. For example, Thomson Electronics bought RCA, Philip Morris obtained General Foods, Schweppers merged with Cadbury, and Nestle absorbed Rowntree Mackintosh.

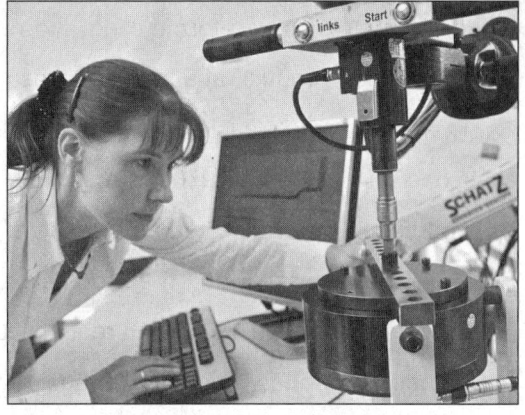

Such **acquisitions**[2] can be **tricky**[3] — the company must be certain that the acquired products blend with its current products and that the firm has the skills and resources needed to continue to run the acquired brands profitably. Acquisitions can run into **snags**[4] with government regulators. For instance, even under the Reagan Administration's loose antitrust policy, regulators did not allow Pepsi to acquire 7-Up. Finally, such acquisitions have high price tags. Philip Morris coughed up $5.7 billion for General Foods and Nestle forked out over $2.5 billion for Rowntree Mackintosh. But despite high initial **outlays**[5], buying established brands may be cheaper in the long run than paying the enormous costs of trying to create well-known brands from scratch. Moreover, acquiring proven winners eliminates almost all the risks of new-product failure. Acquisitions also provide a quick and easy way to gain access to new markets or strengthen positions in current markets.

Developing "Me-too" Products

In recent years, many companies have used "me-too" product strategies—introducing **imitations**[6] of successful competing products. Thus, Tandy, Sanyo, Compaq and many others produce IBM-compatible personal computers. These "clones" sometimes sell for less than half the price of the IBM models they emulate. Imitation is now fair play for products ranging from soft drinks to **toiletries**[7].

Me-too products are often quicker and less expensive to develop. The market-leader pioneers the technology and bears most of the product development costs while the imitative product can sometimes offer more value than the market-leading originals. Furthermore, me-too products are less costly and risky to introduce — they enter a proven market, riding on the **coattails**[8] of the market-leader.

On the other hand, a me-too strategy has some drawbacks. The imitating company enters the market late and must battle a successful, firmly **entrenched**[9] competitor.

Reviving Old Brands

Many companies have found "new gold in the old" by reviving once-successful brands that are now dead or dying. Many old and **tarnished**[10] brand names still hold magic for consumers.

注释

4. **snag** [snæg] n. 隐伏的困难；未料到的障碍；尖利的突出物

5. **outlay** ['aʊtˌleɪ] n. （用于某一目的的）花费，开支

6. **imitation** [ˌɪmɪ'teɪʃən] n. 模仿，仿效；模仿品，仿制物

Often, simply reviving, reformulating and repositioning an old brand can give the company a successful "new product" at a fraction of the cost of building new brands.

There are some classic examples of brand revivals. For example, Ivory Soap reversed its sales decline in the early 1970s when it was re-promoted for adult use rather than just for babies. Dannon yogurt sales rocketed as a result of linking it to healthy living. Warner-Lambert revived Black Jack gum by playing on the nostalgia of its 110-year old name; Coca-Cola rejuvenated Fresca by adding Nutra Sweet and real fruit juices.

Sometimes a dead product rises again with a new name, as happened with one of Nestle's cookery brands. Some years ago, Nestle withdrew a product when it failed in test market, but later revived the line under the Lean Cuisine brand to fit with today's health-conscious consumers.

Nevertheless, there are dangers with reviving old brands. Perhaps the biggest of them is that it can encourage marketers to look back rather than forwards.

原文翻译

开发并推广主要新产品的平均成本费用已激增到大大超过 1 亿美元。更为糟糕的是，许多这些成本高的新产品都失败了。所以，一些公司正在推行比开发崭新品牌成本低、风险小的新产品策略。这里我们描述三种新产品策略：获得新品牌、开发仿制产品和重塑传统品牌。

获得新品牌

一家公司可购买另一家公司及其确立的品牌，而不是从头开始开发它自己的新产品。20 世纪 80 年代中期，人们目睹了大公司吞并其他公司的戏剧性浪潮。比如，汤姆森电器公司买下了美国无线电公司，菲利浦·莫里斯公司收购了食品总公司，史威士公司与吉百利公司合并了，雀巢公司并吞了朗特·利马金托什公司。

这样的公司合并可能很棘手 —— 兼并公司必须弄清楚它所获得的产品与它目前的产品能融为一体，还要弄明白公司具备继续营利性地经营获得的品牌所需的技术和资源。此外，公司兼并可能受到政府管理部门的阻碍。例如，即使在里根政府实施宽松的反托拉斯政策的情况下，管理部门也没有允许百事可乐公司收购七喜公司。最后的棘手问题是，被兼并的公司标价都很高。菲利浦·莫里斯公司付出了 57 亿美元收购了食品总公司，雀巢公司支付了 25 亿多美元才得到了朗特·利马金托什公司。但是，尽管购买名牌最初支出的费用是很昂贵的，但从长远来看，可能比想方设法从零开始打造著名品牌所需的巨额费用便宜一些。况且，获得了确实很成功的公司就避免了冒新产品可能失败所导致的几乎所有的风险。获得名牌还可以提供打入新市场、巩固目前市场地位的便捷途径。

开发仿制产品

注释
7. **toiletry** ['tɔɪlɪtrɪ] n. 盥洗用具；梳妆用品，化妆用品　　　　牢固地位
8. **coattail** ['kəʊteɪl] n.（男人晚礼服的）燕尾形后摆　　10. **tarnish** ['tɑːnɪʃ] vt. 使晦暗；使变色；使失去光泽
9. **entrench** [en'trentʃ] vt. 使牢固地处于特定位置；处于

最近几年，许多公司都运用仿制产品策略 —— 引进竞争力很强的成功产品的仿制品。这样，天迪公司、三洋公司、康柏公司和许多其他公司都生产 IBM 兼容性个人电脑。这些"克隆制品"有时以低于他们仿效的 IBM 型号的半价出售，对于从软饮料到化妆品的产品来说，仿制现在是一种正当的行为。

仿制产品的开发往往比较快，而且成本也比较低。市场开拓者开创新技术并承担大多数产品开发的费用，而仿制产品有时却能比领先市场的原产品提供更多的价值。再者，推广仿制产品花费较少，风险也较小。仿制产品借助市场开拓者的声望进入已经被确认的市场。

另一方面，实施仿制品策略也有一些缺陷。仿制产品公司进入市场较晚，必须与成就斐然、地位牢固的对手竞争，打一场硬仗。

重塑传统品牌

许多公司在重新塑造曾经颇为成功、但现已被废弃或正在消亡的品牌的过程中，发现"传统品牌有闪光的金子"。许多失去光泽的老品牌对消费者仍然有魅力。通常的情况是，对传统品牌进行简单的更新，重新阐述并重新定位，只需要打造新品牌的一小部分费用，就会给公司带来成功的新产品。

有一些关于品牌重塑的典型例子。例如，20 世纪 70 年代早期，象牙肥皂制造厂将其产品作为成人用品而不仅仅是作为婴儿用品重新促销，扭转了其销售下滑的趋势；达能奶业公司把酸奶跟健康生活密切联系起来，使其酸奶销售量扶摇直上；华纳－兰勃特利用人们对拥有 110 年历史的老品牌的怀旧情愫重塑了黑杰克口香糖品牌；可口可乐公司通过增加天然食糖和纯正的水果汁，给清桑可乐品牌重新注入了活力。

有时，一种废弃的产品随着一个新名字而重新崛起。如雀巢的一种烹调品牌换了个新名字就再次兴旺起来了。几年前，雀巢撤回一种在市场试销中失败了的产品，后来将其改为适应具有现代健康意识消费群体的"减肥食品"品牌，这种产品又复苏了。

不过，重塑传统品牌也有风险。也许，最大的风险在于它可能会鼓励市场营销者向后看而不是朝前看。

文化点滴

Pepsi

百事公司（Pepsico., Inc.）是一家饮料和休闲食品公司，在全球 200 多个国家和地区拥有 14 万雇员，2004 年销售收入达 293 亿美元，为全球第四大食品和饮料公司。公司总部设在美国纽约市。公司附属机构近百个，主要有百事可乐饮料公司、弗利托－莱公司（快餐馆）、啤咂餐馆（供应意大利式烘馅饼等）、北美运输公司和威尔逊体育用品公司等。该公司子公司分布很广，美国国内涉及 48 个州，国外涉及 100 多个国家和地区。

Sanyo

日本三洋电器集团是一家有 60 多年历史的大型企业集团，总部位于日本大阪，产品涉及显示器、手机、数码相机、机械、生物制药等众多领域。

三洋电机由井植岁男（1902—1969）于 1947 年成立，并于 1950 年组成株式会社，创办人为松下幸之助的内弟以及松下电器前雇员。"三洋"意思为"三个海洋"，指的是该公司的创办人有将他们的产品销售到世界各地，横跨大西洋、太平洋与印度洋的抱负。

写作特点

本文是典型的总—分—总式的结构，开篇即"Here we describe three new product strategies: acquiring new brands, developing "me-too" products, and reviving old brands.", 然后分别叙述三种策略, 即"acquiring new brands, developing "me-too" products, and reviving old brands"。文章的最后再次总结: Nevertheless, there are dangers with reviving old brands. Perhaps the biggest of them is that it can encourage marketers to look back rather than forwards. 总—分—总的结构能在最短时间内让读者了解最重要的信息，将文章要点一开始就交代清楚，总—分—总结构还能稳定读者情绪。

品味鉴赏

新产品开发，是指从研究选择适应市场需要的产品开始，到产品设计、工艺制造设计，直到投入正常生产的一系列决策过程。从广义而言，新产品开发既包括新产品的研制，也包括原有老产品的改进与换代。新产品开发是企业研究与开发的重点内容，也是企业生存和发展的战略核心之一。不断开发新产品是形成竞争优势的一个主要因素。如何缩短新产品开发周期，是成功推出新产品的关键。市场营销学中使用的新产品概念不是从纯技术角度理解的，产品只要在功能或形态上得到改进，与原产品产生差异，并为顾客带来新的利益，即视为新产品。企业新产品开发的实质是推出不同内涵与外延的新产品。对大多数公司来说，新产品开发是改进现有产品，而非创造全新产品。

美文感悟

幸福感是一种心理体验，它既是对生活的客观条件和所处状态的一种事实判断，又是对于生活的主观意义和满足程度的一种价值判断，它表现为在生活满意度基础上产生的一种积极的心理体验。而幸福感指数，就是衡量这种感受具体程度的主观指标数值。"幸福感指数"的概念起源于30多年前，最早是由不丹国王提出并付诸实践的。20多年来，在人均GDP仅为700多美元的南亚小国不丹，国民总体生活得较幸福。"不丹模式"引起了世界的关注。

Happiness Index
幸福指数

作者简介：

大卫·弗朗西斯（David Francis，1850—1927），美国政治家。他曾在很多部门供职，包括任圣路易斯市市长、第27届密苏里州官员和美国下议院秘书；1916至1917年间，他是美国驻苏联大使。

In terms of happiness, your spouse—if you have one—is worth $100,000 a year.

That's the finding of two economists who have tried to put a monetary value on happiness, measuring the emotional value of everything from religion to racial discrimination in dollars.

Such a **calculation**[1], admits economist David Blanchflower, is "a little bit off-the-wall" and may **prompt**[2] **wry**[3] comments within some marriages on "cashing in."

The two economists are, of course, speaking of averages. They have used an annual survey of some 1,500 Americans from 1972 to 1998 to measure self-reported happiness and the factors that go with it. But it turns out that the happiness value of a stable marriage is "incredibly high," says Dr. Blanchflower, a professor at Dartmouth College in Hanover, N.H., whose study has

注释　**1. calculation** [ˌkælkjəˈleɪʃən] *n.* 计算，盘算；估计；计算的结果　　**2. prompt** [prɒmpt] *a.* 敏捷的；迅速的；立刻的　*v.* 提示；指点；促进；激起，唤起

just been published by the National Bureau of Economic Research in Cambridge, Mass. "Don't give it up lightly."

Blanchflower and his partner Andrew Oswald, an economist at Warwick University in Britain, begin with this question: "Taken all together, how would you say things are these days — would you say that you are happy, pretty happy, or not so happy?"

The survey results include detailed characteristics of those surveyed—married, divorced, single, income level, race, gender, etc.

With that data, they found which factors are associated with greater happiness.

Extra money does buy some happiness. But not as much as many would suspect. Constructing a sort of happiness index that assigns 3 to "very happy," 2 to "pretty happy," and 1 to "not too happy," the two **reckon**[4] that an extra dollar provides 0.00000409 in additional happiness. Or $10,000 would give you 0.04 units of extra happiness.

The two economists, using this index, assign a dollar value to other factors associated with more or less happiness.

Using that device, a lasting marriage is worth $100,000 per year compared with being widowed or divorced. Being "separated" is the greatest **depressant**[5] of happiness, followed closely by the death of a spouse.

Second and **subsequent**[6] marriages are less happy than first marriages — on average.

A 16-year-old whose parents divorced has a lower level of well-being in adulthood.

"Marriage is believed by psychologists and **psychiatrists**[7] to provide a protective effect to mental well-being," the authors note.

Blanchflower suspects the decline in the happiness level of Americans from the early 1970s to the late 1990s, despite rising incomes, may be attributed to the rise in divorce.

Other findings include:

*To bring African-Americans up to average happiness levels, they would need an extra $30,000 in annual income.

This, the authors speculate, may be the impact of racial discrimination. Over the past few

---

注释

3. **wry** [raɪ] *a.* 扭曲的，歪斜的；嘲弄的
4. **reckon** ['rekən] *vt.* 测算，估计；认为；计算
5. **depressant** [dɪ'presənt] *n.* 镇静剂
6. **subsequent** ['sʌbsɪkwənt] *a.* 后来的；随后的

decades, however, their happiness level has risen. "Blacks have made up some ground," they say.

*Unemployment is highly damaging to men's happiness. It would take $60,000 a year to offset being jobless.

*Men's happiness has trended up. Women's sense of well-being, though higher than that of men, has fallen "noticeably."

Policies aimed at ending discrimination against women apparently have not boosted their happiness overall.

*The educated tend to be happier than those less educated, even when separated from the higher income that often accompanies greater education.

*Happiness and life satisfaction are U-shaped according to age. In the United States, people's sense of well-being sinks to a low around 40 and then rises.

Perhaps, the authors suggest, people adapt to their circumstances, **relinquish**[8] some unfulfilled **aspirations**[9] by the middle of their lives, and enjoy life more.

*Being religious has a positive effect.

*Overall, the number of children and **siblings**[10] a person has doesn't have an impact on their happiness. But for those under 30, happiness decreases proportionately to the number of both children and siblings, Blanchflower and Mr. Oswald found in a separate study, "The Rising Well-Being of the Young."

Blanchard suspects this has to do with the stress associated with having lots of kids.

Surveys in Britain give "noticeably similar results" to those in the US. But people's level of satisfaction has remained about the same from the early 1970s to the late 1990s.

原文翻译

从幸福角度讲，你的配偶——如果你已经成家的话——价值每年10万美元。

这是两位经济学家的发现。他们试图用金钱为幸福估价，用美元衡量从宗教到种族歧视的所有问题的情感价值。

经济学家大卫·布兰奇弗劳尔承认，这种计算"有点离奇"，并可能引起不当的想法，认为有些人结婚是为了"从中捞取好处"。

当然，这两位经济学家是就一般人而言的。他们参考了1972至1998年对大约1500名美国人进行的年

注释

7. **psychiatrist** [saɪˈkaɪətrɪst] n. 精神病专家，精神病医生

8. **relinquish** [rɪˈlɪŋkwɪʃ] vt. 放弃，让出（权利、财产等）；放开，松手；撤离

9. **aspiration** [ˌæspəˈreɪʃən] n. 强烈的愿望；吸气，吸入

10. **sibling** [ˈsɪblɪŋ] n. 兄弟，姐妹

度调查。情况表明，稳固婚姻中的幸福价值"高得惊人"。在新罕布什尔州汉诺威的达特茅斯学院担任教授的布兰奇弗劳尔博士说。马萨诸塞州剑桥的全国经济研究局刚刚发表了他的研究成果。他还说："不要轻易放弃婚姻。"

布兰奇弗劳尔和他的合作伙伴、英国华威大学的经济学家安德鲁·奥斯瓦尔德是以这个问题开始他们的调查的："总的来说，你会怎样描述近况——是快乐、相当快乐，还是不怎么快乐？"

调查结果包括被调查对象的详细特征——已婚、离异、单身、收入水平、种族和性别等。

他们运用这些数据找出了那些与更高程度幸福相关的因素。

额外的金钱的确可以买到某种幸福，但是并不像许多人料想的那么多。他们设计了一种幸福指数：3 表示"非常幸福"，2 表示"相当幸福"，1 表示"不太幸福"。这两位经济学家认为，每增加 1 美元，只能多获得 0.00000409 个单位的幸福。或者说 1 万美元可以使你的幸福增值 0.04 个单位。

这两位经济学家用这种指数以美元为单位对与大大小小的幸福相关的其他因素进行了估价。

采用这种方法可以算出，与鳏寡或者离异相比，持久的婚姻每年价值 10 万美元。"与配偶分居"是对幸福最大的抑制剂，紧随其后的是丧偶。

一般来说，二婚或者此后的婚姻都不如第一次婚姻幸福。

一个父母离异的 16 岁青少年在成年之后会拥有较低程度的幸福。

这两位作者指出："心理学家和精神病学家认为婚姻是对精神健康的一种保障。"

布兰奇弗劳尔认为，尽管从 20 世纪 70 年代初到 90 年代末期美国人的收入增加了，但是他们的幸福程度却降低了，这可能与离婚率的升高有关。

其他的发现包括：

※ 要使非洲裔美国人的幸福指数上升到平均水平，他们的年收入还需要增加 3 万美元。

这两位作者认为，这种较低的幸福程度可能是种族歧视的结果。然而，在过去的几十年中，他们的幸福程度已经上升了。两位作者说："黑人已经取得了一些进展。"

※ 失业对男人的幸福损伤极大。要补偿这种无业状况一年需要 6 万美元。

※ 男人的幸福程度越来越高了。女人的幸福感虽然比男人的要高一些，但已有"明显"下降。

那些旨在消除女性歧视的政策显然还未从总体上提高她们的幸福程度。

※ 受教育多的人趋于比受教育少的人更幸福，即使在拿不到高薪时也如此，虽然高薪常常与高学历相关。

※ 幸福程度与对生活的满意程度随着年龄的增加而呈 U 形曲线。在美国，人们的幸福感在 40 岁左右降至谷底，然后又开始上升。

这两位作者建议人们也许应该适应环境，到中年时放弃一些仍未实现的抱负，从而幸福地享受人生。

※ 宗教信仰对人有积极影响。

※ 总体上来讲，一个人所有的孩子和兄弟姐妹的数量对他们的幸福并没有影响。但是，布兰奇弗劳尔和奥斯瓦尔德先生在另一项名为"年轻人日益增高的幸福感"的课题研究中发现，对于那些 30 岁以下的人来说，幸福感会因孩子和兄弟姐妹的增多而成比例地下降。

布兰彻德认为，这必定是由于孩子多而压力增大的缘故。

在英国的调查得出了与在美国的调查"明显相似的结果"。但是，从 20 世纪 70 年代初到 90 年代末期，人们的满意程度几乎一直没有变化。

Chapter 4 热门话题

文化点滴

Happiness Index

幸福感是一种心理体验，它既是对生活的客观条件和所处状态的一种事实判断，又是对于生活的主观意义和满足程度的一种价值判断，它表现为在生活满意度基础上产生的一种积极的心理体验。而幸福感指数，就是衡量这种感受具体程度的主观指标数值。"幸福感指数"的概念起源于 30 多年前，最早是由不丹国王提出并付诸实践的。20 多年来，在人均 GDP 仅为 700 多美元的南亚小国不丹，国民总体生活得较幸福。"不丹模式"引起了世界的关注。

racial discrimination

种族歧视在古代即已存在，但其现代形式是从资本原始积累时期开始的。至今，在世界上若干地区仍存在种族歧视现象。这种现象是由反动统治阶级采取立法、行政和其他措施，鼓吹和散布种族优越和种族仇恨学说等造成的。种族歧视是对人类尊严的凌辱，受到了国际舆论和国际组织的一再谴责。1973 年 11 月 30 日，联合国通过《禁止并惩治种族隔离罪行国际公约》，再次明确宣布，凡犯有种族隔离行为的组织、机构或个人，即为犯罪，应负国际罪责。

写作特点

本文叙述了许多调查研究的结果，并对它们给予评述。例如："To bring African-Americans up to average happiness levels, they would need an extra $30,000 in annual income. This, the authors speculate, may be the impact of racial discrimination. Over the past few decades, however, their happiness level has risen. 'Blacks have made up some ground,' they say." 这种写作手法可以更好地和读者交流沟通，让作者第一时间清楚作者的观点感受，易于产生共鸣。

品味鉴赏

本文写法新奇，试图从金钱的角度来衡量幸福，听起来有点不可思议。但是，通过细致的调查研究，金钱、幸福、宗教信仰、种族歧视之间都有一定的关系，并且文章对这些关系进行量化，最终突出体现出"不要轻易放弃婚姻"。

美文感悟

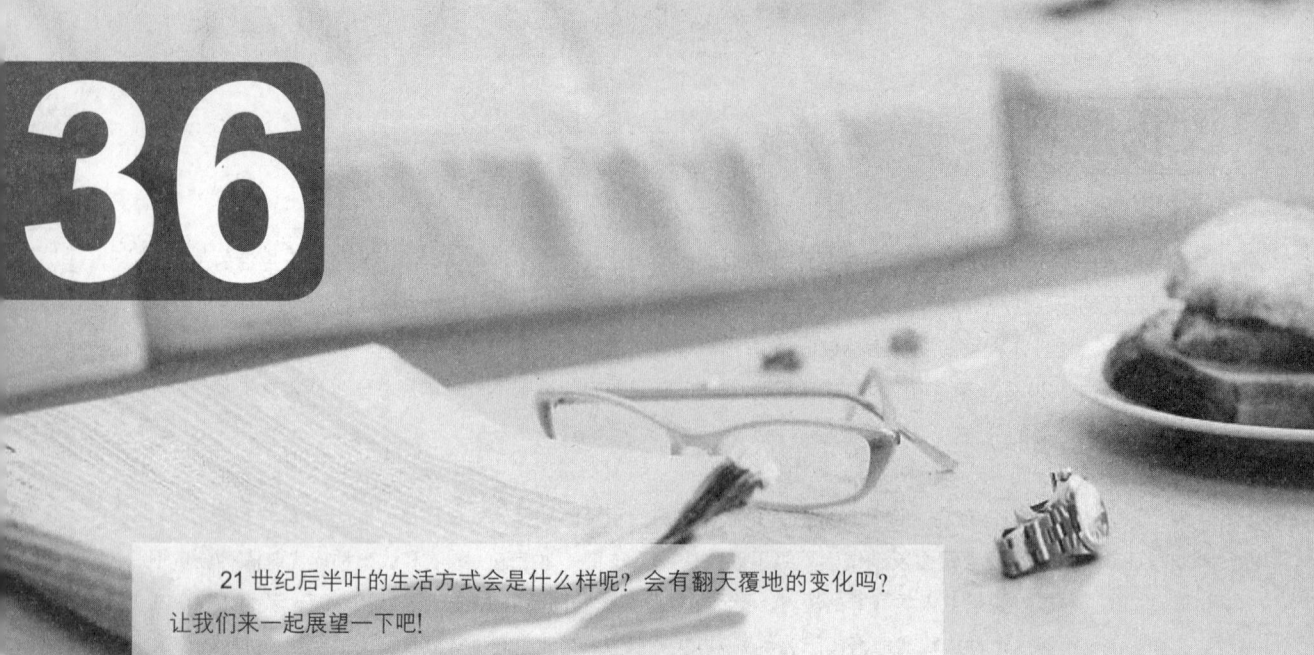

21世纪后半叶的生活方式会是什么样呢？会有翻天覆地的变化吗？让我们来一起展望一下吧！

Life-styles of the 21st Century
21世纪的生活方式

Americans in the future will probably not live as Americans do today. **Fusion**[1] power will be capable of producing energy without limits while saving natural resources. People may live well past a hundred years, be equipped with plastic body parts, and eat man-made foods. Space travelers will walk on the planets. These factors of life were science fiction images a few decades ago. Today such events are already discussed as if real.

How do people imagine life in the United States in the future? Below are some predictions made by Richard N. Farmer, who gave his light-hearted opinion of the "World of 2084".

Since no one wants to do the dirty, uninteresting factory-line work any more, we decide not to. So we take some **chimpanzees**[2], or if we really want some strength, some great **apes**[3], do a bit of scientific engineering here and there, and we create some animals, which are made for the factory line. They work their eight hours a day, and don't mind the repetition a bit.

Jack Baxter, a common American of 2084, glanced at his **stop-watch**[4]. He was slowing down; he could only run the kilometer in four minutes flat now, and when he was 80, he could do it in three-fifty. But, being 140 years old made a difference, **regardless of**[5] what his doctor said.

注释
1. fusion ['fjuːʒən] n. 融合；熔化
2. chimpanzee [ˌtʃɪmpænˈziː] n. 黑猩猩
3. ape [eɪp] n. 猿
4. stop-watch 记秒表；跑表，停表

Jack had received his first cancer shot in 1981; he had received his man-made heart in 2014, before they really got those human ones perfected, so he wasn't a very good example of a complete human. But he felt pretty good; he had been one of the lucky ones, who had received his shots to make him young again before he turned 40, so he was still a young-looking fellow. Of course, he looked  old in his world, since no one got much beyond 30-looking any more. And, of course, he would die; right now, fellows pushing 200 were in poor shape and kicking off.

Death used to be a pretty simple thing. Body processes stopped, and you left us. But nowadays even, it is not uncommon for a person to be brought back with heart massage perhaps a full hour or more after he's "dead." By 2084, if we can store a dead body in a cold refrigerator room soon enough, lots of people who now would die may not. Now we all die, sooner or later; maybe by 2084, we won't die until we are good and ready. And that would be a new freedom indeed.

Johnny, who's almost 10, can't read, but no one is worried. Indeed, Johnny has been going to school since he was 3, but it hasn't been the kind of school that we are familiar with. The kids learn all sorts of things about living together and getting along with each other, but nothing about school subjects. You see, we have figured out that age ten is about the time that a child can really put reading and mathematical skills to use. So, on his tenth birthday, Johnny goes to the brain-control center. He sits for an hour or so under a machine that looks something like a hair-dryer, with him attached to it. When he finishes, the entire reading, writing, and math patterns he needs to know are impressed right on his brain. Why fool around for years drilling kids, when all education really is made up of is a set of very mixed brain patterns? Just add them straight onto the brain, and you save lots of time and money. And if you want to teach any other kind of skills, like electrical theory for electricity workers, well, there's a pattern for that too.

注释

5. **regardless of** 不顾，不管

原文翻译

　　美国人在未来可能不会像现在的美国人一样生活了。核聚变所产生出的能源是无限的,同时可以节省天然资源。100 年之后人们可能会生活得很好,身体上配有塑料的身体零件,吃人造食品。太空旅行者行走在行星上。几十年前这些生活方式还是科幻小说里的情节。今天,人们对这些生活方式已经开始展开讨论了,仿佛一切已经成真。

　　人们对美国未来的生活是如何展望的呢?下面由理查德 N. 法莫所做出的一些预测,他展示给大家在"2084 年的世界"人们过着轻松愉快的生活。

　　既然没有人愿意做既脏又乏味的工厂生产线上的工作,我们就不去做。我们可以让黑猩猩去做,或者如果我们真的想要一些外援,一些类人猿,我们可以尝试进行一点科学工程来创造一些动物,让它们在生产线上劳作。他们每天工作 8 小时,对重复的工作感觉不到厌倦。

　　2084 年,一个普通的美国人杰克·巴克斯特,瞥了一眼他的秒表。他放慢速度,他在 4 分钟内只能跑 1 公里。他 80 岁时,用 3 分 50 秒就能跑完 1 公里。但是,无论他的医生用什么话语来安慰他,他毕竟已经 140 岁了,今非昔比了。在 1981 年,杰克接受了他第一次治疗癌症的医疗注射,在 2014 年安装了一颗人造心脏,在这两项治疗与他的身体完美地融合前,他不算是一个完整的人。但他觉得还不错,他是一个幸运的人,40 岁之前他接受使他重返青春的医疗注射,所以他看上去仍然是一个年轻人。当然,在他的生活圈子里他看上去是老的,因为没有人看上去超过 30 岁了。当然,他也会死。现在快 200 岁的人身体才会出现不好的状况,才会死去。

　　死亡在过去是一件相当简单的事情。身体机能停止,你离开了我们。但现在一个人"死"后接受一个小时或一个多小时的心脏按摩后又重生了是非常平常的一件事。到 2084 年,如果我们能及时地将尸体存放到寒冷的冷藏库里,很多现在会死的人可能在当时不会死。现在,我们所有人迟早都会死,也许在 2084 年,直到我们都准备好了,我们才会死去。这确实将是一种新的自由。

　　约翰尼快 10 岁了,但还不识字,但没人担心这点。事实上,约翰尼自从 3 岁就已经开始上学了,但那所学校并不是我们所熟悉的那种学校。孩子们学习各种关于如何生活在一起、如何彼此相处的知识,但没有任何学习的科目。你看,我们已经想通了,10 岁才是孩子可以真正应用到阅读和数学技能的时候。因此,在约翰尼的第 10 个生日的时候,他来到大脑控制中心。他坐在一台看起来像吹风机的机器下面大约 1 个小时,这台机器与他连接到一起。1 个小时左右过后,他所需要的所有阅读、写作和数学模式嵌入到他的大脑。既然所有的教育都是由一组很复杂的大脑模式组成的,为什么还浪费那么多年来训练孩子这些技能?只需将其添加到大脑里,这样可以节省大量的时间和金钱。如果你想教任何其他的技能,如电力工人要掌握的电气原理,同样有电气原理的模式。

文化点滴

Richard N. Farmer，美国印第安纳大学的管理学家，著有《国际管理》一书。

写作特点

本文是一篇说明文，是以说明为主要表达方式来解说事物、阐明事理而给人以知识的文章，它通过对实体事物的解说，或对抽象真理的阐释，使人们对事物的形态、构造、性质、种类、成因、功能、关系或对事理的概念、特点、来源、演变、异同等有所认识，从而获得有关的知识。以说明为主是说明文与其他文体在表达方式上相区别的标志。本文用具体的例子来说明未来的生活方式是什么样的。

品味鉴赏

21世纪是人类的生活方式将发生巨大变革的世纪，无论人与环境、人与世界、人与技术，还是人与人的关系都面临着新的问题，传统受到极大的挑战。在这一巨大变革面前，我们应该具有新的价值理念，即人与万物共存共赢。共存，就是人与万物共同存在于一个世界性的统一体平台上；共赢，就是矛盾的每一方在相互交往的过程中，都从其他各方吸取有利于自身发展的营养和因子，从而实现共赢。共存共赢，是21世纪人类新的生活方式的精髓和灵魂。

21世纪中国社会的生活方式将以合理、自由和丰富为原则，以文明、健康、科学为主要特征。社会赋予中国人以更多的时空和物质消费资源，人们可以更自由地安排丰富多彩的生活。

美文感悟

外星人真的存在吗？他们在哪里？这些问题一直困扰着我们。长久以来，人类利用各种方式来找寻外星人。

Human Seeks Alien
寻找外星人

作者简介：

蒂莫西·费里斯（Timothy Ferriss, 1944—）美国科学作家，撰写过12部最佳畅销书，其中包括《自由的科学》（2010）和《银河系简史》（1988）。后者曾获美国物理科学学院奖并获普利策提名。

Humans have long speculated that we're not alone in the universe, but the 21st century could be the time when these speculations are at last replaced by fact.

Mars, long regarded as the most promising place in the solar system to look for **extraterrestrial**[1] life, is to be visited by a **flotilla**[2] of automated invaders, starting with the Mars Surveyor Lander 2001, which will sniff the soil to help determine its suitability for life. Other future probes include a soil-return mission, Mars balloons, and long-range rovers capable of exploring the Martian surface for years **on end**[3].

Whether or not unmanned probes find signs of life on Mars, we're going to want to follow up by sending humans to the Red Planet. If there is evidence of life there, the astronauts' mission

注释
1. **extraterrestrial** [,ekstrətə'restri:əl] *adj.* 地球外的
2. **flotilla** [fləʊ'tɪlə] *n.* 小舰队、小型船队
3. **on end** 连续地；直立着，竖立着
4. **auspicious** [ɔː'spɪʃəs] *adj.* 有前途的；有希望的；有

will be to learn more about it. If not, they will want to dig deeper and—if Mars does prove to be sterile—prepare it for human habitation.

Another **auspicious**[4] target in the search for life is the ocean thought to lie beneath the global ice cap covering Jupiter's moon Europa. For such an ocean to exist, scientists theorize, Europa must have a molten core and thermal vents that keep the water warm. Here on Earth, such vents are abloom with strange life forms; some researchers propose that terrestrial life might have originated there, without benefit of sunlight.

To see if there is aquatic life on Europa, we could dispatch a lander capable of melting a hole in the ice—which is estimated to be at least kilometers thick—and releasing small submarines into the ocean to seek out thermal vents. NASA's Europa Orbiter, scheduled for launch in 2003, is a first step: It will look for tidal bending of the ice crust, which would confirm the presence of an ocean below.

Saturn's mysterious satellite Titan—which has a dense, cloudy atmosphere thought to be rich in organic molecules—may replicate conditions on the early Earth when life began. The Cassini spacecraft, due to orbit Saturn in 2004, will parachute a probe onto Titan's surface. The probe could be followed up by a Titan orbiter equipped with a brace of small landers. Such missions could **shed light on**[5] the origins of life in general, even if there is no life on Titan itself.

Space probes passing Earth on their way to the outer planets have already detected spectral evidence of terrestrial life, proving that this approach can work. Earth's spectral lines signal the presence of chlorophyll, molecular oxygen (plants recirculate oxygen, which otherwise would combine with the soil and fade from sight), and methane (which would soon be gobbled up by the oxygen, were it not constantly being burped into the atmosphere by ruminating cattle and bubbling swamp gas). If similar spectra are found for another planet, we will be on the verge of the greatest scientific discovery in all history—that there is indeed life beyond Earth.

注释 利的；吉利
5. **shed light on** 为……提供线索；对……透露情况；使……清楚地显出；阐明……

原文翻译

　　长久以来，人类一直在这样推测，自己在茫茫宇宙中并非孤孤单单，而21世纪或许正是这类推测最终得以证实的时候。

　　火星一直被认为是太阳系中最有希望找到天外生命的地方。人类将发送一系列自动驾驶的探测器探访该星球。首先前往的是火星勘测登陆器2001号，它将采集那里的土壤，帮助人类确定它是否适合生命存在。未来要进行的其他探索包括土壤回运、发射火星探测气球以及发射能常年观测火星表面的远程漫游卫星。

　　不论不载人的探测器能否在火星上发现生命迹象，接下去我们还准备派人类前往这颗红色行星。一旦发现有生命活动的迹象，宇航员们将对它作进一步的了解。如果没有发现生命迹象，他们将作更深入的挖掘探索。如果确实证实火星上没有生命存在，宇航员们会为人类在火星上居住做准备工作。

　　另一个有望找到生命的目标是木星的卫星木卫二。人们认为，在木卫二的表面冰帽之下是海洋，而海洋中可能存在生命。科学家们从理论上推断，木卫二上可能存在这样一个海洋，其核心部分必定是熔岩，而且必定有通道传送出热能来保持水温。在地球上，这样的通道里满是各种奇异的生命形态；一些研究者认为，地球上的生命可能并非得益于阳光而产生，而是源于这些通道。

　　要搞清木卫二上是否有水中生命存在，我们可以发送一枚登陆器到那里，该登陆器可以在估计至少3公里厚的冰层上熔出一个洞，然后由小型潜水艇潜入海洋去寻找热能通道。美国国家宇航局第一步计划于2003年发射木卫二轨道飞行器，该飞行器将在冰壳上寻找潮水冲刷而成的弯曲痕迹，若发现这种痕迹，我们便可以确定木卫二的冰壳下面有海洋存在。

　　土星的神秘卫星土卫六可能重现了地球早期生命产生之时的环境。该卫星被浓密的大气层所覆盖——人们认为大气层中富含有机分子。卡西尼号航天飞机计划于2004年绕土星飞行，届时它将向土卫六表面伞降一枚探测器。继该探测器之后，人们还将发射配有一对小型着陆器的木卫二轨道飞行器。即使这一系列探测最后证实木卫二本身并无生命，它们也能告诉人们生命起源的大致情况。

　　前往其他行星的空间探测器在经过地球时，已经发现了表明地球生命迹象的光谱证据，这证明通过光谱寻找生命的办法是可行的。地球的光谱线表明，地球上存在叶绿素、分子氧（是植物使氧气得以循环利用，否则氧气将与土壤结合而隐匿不见）和甲烷（如果不是从反刍的动物口中和噗噗往外冒的沼气中不断有甲烷释放到大气中去，这种气体将很快为氧气所吞噬）。假如能在其他行星上发现类似的光谱，我们就离人类有史以来最伟大的科学发现不远了——那就是，地球之外确实存在生命。

文化点滴

Europa

　　木卫二。在1610年被伽利略发现，是木星的第六颗已知卫星，是木星的第四大卫星，在伽利略发现的卫星中离木星第二近。木卫二比地球的卫星月球稍微小一点，直径达到3100公里，是太阳系天体系统中的第六大卫星和第十五大天体。哈勃望远镜的观察揭示出木卫二有一个含氧的稀薄大气。

写作特点

本文使用了举例的写作方法。举例是列举有代表性的恰当的事例来进行说明。这是常用的说明方法，例子前面常有"比如""例如""如"或某年某月等标志性词语。例子的作用是反映一般情况，具体、有力地说明事物。本文把火星、木星的卫星木卫二及土卫六作为具体的例子来说明在这3个星球上可能存在外星生命。

品味鉴赏

古今中外一直有关于"外星人"的假想，在各国史书中也有不少疑似"外星人"的奇异记载，但现今人类还无法确定是否有外星生命，甚至是"外星人"的存在。

孤独的地球人在茫茫宇宙中寻找任何可能存在的友好的天外智慧生命，期望能与之建立长久的联系。本文分析了太阳系内部分天体存在生命的可能性，告诉大家科学家们将对它们进行一系列考察，并乐观地预言，观测手段的进步将有助于人类尽早发现天外生命。

美文感悟

地球环境日趋恶化，种种令人担忧的问题层出不穷，如：臭氧层的破坏、地球温室效应、酸雨、海洋污染、有害废弃物的越境转移、热带雨林的减少、野生动植物濒临灭绝、地球沙漠化……

Home Wreckers
家园正遭破坏

作者简介：

保罗·雷伯恩（Paul Raeburn, 1950—），美国《商业周刊》的科学编辑及资深作者，美联社的科学编辑及资深科学记者。

Biosphere II was a spectacular failure. The gleaming glass-and-concrete habitat sprawling across the desert in Oracle, Arizona, was supposed to support eight human "biospherians" for two years, but the seal had to be broken before the experiment ended in 1993. Oxygen had fallen to levels normally seen at an elevation of 17,500 feet. **Nitrous oxide**[1] had risen to the point where it threatened to cause brain damage. The fresh water supply became contaminated, and vines smothered food plants. Insect **pollinators**[2] and many other species became extinct. By the end, Biosphere II was overrun with swarms of ants and cockroaches.

注释

1. **nitrous oxide** ['naɪtrəs'ɒksaɪd] *n.* 一氧化二氮，笑气
2. **pollinator** ['pɒlɪneɪtə] *n.* 传粉者，传粉媒介，传粉昆虫
3. **spasm** ['spæzəm] *n.* 痉挛；抽搐；（能量、行为等的）突发；发作
4. **boreal** ['bɔːriːl] *adj.* 北的；北方的；北方地区的；北风的

Scientists who gathered recently to review the Biosphere II experiment reached a disturbing conclusion: "No one yet knows how to engineer systems that provide humans with the life-supporting services that natural ecosystems produce for free."

The problem is that these ecosystems are undergoing wrenching changes. Water and air quality, while improving in some regions, are deteriorating in many others. Carbon dioxide levels in the atmosphere are climbing. The world's population could reach 10 billion by 2050. And famed Harvard biologist Edward O. Wilson says the current rate of species losses puts us "in the midst of one of the great extinction **spasms**[3] of geological history. " All of which makes many ecologists wonder whether humans too will soon become extinct.

"It's an incredibly important but incredibly difficult question," says David Tilman of the University of Minnesota, one of the scientists who reviewed the Biosphere II experiment. "If we continue on this course, we're heading for a world in which agriculture will have immense impacts on the entire globe," he says. "Humans will consume the vast majority of the [surface fresh] waters of the world, especially for irrigation. Pesticide use could double in the next 50 years."

Because of these human impacts, Tilman says, "We're heading for a world in which we will have to engineer services we've always received for free from nature." That's why the failure of Biosphere II was so disturbing: It proves that we don't yet know how to do that.

Tilman is not an environmental activist; he is a scientist. His concerns about the future arise from the years he had spent doing experiments at a 9-square-mile study site called Cedar Creek, about 30 miles north of Minneapolis. Three distinct ecosystems meet there: northern, or **boreal**[4] forest; **deciduous**[5] forest; and prairie. Tilman has studied how different areas in Cedar Creek respond to drought, changes in nitrogen levels in the soil, and changes in the numbers and kinds of species living in these areas.

The experiments have shown that ecosystems with the most species are most resistant to drought, soil degradation, and wild fluctuations in plant growth. Tilman's research has also shown that high levels of nitrogen—the key component in agricultural fertilizers—can lead to the

---

注释

5. **deciduous** [dɪ'sɪdʒuəs] *adj.* （指树木）每年落叶的
6. **deplete** [dɪ'pliːt] *v.* 耗尽、用尽
7. **Permian** ['pɜːmɪən] *n.& adj.* 二叠纪（的）
8. **Homo sapiens** [ˌhəʊməˈsæpɪenz] *n.* 智人（现代人的学名）

extermination of certain plant species.

"We are heading for a biologically simpler world, with many fewer species in it," he says. If the ecological principles established at Cedar Creek hold true elsewhere, that means we'll be living in a world with **depleted**[6] soils, vulnerability to drought, and unpredictable changes in plant growth—which could lead to years of bounty and years of famine.

And the services that nature provides will begin to crumble. "The production of clean water and fertile soils, the pollination of crops, the disposal of humanity's waste products—these are all things that have been done for us," says Tilman. As the world loses its biological diversity, these needs will no longer be met.

"To get off this course, we have to realize our interdependence with other organisms in this world, " Tilman says. For example, letting cattle graze on grasslands to turn low-quality food (grass) into high-quality food (protein) is more efficient than keeping cattle in pens and feeding them grain, he says. "It takes a lot of land to produce that grain."

But changes in farming alone will not be enough. "We also have to have major changes in lifestyle," Tilman says. "We can't all live like Westerners. We're going to have to go in the other direction—living more like Asians."

The Biosphere II experience demonstrated that maintaining human life is a tricky proposition—especially if we can no longer rely on the services provided by natural ecosystems. If we are currently living through a mass extinction, as Wilson believes, we should consider tha past. In the great **Permian**[7] extinction 245 million years ago, 96 percent of species perished. Eventually, the Earth was repopulated with a rich collection of new species—but it took 100 million years. "That should give pause to anyone who believes that what **Homo sapiens**[8] destroys, nature will redeem," Wilson says. "Maybe so, but not within any length of time that has meaning for contemporary humanity."

原文翻译

生物圈 2 号彻底宣告失败。这个闪闪发光的玻璃与混凝土构筑的模拟生态圈位于亚利桑那州奥拉克尔的沙漠中，按照原实验计划，有 8 名"生态圈人"将在里面生活 2 年，实验本应于 1993 年结束，但结果改模拟生物圈却不得不提前封闭。因为圈内氧气的浓度很低，已降至通常在海拔 1.75 万英尺高空才会有的稀薄程度。一氧化二氮的含量却已达到可能引起脑损伤的地步。淡水资源遭到污染，赖以为生的植物枝蔓缠绕，传播花粉的昆虫和许多其他物种灭踪绝迹。到最后，生物圈 2 号内到处是蚂蚁横行，蟑螂乱爬。

科学家们最近聚在一起回顾探讨生物圈 2 号实验计划，得出这样一个令人担忧的结论："迄今为止，无人知道如何去操纵管理为人类提供生活保障的各种系统，而自然界的各类生态系统却可以无偿为人类提供一切所需。"

问题在于，自然界的这些自然生态系统正在发生令人痛心的变化。空气和水的质量尽管在某些地区得到了改善，却在其他许多地区恶化起来。大气中二氧化碳的含量在上升。世界人口到2050年有可能达到100亿。哈佛大学的著名生物学家爱德华·欧·威尔逊说，目前物种消失的比例之大，已使我们人类处于"地质史上最为严重的物种灭绝时期之一"中。所有这一切令许多生态学家担心，人类是否也将很快走向灭绝？

"这是一个无比重要但又无比难以回答的问题，"明尼苏达大学的戴维·蒂尔曼说。他是参与回顾探讨生物圈2号实验的科学家之一。"如果我们继续这样下去，就意味着我们是在进入这样一个世界——农业将对全球产生巨大影响：人类将消耗掉世界上绝大多数的（地表淡）水，主要用于灌溉。今后50年，农药的使用量可能会增加一倍。"

蒂尔曼说，正是因为人类的这些影响，"我们正步入这样一个世界——在这个世界里我们必须将学会自我管理，为自己提供我们一向无偿取之于大自然的各种服务"。这也正说明了为什么生物圈2号实验的失败如此令人惶恐：它证明我们人类还不知道如何去自力更生。

蒂尔曼不是环保积极分子，他是科学家。他对未来的关注始于他参与雪松溪研究基地的实验之时。该基地位于明尼阿波利斯北部约30英里处，占地9平方英里。那里有三种生态系统交汇：北部或者叫北方林区、落叶林区和草原区。蒂尔曼的研究课题是，这三个区域在面对干旱、土壤氮含量的变化和生活在这些区域的物种数量及种类的改变时，各自会发生什么变化。

实验结果表明，生物物种数量最多的生态系统最能够抵御干旱及土质下降和植物生长过程中的剧烈变动。蒂尔曼的研究同时也显示，如果农用肥料中的主要成分——氮的浓度过高，有可能导致某些植物物种的灭绝。

蒂尔曼说，"我们正在进入一个生态环境越来越单一、物种越来越稀少的世界"。如果雪松溪的生态规律适用于其他地区，那就意味着我们生活的环境会变成这副样子：土地资源枯竭，动辄就出现旱灾，作物生长情况难以预测——收成时好时坏，几年丰收，几年饥荒。

而大自然所提供的各种服务也将随之消失。"水的净化，沃土的提供，农作物的授粉，垃圾的处理——大自然为我们做了所有这一切，"蒂尔曼说。而随着生态环境越来越缺乏多样性，它将再也无法满足人类的这些需求。

"要摆脱这种环境恶化的趋势，我们必须先要意识到这一点：人类与世界上的其他生物系统是相互依存的，"蒂尔曼说。例如，我们可以在草地上放牧，让牲口把低质量的食物（草）变成高质量的食物（蛋白质）。这样做比把牲口关在圈里喂谷物效果要好得多，因为"生产那些谷物要占用大批土地"，蒂尔曼说。

但是仅仅在农业方面做些改变是不够的。"我们的生活方式也应当有重大变化，"蒂尔曼说。"我们不能完全像西方人那样生活。我们要朝另一个方面努力——更多地像亚洲人那样生活。"

生物圈2号一事表明，维持人类生存是个棘手的问题——特别是假如我们无法再依靠自然生态系统来为我们提供各种服务的话。如果像威尔逊所认为的那样，我们目前正生活在一个物种大规模灭绝的时期，那我们应当回过头去看看过去发生的事。2.45亿年前的那次二叠纪物种大灭绝中，96%的物种销声匿迹。后来，地球上再次出现大量新物种——但这一过程花了1亿年时间。"此事值得那些认为智人破坏的一切，大自然会重新恢复起来的人好好考虑考虑，"威尔逊说。"或许他们说得对，但是恢复时间之长，对于我们当代人来说是毫无意义的。"

文化点滴

Biosphere II

生物圈2号。人们居住的地球被称为生物圈1号，建在美国亚利桑那州图森市郊的一个建筑面积为1.2公顷的特殊建筑物称为生物圈2号。在生物圈2号里面，有模仿地球各自然区的海洋、热带雨林、热带草原地带、沙漠地带、灌木丛地带、温带草原和作物集约耕作区。该实验最后以失败告终。目前，原先作为人类栖息地的区域被辟为旅游区，其余各部分仍在供科学家进行其他研究。

写作特点

引用是指写文章时，有意引用成语、诗句、格言、典故等，以表达自己的思想感情，说明自己对新问题、新道理的见解。引用的作用是使论据确凿充分，增强说服力，富启发性，而且语言精练，含蓄典雅。本文大量引述了参与回顾探讨生物圈2号实验的科学家之一、明尼苏达大学的戴维·蒂尔曼的话语来加强说服力。

品味鉴赏

生物圈2号的失败使人得出这样一个令人担忧的结论：迄今为止，无人知道如何去操纵管理为人类提供生活保障的各种系统。被称为生物圈1号的地球是人类目前唯一的栖息地，而环境的恶化正愈演愈烈。如果再不采取措施，我们将面临灭绝的威胁，因为我们无处可去。

美文感悟

是一种什么力量让我们如此害怕，以致看见在地上挣扎、抽搐的"小悦悦"都赶紧绕开走掉，甚至陈阿姨去救助的时候都还劝她不要多事？这种神秘的力量，你到底是谁？来自何处？是个什么面目？以什么手段叫我们的生命和人格变得如此萎缩卑微、毫无尊严？

The "Little Yue Yue" Incident as a Source of Complete Despair and a Glimpse of Hope
"小悦悦"事件：彻底的绝望和希望的一瞥

The chilling video of little YueYue being run over and ignored by passengers cannot be ignored. China is still recovering, trying to understand what went wrong in social values. Many shocking incidents come and go in China, as corruption, socioeconomic gaps within society and lack of infrastructure can often lead to "interesting" events in such a huge country, but the 'little Yue Yue' incident isn't so clear-cut; it doesn't allow people just to point fingers at corrupted official or evil criminals, it leads people to **introspection**[1].

On October 13, 2011 in the city of Foshan, in the southern Guangdong Province, a two years old **toddler**[2], Wang Yue (nicknamed "Yue Yue") was hit by a vehicle. But the hit-and-run accident was only the introduction to a shocking scene, in which 18 pedestrian passengers ignored the

---

注释
1. **introspection** [ˌɪntrəˈspekʃən] n. 反省，内省；自我反省
2. **toddler** [ˈtɒdlə] n. 蹒跚行走的人；幼童装；学步的幼儿
3. **extort** [ɪkˈstɔːt] vt. 敲诈；曲解

injured child and walked away, before Chen Xianmei, a 57 years old woman, noticed the child while she was collecting trash, picked Yue Yue up and looked for her parents.

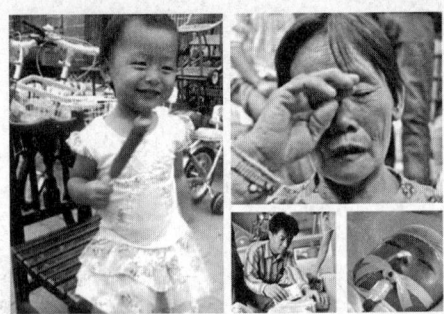

What went wrong? How come nobody noticed the injured child? Is it a matter of lack of attention? Does it have to do with the Foshan culture? Are Chinese lacking minimal compassion? Does this have to do with the soul-corrupting modernity or rather the fear of authorities? Or perhaps the passengers could not know for sure that the child was indeed seriously injured?

Some Chinese netizens, when discussing the incident, claimed that picking up and injured child can be scary; what if she dies? How can one be certain he/ she won't be blamed of the child's death and be **extorted**[3]? These thoughts of not having confidence in the system, to the extent of not allowing oneself get into a mess of helping the other (no wonder the woman who did attempt to rescue Yue Yue was a poor peasant that had "nothing to lose"), should be rethought by officials. Suggestions for legislation of Good Samaritan Laws, which will protect aiding bystanders, have been expressed throughout China.

Citizen response shows that apathy is strongly condemned by both officials and commoners. How the strong sense of empathy, experienced when watching the painful Yue Yue video, can be translated into positive initiative when witnessing "live" incidents can be discussed limitlessly.

原文翻译

我们对令人心寒的"小悦悦"被车撞倒、路人冷漠的视频不能漠视。

中国还在对这一事件带来的伤痛中恢复,试图了解我们的社会价值观到底出了什么问题。在中国出现许多令人震惊的事件,如腐败、贫富差距及基础设施的缺乏,在这样一个巨大的国家里常可导致"有趣"的事件,但"小悦悦"事件也不是那么鲜明,它不只是让人们手指指向贪官污吏或邪恶的罪犯,它会让人们反省。

2011年10月13日,在广东省南部佛山市,一个两岁的孩子王悦(昵称"悦悦")被车撞倒。但是这起交通事故逃逸事件只是为后面令人震惊的场面拉开了序幕,18个路人从受伤的孩子身边冷漠地走过,之后一位57岁的老人陈贤妹,在她收垃圾的时候注意到了孩子,抱起悦悦去找她的父母。

出了什么问题?怎么会没有人注意到受伤的孩子呢?是因为忽视吗?这就是佛山的文化吗?中国人缺乏最低限度的同情吗?或者,也许路人不知道孩子确实受了重伤?

一些中国网民在讨论此事时,声称救起受伤的孩子是可怕的,如果她死了怎么办?一个人怎么能确定他或她将不会被指责对孩子的死亡负责并受到勒索?这些想法表明对制度缺乏信心,不想因为帮助别人而惹麻烦(难怪救起"小悦悦"的是一个贫穷的农民,她没有什么可失去的),政府官员应该反思。建议为见义勇为的行为立法,这将保护伸出援助之手的人,全中国都支持这个建议。

市民的反应表现出此事件中路人的冷漠受到政府官员和普通百姓的强烈谴责。如何将在观看令人痛心的"小悦悦"视频时的强烈同情心转化为积极主动的情绪,是值得深刻探讨的。

文化点滴

Foshan, Guangdong Province

佛山市位于中国广东省中南部，地处珠江三角洲腹地，东经113°06'，北纬23°02'，珠江水系中的西江、北江及其支流贯穿全境。东倚广州，距离香港约231公里，距澳门约140公里。佛山气候温和，雨量充足，自古就是富饶的鱼米之乡。佛山市的常住人口为603万人（2011年数据），其中户籍人口370.89万人。佛山还是著名侨乡，旅外侨胞达140万人。

写作特点

本文大量地使用了反诘。如："出了什么问题？怎么会没有人注意到受伤的孩子呢？是因为忽视吗？这就是佛山的文化吗？中国人缺乏最低限度的同情吗？或者，也许路人不知道孩子确实受了重伤？"反诘有反问的意思，但又不同于反问，它有追问、责问的意味。反诘是用疑问的形式表达确定的意思，以加强语气。

品味鉴赏

很多人说那18个路人冷漠，但我想他们更多的或许是害怕，怕被冤枉，怕跟政府部门特别是警察打交道，怕无穷无尽的麻烦……陈贤妹阿姨说："我一个捡垃圾的怕什么呢？"陈阿姨的不怕，以及当时有人劝她不要多事，都反证出那18个路人更多的是怕。

之所以说他们不是冷漠，是因为我相信我们中国人内心深处存在几乎与生俱来的道德感，中国几千年儒家文化的最大功效就是培养了我们的这种道德感：人应该做个有德之人，社会应该是个有道德的社会。这形成了我们民族性格中最主要的特质，我甚至认为这也是我们异于他族的最显著之处。

因此，在"小悦悦"事件中，我认为是"害怕"战胜了我们的道德感。谴责他们怯弱其实没有什么道理，因为我们自己也未尝不是如此；更毫无意义，因为这丝毫无改于"小悦悦"的遭遇，而且这样的事也必定还会在中国大地上出现。

根本的拯救，还是要找出那个令我们害怕的神秘力量，消解它，根除它，只有这样我们才不再害怕，我们心底的道德感才会焕发力量和光辉，"小悦悦"这样的遭遇才可望避免，生命的尊严才有望回归，而我们，也可以终于活得像个人样。

这样的拯救，除了我们自己，别无他人。

美文感悟

Chapter 5

世界名人

本章节选了10篇关于10位世界名人的相关传记、故事及其著名演讲。世界名人,或以其深邃的思想推动了世界文明的进步,或以其叱咤风云的政治生涯影响了历史的进程,或以其在自然科学领域中的巨大成就造福于人类。了解他们的生平、思想、智慧以及人格魅力,必然会对我们的人生产生重大的影响。

Magic Mama – J.K. Rowling
魔法妈妈——J.K. 罗琳

背景介绍：

乔安妮·凯瑟琳·罗琳，作家，代表作品《哈利·波特》系列小说。1965年7月31日生于英国的格温特郡的 Chipping Sodbury 综合医院。毕业于英国 University of Exeter（埃克塞特大学），学习法语和古典文学，获文理学士学位。毕业后曾在英国曼彻斯特接受教学培训。

Like that of her own character, Harry Potter, J.K. Rowling's life has the **luster**[1] of a fairy tale. Divorced, living on public assistance in a tiny Edinburgh flat with her infant daughter, Rowling wrote *Harry Potter and the Sorcerer's Stone* at a table in a cafe during her daughter's naps —

注释

1. **luster** ['lʌstɚ] *n.* 光泽；光辉；光彩；荣耀

and it was Harry Potter that rescued her.

Joanne Kathleen Rowling entered the world in Chipping Sodbury General Hospital in Bristol, England, a fitting beginning for someone who would later enjoy making up strange names for people, places and games played on flying **broomsticks**2. Her younger sister Di was born just under two years later.

Rowling remembers that she always wanted to write and that the first story she actually wrote down, when she was five or six, was a story about a rabbit called Rabbit. Many of her favorite memories center around reading—hearing *The Wind in the Willows*3 read aloud by her father when she had the **measles**4, enjoying the **fantastic**5 adventure stories of E. Nesbit, **reveling**6 in the magical world of C. S. Lewis's *Narnia*, and her favorite story of all, *The Little White Horse* by Elizabeth Goudge.

At Exeter University Rowling took her degree in French and spent one year studying in Paris. After college she moved to London to work for **Amnesty**7 International as a researcher and **bilingual**8 secretary. The best thing about working in an office, she has said, was typing up stories on the computer when no one was watching. During this time, on a particularly long train ride from Manchester to London in the summer of 1990, the idea came to her of a boy who is a **wizard**9 and doesn't know it. He attends a school for wizardry—she could see him very plainly in her mind. By the time the train pulled into King's Cross Station four hours later, many of the characters and the early stages of the plot were fully formed in her head. The story took further shape as she continued working on it in pubs and cafes over her lunch hours.

In 1992 Rowling left off working in offices and moved to Portugal to teach English as a Second Language. In spite of her students making jokes about her name (this time they called her "Rolling Stone"), she enjoyed teaching. She worked afternoons and evenings, leaving mornings free for writing. After her marriage to a Portuguese TV journalist ended in divorce, Rowling returned to Britain with her infant daughter and a suitcase full of Harry Potter notes and chapters. She settled in Edinburgh to be near her sister and set out to finish the book before looking for a teaching job. Wheeling her daughter's carriage around the city to escape their tiny, cold apartment, she would **duck**10 into coffee shops to write when the baby fell asleep. In this way she finished the book and started sending it to publishers. It was rejected several times before she found a London agent, chosen because she liked his name—Christopher Little.

Rowling was working as a French teacher when she heard that her book about the boy wizard had been accepted for publication. *Harry Potter and the Philosopher's Stone* was

注释	2. **broomstick** ['bru:m,stɪk] *n.*（童话故事中女巫常骑于空中的带柄的）扫帚	作乐；喧闹的宴会或庆典
		7. **amnesty** ['æmnɪstɪ] *n.* 大赦，特赦
	3. **willow** ['wɪləʊ] *n.* 柳树；柳木制品	8. **bilingual** [baɪ'lɪŋgwəl] *a.* 双语的，两种语言的，能说两种语言的
	4. **measles** ['mi:zəlz] *n.* 麻疹	
	5. **fantastic** [fæn'tæstɪk] *a.* 空想的，异想天开的；奇异的，古怪的；极好的	9. **wizard** ['wɪzəd] *n.*（尤指故事中的）男巫；术士
		10. **duck** [dʌk] *n.* 鸭子，野鸭 *vt. & vi.* 躲避，回避；潜入
	6. **revel** ['revəl] *vi.* 陶醉，狂欢作乐；扬扬得意 *n.* 狂欢，	

published in June 1997 and achieved almost instant success. With the publication of the American edition, in 1998, Rowling's books continued to make publishing history. Harry Potter climbed to the top of all the bestseller lists for children's and adult books. Indeed, the story of the boy wizard, his Cinderlad[11] childhood, and his adventures at Hogwarts School of Witchcraft and Wizardry caught the imagination of readers of all ages. In Britain a separate edition of the first book appeared with a more "adult" dust jacket so that grown-ups reading it on trains and subways would not have to hide their copy behind a newspaper.

J. K. Rowling lives in Edinburgh, Scotland, with her daughter Jessica and continues to work on writing the seven-book saga of Harry Potter.

原文翻译

J. K. 罗琳的生活展现出童话般的光芒，如同她所创造的魔法小巫师——哈利·波特。经历了一次失败的婚姻后，这个靠救济金过日子、独自抚养女儿的单亲妈妈和出生不久的女儿搬到了爱丁堡的一个狭小的公寓里。她常待在公寓附近的咖啡馆里，待女儿熟睡后开始写作。就在这个小咖啡馆里，她写出了《哈利·波特与魔法石》，塑造了那个将她带离窘境的小巫师。

乔安·凯瑟琳·罗琳出生在英格兰布里斯托的奇伏索德伯里综合医院里，这对一个喜欢给别人起奇怪名字、喜欢坐着扫帚满场飞奔的小姑娘来说，是个合适的开始。她的妹妹迪两年后来到这个世上。

罗琳回忆自己从小就喜欢写作，五六岁时就写了一篇跟兔子有关的故事。小时候美好的记忆似乎总是围绕阅读的——得麻疹时听爸爸大声讲《柳树里的风》的故事，读伊迪丝·内斯比特的奇异的冒险故事，沉浸在 C. S. 路易斯的《纳尼亚》和伊丽莎白·古奇的《小白马》的奇妙故事世界里。

在埃克塞特大学里，罗琳主修法语，在巴黎留学一年。毕业后，她搬去伦敦担任大赦国际的调查员和双语秘书。罗琳回忆说，那段时间最有趣的事情就是趁没人的时候在电脑上打小说。1990 年，时值 24 岁的罗琳坐在由曼彻斯特出发前往伦敦的火车上，写一个是巫师然而却自己不知晓的男孩的故事的想法闯入了她的生命。她可以在脑海里清晰地勾画他的模样，看到他进入魔法学校。4 小时后，当火车驶入国王十字车站时，大部分人物和故事的前期框架已经在她的脑海里形成了。当她午餐时间坐在咖啡馆里继续构思时，故事的结构变得更加清晰。

1992 年，罗琳结束了白领生涯，前往葡萄牙做英语教师。尽管学生们常拿她的名字开玩笑，叫她"滚石"（英语中 Rowling 与 rolling 同音），她仍然非常喜欢教书。她在下午和晚上去学校工作，上午用来写作。不久后，她与一名葡萄牙的电视台记者结婚，但这段婚姻最终以离婚告终。离婚后，罗琳带着女儿和满满一箱子哈利·波特的笔记与手稿回到了英国。为了能住得靠近妹妹，罗琳在爱丁堡定居下来，准备在找新工作前完成这部小说。她常常推着女儿的手推车四处闲逛，只是为了逃离又小又冷的公寓。她会躲到咖啡馆里，趁女儿睡着时写作。就这样，罗琳在咖啡馆里完成了哈利·波特的创作，开始寻找出版商。但她的稿件被多次退回，直到她找到了一个伦敦的经纪人。罗琳之所以会找到他，仅仅是因为喜欢他可爱的名字——克里斯多夫·里特（Christopher Little）。

当罗琳得知这本关于小巫师的小说被出版商接受时，她正在一所学校教法语。《哈利·波特与魔法石》在 1997 年 6 月甫一出版，就大获成功。随着 1998 年在美国的出版，罗琳的书继续创造着出版界的历史。哈利波特登上了儿童与成人书籍的最佳销售榜的首位。确实，这个小巫师的故事、他灰姑娘一样的童年和他在霍格华兹魔法学校的历险，引发了各个年龄读者的丰富想象力。在英国，出版商出版了一种更成人化封面的版本，使得大人们能在火车或者地铁里阅读而不用把书藏在报纸后面。

现在，J. K. 罗琳和她的女儿杰西卡住在苏格兰的爱丁堡，继续完成哈利·波特的冒险故事。

注释

11. Cinderlad ['sɪndəlæd] n. 灰姑娘一样

文化点滴

E. Nesbit

伊迪丝·内斯比特（婚后姓名为 Edith Bland，1858—1924），英国小说作家和诗人，在儿童文学的出版上使用 E. Nesbit 为名。其最著名的文学作品为曾经改编成电影《沙仙活地魔》(*Five Children and It*, 2004) 的奇幻魔法故事系列：《五个孩子和一个怪物》、《五个孩子和凤凰与魔毯》、《五个孩子和一个护身符》三部曲，和《铁路边的孩子们》(*The Railway Children*, 1970)。

C. S. Lewis

C. S. 路易斯（1898-1963），是 20 世纪英国一位具有多方面天才的作家。他 26 岁即登牛津大学教席，被当代人誉为"最伟大的牛津人"。1954 年他被剑桥大学聘为中世纪及文艺复兴时期英语文学教授，这个头衔保持到他退休。他在一生中完成了三类很不相同的事业。他被称为"三个 C. S. 路易斯"：一是杰出的牛津剑桥大学文学史家和批评家，代表作包括《牛津英国文学史·16 世纪卷》；二是深受欢迎的科学幻想作家和儿童文学作家，代表作包括《太空》三部曲和《纳尼亚传奇》七部曲；三是通俗的基督教神学家和演说家，代表作包括《天路回归》《魔鬼家书》《返璞归真》《四种爱》等等。他一生著书逾 30 部，有学术著作、小说、诗集、童话，他在全世界拥有庞大的读者群，时至今日，他的作品每年仍吸引着成千上万的新读者。

Elizabeth Goudge

伊丽莎白·古奇（1900—1984），英格兰小说作家、短篇故事和儿童文学作家。最著名的文学作品为 1946 年的《小白马》(*The Little White Horse*)，同年荣获卡内基奖章（Carnegie Medal）。1944 年的小说 *Green Dolphin Country* 在美国出版的书名为 *Green Dolphin Street*（《绿豚街》），1947 年改编成同名电影 *Green Dolphin Street* 上映。

写作特点

本文是一篇人物介绍，人物介绍属于记叙文（narration）的写作范畴，写作时要围绕人物组织材料。所写短文中应包括人物（who）、时间（when）、地点（where）、主要事件（what）等内容。写作时，要做到主题鲜明，内容清楚，并注意结构的完整性。

常见可运用句型：

sb. is considered to be one of the greatest ...

Well known as ..., he ...

Born in a poor family, he had to ...

When he was a small boy, he showed a great interest in ...

Thanks to the help of ..., he was able to continue his education.

Between ... and ..., he studied at ...

From ... to ..., he first worked as ..., and then he became ...

He was praised/honored for ...

She devoted herself to scientific research and made great contributions to ...

She was awarded the Nobel Prize in Chemistry for her scientific achievements.

His achievements are worthy of praise.

品味鉴赏

　　J.K. 罗琳从小喜欢写作和讲故事。开始构思哈利·波特的故事是在 1990 年，24 岁的她在前往伦敦的火车旅途中，火车因故障停车，车外的草地上有一群牛，灵感突然迸发了，并且在后来的途中，一个瘦弱、戴着眼镜的黑发小巫师一直在车窗外对着她微笑。罗琳把这个叫哈利·波特的男孩故事推向了世界。于是，哈利·波特诞生了——一个 11 岁小男孩，瘦小的个子，黑色乱蓬蓬的头发，明亮的绿色眼睛，戴着圆形眼镜，前额上有一道细长、闪电状的伤疤……哈利·波特成为风靡全球的小说人物。

　　作为单身母亲，罗琳母女的生活极其艰辛。她的第一本书《哈利·波特与魔法石》前后共写了 5 年，这期间，她从葡萄牙回到了爱丁堡。罗琳因为自家的屋子又小又冷，时常到住家附近的一家咖啡馆里，据罗琳说，她喜欢咖啡馆的氛围。她将女儿放在桌边的婴儿车上，就在女儿的吵闹声里写作，把哈利·波特的故事写在小纸片上。故事成文后，罗琳多次呈上书稿均遭拒绝不果。不过，她的努力终于得到了回报。在一所小印刷厂 Bloomsbury 接下印刷权后，童话一出版便备受瞩目，好评如潮，其中包括英国国家图书奖、儿童小说奖，以及斯马蒂图书金奖章奖，她的生活发生了天翻地覆地变化，她自己也成了英国第三富婆。

　　随后，罗琳又分别于 1998 年与 1999 年创作了《哈利·波特与密室》和《哈利·波特与阿兹卡班囚徒》，进一步轰动世界。2000 年 7 月，随着第四部《哈利·波特与火焰杯》的问世，世界范围的哈利·波特热持续升温，创造了出版史上的神话。而根据小说拍摄的电影自从最近上映以来，也纷纷在世界不少地方打破当地的票房纪录。哈利·波特系列小说第五部《哈利·波特与凤凰社》于 2003 年 6 月 21 日在全球同步发行，掀起了又一轮哈利·波特的热潮。哈利·波特系列小说第六部《哈利·波特与"混血王子"》于 2005 年 7 月 16 日在全球同步发行，该书的中文版已于 2005 年 10 月 15 日前发行。

　　到了 2007 年 7 月 21 日，哈利·波特系列的最后一部小说，《哈利·波特与死亡圣器》发行，为这一系列小说画上了句号。

美文感悟

10 Lessons Learned from Facebook Founder Mark Zuckerberg
从"脸书"创始人马克·扎克伯格那里学到的10课

背景介绍：

马克·扎克伯格（1984—），美国社交网站 Facebook 的创办人，被人们冠以"盖茨第二"的美誉。哈佛大学计算机和心理学专业辍学生。据《福布斯》杂志保守估计，马克·扎克伯格拥有 135 亿美元身家，是 2008 年全球最年轻的单身巨富，也是历来全球最年轻的自行创业亿万富豪。2012 年 5 月 19 日和华裔女友普莉希拉－陈成婚。

Mark Elliot Zuckerberg is an American computer programmer and Internet **entrepreneur**[1]. He is best known as one of four co-founders of the social networking site Facebook, of which he is

注释	1. **entrepreneur** [ˌɒntrəprəˈnɜː] n. 企业家，主办人，承包人	3. **flexibility** [ˌfleksəˈbɪləti] n. 柔韧性，机动性，灵活性
	2. **shareholder** [ˈʃeəˌhəʊdə] n. 股东，股票持有者	4. **inherent** [ɪnˈhɪrənt] a. 固有的，内在的

chairman and chief executive. It was co-founded as a private company in 2004 by Zuckerberg and classmates Dustin Moskovitz, Eduardo Saverin, and Chris Hughes while they were students at Harvard University. Zuckerberg is the largest individual **shareholder**[2] with 28.4 percent of the common stock and controls 56.9 percent of the voting power. As of 2012, his personal wealth was estimated at more than $19.1 billion, making

him one of the world's youngest billionaires. Zuckerberg is one of the 30 richest people on Earth. He was named four times in Time 100: in 2009 as one of the 100 influential people of the world, in 2010 as Time magazine's Person of the Year, in 2011 as one of the 100 influential people of the world and in 2012 in "The All-Time TIME 100 of All Time" by Joel Stein in Time.

Lesson 1: Be open to change without losing sight of your goals.

Facebook grew because of Zuckerberg's **flexibility**[3] and willingness to change his product based on consumer demands and financial opportunities. At no point did he charge users to take advantage of the networking service – profits came purely from advertisements. Because of this, Facebook stands as a perfect example of exercising a great deal of adaptability without ever having betrayed its initial intentions.

Lesson 2: Engage people.

What Zuckerberg did right is use humanity's **inherent**[4] need for interaction and allowed them a venue through which they can connect with loved ones without ever having to pay a cent. Over time, the site expanded its offerings to let them share pictures, chat, play games, take quizzes, and send gifts to one another, acting as a one-stop shop for long-distance or schedule-blocked friendship.

Lesson 3: People yearn for true friendships.

The biggest social networking site Facebook with over half a billion members show us that all of us human beings, deep down in our hearts, need friends. We humans need to be connected to others or to somehow belong to a group or community. It's good to have lots of online "friends" in Facebook, but we should not forget to cultivate offline friends in the real world too.

Lesson 4: Embrace technology.

Zuckerberg's project succeeded not only because of its emphasis on community and connectivity, but because it understood the potential inherent in emerging and developing technologies and did its best to take advantage of them. As a result, it becomes one of the **cornerstones**[5] of the so-called Web 2.0 movement.

注释

5. cornerstone ['kɔːnəˌstəʊn] n. 奠基石，基础；最重要部分，柱石

6. cohort ['kəʊhɔːt] n. （古罗马军队的）步兵大队，军队；一群人，同伙

7. vacuum ['vækjuəm] n. 真空，空白；<口>真空吸尘器；空间；空虚

Lesson 5 : Stick with what you know.

It is also a good idea to stay within known abilities. Never try and push something that does not fit. Zuckerberg and his small band of **cohorts**[6] succeeded because they started a project based on their strengths and experiences. Their computer science background led to a computer science undertaking.

Lesson 6: Do not be afraid to ask questions.

Zuckerberg did not become a billionaire in a **vacuum**[7]. He started off by collaborating with computer scientists, and while the questions themselves remain unknown, it is a safe assumption that all cooperative efforts involve a series of problems, questions, answers, and solutions.

Lesson 7: Ideas change the world.

Innovation and new ideas continuously bring out new global icons like Mark Zuckerberg because of sheer creativity, with the phenomenon Facebook co-created by him just in 2004 in his Harvard dorm room. Before, we thought Microsoft and Apple were the ultimate; then came Yahoo, then Google, and now Facebook.

Lesson 8: Be kind to all, never underestimate anyone.

Be kind to every person, especially those without friends in school, in the office or in your neighborhood, the loners or the problematic. Be kind not because he or she might b++ecome unexpectedly a future success like the campus **nerds**[8] Bill Gates or Mark Zuckerberg, but because it is the civilized and **Christian**[9] way to live.

Lesson 9 : Have passion!

Zuckerberg had passion, believed in what he was and what he is still doing. Why would Zuckerberg stay up until the **wee**[10] hours of the morning, programming code on his laptop while his colleagues were out partying? Isn't it all ultimately because of sheer passion?

Lesson 10 : Simplicity and community.

In the end, Mark Zuckerberg never really did anything too complex to rake in his fortune. Simplicity and community dictated the route he eventually took towards billionaire status, and these relatively **straightforward**[11] goals have plenty to offer college students **aspiring**[12] to create their own businesses and services.

注释	8. **nerd** [nɜːd] *n.* 讨厌的人，卑微的人	11. **straightforward** [streɪt'fɔːwəd] *a.* 直截了当的，坦率的，明确的
	9. **Christian** ['krɪstʃən] *a.* 信基督教的，基督教的，基督教徒的	
	10. **wee** [wiː] *a.* 很小的，极小的	12. **aspiring** [əs'paɪərɪŋ] *a.* 有志气的，有抱负的；高耸的

原文翻译

马克·埃利奥特·扎克伯格是美国软件设计师和互联网企业家,是著名的社交网站"脸书"的四位联合创始人之一,他是"脸书"的主席和首席执行官。"脸书"是他和哈佛大学的同学达斯汀·莫斯科维兹、爱德华多·萨维林、克里斯·休斯于2004年共同创立的一家私人公司。扎克伯格是最大的股东,占有28.4%的股份和控制56.9%的投票权利。到2012年,他的个人财富估计超过了191亿美元,这使得他成为世界上最年轻的亿万富翁。扎克伯格是世界上30位最富有的人之一。他被时代100四次提名:2009年世界上最有影响力的100人之一,2010年《时代》杂志年度人物,2011年世界上最有影响力的100人之一以及2012年被《时代》杂志乔尔·斯坦恩选入"史上时代100"。

第一课:盯住目标,敢于改变。

"脸书"的增长,是由于扎克伯格根据消费者的需求和金融机会的灵活性和愿意改变自己的产品。在任何时候,他绝不利用网络服务收取用户费用——利润纯粹来自广告。正因如此,"脸书"成为没有背叛初衷而展现出极大的适应性的完美例子。

第二课:吸引顾客。

扎克伯格做对的一点是利用人类互动的内在需要,并提供给人们的场所,通过这些场所,人们可以与喜爱的人连线而无需支付一分钱。随着时间的推移,该网站扩大其服务,人们可以分享照片、聊天、玩游戏、参加测验并互送礼品,就好像在为被时空阻碍的友谊提供一站式服务。

第三课:人们渴望真正的友谊。

在最大的社交网络"脸书"上有5亿成员,这显示出我们人类在我们的内心深处需要朋友。我们人类需要和他人联通或者在某种程度上属于一个组群或者群体。在"脸书"上拥有许多"朋友"是很好的事情,但是我们不应该忘记在线下的真实世界里培养友谊。

第四课:拥抱技术。

扎克伯格不单是因为"脸书"强调社区性和联通性,而且因为它明白开发技术的潜在的重要性,并且尽最大的努力利用好技术。结果就是,"脸书"成为所谓的网页2.0运动最重要的部分之一。

第五课:坚持你所知道的。

保持在已知的范围内是个好想法。永远不要尝试和推动那些不适合的东西。扎克伯格和他的小组取得成功,因为他们基于自身的力量和经验来开始他们的事业。他们的电脑科技背景致使一个电脑科技企业的兴起。

第六课:勇于提问。

扎克伯格成为亿万富翁并非浪得虚名。他以与计算机科学家合作开始,而问题本身却不得而知,这里可以假设,所有的合作努力一定涉及一系列问题、提问、答案和解决方案。

第七课:想法改变世界。

创新的和新鲜的想法不断为世界产生像扎克伯格这样的新偶像,因为纯想象力和"脸书"只是在2004年他在哈佛的寝室里和伙伴共同创造出来的这么个现象。在此之前,我们认为微软和苹果是极限的了,然后出现雅虎,然后谷歌,现在是"脸书"。

第八课:待人友善,不要低估别人。

友善地对待每一个人,尤其是那些在学校、办公室或者邻里没有朋友的人,还有孤独者或者有麻烦的人。对他们友善不是因为他们可能在不经意间成为未来的成功者,就像校园里的傻瓜比尔·盖茨或者马克·扎克伯格,而是因为这是文明的、高尚的生活方式。

第九课:拥有热情。

扎克伯格拥有热情，他相信他自己和他正在做的事情。为什么当扎克伯格的同事们外出聚会时他却情愿熬夜到清晨用笔记本电脑编程呢？这一切难道最终不就是因为纯粹的热情吗？

第十课：简单和社会团体。

最终，马克·扎克伯格并没有做任何一件复杂的事情来碰运气。简单和社会团体控制着他最终成为亿万富翁的道路，而且这些相对直接的目标足以给大学生渴望去开创自己的事业。

文化点滴

Facebook

Facebook 是一个社交网络服务网站，于 2004 年 2 月 4 日上线。从 2006 年 9 月到 2007 年 9 月间，该网站在全美网站中的排名由第 60 名上升至第 7 名。同时，Facebook 是美国排名第一的照片分享站点，每天上载 850 万张照片。随着用户数量的增加，Facebook 的目标已经指向另外一个领域：互联网搜索。2012 年 2 月 1 日，Facebook 正式向美国证券交易委员会提出首次公开发行（IPO）申请，目标融资规模达 50 亿美元，并任命摩根士丹利、高盛和摩根大通为主要承销商。这将是硅谷有史以来规模最大的 IPO。2012 年 5 月 18 日，Facebook 正式在美国纳斯达克证券交易所上市。

Time magazine

《时代》（又译《时代周刊》、《时代杂志》）美国出版的时事周刊，被誉为当代最具代表性与影响力的刊物。《时代》的注册商标为大写的"TIME"。在一些广告中，《时代》将"TIME"定义为"报道国际重要事件的杂志"（The International Magazine of Events 缩写）作为它的刊物定位。

Microsoft

微软公司是世界 PC（Personal Computer，个人计算机）机软件开发的先导，由比尔·盖茨与保罗·艾伦创始于 1975 年，总部设在华盛顿州的雷德蒙市（Redmond，邻近西雅图），目前是全球最大的电脑软件提供商。微软公司现有雇员 6.4 万人，2005 年营业额 368 亿美元。其主要产品为 Windows 操作系统、Internet Explorer 网页浏览器及 Microsoft Office 办公软件套件。1999 年推出了 MSN Messenger 网络即时信息客户程序，2001 年推出 Xbox 游戏机，参与游戏终端机市场竞争。

Apple

苹果公司，原称苹果电脑公司，是全球第一大手机生产商，是全球主要的 PC 厂商，也是世界市值最大的上市公司，其核心业务是电子科技产品。苹果的 Apple II 于 20 世纪 70 年代助长了个人电脑革命，其后的 Macintosh 接力于 20 世纪 80 年代持续发展。最知名的产品是其出品的 Apple II、Macintosh 电脑、iPod 音乐播放器、iTunes 商店、iMac 一体机、iPhone 手机和 iPad 平板电脑等，在高科技企业中以创新而闻名。2012 年 2 月底，苹果市值在派息预期的刺激下大涨，一举突破 5000 亿美元关口。

Yahoo

雅虎是美国著名的互联网门户网站，20 世纪末互联网奇迹的创造者之一。其服务包括搜索引擎、电邮、新闻等，业务遍及 24 个国家和地区，为全球超过 5 亿的独立用户提供多元化的网络服务；同时也是一家全球性的因特网通讯、商贸及媒体公司。2012 年 4 月 4 日，美国雅虎公司宣布将裁员 2000 人，约相当于雅虎全球员工数量的 14%。

Google

谷歌是一家美国上市公司（公有股份公司），于 1998 年 9 月 7 日以私有股份公司的形式创立，以设计并管理一个互联网搜索引擎。谷歌公司的总部称作"Googleplex"，它位于加利福尼亚山景城。谷歌目前被公认为是全球规模最大的搜索引擎，它提供了简单易用的免费服务。"不作恶"（Don't be evil.）是谷歌公司的一项非正式的公司口号，最早是由 Gmail 服务创始人在一次会议中提出。2012 年 5 月，谷歌以 125 亿美元收购摩托罗拉移动。

写作特点

本文对于这10课的介绍使用了举例法，下面对英文写作中举例法的应用做个简单的介绍。

举例子（举例说明法），举出实际事例来说明事物，使所要说明的事物具体化，以便读者理解。这种说明方法叫举例法。

运用举事例的说明方法说明事物或事理，一要注意例子的代表性，二要注意例子的适量性。举例法使文章表达的意思更明确，读者更明白，增强说服力。

品味鉴赏

20岁的扎克伯格虽然考入了知名的哈佛大学，但却是该学校计算机和心理学系的辍学生。2004年，他在哈佛的大学宿舍创办了Facebook。短短数年，这一网站迅速风靡全世界，如今，它已成为世界上最重要的社交网站之一，就连美国总统奥巴马、英国女王伊丽莎白二世等政界要人都成了Facebook的用户。媒体称，Facebook的市值已高达1800亿美元，扎克伯格本人也因这一成功创业，成为世界上最年轻的亿万富翁，同时也是最积极从事慈善事业的美国富豪之一。

扎克伯格曾表示："一些人等到事业晚期才回馈（社会）。可现在就有那么多事情需要做，为何要等待？我们中一些人很可能在人生早期回馈社会，见证我们慈善努力的影响。"2013年9月23日，扎克伯格宣布捐赠1亿美元，赞助新泽西州纽瓦克市修缮学校。这次捐赠创下美国青年人慈善捐款纪录。

外界一提到扎克伯格时，总是将其同微软创始人比尔·盖茨做比较，因为他们都是从哈佛大学辍学的"坏学生"，都是白手起家，在互联网上创业，从而影响全世界。

美文感悟

Starbucks: 19,555 Stores in 58 Countries and Still Growing

星巴克：58个国家的19,555家店面并且还在增长

> **背景介绍：**
>
> 星巴克（Starbucks）是美国一家连锁咖啡公司的名称，1971年成立，为全球最大的咖啡连锁店，其总部坐落在美国华盛顿州西雅图市。除咖啡外，星巴克亦有茶、馅皮饼及蛋糕等商品。星巴克在全球范围内已经有近12,000间分店遍布南北美洲、欧洲、中东及太平洋地区。2012年3月，星巴克在美国的两款甜点被曝用胭脂虫当着色剂，专家称或令哮喘者过敏。2012年4月，星巴克表示停用该着色剂。
>
>

Starbucks Corporation is an international coffee company and **coffeehouse**[1] chain based in Seattle, Washington. Starbucks is the largest coffeehouse company in the world, with 19,555

注释
1. **coffeehouse** ['kɒfɪˌhaʊs] *n.* 咖啡馆
2. **vendor** ['vendə] *n.* 摊贩、小贩
3. **brew** [bru:] *vt.* 酿造；泡，煮；策划；酿成
4. **groundwork** ['graʊndˌwɜːk] *n.* 基础、基本原理

stores in 58 countries, including 12,811 in the United States, 1,248 in Canada, 965 in Japan, 766 in Great Britain, 580 in China and 420 in South Korea.

Chances are you've enjoyed a cup of coffee from Starbucks. Since the opening of the first Starbucks in 1971 as a **vendor**[2] of high-quality coffee beans and **brewing**[3] equipment, the company has expanded to become the most popular coffeehouse chain in the world. Its 14,000 stores in 43 countries sell coffee beverages, beans, teas, brewing equipment, pastries, and more. How did this happen?

Starbucks Chairman Howard Schultz took over the company in 1987. He recognized an untapped market in busy individuals in urban areas who could afford fine coffees. In 1995, Schultz hired Anna Niess and Will Chassaing to redesign his booming chain. In addition to laying the **groundwork**[4] for Starbucks' well-known symbols and distinctive style, they created a program that led to opening one store per day throughout the 1990s.

One thing that makes Starbucks so popular is the company's vision of their stores as a "third place" to spend time in addition to work and home. It's a **cozy**[5] environment that serves as a meeting place. This attracts a loyal following of customers that come not only to drink coffee, but to relax, work, socialize, and attend cultural events.

Schultz still sees a great deal of **potential**[6] for his company. Starbucks plans to have 40,000 stores worldwide with 20,000 in the US and Canada. Starbucks is not always welcomed with open arms, of course. The store located inside Beijing's Forbidden City was finally closed in July 2007 due to protests that it was **trampling**[7] on Chinese culture. Despite this setback, the company has been a huge success and is now a household name around the world.

Schultz first experienced Starbucks as a salesman for Swedish drip coffeemakers on a trip to visit the Seattle company that had been buying his products. A year later, he joined the company. Conflict arose when Schultz **recommended**[8] Starbucks sell brewed coffee in addition to beans and equipment. The owners disagreed, and in 1985, Schultz went on to start his own coffee shop. In 1987, the original Starbucks owners sold their company to Schultz, and refocused their attention on selling coffee beans and teas.

Schultz promoted an aggressive expansion of Starbucks throughout the US and Canada. When Starbucks began selling stock shares in 1992, he had already grown the chain to 165 stores. Throughout the expansion of Starbucks, Schultz has held strong principles of social responsibility. Starbucks takes good care of its employees with health insurance, stock options, and stable hours. In fact, under Schultz, Starbucks has been consistently ranked one of the best

注释
5. **cozy** ['kəʊzɪ] *a.* 舒适的，安逸的，惬意的
6. **potential** [pə'tenʃəl] *a.* 潜在的，有可能的 *n.* 潜力
7. **trample** ['træmpl] *vt.* 践踏，蹂躏，无视，蔑视
8. **recommend** [ˌrekə'mend] *vt.* 推荐，劝告；使显得吸引人；托付
9. **reputation** [ˌrepju'teɪʃən] *n.* 名气，名声，好名声，信誉

places to work in the US and UK.

Commitments to environmentalism, fair pay for coffee bean growers, and a positive contribution to society contribute to Schultz's **reputation**[9] as a truly ethical businessman. That means with Schultz in charge of Starbucks, you can enjoy your coffee with a clear **conscience**[10].

His Strengths

Starbucks Corporation is a very profitable organization, earning in excess of $600 million in 2004. The company generated revenue of more than $5000 million in the same year.

It is a global coffee brand built upon a reputation for fine products and services. It has almost 9000 cafes in almost 40 countries.

Starbucks was one of the *Fortune* Top 100 Companies to Work For in 2005. The company is a respected employer that values its workforce.

The organization has strong **ethical**[11] values and an ethical mission statement as follows, "Starbucks is committed to a role of environmental leadership in all facets of our business."

His Opportunities

Starbucks are very good at taking advantage of opportunities.

In 2004 the company created a CD-burning service in their Santa Monica (California USA) cafe with Hewlett Packard, where customers create their own music CD.

New products and services that can be retailed in their cafes, such as Fair Trade products.

The company has the opportunity to expand its global operations. New markets for coffee such as India and the Pacific Rim nations are beginning to emerge.

Co-branding with other manufacturers of food and drink, and brand **franchising**[12] to manufacturers of other goods and services both have potential.

原文翻译

星巴克公司是一个国际咖啡公司和咖啡厅连锁店，总部在美国华盛顿州西雅图市。星巴克是世界上最大的咖啡厅公司，在58个国家拥有19,555家店面，包括有12,811家在美国，1,248家在加拿大，965家在日本，766家在英国，580家在中国和420家在韩国。

你可能曾享用过一杯星巴克的咖啡。自从第一家星巴克以小贩的形式于1971年开始贩售优质咖啡豆与滴滤器具至今，该公司已扩展成为全球最受欢迎的连锁咖啡厅。他们在43个国家共14,000间分店中贩卖咖啡饮品、咖啡豆、茶、滴滤式咖啡机、糕饼及其他产品。这一切是怎么发生的呢？

星巴克主席霍华德·舒尔茨在1987年接管了公司。他在喝得起优质咖啡的忙碌都市人中，发现了一个未开发的市场。1995年，舒尔茨聘请安娜·尼斯和威·查赛因为这间蓬勃发展的连锁店重新设计风格。除

注释　声望，荣誉，名望　　　　　　　　　　　　12. franchise ['fræn,ʃaɪz] n. 选举权，参政权，特许权，
10. **conscience** ['kɒnʃəns] n. 良心，道德心　　　　　经销权
11. **ethical** ['eθɪkəl] a. 伦理学的，道德的，伦理的

了为星巴克著名的标志与特色奠定基础之外，他们还创造出一套方案，这使他们在 20 世纪 90 年代每一天就能开一家新分店。

让星巴克如此受欢迎的一点在于，它将自己定位为工作与家之外"第三个"消磨时间的地方。它环境舒适，是聚会的好去处。这吸引了一群忠实的老主顾，来不只为喝咖啡，也为了放松、工作、社交或参加文化活动。

舒尔茨看见公司仍然有许多潜力。星巴克计划在全球开设 4 万家分店，其中 2 万家在美国与加拿大。当然，并不是所有人都张开双臂欢迎星巴克。位于北京紫禁城内的星巴克，就因破坏中华文化的反对声浪于 2007 年 7 月关门大吉。尽管受到这波挫折，星巴克还是极为成功，成为全球家喻户晓的品牌。

霍华德·舒尔茨第一次接触到星巴克咖啡时，是一家瑞典滴滤式咖啡机公司的业务员，他前往西雅图拜访这家客户。一年后，他加入了这家公司。舒尔茨建议星巴克除了咖啡豆与咖啡机以外，也应该贩卖现煮咖啡，此举引起双方冲突。老板不同意，而在 1985 年，舒尔茨接着开设自己的咖啡厅。1987 年，星巴克原来的老板将公司卖给舒尔茨，将焦点重新放在贩卖咖啡豆与茶上。

舒尔茨以积极的手法将星巴克扩展至全美与加拿大。当星巴克在 1992 年开始卖出股票，舒尔茨已让连锁总数成长至 165 家店。在星巴克的扩展过程中，舒尔茨具有强烈的社会责任。星巴克提供保健、认股与稳定工时来善待员工。事实上，在舒尔茨的领导下，星巴克一直名列英美两国最佳就业环境之一。

致力于环保、给予咖啡农合理酬劳，并正面回馈社会，使舒尔茨建立起道德企业家的声望。这代表在舒尔茨领导下的星巴克，你不必昧着良心也可以享受好咖啡。

星巴克的优势

星巴克公司是一个非常能获利的组织，在 2004 年收入超过 6 亿元，该公司在同一年所产生的收入超过 50 亿美元。

它是一个建立在具有良好声誉的产品和服务基础上的全球性的咖啡品牌，它已差不多在近 40 个国家有 9000 家咖啡厅。

在 2005 年，星巴克就是《财富》100 强公司之一。这是一家看重劳动力的、受尊重的公司。

该组织具有很强的道德价值观念和道德使命，星巴克致力于做行业的佼佼者。

星巴克的机遇

星巴克非常善于利用机遇。

在 2004 年，公司创建了一个 CD 刻录服务，他们在圣莫尼卡（美国加州）咖啡馆与惠普公司一起，那里的顾客建立他们自己的音乐 CD 。

在它的咖啡店里提供新的产品和服务，如平价产品。

该公司有机会扩大其全球业务。新的咖啡市场，如印度和太平洋沿岸地区的国家都开始出现。

共同品牌与其他厂商的食物和饮料，和品牌特许经营权的制造商的其他商品和服务都具有的潜力。

文化点滴

Howard Schultz

霍华德·舒尔茨是星巴克的董事长和首席战略总监。1952 年，霍华德·舒尔茨出生在纽约的布鲁克林区，美国北密歇根大学毕业。1975 年进入施乐公司工作，1982 年成为星巴克的市场部和零售部经理。1986 年，离开星巴克开设了自己的第一家咖啡店。1987 年，舒尔茨召集一批投资者买下星巴克公司。1992 年，星巴克在美国上市。星巴克咖啡 1999 年进入中国，积极致力于将中国做成在美国之外最大的国际市场。2006 年，舒尔茨跻身《福布斯》400 富豪榜，身家在 10 亿美元以上。

Forbidden City

紫禁城是中国明、清两代24个皇帝的皇宫。明朝第三位皇帝朱棣在夺取帝位后，决定迁都北京，即开始营造紫禁城宫殿，至明永乐十八年（1420年）落成。依照中国古代星象学说，紫微垣（即北极星）位于中天，乃天帝所居，天人对应，于是皇帝的居所又称紫禁城。

写作特点

本文是一篇说明文。下面对英文写作中的说明文的写法做个简单的介绍。

说明文是阐述事物的特征、本质、性能、结构、用途或科学原理的一种文体。其说明的对象可以是具体的，如自然环境、仪表设备等，也可以是抽象的，如概念定律等。

英语说明文的写作相对于英语论说文来说，有一定的套路可循，因此不是十分复杂。说明科技方面的内容，常用定义法、比较对比法、分类法、因果法等；说明自然环境方面的内容，常用时间次序法、分类法等。当然，随着对象的不同，具体应该采用的方法也会有所不同。

英文说明文的写作应该注意的事项有下面几点：

（1）语言简明扼要，通俗易懂，避免夸张华丽的辞藻，要把真实的一面展现在读者面前。

（2）说明时一定要把握一个中心主题。说明文中细枝末节较多，但不能喧宾夺主。

（3）说明的次序非常重要。合理的次序会使文章条理清楚，脉络明晰。因此，练习时可以尝试不同的次序进行写作，找出最合理的一种。

（4）由于说明文写实性较强，有时难免会让人感到没有生气。因此，可以适当使用一些比喻、拟人等修辞手段，来增加文章的色彩。

美文感悟

_____
_____
_____
_____

Warren Edward Buffett
沃伦·爱德华·巴菲特

背景介绍:

沃伦·爱德华·巴菲特（1930—），全球著名的投资商，生于美国内布拉斯加州的奥马哈市。在 2008 年的《福布斯》排行榜上财富超过比尔·盖茨，成为世界首富。在第十一届慈善募捐中，巴菲特的午餐拍卖达到创纪录的 263 万美元。2010 年 7 月，沃伦·巴菲特再次向 5 家慈善机构捐赠股票，依当前市值计算相当于 19.3 亿美元。这是巴菲特 2006 年开始捐出 99% 资产以来，金额第三高的捐款。2011 年 12 月，巴菲特宣布，他的儿子霍华德会在伯克希尔·哈撒韦公司中扮演继承人的角色。

Warren Edward Buffett was born on August 30, 1930. He is an American business **magnate**[1], investor, and **philanthropist**[2]. He is widely considered the most successful investor of the 20th century. Often introduced as "**legendary**[3] investor", Warren Buffett is the primary shareholder,

注释
1. **magnate** ['mæɡˌnet] *n.* 富豪，权贵，巨头
2. **philanthropist** [fə'lænθrəpɪst] *n.* 慈善家
3. **legendary** ['ledʒənˌderɪ] *a.* 传说的，传奇的，极其著名的

chairman and CEO of Berkshire Hathaway. He was ranked as the world's wealthiest person in 2008 and is the third wealthiest person in the world as of 2011. In 2012, American magazine *Time* named Buffett one of the most influential people in the world.

Buffett is called the "Sage of Omaha" and is noted for his adherence to the value investing philosophy and for his personal **frugality**[4] despite his immense wealth. As a notable philanthropist, he has **pledged**[5] to give away 99 percent of his fortune to philanthropic causes, primarily via the Gates Foundation. On April 11, 2012, he was diagnosed with prostate cancer.

Warren Buffet's incredible successful career began as an entrepreneur at an early age. He was the only boy in his family and the second of three children. He displayed an amazing **aptitude**[6] for both money and business at a very early age. At only six years old, Buffett purchased six packs of Coca Cola from his grandfather's grocery store for twenty five cents and resold each of the bottles for a nickel, pocketing a five cent profit. While other children of his age were playing, Warren was making money. At 14, he and a fellow high school student started a pinball machine installation company. He eventually sold his stake for $1,200 and used the money to buy 40 acres of farmland which he rented to farmers. He graduated near the top 20 in his class. At the age of 16 and despite having already proved to himself his future potential as an entrepreneur, he reluctantly followed his father's advice. Buffett first enrolled at The Wharton School, University of Pennsylvania (1947—1949). In 1950, he transferred to the University of Nebraska. Buffett then enrolled at Columbia Business School after learning two well-known securities analysts. He then received a M.S. in Economics from Columbia University in 1951. In 2008, Buffett became the richest man in the world **dethroning**[7] Bill Gates, who had been number one on the *Forbes* list for 13 **consecutive**[8] years.

Unlike many billionaires, Buffet lives a relatively humble life, continuing to live in the same house in Nebraska which he bough in 1958 for $31,500. What Warren Buffett will be remembered for, for many years to come is his decision to donate his wealth to charity, with 83% of it going to the Bill and Melinda Gates Foundation. The donation amounts to approximately US$30 billion, the largest charitable donation in history.

His pastime after he gets home is to make himself some pop corn and watch television. Warren Buffet does not carry a cell phone, nor has a computer on his desk.

He has given his CEO's only two rules.

注释

4. **frugality** [fru'gæləti] *n.* 节约，朴素，节俭
5. **pledge** [pledʒ] *n.* 保证，誓言 *vt.* 许诺，用……担保
6. **aptitude** ['æptɪtud] *n.* 才能、资质、天资
7. **dethrone** [dɪ'θrəʊn] *v.* 废黜，废位；赶出
8. **consecutive** [kən'sɔkjətɪv] *adj.* 连续的，连贯的

Rule 1: Do not lose any of your shareholder's money.

Rule 2: Do not forget rule number 1.

Other famous sayings:

Money doesn't create man but it is the man who created money.

Live your life as simple as you are.

Don't go on brand name; just wear those things in which you feel comfortable.

Don't waste your money on unnecessary things; just spend on them who really in need rather.

After all it's your life then why gives chance to others to rule our life?

原文翻译

沃伦·爱德华·巴菲特生于 1930 年 8 月 30 日。他是一位美国商业巨头、投资者和慈善家。他被认为是 20 世纪最成功的投资者。作为"传奇投资者",沃伦·巴菲特是伯克希尔·哈撒韦公司的大股东、董事长兼首席执行官。在 2008 年,他被评为世界上最富有的人;2011 年,世界上第三富有的人。美国《时代》杂志在 2012 年称巴菲特是世界上最有影响力的人之一。

"奥马哈圣人"——沃伦·巴菲特因坚持价值投资理念和他的节俭而出名,尽管他拥有巨大的财富。作为一个著名的慈善家,他已承诺放弃他财富的 99%;通过盖茨基金会捐给慈善事业。2012 年 4 月 11 日,他被诊断出患有前列腺癌。

沃伦·巴菲特令人难以置信的成功的职业生涯是小时候作为一个企业家开始的。他是他家 3 个孩子中唯一的男孩,排行老二。在很小的年纪,他就显示出了惊人的资金和商业天赋。6 岁时,他从祖父的杂货店花了 25 美分购买了 6 瓶可口可乐,转而以每瓶 5 分镍币售出,赚得 5 分钱的利润。同年龄的其他孩子正在玩耍,而沃伦却在赚钱。14 岁,他和另一位高中学生开始了弹球机安装公司,最终以 1200 美元卖了他的股份。他用这些钱购买了 40 亩农田租给农民。16 岁他以班级排名前 20 位毕业,尽管已经证明了自己作为一个未来企业家的潜力,但他没有遵循父亲的意见成为一名企业家。1947—1949 年,巴菲特就读于宾夕法尼亚大学沃顿商学院。1950 年,他到了内布拉斯加大学。然后巴菲特就读于哥伦比亚商学院,跟两个知名的证券分析师学习。他于 1951 年获得哥伦比亚大学经济学理科硕士学位。2008 年,巴菲特力压连续 13 年在《福布斯》财富榜上排名第一的比尔·盖茨,成为世界首富。

不像其他亿万富翁,巴菲特过着相对简朴的生活,继续住在 1958 年在内布拉斯加州以 31,500 美元买的房屋中。今后,巴菲特将被记住的是他决定把他的财富捐给慈善机构,其中 83% 捐赠到比尔和梅林达·盖茨基金会。此次捐赠金额约 300 亿美元,有史以来规模最大的慈善捐款。

回家后为自己做一些爆米花和看电视,以此打发闲暇时间。沃伦·巴菲特不带手机,办公桌上也没有电脑。

他给他的首席执行官两个规则。

规则 1:不要失去任何股东的钱。

规则 2:不要忘记规则 1。

其他著名的格言:

钱不会创造人,而是人创造了金钱。

活得越简单越好。

不要追求名牌,穿你觉得舒服的。

不要把钱浪费在不必要的事情上,把钱花在真正需要它的人身上。

毕竟这是你的生命,那么为什么给别人统治我们的生活提供机会?

文化点滴

Berkshire Hathaway

伯克希尔·哈撒韦公司由沃伦·巴菲特于1956年创建，是一家世界著名的保险和多元化投资集团，总部在美国。该公司主要通过国民保障公司以及再保险巨头通用、科隆再保险公司等附属机构从事财产/伤亡保险、再保险业务，在其他许多领域也有商业活动。其中最重要的业务是以直接的保险金和再保险金额为基础财产及灾害保险。伯克希尔·哈撒韦公司设有许多分公司。其中包括GEICO公司，是美国第六大汽车保险公司；General Re公司，是世界上最大的4家再保险公司之一。

prostate cancer

前列腺癌就是发生于男性前列腺组织中的恶性肿瘤，是前列腺腺泡细胞异常无序生长的结果。前列腺癌的发病率具有明显的地理和种族差异。在欧美等发达国家和地区，它是男性最常见的恶性肿瘤，其死亡率居各种癌症的第二位；在亚洲，其发病率低于西方国家，但近年来呈迅速上升趋势。

pinball machine 弹球机

自从1947年（Gottlieb）公司推出第一款真正的弹球机游戏Humpty Dumpty以来，弹球机游戏开始风靡全球。人们控制着球桌上的银色小球，让它去撞击目标，让它在斜坡上飞奔……弹球游戏机，其弹球付出效率良好，游戏进行时不会中断，游戏者的兴致不受影响。其弹球从补给管道经连通构件直接送入弹球计数装置，计数装置付出的弹球先经溢流构件的前盘用通道进入前盘，前盘满后又经下盘通道进入下盘，下盘满后，或把溢出的弹球经计数用通道导入持有弹球计数装置进行计数，并显示于持有球数显示装置，或由检测装置测知下盘装满，经控制装置使计数装置停止付出，并在显示装置上显示应付出的弹球余数。

M.S.

M.S. 是 Master of Science 的英文缩写，即理学硕士。

写作特点

本文主要是人物介绍。下面对英文写作中的人物介绍的写法做个简单的介绍。

（1）人物简介的写作步骤

- Birthday and birth place
- Family background
- Education
- Big events in his or her life (in order of time)
- Evaluation

（2）人物简介写作中常用的词组及句子：

- Birthday and birth place
- Family background
    1) a poor / rich family;
    2) his (her) family was so poor that…

3) with the help of his parents;

4) his father was very strict with him…

5) the son of a poor family;

6) when he was a small boy;

7) as a child;

8) during his (her) childhood;

9) spend his childhood in…

10) live a happy (hard) life;

11) a boy of 15

· Education

1) graduate from…department of…university;

2) When at college, he majored in…

3) receive a doctor's degree;

4) get higher education;

5) go abroad for further studies;

· Big events in his life

1) be interested in…; 2) work hard at…; 3) devote his lifetime to…; 4) do research about/into… ; 5) make a big decision/make up one's mind to do sth; 6) do sth with great determination and perseverance; 7) be fond of…; 8) be strict in sth; 9) have a…way of doing sth; 10) try one's best to do sth; 11) encourage sb to do sth; 12) fight for, give up one's life for sb/sth; 13) win a prize in…competition; 14) be good at; 15) make rapid progress in…; 16) set a new world record of…; 17) become a member of … ; 18) study hard/train hard; 19) win a gold medal; 20) work so hard as to improve…; 21) have a gift for…

· Evaluation

1) one of the best (most important)… ; 2) set sb a good example; 3) a model teacher; 4) be respected by everyone; 5) sing high praise for… speak (think) highly of… ; 6) his hard work brought him great success; 7) his heroic story spread all over the city; 8) remember sb forever; 9) be honored as… ; 10) be famous as…; 11) be regarded as…; 12) become a world champion at… Championships; 13) He became famous for his new theory; 14) The people had come to love him as an inspiring leader; 15) Lei Feng has been praised for his communist spirit. 16) People spoke highly of him and all respected him

品味鉴赏

沃伦·巴菲特是全球著名的投资商，举世公认的投资大师，生于美国内布拉斯加州的奥马哈市。在2008年的《福布斯》排行榜上，巴菲特超过比尔·盖茨成为世界首富。

巴菲特创造了不计其数的投资传奇。

Chapter 5 世界名人

1968年，巴菲特公司的股票增长了46%，而道·琼斯指数才增长了9%。

1972年，巴菲特投资报刊业。他的介入使《华盛顿邮报》利润大增，每年平均增长35%。10年之后，巴菲特投入的1000万美元升值为两个亿。

1980年，他用1.2亿美元，以每股10.96美元的单价买进可口可乐7%的股份。到1985年，可口可乐改变了经营策略，开始抽回资金，投入饮料生产。其股票单价已涨至51.50美元，翻了5倍。

1992年，巴菲特以每股74美元购下435万股美国高技术国防工业公司——通用动力公司的股票，到年底股价上升到113美元。

巴菲特是有史以来最伟大的投资家，他依靠股票、外汇市场的投资，成为世界上数一数二的富翁。他倡导的价值投资理论风靡世界。巴菲特曾将价值投资归结为三点：把股票看成许多微型的商业单元，把市场波动看作你的朋友而非敌人，购买股票的价格应低于你所能承受的价位。"从短期来看，市场是一架投票计算器。但从长期看，它是一架称重的机器。"事实上，掌握这些理念并不困难，但很少有人能像巴菲特一样数十年如一日地坚持下去。

一生能够积累多少财富，不取决于你能够赚多少钱，而取决于你如何投资理财。钱找人胜过人找钱，要让钱为你工作，而不是你为钱工作。

美文感悟

"责任、荣誉、国家",简短 6 个字的校训,成为西点军人做人的准则,也成为世人所称道的西点精神的结晶。这种重责任、重荣誉、重爱国主义教育的独到教育方针,成为许多国家军校争相效法的办校宗旨。

Duty, Honor, Country
责任、荣誉和国家

背景介绍:

道格拉斯·麦克阿瑟(Douglas MacArthur,1880—1964),华语界常称其为"麦帅",是美国著名军事将领,官至五星上将,并且曾任菲律宾陆军元帅。20 世纪 30 年代任美国陆军参谋长,是太平洋战争中盟军主要指挥官之一,1919 年,他被任命为美国西点军校的校长。1962 年,在其生涯最后一次参访西点军校,在校方颁赠给麦克阿瑟将军勋章和奖状,并于参加阅兵庆典后,发表以西点军校校训为题的著名演说——《责任、荣誉、国家》。本文则是这篇演讲稿的节选。

  In battle and in the face of danger and death, he discloses those **divine**[1] attributes which his Maker gave when he created man in his own image. No physical courage and no brute instinct can take the place of the Divine help which alone can sustain him.

注释
1. **divine** [dɪ'vaɪn] *a.* 神圣的,神的
2. **thrust** [θrʌst] *vt.& vi.* 猛推;逼迫;强行推入;延伸
  n. 刺;推力;[军]突击;[地]逆断层
3. **unfathomed** [ˌʌn'fæðəmd] *a.* 未探测深度的;尚未测

However horrible the incidents of war may be, the soldier who is called upon to offer and to give his life for his country is the noblest development of mankind.

You now face a new world—a world of change. The **thrust**² into outer space of the satellite, spheres, and missiles mark the beginning of another epoch in the long story of mankind. In the five or more billions of years the scientists tell us it has taken to form the earth, in the three or more million years of development of the human race, there has never been a more abrupt or staggering evolution. We deal now not with things of this world alone, but with the illimitable distances and as yet **unfathomed**³ mysteries of the universe. We are reaching out for a new and boundless frontier.

We speak in strange terms: of **harnessing**⁴ the cosmic energy; of making winds and tides work for us; of creating unheard synthetic materials to supplement or even replace our old standard basics; to purify sea water for our drink; of mining ocean floors for new fields of wealth and food; of disease preventatives to expand life into the hundreds of years; of controlling the weather for a more equitable distribution of heat and cold, of rain and shine; of space ships to the moon; of the primary target in war, no longer limited to the armed forces of an enemy, but instead to include his civil populations; of ultimate conflict between a united human race and the sinister forces of some other planetary galaxy; of such dreams and fantasies as to make life the most exciting of all time.

And through all this **welter**⁵ of change and development, your mission remains fixed, determined, **inviolable**⁶: it is to win our wars.

Everything else in your professional career is but **corollary**⁷ to this vital dedication. All other public purposes, all other public projects, all other public needs, great or small, will find others for their accomplishment. But you are the ones who are trained to fight. Yours is the profession of arms, the will to win, the sure knowledge that in war there is no substitute for victory; that if you lose, the nation will be destroyed; that the very obsession of your public service must be: Duty, Honor, Country.

Others will debate the controversial issues, national and international, which divide men's minds; but serene, calm, aloof, you stand as the Nation's war-guardian, as its lifeguard from the raging tides of international conflict, as its **gladiator**⁸ in the arena of battle. For a century and a half you have defended, guarded, and protected its hallowed traditions of liberty and freedom, of right and justice.

注释
量的
4. harnessing ['hɑːnɪsɪŋ] n. 马具，挽具

5. welter ['weltə] vi. 滚；打滚；浸；浸湿 n. 混乱；杂乱混合，大杂烩

Let civilian voices argue the merits or demerits of our processes of government; whether our strength is being sapped by deficit financing, indulged in too long, by federal **paternalism**[9] grown too mighty, by power groups grown too arrogant, by politics grown too corrupt, by crime grown too rampant, by morals grown too low, by taxes grown too high, by extremists grown too violent; whether our personal liberties are as thorough and complete as they should be. These great national problems are not for your professional participation or military solution. Your guidepost stands out like a **ten-fold**[10] beacon in the night: Duty, Honor, Country.

You are the **leaven**[11] which binds together the entire fabric of our national system of defense. From your ranks come the great captains who hold the nation's destiny in their hands the moment the war tocsin sounds. The Long Gray Line has never failed us. Were you to do so, a million ghosts in olive drab, in brown khaki, in blue and gray, would rise from their white crosses thundering those magic words: Duty, Honor, Country.

This does not mean that you are war mongers.

On the contrary, the soldier, above all other people, prays for peace, for he must suffer and bear the deepest wounds and scars of war.

But always in our ears ring the ominous words of Plato, that wisest of all philosophers: "Only the dead have seen the end of war."

The shadows are **lengthening**[12] for me. The twilight is here. My days of old have vanished, tone and tint. They have gone glimmering through the dreams of things that were. Their memory is one of wondrous beauty, watered by tears, and coaxed and caressed by the smiles of yesterday. I listen vainly, but with thirsty ears, for the witching melody of faint bugles blowing **reveille**[13], of far drums beating the long roll. In my dreams I hear again the crash of guns, the rattle of **musketry**[14], the strange, **mournful**[15] mutter of the battlefield.

But in the evening of my memory, always I come back to West Point.

Always there echoes and re-echoes: Duty, Honor, Country. Today marks my final roll call with you, but I want you to know that when I cross the river my last conscious thoughts will be of The Corps, and The Corps, and The Corps.

I bid you farewell.

原文翻译

在战斗中，面对着危险与死亡，他显示出造物主按照自己意愿创造人类时所赋予的品质。只有神明能帮助他、支持他，这是任何肉体的勇敢与动物的本能都代替不了的。

无论战争如何恐怖，招之即来的战士准备为国捐躯是人类最崇高的进化。

现在，你们面临着一个新世界——一个变革中的世界。人造卫星进入星际空间。卫星与导弹标志着人类漫长的历史进入了另一个时代——太空时代。自然科学家告诉我们，在50亿年或更长的时期中，地球形成了；

注释
6. **inviolable** [ɪnˈvaɪələbəl] *a.* 不可侵犯的
7. **corollary** [kəˈrɒləri] *n.* 必然结果
8. **gladiator** [ˈglædɪˌeɪtə] *n.* 角斗士
9. **paternalism** [pəˈtɜːnəˌlɪzəm] *n.* 家长式管理

在300万年或更长的时期中，人类形成了；人类历史还不曾有过一次更巨大、更令人惊讶的进化。我们不单要从现在这个世界，而且要从无法估算的距离，从神秘莫测的宇宙来论述事物。人们正在认识一个崭新的无边无际的世界。

我们谈论着不可思议的话题：控制宇宙的资源；让风力与潮汐为我们所用；创造空前的合成物质以补充甚至代替古老基本物质；净化海水以供我们饮用；开发海底以作为财富与食品的新基地；预防疾病以使寿命延长几百岁；调节空气以使冷热、晴雨分布均衡；登月宇宙飞船；战争中的主要目标不仅限于敌人的武装力量，也包括其平民；团结起来的人类与某些星系行星的恶势力的最根本的矛盾；使生命成为有史以来最扣人心弦的那些梦境与幻想。

为了迎接所有这些巨大的变化和发展，你们的任务将变得更加坚定而不可侵犯，那就是赢得我们战争的胜利。

你们的职业要求你们在这个生死关头勇于献身，此外，别无所求。其余的一切公共目的、公共计划、公共需求，无论大小，都可以寻找其他办法去完成；而你们就是受训参加战斗的，你们的职业就是战斗——决心取胜。在战争中最明确的目标就是为了胜利，这是任何东西都代替不了的。假如你失败了，国家就要遭到破坏，因此你的职业唯一要遵循的就是责任、荣誉、国家。

其他人将纠缠于分散人们思想的国内外问题的争论，可是你将安详、宁静地屹立在远处，作为国家的卫士，作为国际矛盾怒潮中的救生员，作为硝烟弥漫的竞技场上的格斗士。一个半世纪以来，你们曾经防御、守卫、保护着解放和自由、权利与正义的神圣传统。

让平民百姓去辩论我们政府的功过：我们的国力是否因长期财政赤字而衰竭，联邦的家长式传统是否势力过大，权力集团是否过于骄横自大，政治是否过于腐败，犯罪是否过于猖獗，道德标准是否降得太低，捐税是否提得太高，极端分子是否过于偏激，我们个人的自由是否像应有的那样完全彻底。这些重大的国家问题与你们的职业毫不相干，也无需使用军事手段来解决。你们的路标——责任、荣誉、国家，比夜里的灯塔要亮10倍。

你们是联系我国防御系统全部机构的纽带。当战争警钟敲响时，从你们的队伍中将涌现出手持国家命运的伟大军官。还从来没有人打败过我们。假如你也是这样，上百万身穿橄榄色、棕色、蓝色和灰色制服的灵魂将从他们的白色十字架下站起来，以雷霆般的声音喊出那神奇的口号——责任、荣誉、国家。

这并不意味着你们是战争贩子。

相反，高于众人之上的战士祈求和平，因为他忍受着战争最深刻的伤痛与疮疤。可是，我们耳边经常响起那位大智大慧的哲学之父柏拉图的警世之言："只有死者才能看到战争的终结。"

我的生命已近黄昏，暮色已经降临。我昔日的风采和荣誉已经消失。它们随着对昔日事业的憧憬，带着那余晖消失了。昔日的记忆奇妙而美好，浸透了眼泪和昨日微笑的安慰和抚爱。我尽力但徒然地倾听，渴望听到军号吹奏起床号的那微弱而迷人的旋律，以及远处战鼓急促敲击的动人节奏。我在梦幻中依稀又听到了大炮在轰鸣，又听到了滑膛枪在鸣放，又听到了战场上那陌生、哀愁的呻吟。

然而，晚年的回忆经常将我带回到西点军校。

我的耳旁回响着，反复回响着：责任、荣誉、国家。今天是我同你们进行的最后一次点名。但我愿你们知道，当我到达彼岸时，我最后想的是学员队，学员队，还是学员队。

我向大家告别。

注释	10. **ten-fold** *adv.& adj.* 十倍地（的）	13. **reveille** ['revəli] *n.* 起床号
	11. **leaven** ['levən] *n.* 发酵，影响力	14. **musketry** ['mʌskɪtrɪ] *n.* 步枪射击
	12. **lengthen** ['leŋθən] *v.* （使）加长、延长	15. **mournful** ['mɔːnfəl] *a.* 悲伤的

文化点滴

Duty, Honor, Country
西点军校的校训:"责任、荣誉、国家"。

The Long Gray Line
《西点军魂》:美国军教片的始祖,根据爱尔兰移民马提马哈的自传改编拍摄。描述主人公在青年时代进入西点军校当体育教官,前后服务了 50 年,成为不少军校学生的良师益友。全片通过一个小人物的日常生活来反映被誉为美军精神堡垒的西点军校在 20 世纪前半期的整个历史演变,亲切自然。

Plato
柏拉图(约公元前 427 年—公元前 347 年),古希腊伟大的哲学家,也是全部西方哲学乃至整个西方文化最伟大的哲学家和思想家之一,他和老师苏格拉底、学生亚里士多德并称为古希腊三大哲学家。

West Point
美国军事学院(The United States Military Academy at West Point),常被称为西点军校。西点军校是美国第一所军事学校,位于纽约州西点(哈德逊河西岸),距离纽约市约 80 公里。学校占地 16,000 英亩(约 6,500 公亩)。该校是美国历史最悠久的军事学院之一。它曾与英国桑赫斯特皇家军事学院、俄罗斯伏龙芝军事学院以及法国圣西尔军校并称世界"四大军校"。

写作特点

本文第四段使用了大量的排比句。下面对英文写作中排比句的应用做个简单的介绍。

英文中的排比句式整齐而有气势,不会使人感到单调。

如"读书使我们聪明,锻炼使我们强健",可以这样表达:

Reading makes us wise while exercises make us strong.

(1) 名词排比:

Three passions, simple but overwhelmingly strong, have governed my life: the longing for love, the search for knowledge, and unbearable pity for the suffering of mankind.

(2) 形容词或副词排比:

形容词排比:

a small and peaceful town

a stupid and incorrigible decision

a direct and simple yet magically effective method

副词排比:

A conscientious professor always prepares his lecture carefully, intelligently and prudentially.

(3) 比较级的并列:

The impact that technology has had on our daily life and society, in general, is undeniable. It will become even greater as computers get faster, smaller, smarter, and so inexpensive that virtually everyone will be able to own one.

（4）动词排比：

As one of modern college students, I get online everyday to acquire the information I need, to download the music and movie I like, and to chat with the friends I miss.

（5）介词短语排比：

Studies server for delight, for ornament, and for ability.

a government of the people, by the people and for the people

品味鉴赏

"责任、荣誉、国家"，简短6个字的校训，成为西点军人做人的准则，也成为世人所称道的西点精神的结晶。这种重责任、重荣誉，重爱国主义教育的独到教育方针，成为许多国家军校争相效法的办校宗旨。

从某种意义上说，麦克阿瑟的演讲，是对西点校训的最好注解，是对西点教育方针的最好说明，是对西点培养"完整人"目标的最直观阐述。

责任，是西点军校对其学员的基本要求。它要求所有的学员从入校的那天起，都要以服务的精神自觉自愿地去做那些应该做的事，都有义务、有责任履行自己的职责，而且在履行职责时，其出发点不应是为了获得奖赏或避免惩罚，而是出于发自内心的责任感。正是西点军校多年来向其学员实施的这种责任感的教育，为学员毕业后忠实地履行报效祖国的职责和义务奠定了坚实的思想基础。

荣誉，是西点军校对其学员在道德行为方面的要求。军校从建校之初，就着手制定了《荣誉准则》和《荣誉制度》，并专门成立了执行与监督机构——学员荣誉委员会，从而形成了西点军校独特的荣誉体系。荣誉准则的基本内容是："每个学员决不说谎、欺骗或者偷窃，也决不容忍此类行为者。"多年来，西点军校使学员始终生活在荣誉准则和荣誉制度的环境中，对形成学员诚实、自信、信任和相互尊重的良好的道德品格起了重要的推动作用。

"国家"一词，旨在唤起一种为美国国家利益和民族理想服务的献身精神。这是军校培养学员的终极目标和最高要求，是西点军校办校基本方针的最本质体现。100多年来，西点军人正是遵循这一校训，忠于国家、献身疆场，英勇顽强，前赴后继，为维护美国的国家利益忠实地履行职责，作出了巨大贡献。

美文感悟

Getting to Know Steven Allen Spielberg
认识史蒂文·阿兰·斯皮尔伯格

背景介绍：

史蒂文·斯皮尔伯格（1946—），生于美国俄亥俄州的辛辛那提市，犹太人血统，美国著名电影导演、编剧和电影制作人。在电影生涯中，斯皮尔伯格曾触及多种主题与类型，有犹太人大屠杀、奴隶制度、战争与恐怖主义等题材。斯皮尔伯格曾两度荣获奥斯卡最佳导演奖，他有三部电影：《大白鲨》（1975）、《E.T.外星人》（1982）与《侏罗纪公园》（1993），打破票房纪录，成为当时最卖座的电影。至今，斯皮尔伯格执导的电影收入在全球已超过85亿美元。《时代》杂志将他列入世纪百大最重要的人物的一员，《生活》杂志将他评为他同代中最有影响力的人物。

Steven Allan Spielberg (1946-) is an American film director, screenwriter, producer, video game designer, and studio entrepreneur. In a career of more than four decades, Spielberg's films have covered many themes and genres. Spielberg's early science-fiction and adventure films

---

注释

1. **blockbuster** ['blɒk,bʌstə] n. 重磅炸弹；了不起的人或事；大片；风靡一时的事物
2. **holocaust** ['hɒlə,kɔːst] n. 大屠杀，浩劫，毁灭
3. **terrorism** ['terə,rɪzəm] n. 恐怖主义、恐怖手段，威吓

were seen as archetypes of modern Hollywood **blockbuster**[1] filmmaking. In later years, his films began addressing such issues as the **Holocaust**[2], slavery, war and **terrorism**[3]. He is considered one of the most popular and influential filmmakers in the history of cinema. He is also one of the co-founders of DreamWorks movie studio.

Spielberg won the Academy Award for Best Director for *Schindler's List* (1993) and *Saving Private Ryan* (1998). Three of Spielberg's films—*Jaws* (1975), *E.T. the Extra-Terrestrial* (1982), and *Jurassic Park* (1993)—achieved box office records, each becoming the highest-grossing film made at the time. To date, the unadjusted **gross**[4] of all Spielberg-directed films exceeds $8.5 billion worldwide, the highest for any filmmaker in history. *Forbes* puts Spielberg's wealth at $3.0 billion. *Time* magazine listed him as one of the 100 greatest people of the 20th Century. *Life* named him the most influential person of his generation.

Spielberg, whose mother was a music teacher, was born in Cincinnati, Ohio, in 1946. He was interested in movies and started making short films when he was very young. At 12, he made a 9-minute film to earn his Boy Scout photography **badge**[5]. This was a film in which Spielberg used real actors instead of toys. In 1959 when he was 13 years old, he won a prize for a 40-minute war movie. He wrote the scripts for the films himself. A few years later, when he was 16, he filmed a 2-hour science-fiction epic called *Firelight*. He set his sights on Hollywood.

When Spielberg was young, his dream was to go to the Film Academy, but he couldn't. Spielberg failed to get into film school because of his high school grades. He was undeterred and went directly to Universal Studios, where he got a position as an intern at a film studio. In 1968, he made a short film that caught the attention of Universal's vice president. Spielberg became Hollywood's youngest ever director. This was the moment when Spielberg's career really took off.

Spielberg's first major movie was the shark horror film *Jaws*. It was a real blockbuster. It is about a big white shark that attacks swimmers who are spending their holidays in a small village by the sea. Many people who saw the film were afraid to swim in the sea when they remembered the scenes in which people were eaten by the shark. It was a **sensational**[6] hit and made Spielberg a household name. He has since made many blockbusters that have become a part of world culture. Spielberg has made two films about creatures that come to the earth from outer space. For example, *E.T.* (1982) is about a young boy called Elliot who makes friends with a small creature from outer space and helps him to find a way to go home. The world of adult is cold. Scientists want to find ET to cut him into pieces to do research. But in the world of children and the world where ET comes from, love and friendship are the most important things in life. *Jurassic Park*, which Spielberg made in 1993, is about a park where a very rich man keeps different kinds of dinosaurs. When the park is hit by a storm, things start going wrong. The film

注释　4. gross [grɒs] *n.* 总额　　　　　　　　　　6. sensational [sen'seɪʃənəl] *a.* 轰动的，耸人听闻的，
　　　5. badge [bædʒ] *n.* 徽章，像章，奖章；象征，标记　　　极好的，绝妙的

becomes very exciting when the children are hunted by meat-eating **dinosaurs**[7].

Spielberg has also dealt with serious issues such as slavery, the Holocaust and terrorism. He has also ventured into video game production. His later films such as *Schindler's List* and *Saving Private Ryan* are about the **cruelty**[8] of war. In his war films, he has shown that love and peace will win over war in the end.

Steven Spielberg is one of the top directors in the film industry and also has many fans in China. When asked about the secret of his success, Steven Spielberg said that he owes much of his success and happiness to his wife and children. He met Kate Capshaw, who is an actress, when he was working on one of his films. After that it still took seven years before they finally got married. The couple has seven children in all.

原文翻译

史蒂文·阿兰·斯皮尔伯格是一位美国电影导演、电影编剧、制片人、视频游戏设计师和电影制片厂企业家。在他40多年的电影生涯中，斯皮尔伯格的电影涵盖了许多主题与类型。斯皮尔伯格的早期科幻小说与冒险电影，被视为现代好莱坞大片的典范。斯皮尔伯格后来的作品则开始将触角延伸至犹太人大屠杀、奴隶制度、战争与恐怖主义等题材。他被认为是电影史上最受欢迎和最有影响力的电影制作者之一。他也是梦工厂电影制作室的合创人之一。

斯皮尔伯格在《辛德勒的名单》（1993）和《拯救大兵瑞恩》（1998）中赢得了奥斯卡奖最佳导演。斯皮尔伯格的三部电影《大白鲨》（1975）、《E.T. 外星人》（1982）和《侏罗纪公园》（1993），取得了票房纪录，每一部都是当时最卖座的电影。至今，斯皮尔伯格执导的电影收入在全球粗估已超过85亿美元，是历史上最高的。《福布斯》统计斯皮尔伯格拥有30亿美元的财富。《时代》杂志将他列为20世纪最伟大的100人之一，《生活》杂志将他命名为在他那一代最有影响力的人。

斯皮尔伯格1946年出生在俄亥俄州的辛辛那提，他的母亲是一位音乐教师。他很小的时候就对电影非常有兴趣，并开始制作短片。 12岁时，他制作了一部9分钟的电影，赢得了童子军摄影徽章。在这部电影中，斯皮尔伯格使用了真正的演员，而不是玩具。1959年他13岁，他拍摄了一部40分钟的战争片并获奖。他自己写电影脚本。几年后，当他16岁时，他拍摄了一部两个小时的叫作《火光》的科幻史诗。他把他的目光投在好莱坞。

当斯皮尔伯格年轻的时候，他的梦想是去电影学院，但他不能。斯皮尔伯格未能进入电影学校是因为他的高中成绩。他不为所动，直接去了环球影城，在那里他得到了一个电影制片厂实习生的位置。在1968年，他制作了一部短电影，吸引了环球公司副总裁的注意。斯皮尔伯格成为好莱坞有史以来最年轻的导演。这是斯皮尔伯格的事业真正起飞的那一刻。

斯皮尔伯格的第一部主要电影是鲨鱼恐怖片《大白鲨》。这是一个真正的重磅炸弹。它是关于一条白色的大鲨鱼袭击在海边的一个小村庄度假的泳客的故事。许多看过电影的人想起鲨鱼吃人的场景都不敢在海里游泳。这是一个极大的成功，并使斯皮尔伯格成为一个家喻户晓的名字。从那时起，他拍了许多大片并成为世界文化的一部分。斯皮尔伯格拍过两部关于来自外太空生物的电影。例如，《E.T.》（1982）是关于一个叫作埃利奥特的小男孩和一个来自外太空的小生物成为朋友，并帮助他找到回家的路的电影。成人的世界是冷漠的。科学家希望找到E.T.并将其切成片做研究。但在儿童和E.T.的世界里，爱和友谊是一生中最重要的事情。斯皮尔伯格1993年拍摄的《侏罗纪公园》，是关于一个非常富有的人在一个公园里养了不同种类的恐龙。当公园被风暴雨袭击，事情开始麻烦了。当孩子们被肉食恐龙追杀时，电影令人惊心动魄。

斯皮尔伯格也拍过严肃主题的电影，如奴隶制度、犹太人大屠杀和恐怖主义。他还涉足视频游戏生产。

注释
7. dinosaur ['daɪnəsɔː] *n.* 恐龙
8. cruelty ['kruːəltɪ] *n.* 残忍，残忍的行为，残酷行为，虐待

他晚期的电影,如《辛德勒的名单》和《拯救大兵瑞恩》体现了战争的残酷。在他的战争电影中,他表明,爱与和平将最终超越战争。

斯蒂文·斯皮尔伯格是电影界的顶级导演之一,在中国也有很多影迷。当被问到成功的秘诀时,他说,他的成功和幸福归因于他的妻子和孩子。他遇到女演员凯特·卡普肖时正在拍摄一部电影。之后,过了7年他们才终于结婚。这对夫妇共有7个孩子。

文化点滴

Hollywood
好莱坞是全球最著名的影视娱乐和旅游热门地点,位于美国加利福尼亚州洛杉矶市西北郊。现"好莱坞"一词往往直接用来指美国加州南部的电影工业。

DreamWorks
梦工厂是美国排名前10位的一家电影洗印、制作和发行公司,同时也是一家电视游戏、电视节目制作公司。参与制作或发行的电影,在北美票房方面,有2部4亿,5部3亿。在短短10多年中,超过30部电影过亿。曾出品过经典动画《史莱克》《马达加斯加》《驯龙记》《功夫熊猫》等,出品过《美丽心灵》《美国丽人》《角斗士》《拯救大兵瑞恩》《追梦女郎》等优秀电影,同时也出品过《变形金刚》《逃出克隆岛》等商业大作。

写作特点

本文是一篇人物通讯。下面对英文写作中的人物通讯方面的注意事项做个简单的介绍。

人物通讯的功能在于具体、生动、客观报道新闻人物的典型事迹。新闻人物既可是正面典型,也可是反面典型;既可是个体人物,也可是以团体为对象的集体人物,如某个组织、单位等。

(1)人物通讯切忌刻意编造"显著性事迹"。

在报道新闻人物时,不能对人物不加分析地全盘肯定或全盘否定。如写先进人物时,往往写得不近人情,编造诸如"父母去世不回家"等事迹;而写反面人物时却又写得恶贯满盈,一无是处。如此编造典型"显著性事迹",不仅使得人物事迹缺乏新意、毫无特点,也有损新闻真实,引起读者怀疑甚至反感。编造"显著性事迹",主要是对新闻人物不够了解,采访不够深入,或者采访时"先入为主",以挖掘"显著性事迹"为采访目标。因此,要避免"显著性事迹"造成新闻人物"失真",应深入采访,了解新闻人物的全貌及相关事件、语言、细节等,筛选出其中"与众不同"的内容。

(2)人物通讯选材切忌模式化。

人物通讯要善于截取新闻人物个性化的语言、行动、细节等读者意想不到(未知)的素材来表现人物,切忌模式化。在人物通讯写作过程中,存在以下几种模式化倾向:

一是人物形象刻板化,只顾工作,不顾身体;只为别人,不为家人。

二是典型事迹虚构化,"高大全"难掩"假大空"。

三是新闻细节想象化,违背新闻写作客观原则。

品味鉴赏

　　称史蒂文·斯皮尔伯格（Steven Spielberg）为"电影织梦者"一点也不为过，他是以影片《辛德勒名单》而荣获奥斯卡金像奖的大导演，他的《大白鲨》、《E.T.》、《侏罗纪公园》等著名的商业娱乐片却为更多的电影迷们所知，当人们带着这种印象涌向电影院去欣赏那部黑白电影《辛德勒名单》时，却发现了斯皮尔伯格的另一个世界，一个充满智慧和理性的世界，一个真正的电影艺术的世界。

　　1994年3月2日，第66届奥斯卡颁奖晚会上，影片《侏罗纪公园》（*Jurassic Park*，1993）和《辛德勒名单》（*Schindler's List*，1993）囊括了共9项奖项。当这两部杰作的共同导演斯皮尔伯格登上领奖台时，全场起立，掌声不息，在这个属于斯皮尔伯格的夜晚，一向镇定含蓄的他也不禁潸然泪下。

　　斯皮尔伯格曾经两次荣获奥斯卡奖，并且是有史以来电影总票房最高的导演（数据截至2009年）。《福布斯》杂志估计斯皮尔伯格的净资产大约为30亿美元。2006年，《首映》将他列为电影业最有权势和影响力的人物。他位列《时代》"本世纪最伟大的100人"名单中，并在20世纪末被《生活》杂志评选为他那个时代最有影响力的人物。

美文感悟

Nicholas Sparks and His *Dear John*
尼古拉斯·斯帕克斯和他的《分手信》

背景介绍：

尼古拉斯·斯帕克思（1965—）是美国著名畅销书作家，著有多部小说，作品被翻译成超过 35 种语言，全球销量超过 4500 万册！他与《哈利·波特》系列作者 J. K. 罗琳，是仅有的两位同时有精装和平装作品在《纽约时报》排行榜上停留超过一年的作者。他被称为美国"纯爱小说教父""纯爱小说天王""催泪弹"。《瓶中信》是斯帕克斯的经典代表作，也是他最畅销的一部小说。这部小说的灵感来自尼古拉斯·斯帕克斯自己的父亲。母亲亡故后，父亲的哀恸让他开始思考，人生是否能第二度找到真爱？据此改编的电影由凯文·科斯特纳、罗宾·莱特以及保罗·纽曼主演。尼古拉斯·斯帕克斯其他已出版的简体中文版作品有《忠实信徒》《手札情缘》《分手信》《幸运符》《罗丹岛之恋》《抉择》《最后的歌》《避风港》等。

Nicholas Charles Sparks is an internationally bestselling American novelist and screenwriter. He has 16 published novels, with elements including cancer, death, **pirates**[1], and love. Nine

---

注释
1. **pirate** ['paɪərɪt] *n.* 海盗，强盗
2. **starring** ['stɑːrɪŋ] *n.* 领衔主演
3. **theatrically** [θɪ'ætrɪkəlɪ] *ad.* 戏剧化地
4. **adaptation** [ædæp'teɪʃən] *n.* 适应，顺应，改编

have been adapted to films, including *Message in a Bottle*, *Nights in Rodanthe*, *Dear John*, *A Walk to Remember*, *The Notebook*, *The Last Song*, and most recently *The Lucky One*.

Dear John is a 2010 American romantic drama-war film **starring**² Amanda Seyfried and Channing Tatum. It was released **theatrically**³ in North America on February 5, 2010. The film was directed by Lasse Hallström, and it is an **adaptation**⁴ of Nicholas Sparks's novel of the same name. It follows the life of a soldier (Channing Tatum) after he falls in love with a young woman (Amanda Seyfried). They decide to exchange letters to each other after he is **deployed**⁵ to the war. The movie was filmed in 2009 in Charleston, South Carolina.

Despite receiving negative reviews, the film made a strong box office performance, knocking off *Avatar* after seven weekends in first place and grossing a total of $114,977,104 worldwide. The film was released on May 25, 2010 on DVD and Blu-ray.

A "Dear John Letter" is a letter written to a husband or boyfriend to inform him their relationship is over, usually because the author has found another lover. Dear John letters are often written out of an inability or unwillingness to inform the man in person. The **reverse**⁶ situation, in which someone writes to his wife or girlfriend to break off the relationship, is referred to as a "Dear Jane letter".

While the exact origins of the phrase are unknown, it is commonly believed to have been coined by Americans during World War II. Large numbers of American troops were **stationed**⁷ overseas for many months or years, and as time passed many of their wives or girlfriends decided to begin a relationship with a new man rather than wait for their old one to return.

As letters to servicemen from wives or girlfriends back home would typically contain **affectionate**⁸ language (such as "Dear Johnny", "My dearest John", or simply "Darling"), a serviceman receiving a note beginning with a **curt**⁹ "Dear John" would instantly be aware of the letter's purpose.

A writer summed it up in August 1945, "Dear John," the letter began. "I have found someone else whom I think the world of. I think the only way out is for us to get a divorce," it said. They usually began like that, those letters that told of infidelity on the part of the wives of servicemen... The men called them "Dear Johns".

Classic Dialogue:

There's something I wanna tell you.

After I got shot...you wanna know the very first thing that entered my mind...

...before I blacked out?

Coins.

注释

5. **deploy** [dɪˈplɔɪ] *vt.&vi.* （尤指军事行动）使展开，施展，有效地利用

6. **reverse** [rɪˈvɜːs] *a.* 反面的，颠倒的，倒开的

7. **station** [ˈsteɪʃən] *vt.* 配置，安置，驻扎

8. **affectionate** [əˈfekʃənɪt] *a.* 深情的，挚爱的，慈爱的，有感情的

I'm 8 years old again on a tour of the U.S. **Mint**[10].
I'm listening to a guide explain how coins are made.
How they're punched out of sheet metal.
How they're **rimmed**[11] and **beveled**[12].
How they are stamped and cleaned.
And how each and every batch of coins are personally examined.
Just in case any have slipped through with the slightest imperfection.
That's what popped into my head.
I am a coin in the United States Army.
I was minted in the year 1980. I've been punched from sheet metal.
I've been stamped and cleaned.
My ridges have been rimmed and beveled.
But now I have two small holes in me.
I'm no longer in perfect condition.
So there's something else I wanna tell you.
Right before everything went black...
...you wanna know the very last thing that entered my mind?
You.

原文翻译

尼古拉斯·查尔斯·斯帕克斯是一位美国国际畅销书作家和电影编剧。他已经出版了16部小说，主题包括癌症、死亡、基督、海盗和爱情。其中6部已被拍成了电影，分别为《瓶中信》《罗丹岛之恋》《分手信》《初恋的回忆》《恋恋笔记本》《最后一支歌》和最近的《幸运符》。

《分手信》是一部在2010年由阿曼达·西耶弗里德和查宁·塔图姆主演的浪漫戏剧战争电影。2010年2月5日在北美上映。本片由莱塞·霍尔斯道姆执导，改编于尼古拉斯·斯帕克斯的同名小说。电影讲述了一位士兵（查宁·塔图姆饰演）同一位年轻女士（阿曼达·西耶弗里德饰演）坠入爱河后的故事。他们决定在他去打仗之后互相通信。电影于2009年拍摄于南卡罗来纳州的查尔斯顿。

尽管受到负面评论，电影的票房收入表现强势。将《阿凡达》推掉后，该片7周排在榜首，在全球总共获利114,977,104美元。该片2010年5月25日发布了DVD和蓝光版。

所谓"Dear John letter"，是指一个女子写给丈夫或男友表示分手的信件，通常是在写信人另有所爱的情况下所写，且往往写信人不能够或不想要当面告知男方这一情况。反之，如果是写给妻子或女友告知分手的信，则被称作"Dear Jane letter"。

分手信为什么叫Dear John letter，确切的起源还真不可考证，但人们普遍认为这个词由美国人缔造于"二战"时期。当时大量的美军部队被派往海外，短则数月，长则数年。光阴流转，军嫂们或者在家的女朋友不愿再独守空闺，盼着良人归来，决定开始一段全新的感情。

而这些服役军人们的妻子或女友通常都是以充满爱意的称谓，比方"亲爱的强尼""我最亲爱的约翰"

注释
9. **curt** [kət] *a.* 简短的、三言两语的、草率的、敷衍了事的
10. **mint** [mɪnt] *n.* 薄荷；铸币厂
11. **rim** [rɪm] *vt.* 环绕（圆形或环形物的）边缘，镶边
12. **bevel** [ˈbevəl] *vt.* 把（某物）切成或磨成斜边或斜角

或者"亲爱的"开始她们残酷的分手信,军人们收到如此生硬开头的信件,往往都有所警觉:是不是要分手了?

1945年8月,一位作家总结道:"亲爱的约翰,"信是这么开头的,"我找到了另一个人,我愿意与他共度一生。唯一的解决方案就是,咱俩离婚吧。"这类信通常都是这么写的,这些军嫂们婉转坦白自己背叛的信件。而那些被一脚踢开的男人们,称自己为"亲爱的约翰们。"

经典对白:

我想跟你说些事,

在我中弹之后……

……你想知道第一个闪进我脑海里的念头是什么吗?……

……在我昏倒之前,

硬币,

我又回到了8岁那年去参观美国造币厂的时候,

我听着向导向我们解释硬币是如何造出来的,

金币如何从金属薄片中穿孔造出的,

如何被打磨得有棱有角,

如何被戳印和清洗,

和如何对每一个和每一批硬币进行人工分拣,

只是为了防范有任何小瑕疵的硬币溜出去,

那就是突然闪现在我脑海里的东西。

在美国陆战军里我就是一个硬币。

1980年,我被从金属薄片中穿孔铸造出来,

被戳上印记,接受洗礼,

我的棱角被打磨有致,

但是现在我身上有两个小洞,

我不再处在完美状态,

所以我想告诉你另外一些事,

就在一切昏暗之前……

…你想知道最后闪入我脑海的事吗?

是你。

文化点滴

Avatar

《阿凡达》是一部科幻电影,由著名导演詹姆斯·卡梅隆执导,20世纪福克斯出品,该片有2D、3D和IMAX-3D三种制式供观众选择。影片的预算超过5亿美元,成为电影史上预算金额最高的电影。此外,由导演詹姆斯·卡梅隆监制的全平台同名游戏《阿凡达》(James Cameron's Avatar: The Game)于2009年12月1日推出,游戏类型为TPS(第三人称科幻射击动作游戏),支持3D显示器。另外还有一些《阿凡达》周边产品及同名作品。

Blu-ray

蓝光光碟(Blu-ray Disc,简称BD)是DVD之后的下一代光盘格式之一,用以存储高品质的影音以及高容量的数据存储。蓝光光碟的命名是由于其采用波长405纳米(nm)的蓝色激光光束来进行读写操作(DVD采用650纳米波长的红光读写器,CD则是采用780纳米波长)。一个单层的蓝光光碟的容量为25或是27GB,足够录制一部长达4小时的高解析影片。2008年2月19日,随着HD DVD领导者东芝宣布在3月底退出所有HD DVD相关业务,持续多年的下一代光盘格式之争正式画上句号,最终由SONY主导的蓝

光光碟胜出。

写作特点

　　本文最后的部分使用了大量的电影原文经典对白。近年来，越来越多的人开始通过英语电影来学习英语，尤其是口语。但要真正看懂电影，不仅需要一定的语言、文化知识的储备，更重要的是对英语电影对白的语体特征有一定的了解。英语电影对白体的根本特征是简洁，促成简洁的重要手段是省略句式和缩略语的使用。理解把握这种简洁语体是我们看懂英语电影、培养地道英语语感的基础。大多数电影的对白都力求简洁，即用最少的词句表达最丰富的内容。为做到这一点，电影编剧除了在句式上采用结构简单、清晰明了的短句，在选词上尽量选择短小的生活词汇外，广泛地使用省略句式是电影对白的一大特点。

品味鉴赏

　　尼古拉斯·查尔斯·斯帕克斯于 1965 年 12 月 13 日生于美国内布拉斯加。他是当代首屈一指的美系纯爱小说畅销天王，当代两位同时有精装和平装作品在榜上停留超过一年的作者，另外一个是 J. K. 罗琳。他的作品，在全美发行超过 5000 万册，海外销量超过 1200 万册，全球销量逾 4500 万册，在 35 个国家和地区发行。同时，他的作品也是电影导演的最爱，《手札情愿》、《瓶中信》、《留住一片情》、《分手信》都赢得了不俗的票房。2008 年 9 月 26 日，《罗丹岛之恋》全球首映，被称为是继《廊桥遗梦》后最值得期待的情感大片。

　　斯帕克斯历年编剧作品：

　　1999 年 《瓶中信》

　　2002 年 《初恋的回忆》

　　2004 年 《恋恋笔记本》

　　2008 年 《罗丹岛之恋》

　　2010 年 《分手信》

　　2010 年 《最后一支歌》

　　2010 年 《避风港》

美文感悟

47

Whitney Elizabeth Houston Remembered
铭记惠特妮·伊丽莎白·休斯顿

背景介绍：

惠特妮·休斯顿（1963—2012）是美国乐坛巨星，她以强而有力的嗓音、一字多转音的感染力与宽广的音域，被誉为美国第一嗓。惠特妮在全世界有超过1.7亿张专辑的销售纪录。她是首张专辑销量最高和单张专辑销量最高的女歌手。惠特妮也是Billboard音乐排行榜第一位连续缔造7首冠军单曲的女歌手。根据《吉尼斯世界纪录》，惠特妮是获奖最多的女歌手（获奖416次，提名562次）。美国时间2012年2月11日在比弗利希尔顿酒店被宣布死亡，死因是心脏病发滑入浴缸溺水而亡，终年48岁。

Saturday, hundreds of people will gather in Newark, New Jersey, for the **funeral**[1] of Whitney Houston. The forty-eight year old performer died a week earlier at a hotel in California.

People in her hometown of Newark say she never forgot where she came from. Her close

注释
1. **funeral** ['fjuːnərəl] *n.* 葬礼
2. **gospel** ['ɡɒspəl] *n.* 真理，信条，福音音乐
3. **basement** ['beɪsmənt] *n.* 地下室
4. **Baptist** ['bæptɪst] *n.* 浸礼会教友，施浸礼者

friend and **gospel**² singer Marvin Winans recently said that below the surface Whitney Houston was still the same little girl from New Jersey.

A childhood friend of the star, Gregory Whittle, remembers growing up with her. "A lot of time in the **basement**³ you could hear her singing. She had a gift. It was strictly from God."

Marvin Winans is to speak at the funeral. It will be held at the New Hope **Baptist**⁴ Church. Whitney Houston attended that church while growing up. It was also the first place she sang publicly. She was a member of the church **choir**⁵.

A 22 year-old Whitney Houston performing in Boston, Massachusetts, in 1986. As a teenager, Whitney Houston performed as a back-up singer for Chaka Khan, Lou Rawls and other artists. But she also had a successful modeling career by the time she was twenty. Her picture appeared on the cover of *Seventeen* and inside magazines including *Glamour* and *Cosmopolitan*.

In 1983, Clive Davis, the head of Arista records, heard Whitney Houston singing in New York City. He offered her a recording agreement soon after. For the next two years, Whitney Houston worked on her first record **album**⁶. *Whitney Houston* was released in 1985. Slowly but surely, it became a huge hit. It stayed in the number one position on *Billboard* magazine's Top Two Hundred Albums chart for fourteen weeks. The first number one single from the album was *Saving All My Love for You*.

Another popular song from that first album was this dance number *How Will I Know*.

The album *Whitney Houston* had seven number one hit singles. It remains the biggest-selling first album by any artist.

The singer followed that success with another. Her album *Whitney* sold twenty million copies. It also made her the first female artist to enter the *Billboard* Top Two Hundred at number one. Whitney Houston was clearing a path of **recognition**⁷ for women artists.

However, her next professional move was her most important. She recorded the **soundtrack**⁸ for and starred in *The Bodyguard*⁹, in 1992.

Kevin Costner played opposite White Houston in the movie. The movie was a big hit, making more than four hundred million dollars in ticket sales worldwide. But the film's **popularity**¹⁰ did not even come close to the success of the album that went with it.

The Bodyguard is the fourth highest selling album of all time. Forty-four million copies have been sold. Among the singles is *I Will Always Love You*, a song written and recorded earlier by Dolly Parton. Whitney Houston's version sold many more copies.

In 1992, Whitney Houston's personal life also grew. She married singer Bobby Brown, of the band New Edition. The marriage surprised many people both in and outside the music industry.

注释

5. **choir** ['kwaɪə] *n.* 教堂的唱诗班，唱诗队；公开表演的合唱团
6. **album** ['ælbəm] *n.* 相册，集邮簿，签名册；唱片
7. **recognition** [ˌrekəɡ'nɪʃən] *n.* 认识，识别，承认，认可

Bobby Brown was considered an industry "bad boy," while Whitney Houston had an **innocence**[11] that led to her nickname the "**prom**[12] queen of soul."

She and Bobby Brown had a daughter, Bobbi Kristina, in 1993. In the late 1990s, Whitney Houston's professional behavior began to come under question. She began to cancel shows and was late for important events. Her appearance changed; she lost weight and looked unhealthy. Her voice also was suffering. Many reports said she was abusing drugs and alcohol.

Whitney Houston and Bobby Brown ended their marriage in 2007. She also publicly admitted to drug abuse. But she entered a treatment program. In 2010, she reported she was drug-free.

But, last Saturday, the singer and actress was found dead in her hotel room in Los Angeles. Officials have not yet released a cause of death. However, news reports say Whitney Houston's family has been told the entertainer died from taking too many **prescription**[13] drugs.

Her seventh and final studio album, *I Look to You*, was released in 2009. Critics generally praised the effort.

Her masterpiece[14]:

I Will Always Love You

If I should stay

I would only be in your way

So I'll go, but I know

I'll think of you every step of the way

And I will always love you

I will always love you

You, my darling you, you

Bitter sweet memories

That is all I'm taking with me

So goodbye, please don't cry

We both know I'm not what you need

And I will always love you

I will always love you

I hope life treats you kind

And I hope you have all you dreamed off

And I wish to you joy and happiness

But above all this I wish to you love

And I will always love you

I will always love you

---

8. **soundtrack** ['saʊnd,træk] n. 声道，音带，声带，声迹，电影配音

9. **bodyguard** ['bɒdɪ,ɡɑːd] n. 保镖，卫士，警卫员

10. **popularity** [ˌpɒpjə'lærɪti] n. 普及，流行，名气，名望，

原文翻译

周六，数百人将聚集在新泽西州纽瓦克，参加惠特尼·休斯顿的葬礼。这位48岁的演员一个星期前在加利福尼亚州的一家酒店去世。

在她的家乡纽瓦克的人说，她永远不会忘记她来自何方。她的亲密朋友和福音歌手马文·威纳斯最近说，惠特尼·休斯顿在外表下仍然是那个来自新泽西州的小女孩。

她的童年朋友格雷戈里·惠特尔，回忆起跟她一起成长的日子。"很多时候，你可以听到她在地下室的歌声。她很有天赋，那是上帝赋予她的。"

马文·威纳斯将在葬礼上发言。葬礼将在新希望浸礼会举行。惠特尼·休斯顿在成长的过程中经常来这个教堂。这也是她首度公开献唱的地方。她是一位教堂唱诗班的成员。

22岁的惠特尼·休斯顿1986年在马萨诸塞州的波士顿演出。作为青年人，惠特尼·休斯顿是歌手夏卡·康、路·洛尔斯和其他艺术家的替补。但当她20岁的时候，她拥有了成功的模特生涯。她的照片出现在《17》杂志的封面和诸如《时尚》和《大都会》杂志里面。

1983年，阿利斯塔唱片公司总裁克莱夫·戴维斯在纽约听到惠特尼·休斯顿演唱。他很快就给了她录制协议。在接下来的两年中，惠特尼·休斯顿打造她的第一张唱片专辑。《惠特尼·休斯顿》这张专辑发布于1985年。慢慢地，但肯定的是，它取得了巨大的成功。它停留在《告示牌》杂志的热门200张专辑的头号位置长达14周。这张专辑的第一首单曲是《把我全部的爱留给你》。

那张专辑另一首流行的歌曲，是这个舞曲《我怎么知道》。

《惠特尼·休斯顿》这张专辑有7支头号单曲。它仍然是最畅销的任何艺术家的第一张专辑。

惠特尼·休斯顿取得一个又一个的成功。她的专辑《惠特尼·休斯顿》卖出了2000万份。这也使她成为《告示牌》杂志热门200第一名的第一位女艺人。惠特尼·休斯顿为女性艺术得到认可开辟了道路。

然而，她的下一个职业改变是最重要的。1992年她录制了电影配乐并出演电影《保镖》。

凯文·科斯特纳在电影中与她演对手戏。这部电影取得了极大的成功，世界范围4000万的票房收入。但是电影的受欢迎程度比不上接下来的专辑。

《保镖》这部专辑是第四卖得最好的专辑。卖出了4400万张。单曲中，《我永远爱你》之前是多莉·帕顿写出并录制的，但是惠特尼·休斯顿的版本卖得更多。

1992年，惠特尼·休斯顿的个人生活也在成长。她和新版本乐队的歌手鲍比·布朗结婚。这个婚姻使得音乐圈内外的许多人吃惊。鲍比·布朗被认为是圈内的"坏小子"，而惠特尼·休斯顿的纯真使她获得了"舞会皇后的灵魂"的昵称。

1993年，她和鲍比·布朗生了一个女儿，名叫波比·克里斯蒂娜。在20世纪90年代后期，惠特尼·休斯顿的职业行为开始受到质疑。她开始取消演出，参加重要事件迟到。她的外表改变了；她瘦了，看着不健康。她的声音也很痛苦。许多报道说她吸毒和酗酒。

惠特尼·休斯顿和鲍比·布朗在2007年结束了他们的婚姻。她还公开承认滥用药物。但她接受了一个治疗方案。2010年，她宣布不再用药。

但是上个周六，这位歌手兼演员被发现在洛杉矶她的旅馆房间里去世。官方还没有宣布死因。然而，有新闻说惠特尼·休斯顿的家人已被告知这位艺人死于服用大量处方药。

她的第七部也是最后一部专辑，《我看着你》，在2009年出版，受到评论家的普遍赞誉。

注释

通俗性，大众性

11. **innocence** ['ɪnəsəns] *n.* 清白，天真无邪，无罪的人

12. **prom** [prɒm] *n.* 正式舞会，毕业舞会

13. **prescription** [prɪsˈkrɪpʃən] *n.* 药方，处方，处方药

14. **masterpiece** ['mɑːstəpiːs] *n.* 杰作，名作，杰出的事

她的代表作:

我永远爱你

如果我留下来,

我只能挡你的路,

所以我走了,但是我知道,

路上的每一步我都会思念你。

我将永远爱你。

我将永远爱你。

你,我亲爱的你!

苦涩而又甜蜜的回忆啊,

那是我所带给自己唯一的东西。

那么,再见吧,请别哭泣。

我们都知道我不是你所要的(那种人)。

我将永远爱你。

我将永远爱你。

我希望生活对你宽容慈悲,

我还希望你能够美梦成真,

我还希望你能够幸福美满,

所有的希望汇成一句话,我希望你爱。

我将永远爱你。

我将永远爱你。

文化点滴

Glamour

Glamour 是美国高端女性时尚周刊,以其独特的编辑理念与视角报道时装、美容、名流及跟女性生活息息相关的一切。读者再也不需要等待一个月才来更新她的头脑和衣橱,每一期杂志都与潮流息息相关,有介绍穿衣风尚的,有关于明星娱乐的,也有一些化妆保养的,内容丰富。每一期都有本土明星排行榜,刊登由网友投票评选出来的明星穿衣榜样和穿衣打扮失败的一些艺人。同时,每一期都有明星的专访,以及号称融"街拍、明星、时尚"为一体的"本周街拍他(她)最潮",还有"你就是时尚评审",主要是对欧美明星的打扮发表意见,另有"欲望清单""封面故事""热力时事"及"本周红黑榜",还有"潮流捕手""编辑精选"等。*Glamour* 近年来发展极快,前不久还推出了男士增刊。

Cosmopolitan

《大都会》杂志是1886年在美国创办的国际知名女性杂志,针对时尚、生活、健身和美容等问题为妇女出谋划策,是世界上最畅销的妇女杂志之一。集合销售、推广、展销、时尚秀的"Cosmopolitan show"在时尚界已有"最佳市场及销售活动"美誉。作为哈斯特集团(Hearst Magazines)的旗舰杂志,以大胆、风趣的美国风格出道的COSMO在全球已经凭借一种"成功而时尚的女性"的共同语言打开市场通道。

《大都会》杂志创办之初是一份家庭杂志,后来偏重于文学,最终在20世纪60年代转变为女性杂志。如今,杂志的内容包括人际关系、性行为、健康、职业、自我提升、娱乐明星以及时尚和美容。《大都会》

杂志目前已有 58 种国际版本，使用 34 种语言印刷，在 100 多个国家发行。

Billboard

1894 年 11 月 1 日，美国俄亥俄州辛辛那提市的一个小酒馆里，两个专门为马戏团、展览会设计告示牌的年轻人威廉·H. 唐纳德森（William H. Donaldson）和詹姆士·F. 亨宁汉（James F. Henningham）酒后兴起，萌生了办刊物的念头，《公告牌》(*Billboard*) 就这样诞生了。

写作特点

本文列出了惠特尼·休斯顿的经典歌曲《我永远爱你》的歌词。英文歌词具有以下的特点：

（1）语音特征。歌曲作为一门听觉艺术，很大程度上需要依靠语音实现其艺术价值，因此歌词具有独特的语音特征。其最显著的语音特征便是押韵。

（2）词汇特征。流行歌曲的主体是普通大众，这决定了它的歌词都是通俗易懂、贴近生活的常用词汇乃至口语、俚语词汇，从而确保歌曲达意顺畅。

（3）语法及词语特征。比如在时态的选择上，好歌往往不会频繁地变换时态，切割听者的注意力，使其在过去、现在和未来时空的转换中疲于奔命，造成欣赏上的断层。

美文感悟

_____
_____
_____
_____
_____
_____

Oprah Winfrey – Talk Show Queen
奥普拉·温弗瑞——脱口秀女王

背景介绍：

奥普拉·温弗瑞（1945—），作为一名黑人，更为当今世界上最具影响力的妇女之一，她的成就是多方面的：通过控股哈普娱乐集团的股份，掌握了超过 10 亿美元的个人财富；主持的电视谈话节目《奥普拉脱口秀》，平均每周吸引 3300 万名观众，并连续 16 年排在同类节目的首位；2009 年 11 月 20 日，据国外媒体报道，在播出了 23 年之后，脱口秀女王奥普拉·温弗瑞的节目《奥普拉脱口秀》将于 2011 年 9 月 9 日结束。

    Oprah Winfrey is an American media **proprietor**[1], talk show host, actress, producer, and philanthropist. She is internationally famous for hosting the most popular talk show on American television. Millions of TV viewers tune in worldwide every day to watch her. She has become a

---

注释
1. **proprietor** [prəˈpraɪətə] n. 所有者，经营者
2. **literacy** [ˈlɪtərəsi] n. 有文化，有教养，有读写能力
3. **abuse** [əˈbjuːz] n. 滥用，虐待，辱骂，陋习，弊端
4. **campaign** [kæmˈpeɪn] n. 战役，（政治或商业性）活动，

household name and is now one of the richest women in the world. She is also famous for raising millions of dollars for charities to help with child **literacy**2.

Oprah was born in 1954 in Mississippi. She experienced child **abuse**3 as she grew up, which led her to **campaign**4 for children's rights later in her life. She helped **draft**5 a bill that President Clinton passed into law. Her career in broadcasting started in 1971 and her big **breakthrough**6 came in 1976 with her own extremely popular TV chat show –*People Are Talking*.

In 1985 movie producer Steven Spielberg offered her a role in *The Color Purple*. She was **nominated**7 for an Oscar at the Academy Awards for her performance. She used her newfound international fame to launch the *Oprah Winfrey Show*. This opened all kinds of doors for her she had never dreamed of. The world was her **oyster**8.

Her chat show is broadcast to over 100 countries. *Life* magazine called her the most influential woman of her generation. She has raised nearly $100 million for charity. She is now a role model for millions of girls around the world. Her latest project is an academy for poor girls, which opened in South Africa in 2007.

Her famous words:

1. Doing the best at this moment puts you in the best place for the next moment.
2. Be thankful for what you have; you'll end up having more. If you **concentrate**9 on what you don't have, you will never, never have enough.
3. I do not believe in failure. It is not failure if you enjoyed the process.
4. Luck is a matter of preparation meeting opportunity.
5. So go ahead. Fall down. The world looks different from the ground.
6. The biggest adventure you can take is to live the life of your dreams.
7. Where there is no struggle, there is no strength.
8. You can have it all. You just can't have it all at once.
9. As you become more clear about who you really are, you'll be better able to decide what is best for you — the first time around.
10. Do the one thing you think you cannot do. Fail at it. Try again. Do better the second time.

注释

竞选运动

5. draft [drɑːft] *n.* 草稿，草案，草图 *vt.* 起草，为……打样，设计

6. breakthrough ['breɪkˌθruː] *n.* 突破

7. nominate ['nɒmɪneɪt] *vt.* 提名，推荐，任命，命名

8. oyster ['ɔɪstə] *n.* 牡蛎，蚝；沉默者

The only people who never **tumble**[10] are those who never mount the high wire. This is your moment. Own it.

11. I always knew I was destined for greatness.
12. I believe that every single event in life happens in an opportunity to choose love over fear.
13. I still have my feet on the ground, I just wear better shoes.
14. I'm black, I don't feel burdened by it and I don't think it's a huge responsibility. It's part of who I am. It does not define me.

原文翻译

奥普拉·温弗瑞是一位美国媒体所有人、脱口秀主持人、演员、制片人和慈善家。她是美国电视上最流行的脱口秀节目的国际著名主持人。数以百万计的电视观众在全世界每天都会调台看她主持。她的名字家喻户晓，她是世界上最富有的女性之一。她也因拿出数百万美元给慈善机构，以帮助孩子识字而出名。

奥普拉1954年出生于密西西比州。在她成长的过程中，她经历了虐待儿童，这导致后来在她的生活中，她为儿童的权利而斗争。她协助起草了一项法案，克林顿总统将该项法案制定成法律。她广播的职业生涯开始于1971年，在1976年她通过极受欢迎的电视聊天节目——《人们都在说》取得了极大的突破。

电影制片人史蒂文·斯皮尔伯格1985年在《紫颜色》中给她一个角色。她因出色的表现在奥斯卡奖中被提名。她用她新建立起的国际声誉，推出《奥普拉·温弗瑞秀》。她做梦也没想到这为她开启了各种通道。世界是属于她的。

她的聊天秀在100多个国家播出。《生活》杂志称她为她这一代最有影响力的女人。她为慈善事业拿出了近1000万美元。她现在是世界各地数百万女孩的榜样。她最新的项目是为贫穷的女孩开设学院，该学院已于2007年在南非开设。

她的名言：
1. 这一刻全力以赴，下一刻成就最佳。
2. 对于你所拥有的，要心存感激，这样你就会拥有更多；对于你所没有的，如果不停强调，你永远都不会满足。
3. 我从不相信失败。如果能享受过程，就没什么失败可言。
4. 幸运，其实就是准备遇到了机会。
5. 所以勇往直前吧！跌倒吧！你会从地上看到一个不同的世界。
6. 你能经历的最大冒险，就是过你梦想的生活。
7. 没有奋斗，你就没有力量。
8. 你可以拥有一切，只是你不可能马上拥有一切。

注释
9. **concentrate** ['kɒnsentreɪt] *v.* 集中，浓缩
10. **tumble** ['tʌmbl] *vi.* 翻倒，摔倒，倒塌 *vt.* 使摔倒

9. 当你更清楚你是谁时,你将能更好地选择最适合你的。

10. 做一件你认为你做不到的事。收获失败。再试一次。第二次做得更好一些。那些不曾跌倒的人是那些不曾走上高压电线的人。这是你的时刻。拥有它吧。

11. 我总是知道我命中注定变得伟大。

12. 我相信,生命中发生的每一个事件都有一个选择,那就是选择爱而不是恐惧。

13. 我依然深深扎根于土地中,我只是穿了更好的鞋子。

14. 我是黑人,我不觉得这是个负担,也不觉得这是个责任。这就是我的一部分。但它不能定义我。

文化点滴

talk show

"脱口秀"是英语词组 Talk Show(口才展示)的音意同译的精彩典范。"脱口秀"是形容人的口才很好,说出的话非常有吸引力,而且谈吐不俗,博得众人的喝彩。在西方,"脱口秀"既是一个视频节目的栏目,也是一种主持风格。我国的相声艺术就被西方国家认为是"脱口秀"。

Academy Awards

奥斯卡金像奖(Academy Award)就是"学院奖",由电影艺术与科学学院(Academy of Motion Picture Arts and Sciences)颁发,1928年设立,每年一次在美国的好莱坞举行。它不仅反映美国电影艺术的发展进程,而且对世界许多国家的电影艺术有着不可忽视的影响。

1927年5月,"好莱坞之王"——米高梅公司总经理梅耶(Louis B.Mayer)在一次晚宴上向在座的同行提出了一个设想:"应该把好莱坞的精英分子们都集中起来,组成一个团体。它包括演员、导演、编剧、摄影师,当然还有制片人,使他们成为好莱坞的支柱,让他们调解纠纷,或者在制片厂里起疏导作用。"一周之后,梅耶草拟了一份关于成立"美国电影艺术与科学学院"(American Academy of Motion Picture Arts and Sciences,简称AMPAS)的提案,学院的首任主席是米高梅旗下的当红影星道格拉斯·范朋克(Douglas Fairbanks)。

于是,他们把工作的重心侧重到了用颁奖的方式来嘉奖在电影摄制方面有显著成就的人士,后来被俗称为"奥斯卡奖"的"学院奖"由此应运而生。1929年5月16日,第一届奥斯卡奖举办。一直到今天,奥斯卡奖就成为美国影艺学院的"主营业务"和该机构的代名词。

写作特点

本文列举了14条奥普拉·温弗瑞的名言,这些名言语言精练,寓意深刻,富有教育意义,值得我们背诵,对我们的生活、工作都起到激励和鼓舞的作用。名言是语言的精华,它包含着丰富的生活经验,蕴含着深刻的人生哲理,闪耀着人类智慧的理性光芒。名人名言不同于谚语,后者属民间创作,前者均出于名家,包括哲学家、思想家、政治家、军事家、科学家、作家等等。名言的语言形式丰富多彩,具有形象性和表现力。许多名言用词巧妙,结构独特,有很强的感染力。最常见的格言是定义式的,即先提出某个现象、事件、概念,然后对之作出判断、评价,揭示其本质,使人从中获得启迪。例如第10句:

Do the one thing you think you cannot do. Fail at it. Try again. Do better the second time. The only people who never tumble are those who never mount the high wire. This is your moment. Own it.

首先提出了现象,然后对其判断、评价,揭示其本质,鼓励人们要不畏困难,大胆尝试,才能成功。温弗瑞的话语通俗易懂,学习和背诵她的话对年轻人励志、成长都大有裨益。

品味鉴赏

　　天命之年、长相平平、肤色黝黑、身材欠佳，笑起来大嘴一咧，谈不上什么优雅。但就是这样一个女人，却占据着《福布斯》2005年度"百位名人"排行榜的头把交椅，令麦当娜、安吉丽娜·朱莉等这一大串光彩照人的女明星难以望其项背。她就是美国"传媒女皇"奥普拉·温弗瑞。奥普拉·温弗瑞，作为一名黑人，更为当今世界上最具影响力的妇女之一，她的成就是多方面的：通过控股哈普娱乐集团的股份，掌握了超过10亿美元的个人财富；主持的电视谈话节目《奥普拉脱口秀》，平均每周吸引3300万名观众，并连续16年排在同类节目的首位；30出头，成为无可争议的"脱口秀女皇"。2002年，被普林斯顿大学授予荣誉博士学位。获"鲍勃·霍普人道主义奖"。2003年获"马里恩·安德森奖"。与一些世界名人共同庆祝曼德拉的85岁生日，成为美国第一位黑人亿万富翁。喜欢奥普拉的人甚至认为如果她去竞选美国总统，获胜的把握也很大。美国伊利诺斯大学更开设了一门课程专门研究奥普拉。2009年11月20日，据国外媒体报道，在播出了23年之后，脱口秀女王奥普拉·温弗瑞的节目《奥普拉脱口秀》将于2011年9月9日结束。

美文感悟

Andrew Carnegie — the King of Steel
安德鲁·卡内基——钢铁大王

背景介绍：

在美国，与"汽车大王"福特、"石油大王"洛克菲勒等大财阀的名字列在一起的，还有一个"钢铁大王"，他就是安德鲁·卡内基。美国工业史上写下了永难磨灭的一页；他征服钢铁世界，成为美国最大钢铁制造商，衣锦还乡，跃居世界首富；而在功成名就后，他又将几乎全部的财富捐献给社会。他生前捐赠款额之巨大，足以与死后设立诺贝尔奖的瑞典科学家、实业家诺贝尔相媲美，由此成为美国人心目中的英雄和个人奋斗的楷模。

Andrew Carnegie (1835 – 1919) was a Scottish-American **industrial**[1] who led the **enormous**[2] expansion of the American steel industry in the late 19th century. He was also one of the most important philanthropists of his era.

注释
1. **industrialist** [ɪnˈdʌstrɪəlɪst] n. 工业家,实业家,工厂主,产业工人
2. **enormous** [ɪˈnɔːməs] a. 巨大的，庞大的
3. **profitable** [ˈprɒfɪtbl] a. 有利可图的
4. **decline** [dɪˈklaɪn] v. 拒绝，n. 衰落
5. **investment** [ɪnˈvestmənt] n. 投资，可获利的东西

He earned most of his fortune in the steel industry. In the 1870s, he founded the Carnegie Steel Company, a step which cemented his name as one of the "Captains of Industry". By the 1890s, the company was the largest and most **profitable**[3] industrial enterprise in the world. Carnegie sold it in 1901 for $480 million to J.P. Morgan, who created U.S. Steel. Carnegie devoted the remainder of his life to large-scale philanthropy, with special emphasis on local libraries, world peace, education and scientific research. His life has often been referred to as a true "rags to riches" story.

Andrew Carnegie, known as the King of Steel, built the steel industry in the United States, and, in the process, became one of the wealthiest men in America. His success resulted in part from his ability to sell the product and in part from his policy of expanding during periods of economic **decline**[4], when most of his competitors were reducing their **investments**[5].

Carnegie believed that individuals should progress through hard work, but he also felt strongly that the wealthy should use their fortunes for the benefit of society. He opposed **charity**[6], preferring instead to provide educational opportunities that would allow others to help themselves. "He who dies rich, dies disgraced," he often said.

Among his more **noteworthy**[7] contributions to society are those that bear his name, including the Carnegie Institute of Pittsburgh, which has a library, a museum of fine arts, and a museum of national history. He also founded a school of technology that is now part of Carnegie-Mellon University. Other philanthropic gifts are the Carnegie **Endowment**[8] for International Peace to promote understanding between nations, the Carnegie Institute of Washington to fund scientific research, and Carnegie Hall to provide a center for the arts.

Few Americans have been left untouched by Andrew Carnegie's **generosity**[9]. His contributions of more than five million dollars established 2,500 libraries in small communities throughout the country and formed the **nucleus**[10] of the public library system that we all enjoy today.

"THE ROAD TO BUSINESS SUCCESS: A TALK TO YOUNG MEN"
From an address to Students of the Curry Commercial College, Pittsburg, June 23, 1885.
The Road to Success

Andrew Carnegie

It is well that young men should begin at the beginning and occupy the most **subordinate**[11] positions. Many of the leading businessmen of Pittsburgh had a serious responsibility thrust

---

注释
6. **charity** ['tʃærɪtɪ] n. 慈善，施舍，慈善团体
7. **noteworthy** ['nəʊtwɜːðɪ] a. 值得注目的，显著的
8. **endowment** [ɪn'daʊmənt] n. 捐赠，捐赠的基金（或财产）；天资；捐款
9. **generosity** [dʒenə'rɒsɪtɪ] n. 慷慨，宽大
10. **nucleus** ['njuːklɪəs] n. 核子

upon them at the very **threshold**[12] of their career, hey were introduced to the broom, and spent the first hours for their business lives weeping out the office. I notice we have **janitors**[13] and janitresses now in offices, and our young men unfortunately miss that salutary branch of a business education. But if by chance the professional sweeper is absent any morning, the boy who has the genius of the future partner in him will not hesitate to try his hand at the broom. It does not hurt the newest comer to sweep out the office if necessary. I was one of those sweepers myself.

Assuming that you have all obtained employment and are fairly started, my advice to you is "aim high". I would not give a fig for the young man who does not already see himself the partner or the head of an important firm. Do not rest content for a moment in your thoughts as head clerk, or foreman, or general manager in any concern, no matter how extensive. Say to yourself, "My place is at the top." Be king in your dreams.

And there is the prime condition of success, the great secret: concentrate your energy, thought, and capital exclusively upon the business in which you are engaged. Having begun in one line, resolve to fight it out on that line, to lead in it, adopt every improvement, have the best machinery, and know the most about it.

The concerns which fail are those which have **scattered**[14] their capital, which means that they have scattered their brains also. They have investments in this, or that, or the other, here, there, and everywhere. "Don't put all your eggs in one basket." is all wrong. I tell you to "put all your eggs in one basket, and then watch that basket." Look round you and take notice, men who do that not often fail. It is easy to watch and carry the one basket. It is trying to carry too many baskets that breaks most eggs in this country. He who carries three baskets must put one on his head, which is apt to tumble and trip him up. One fault of the American businessman is lack of concentration.

To summarize what I have said: aim for the highest; never enter a bar room; do not touch liquor, or if at all only at meals; never speculate; never indorse beyond your surplus cash fund; make the firm's interest yours; break orders always to save owners; concentrate; put all your eggs in one basket, and watch that basket; **expenditure**[15] always within revenue; lastly, be not impatient, for as Emerson says, "No one can cheat you out of ultimate success but yourselves."

原文翻译

安德鲁·卡内基（1835-1919）是一位苏格兰裔美国工业家，他领导了19世纪后期的美国钢铁行业的巨大扩张。他也是他那个时代最重要的慈善家之一。

他在钢铁行业中赢得了他的大部分财富。在19世纪70年代，他创办卡内基钢铁公司，这巩固了他的"行业领袖"之一的名望。到19世纪90年代，该公司是世界上最大的和最有利可图的工业企业。卡内基于1901年把它以4.8亿美元出售给J. P. 摩根公司，后者创造了美国钢铁公司。卡内基把余生致力于大型慈善

注释
11. **subordinate** [sə'bɒdɪnɪt] *a.* 次要的，从属的，下级的
12. **threshold** ['θreʃəʊld] *n.* 开始，开端，极限
13. **janitor** ['dʒænɪtə] *n.* 看门人
14. **scatter** ['skætə] *v.* 分散，散开，撒开，驱散
15. **expenditure** [ɪks'pendɪtʃə] *n.* 支出，花费

事业，特别是当地的图书馆、世界和平、教育和科研。他的生活常常被视为一个真正的"白手起家"的故事。

被称作"钢铁大王"的安德鲁·卡内基在美国建立了钢铁工业。在这个过程中，他变成了美国最富有的人之一。他的成功，部分来自于他销售产品的能力，部分来自于经济萧条时期的扩充策略。在萧条时期，他的多数对手都在缩减投资。

卡内基认为，个人应该通过努力工作来获得进展，但他也强烈地感到有钱人应该运用他们的财富来为社会谋取福利。他反对施舍救济，更愿意提供教育机会，使别人自立。卡内基经常说"富有着死去的人死得可耻。"

他对社会的较重要的贡献都以他的名字命名。这些贡献包括匹兹堡卡内基学校。这个学校有一个图书馆、一个美术馆和一个国家历史博物馆。他还创立了一所技术学校，这所学校现在是卡内基-梅隆大学的一部分。其他的慈善捐赠有为促进国家间了解的卡内基国际和平基金、为科学研究提供经费的华盛顿卡内基学院以及给各种艺术活动提供活动中心的卡内基音乐厅。

安德鲁·卡内基的慷慨大度几乎影响到每个美国人的生活。由于他超过 500 万美元的捐款，2500 个图书馆得以建立起来，遍布在美国各地的小村镇，形成了我们今天还在享用的公共图书馆系统的核心。

"商业成功之道：和年轻人的谈话"
给匹兹堡加里商学院学生的演讲，1885 年 6 月 23 日
成功之道

安德鲁·卡内基

年轻人应该从头学起，担当最基层的职务，这是件好事。匹兹堡有许多大企业家在创业之初都肩负过重任。他们与扫帚结伴，以清扫办公室度过了企业生涯的最初时光。我注意到现在的办公室都配备了工友，这使我们的年轻人不幸丢掉了这个有益的企业教育的一个内容。不过，如果哪一天早晨清扫工碰巧没来，某位具有未来合伙人气质的青年就会毫不犹豫地试着拿起扫帚。在必要时新来的员工扫扫地也无妨，不会因此而有什么损失。我自己就曾经扫过地。

假如你已经被录用，并且有了一个良好的开端，我对你的建议是：要志存高远。一个年轻人，如果不把自己想象成一家大公司未来的老板或者是合伙人，那我会对他不屑一顾。不论职位有多高，你的内心都不要满足于做一个总管、领班或者总经理。要对自己说：我要迈向顶尖！要做就做你梦想中的国王!

成功的首要条件和最大秘诀就是：把你的精力、思想和资本全都集中在你正从事的事业上。一旦开始从事某种职业，就要下定决心在那一领域闯出一片天地来；做这一行的领导人物，采纳每一点改进之心，采用最优良的设备，对专业知识熟稔于心。

失败的企业是那些分散了资金，因而意味着分散了精力的企业。他们向这方面投资，又向那方面投资；在这里投资，在那里投资，到处都投资。"不要把所有的鸡蛋放在一个篮子里"的说法大错特错。我要对你说："把所有的鸡蛋都放在一个篮子里，然后小心地看好那个篮子。"看看你周围，你会注意到：这么做的人其实很少失败。看管和携带一个篮子并不太难。人们总是试图提很多篮子，所以才打破这个国家的大部分鸡蛋。提 3 个篮子的人，必须把一个顶在头上，而这个篮子很可能掉下来，把他自己绊倒。美国商人的一个缺点就是不够专注。

我把所说的话归纳如下：要志在顶峰；千万不要涉足酒吧，不要沾酒，或者仅在用餐时喝点酒；千万不要投机；签署支付的款项时，千万不要超过盈余的现金储备；取消订货的目的永远在于挽救货主；集中精力，把所有鸡蛋放进一只篮子并照管好那只篮子；支出永远小于收入；最后，不要失去耐心，因为正如爱默生所说："除了你自己以外，没有人能哄骗你离开最后的成功。"

文化点滴

American steel industry

美国钢铁公司的前身是成立于 1864 年的卡内基钢铁公司。卡内基钢铁公司是从 19 世纪中叶美国实行关税壁垒之后才强盛起来的,到 1913 年才将这种对美国钢铁工业的关税保护完全取消。在此之前,大部分美国钢铁工业靠关税壁垒在同英国的自由贸易的竞争中取得盈利。卡内基钢铁公司通过白手起家,建成一个生产钢铁的大型钢铁联合企业,且数十年保持世界最大钢铁厂的地位。

该公司在国内拥有数十家子公司,还拥有 30 多条散装货船负责运输。在国外的子公司和联营公司设在加拿大、英国、意大利、德国、西班牙、法国、日本、印度、尼日利亚、巴西等国。该公司生产的范围很广,包括铁矿砂、煤、白云石和其他有色金属的开采,各种钢管、钢板、钢轨的制造、化工产品、石油钻探和采油设备;在坦克车身、重炮等武器制造方面占有重要地位,还参与建筑、造船等业务。

Carnegie-Mellon University

卡内基-梅隆大学是享誉世界的私立顶级研究型大学,学校小巧,学科门类不多,但在其所设立的几乎所有专业都居于世界领先水平。主校区位于美国宾夕法尼亚州(Pennsylvania)的匹兹堡(Pittsburgh)。该校拥有全美第一所计算机学院和戏剧学院,该校的艺术学院、商学院、工学院以及公共管理学院都在全美名列前茅,其计算机科学专业名列全美第一。

卡内基-梅隆大学还是 NASA 航空航天科研任务的主要承制单位之一,该校的机器人研究所从事过自动驾车、月球探测步行机器人、单轮陀螺式滚动探测机器人的研究。

University of Pittsburgh

匹兹堡大学创建于 1787 年,是美国最古老的高等学府之一。到 19 世纪,匹兹堡城成为美国工业革命的中心,匹兹堡大学也因此得到发展,培养了一大批工业革命时代的发明者和创新者。

匹兹堡大学共有 47 个研究中心,15 个研究所,开设了 30 个系科以及拥有商业学院、牙医学院、教育学院、工程学院、信息科学院、法学院、医学院、公共卫生学院、社会科学院等。

写作特点

本文包含了安德鲁·卡内基给匹兹堡加里商学院学生的演讲。演讲是一种社会活动——为了晓喻听众、打动听众、征服听众。演讲要以事实为主,情理为辅;具体形象为实,概括抽象为虚。内容必须要有现实性,作者提出的问题是听众所关心的问题,评论和论辩要有雄辩的逻辑力量——听众所接受并心悦诚服——社会效果。例如:

Opportunities are not windfalls. Opportunities belong to those who dare to take the challenge. Once we are ready, we can and we will be able to transform this evil specter of globalization into a benevolent genie, which means, we will transform the challenges we face into a great opportunity. "Made in China" will not then be a meaning name for inexpensive shoes and clothing, or merely a label for consumer goods and home appliances, but an icon of unsurpassed excellence.

这一段演讲有着沉甸甸的分量,沉实而厚重,精悍而有力,听起来流畅自然,有淋漓尽致之妙,使其演讲推向了最高峰。

演讲稿的写作必须以易说能讲为前提,其词汇、句式和语气都应具有浓厚的口语色彩,通俗易懂,自然流畅，没有太多的公文程式化。写演讲稿是无声的演讲，是以"写"体现"说"的艺术。在语言体裁的抒情上以适合现场表达为尺度。勿追求词藻的华丽，否则会弄巧成拙，很难引起听众的共鸣。例如：

Nowadays, we often see Chinese youngsters walking down the street with dyed blonde hair, wearing a New York Yankees sweater, trying to be cool like those American kids. With more and more cultural exchanges and technological developments, our generation has become more westernized. Someone has described us as a generation coming of age with personal computers, digital videos, and general material prosperity.

演讲者通过通俗易懂的实例及朴实、风趣的语言，把抽象的概念具体化，使其演讲更具说服力和亲和力。

品味鉴赏

在美国，与"汽车大王"福特、"石油大王"洛克菲勒等大财阀的名字列在一起的，还有一个"钢铁大王"，他就是安德鲁·卡内基。他在美国工业史上写下了永难磨灭的一页；他征服钢铁世界，成为美国最大钢铁制造商，衣锦还乡，跃居世界首富；而在功成名就后，放弃了所有的一切，追求另一种自由、无拘束的生活，并为慈善事业作出了巨大的贡献。纽约著名的卡内基音乐厅是他捐资修建的，匹兹堡的卡内基大学是他建立的，还有遍布在世界各地的卡内基图书馆。这就是卡内基，财富对于他而言不是第一位的，享受人生、为社会作出贡献才是他生命的真谛。他将几乎全部的财富捐献给社会。他生前捐赠款额之巨大，足以与死后设立诺贝尔奖的瑞典科学家、实业家诺贝尔相媲美，由此成为美国人心目中的英雄和个人奋斗的楷模。

美文感悟

Chapter 6

灵魂思索

走在由钢筋水泥筑成的城市中，形色匆匆的路人，喧嚣的夜晚，寂寞的自己。有没有那么一刻想要静静地坐在黑夜中，和自己的灵魂对话？你知道自己是谁吗？你想过要成为谁吗？回首往事的时候，心内是否会千回百转？也曾有过飞蛾扑火般的勇气去实现自己的梦想……

Expressing One's Individuality
个性的表现

作者简介：

安诺德·贝奈特（Arnold Bennet，1867—1933），英国著名小说家、批评家和散文家。写过许多以家乡五座工业城镇即"五镇"为背景的小说，主要作品有《五镇的安娜》《老妇人的故事》《克莱汉格》等。

本篇出自作者的《朋友与幸福》（*Friend and Happiness*），属于他为青年们所写的"pocket philosophy"（"袖珍哲学"）之一。

A most curious and useful thing to realize is that one never knows the impression one is creating on other people. One may often guess pretty accurately whether it is good, bad, or indifferent—some people **render**[1] it unnecessary for one to guess, they practically inform others—but that is not what I mean. I mean much more than that. I mean that one has no mental picture corresponding to the mental picture which one's personality leaves in the minds of one's friends. Has it ever struck you that there is a mysterious individual going around, walking the streets, calling at houses for tea, chatting, laughing, grumbling, arguing, and that all your friends know him and have long since added him up and come to a definite conclusion about him without saying more than a chance, cautious word to you; and that person is you? Supposing that you came into a drawing-room where you were having tea, do you think you would recognize yourself

注释 **1. render** ['rendə] *vt.* 致使；提出

as an individuality? I think not. You would be apt to say to yourself as guests do when disturbed in drawing-rooms by other guests: Who's this chap? Seems rather queer. I hope he won't be a bore. And your first telling would be slightly **hostile**[2]. Why, even when you meet yourself in an unsuspected mirror in the very clothes that you have put on that very day and that you know by heart, you are almost always shocked by the realization that you are you. And now and then, when you have gone to the glass  to arrange your hair in the full **sobriety**[3] of early morning, have you not looked on an absolute stranger, and has not that stranger **piqued**[4] your curiosity? And if it is thus with precise external details of form, color, and movement, what may it not be with the vague complex effect of the mental and moral individuality?

A man honestly tries to make a good impression. What is the result? The result merely is that his friends, in the privacy of their minds, set him down as a man who tries to make a good impression. If much depends on the result of a single interview, or a couple of interviews, a man may conceivably force another to accept an impression of himself which he would like to convey. But if the receiver of the impression is to have time at his disposal, then the giver of the impression may just as well sit down and put his hands in his pockets, for nothing that he can do will modify or influence in any way the impression that he will ultimately give. The real impression is, in the end, given unconsciously, not consciously; and further, it is received unconsciously, not consciously. It depends partly on both persons. And it is **immutably**[5] fixed beforehand. There can be no final deception. Take the extreme case, that of the mother and her son. One hears that the son **hoodwinks**[6] his mother. Not he! If he is cruel, neglectful, **overbearing**[7], she is perfectly aware of it. He does not deceive her, and she does not deceive herself. I have often thought: If a son could look into a mother's heart, what an eye-opener he would have! "What!" he would cry. "This cold, impartial judgment, this keen vision for my faults, this **implacable**[8] memory of little slights, and injustices, and **callousnesses**[9] committed long ago, in the breast of my mother!" Yes, my friend, in the breast of your mother. The only difference between your mother and another person is that she takes you as you are, and loves you for what you are. She isn't blind: do not imagine it.

The marvel is, not that people are such bad judges of character, but that they are such good judges, especially of what I may call fundamental character. The wiliest person cannot for ever conceal his fundamental character from the simplest. And people are very **stern**[10] judges, too. Think of your best friends—are you oblivious of their defects? On the contrary, you are perhaps too conscious of them. When you summon them before your mind's eye, it is no ideal creation what you see. When you meet them and talk to them you are constantly making reservations in

注释
2. **hostile** ['hɒstaɪl] *adj.* 有敌意的
3. **sobriety** [sə'braɪətɪ] *n.* 清醒
4. **pique** [piːk] *vt.* 刺激, 激怒
5. **immutably** [ɪ'mjuːtəblɪ] *adv.* 不变地, 永恒地
6. **hoodwink** ['hʊdwɪŋk] *vt.* 欺骗, 蒙蔽
7. **overbearing** [əʊvə'beərɪŋ] *adj.* 傲慢的, 专横的
8. **implacable** [ɪm'plækəbl] *adj.* 难以满足的, 难平息的
9. **callousnesses** ['kæləsnɪs] *n.* 冷淡, 无情
10. **stern** [stɜːn] *adj.* 严厉的, 苛刻的

their disfavor—unless, of course, you happen to be a schoolgirl **gushing**[11] over like a fountain with enthusiasm. It is well, when one is judging a friend, to remember that he is judging you with the same godlike and superior impartiality. It is well to grasp the fact that you are going through life under the **scrutiny**[12] of a band of acquaintances who are subject to very few illusions about you, whose views of you are, indeed, apt to be harsh, even cruel. Above all it is advisable to comprehend thoroughly that the things in your individuality which annoy your friends most are the things of which you are completely unconscious. It is not until years have passed that one begins to be able to form a dim idea of what one has looked like to one's friends. At forty one goes back ten years, and one says sadly, but with a certain amusement: "I must have been pretty **blatant**[13] then. I can see how I must have **exasperated**[14] them. And yet I hadn't the faintest notion of it at the time. My intentions were of the best. Only I didn't know enough." And one recollects some particularly crude action, and kicks one's self...Yes, that is all very well; and the enlightenment which has come with increasing age is exceedingly satisfactory; but you are forty now. What shall you be saying of yourself at fifty? Such reflections foster humility, and they foster also a reluctance, which it is impossible to praise too highly, to **tread**[15] on other people's toes.

A moment ago I used the phrase "fundamental character". It is a **reminiscence**[16] of Stevenson's phrase "fundamental decency". And it is the final test by which one judges one's friends. "After all, he's a decent fellow." We must be able to use that formula concerning our friends. Kindliness of heart is not the greatest of human qualities—and its general effect on the progress of the world is not entirely **beneficent**[17]—but it is the greatest of human qualities in friendship. It is the least dispensable quality. We come back to it with relief from more brilliant qualities. And it has the great advantage of always going with a broad mind. Narrow-minded people are never kind-hearted. You may be inclined to dispute this statement: please think it over; I am inclined to uphold it.

注释

11. gush [gʌʃ] v. 涌出
12. scrutiny ['skruːtɪnɪ] n. 详细审查
13. blatant ['bleɪtənt] adj. 厚颜的，粗鲁的
14. exasperate [ɪɡ'zæspəreɪt] vt. 激怒
15. tread [tred] vt. 践踏
16. reminiscence [remɪ'nɪsns] n. 回想，记忆
17. beneficent [bɪ'nefɪsnt] adj. 慈善的；善行的

原文翻译

　　那么一件让人很奇怪但细想一下又很有好处的事就是：一个人永远不知道自己留给别人的印象是什么。那印象是好，是坏，还是不好不坏，自己通常能够相当准确地猜出来。有些人甚至连猜都不用你猜，他们会直接告诉你。但是我要说的可不是这个，我要说的远远不止这个。我想说的是：一个人头脑中对他自己的印象和他本人在他朋友们头脑中所留下的印象，往往不一致。你曾经想到过吗，世上有那么一个神秘兮兮的人，到处跑来跑去，出街入巷，登门访友，说说笑笑，发发牢骚，争论斗嘴，你的所有朋友都认识他，对他知根知底，早有定论，但平时却只是极其偶然而谨慎地提上一句半句。而你知道吗，那个人正是你！比如说，你走进一个客厅里去喝茶，你敢说你能认出你自己这个人吗？我说你认不出。你很可能会像其他客人那样，当别的客人引起你的注意时，心里会暗想："这家伙是谁？样子怪怪的，但愿他不是个让人厌烦的人。"你这第一反应便是带有敌意的。甚至当你突然在一面非常真实的镜子前看见了你自己，穿着你记得清清楚楚的当天穿上的那身衣服，你还是会因为认出了自己而总是吓一大跳。有时，当你到镜子面前整理一下头发时，尽管是在大清早最清醒的时刻，你不是也仿佛看见了一个完全陌生的人吗？而且这个镜子里的陌生人难道不会激起你的好奇心吗？如果连形式、颜色、动作这类外部的具体细节尚且如此，那么说到心智与道德方面种种飘忽不定的复杂效果又会怎样呢？

　　一个人常会诚心诚意地试图给别人留下个好印象。但结果又怎样呢？结果是，他的朋友们在内心里把他看作一个存心去制造良好印象的人。如果一切只靠一面之缘或仅仅几次会面，一个人完全可以使得他人接受他本人所希望造成的某种印象。但是，如果印象的接受者有充裕的自由时间，那么印象的给予者就只好束手无策地静坐一旁了，因为不管他做什么，也丝毫无法影响、无法改变他最终给别人留下的印象。结论是，真实的印象都是在无意之中而不是有意策划造成的，而且，它也是在无意之间而不是有意地被接受的。印象的形成与双方都有关，而且事先就已确定的，谁也无法蒙混到底。举一个极端的例子，以母子关系为例吧。我们常听说儿子哄骗他的妈妈。但不是他！如果儿子粗暴残忍、专横霸道，母亲是一清二楚的。儿子骗不了她，她也骗不了她自己。我常想：做儿子的如果能够看穿母亲内心的话，他会多么清楚地认识到他自己！"天啊！"他会这么惊叫起来，"这么冷酷无情的判断，对我的缺点洞察入微，很久以前犯下的细小疏忽、失误、冷淡，在我妈妈的心里全都记着呢！"是的，我的朋友，在你母亲的心里全都记着呢。你母亲同别人的唯一不同在于，她能按你本来的面目来看待你，而且尽管你是这样的，她依然爱你。她不是视而不见：可别心存幻想。

　　神奇的是，并不是人们对性格拙于判断，而恰恰相反，人们对性格，尤其是对我所称之为的"基本性格"都非常擅于判断。最狡黠的人也无法在最单纯的人面前长期掩藏他的基本性格。另外，人们评判起来又是相当严格。想想你最好的朋友，你忘记他们的缺点了吗？恰恰相反，你恐怕是太清楚了。当你扪心眼里审视他们的时候，你所看到的决不是一个理想的完人。但当你和他们见面交谈时，你大概总是会不断地把你对他们的负面看法保留起来，当然，除非你碰巧是个无知无畏的小女生，说起话来如江河之水滔滔不绝。当我们评断一个朋友时，最好不要忘记，他也未尝不正以同样神灵般的公正态度在评断着你。你最好认识到这样一个事实：你的一生都是处在一群亲朋故旧的审视之下的，他们对你注定没抱什么幻想，他们对你的看法往往严苛甚至严酷。尤其重要的，你应当彻底理解到，你性格中最容易使你朋友恼怒的东西往往正是你自己完全不曾意识到的东西。常常多少年已经过去了，一个人才会对他曾给自己的朋友们留下的印象有了点模糊认识。一个人40岁的时候回顾10年前的事情，他会悲伤地但又觉得好玩似地说："我那时候一定很莽撞。我一定把他们都惹急了。可我当时是一点也没觉察出来。我也是一番好意呀！只是我知道得太少了。"他回想起一些特别粗鲁的行为，恨不得一脚把自己踢开……当然，这也是件好事；这种随着年龄增长而得来的醒悟实在令人非常快慰；可你已经是40岁的人了。试想，到了50岁时你对自己又会怎么看？这样的反思常会使人变得谦虚，同时也会产生一种谨慎的心态，使人不愿去招惹别人，而这一点正是极为难得的修为。

　　刚才我使用了"基本性格"这个词。这是从史蒂文森的话"基本正派"想起来的。它是我们批判朋友时的最终标准。"毕竟他还是个正派的家伙。"我们必须学会用这个公式来看待我们的朋友。心地善良不一定是人类最伟大的品质，而且对人类发展所起的作用也不完全都是有益的，但是在友谊方面，它却是人类最伟大的品质，是最必不可少的品质。世上不乏更为辉煌的品质，但是我们还是要回到它那里去寻找慰藉。此外，心地善良还有一个与宽广的胸襟相伴的巨大优点。心胸狭窄的人总是缺乏善心。你也许想和我争论一下这种说法：那就请先仔细考虑一下吧，我是倾向于支持这种说法的。

文化点滴

Stevenson

罗伯特·路易斯·史蒂文森（1850—1894），苏格兰小说家、诗人和随笔作家，最著名的小说有《金银岛》（1883）《化身博士》（1886）和《诱拐》（1886）。

写作特点

本文在最后一段引用了史蒂文森的词汇"fundamental decency"（基本正派），即判断朋友的最终标准，对作者说理表情达意都很有帮助，为自己的观点和看法提供有力的论据，增强说服力。

品味鉴赏

朋友相处是一种相互认可、相互仰慕、相互欣赏、相互感知的过程。对方的优点、长处、亮点、美感，都会映在你脑海，尽收眼底。朋友之间贵在互相见谅，"善人者，人亦善之"。对于朋友的优点，不能忌而不学；对朋友的缺点，不能视而不见；对朋友的忠告，不能听而不闻；就是一些过激的言语，或者偏颇的看法，只要是对自己的善言，也不能怒而反讥。一个人，要想多得到真挚的友谊，除了对朋友真诚相待外，还要能够容忍对方的缺点，要学会自己怎样做人，莫辜负朋友的知己之情。

美文感悟

What You See Is the Real You
你所见到的就是真正的你

作者简介：

威拉德·盖林（Willard Gaylin，1925—），美国著名社会学与伦理学家，纽约里兹丁斯社会伦理暨生命科学学院院长，著有 *In the Service of Their Country*（《为国尽忠》）等著作。本文表达了作者对人的内在和外在的独特看法。

It was, I believe, the distinguished Nebraska financier Father J. Flanagan who **professed**[1] to having "never met a bad boy". Having, myself, met a remarkable number of bad boys, it might seem that either our experiences were drastically different or we were using the word "bad" differently. I suspect neither is true, but rather that the Father was appraising the "inner man", while I, in fact, do not acknowledge the existence of inner people.

Since we psychoanalysts have **unwittingly**[2] contributed to this confusion, let one, at least, attempt a small **rectifying**[3] effort. Psychoanalytic data—which should be viewed as supplementary information—is, unfortunately, often viewed as alternative (and superior)

注释
1. **profess** [prəˈfes] *vt.* 公开声称
2. **unwittingly** [ʌnˈwɪtɪŋli] *adv.* 不知情地，无意地
3. **rectify** [ˈrektɪfaɪ] *vt.* 矫正，调整

explanation. This has led to the **prevalent**[4] tendency to think of the "inner" man as the real man and the outer man as an illusion or pretender.

While psychoanalysis supplies us with an incredibly useful tool for explaining the motives and purposes underlying human behavior, most of this has little bearing on the moral nature of that behavior.

Like **roentgenology**[5], psychoanalysis is a fascinating, but relatively new, means of illuminating the person. But few of us are prepared to substitute an X-ray of Grandfather's head for the portrait that hangs in the parlor. The inside of the man represents another view, not a truer one. A man may not always be what he appears to be, but what he appears to be is always a significant part of what he is. A man is the sum total of all his behavior. To **probe**[6] for unconscious determinants of behavior and then define him in their terms exclusively, ignoring his **overt**[7] behavior altogether, is a greater **distortion**[8] than ignoring the unconscious completely.

Kurt Vonnegut has said, "You are what you pretend to be", which is simply another way of saying, you are what we (all of us) perceive you to be, not what you think you are.

Consider for a moment the case of the ninety-year-old man on his deathbed (surely the Talmud must deal with this?) joyous and relieved over the success of his deception. For ninety years he has shielded his evil nature from public observation. For ninety years he has affected courtesy, kindness, and generosity—suppressing all the malice he knew was within him while he calculatedly and artificially substituted grace and charity. All his life he had been fooling the world into believing he was a good man. This evil man will, I predict, be welcomed into the Kingdom of Heaven.

Similarly, I will not be told that the young man who earns his pocket money by mugging old ladies is "really" a good boy. Even my generous and expansive definition of goodness will not accommodate that particular form of self-advancement.

It does not count that beneath the rough exterior he has a heart—or, for that matter, an entire **innards**[9]—of purest gold, locked away from human perception. You are for the most part what you seem to be, not what you would wish to be, nor, indeed, what you believe yourself to be.

Spare me, therefore, your good intentions, your inner sensitivities, your **unarticulated**[10] and unexpressed love. And spare me also those tedious psychohistories which—by exposing the goodness inside the bad man, and the evil in the good—invariably establish a vulgar and **perverse**[11] **egalitarianism**[12], as if the arrangement of what is outside and what inside makes no moral difference.

注释

4. **prevalent** ['prevələnt] *adj.* 普遍的，流行的
5. **roentgenology** [ˌrɒntɡəˈnɒlədʒɪ] *n.* X光线学
6. **probe** [prəʊb] *vt.* 探查；探寻；深挖
7. **overt** [əʊˈvɜːt] *adj.* 公开的，明显的；外在的
8. **distortion** [dɪˈstɔːʃən] *n.* 扭曲，曲解
9. **innards** [ˈɪnədz] *n.* 内脏
10. **unarticulated** [ˌʌnɑːˈtɪkjulɪtɪd] *adj.* 无法言传的
11. **perverse** [pəˈvɜːs] *adj.* 反常的，乖张的
12. **egalitarianism** [ɪˌɡælɪˈteərɪənɪzəm] *n.* 平等主义

Chapter 6 灵魂思索

Saint Francis may, in his unconscious, indeed have been compensating for, and denying, destructive, unconscious Oedipal impulses identical to those which Attila projected and acted on. But the similarity of the unconscious **constellations**[13] in the two men matters precious little, if it does not distinguish between them.

I do not care to learn that Hitler's heart was in the right place. A knowledge of the unconscious life of the man may be an adjunct to understanding his behavior. It is not substitute for his behavior in describing him.

The inner man is fantasy. If it helps you to identify with one, by all means, do so; preserve it, cherish it, embrace it, but do not present it to others for evaluation or consideration, for excuse or **exculpation**[14], or, for that matter, for punishment or disapproval.

Like any fantasy, it serves your purposes alone. It has no standing in the real world which we share with each other. Those character **traits**[15], those attitudes, that behavior—that strange and alien stuff sticking out all over you—that's the real you!

原文翻译

如果我没记错，是内布拉斯加州有名的财政家J.弗拉耐根神甫曾公开表示过他"从没有遇到过坏孩子"。但我自己却曾遇到过相当多的坏孩子。可能是我们两人的经历截然不同吧，或者是我们对"坏"这个字的用法各不相同。不过，我怀疑这两种推测都不是真正的原因，而真正的原因只不过是神甫所评价的是"内在的人"，而我自己则实际上并不承认有所谓"内在的人"存在。

既然我们的心理分析学家们已于无意中引起了这种认识混乱，那么至少得让一个人出来做点纠正的努力。心理分析数据原本只应被视为某种补充性的信息，不幸的是，现在它却常常被视作另一种（和更高级的）解释。这便使人们都倾向于认为"内在的"人才是真正的人，而外在的人只不过是一种假象或假冒者。

尽管心理分析在解释人的行为背后的种种动机和目的方面为我们提供了令人难以置信的有力手段，但其中多数说法却与行为的道德性很少相关。

正像X光线学那样，心理分析在对人的阐释上的确是一种十分诱人且相对较新的手段。但是，我们却很少有人愿意将客厅里挂着的祖父肖像换成一张他老人家的头颅的X光照片。一个人的内在呈现出他的另一副面貌，但那未必是更真实的。一个人不一定总是他所表现的那样，但他所表现的却总是他真正自身的一个重要部分。一个人是他全部行为的总和。只探索人的行为的潜意识的决定因素，然后再用这部分内容来定义这个人，而完全忽略他的外部行为，这一做法要比那种完全忽略潜意识部分的做法荒谬得多。

库尔特·冯内古特曾说过："你就是你假装成的你。"这实际上是说，你就是我们（我们所有人）所见到的你，而不是你自己认为的那个你。

请你用一点时间思考一下这样一个情形：一个九旬老人在临终前的病榻上（当然，犹太教法典里肯定记叙过这类情形？）对于他自己的欺骗成功深感欢喜欣慰。90年来他一直将他的恶毒本性掩藏起来，谁也不曾察觉；90年来他一直假装得彬彬有礼，善良慷慨，一方面将他明知自己心里存在的恶意压制下去，一方面则费尽心机地装出一副优雅仁慈的面孔。他的一生都在欺骗着世人，使全世界的人都相信他是个好人。而这个

注释
13. constellation [ˌkɒnstəˈleɪʃn] n. [心理学]群集；情意丛　　15. trait [treɪt] n. 特点
14. exculpation [ˌekskʌlˈpeɪʃn] n. 开脱，辩解

"恶"人，我敢断言，天国那里也一定会非常欢迎他。

同样，我无法相信，一个平日靠抢劫老妇来挣取零用钱的年轻人会是个"真正的"好青年。即使我对"好"的定义再宽容再扩展，也无法包容这种特殊形式的自我促进。

说一个人粗野的外表下面有一颗纯金般的心或者完整的内在，只不过被锁了起来，别人没法看到，这种话毫无意义。多数情况下你就是你表现出来的那样，并不是你所希望的那样，更不是你自以为的那样。

因此，请你不要给我你的那些善良的好意，你的内在的感情，你的那不曾明示的和不曾表达出来的爱；也请你不要对我进行那冗长乏味的心理分析，那些分析，通过揭露恶人内在之善与善人内在之恶的做法，只会建立一种庸俗的、颠倒是非的无差别论，就好像外部与内部的安排实质上并没有什么不同一样。

圣弗朗西斯也很有可能在他的潜意识里，一直在补偿和否认那带破坏性的无意识的俄狄浦斯式的冲动，这种冲动与阿提拉曾真正设计并实行了的那种冲动是完全相同的。但是，即便在无意识领域的相似性模糊了他们两人的界限，这种相似也没有任何重要性可言。

我对希特勒的那颗心是否长在正确位置并不感兴趣。虽然了解一下他的潜意识生活或许会有助于对他的行为的认识，但在描述此人时决不能用他的潜意识生活替换他的行为。

内在的人只是一种幻觉。如果这种认识能帮助你辨别人，那当然你请便；你尽可以保存它，珍视它，信奉它，只是请不要把它提到他人面前作为评价或考虑、原谅或开脱的根据，或者仅根据这一点来决定惩处。

正像任何其他幻觉那样，这种认识只对满足你个人的目的有用。但在这个你与我共同分享的真实世界中，它却是没有地位的。那些性格特点，那些举止态度，那种行为——那些从你全身冒出的奇特和异样的东西——那才是真正的你！

文化点滴

Father J. Flanagan

美国"青少年城"（Boys Town）的创建人爱德华·约瑟夫·弗拉纳根。该"城"建于1917年，是为无家可归的少年或弃儿所建立的一种救济性慈善机构。

Kurt Vonnegut

库尔特·冯内古特，生于1922年，美国作家，作品在现代生活的暴力和变异中显示同情和幽默。他的小说包括《猫的摇篮》(*Cat's Cradle*, 1963) 和《五号屠宰场》(*Slaughterhouse Five*, 1969)。

Talmud

犹太教法典，古代拉比著作的合集，包括《密西拿》和《革马拉》，构成了正统犹太教中宗教权威的基础。

Saint Francis

圣弗朗西斯，意大利高僧。公元1210年创立弗兰西斯科教派，为中世纪基督教著名教派之一。

Attila

阿提拉（406—453），匈奴帝国国王（433—453），曾侵入罗马帝国并据有欧洲中部20余年，被认为是野蛮入侵者。

写作特点

本文在描述一生都在欺骗着世人的九旬老人和一个平日靠抢劫老妇来挣取零用钱的年轻人的不同人生时用到了对比论证。对比论证是把两种事物加以对照、比较后,推导出它们之间的差异点,使结论映衬而出的论证方法。议论文中常常运用对比论证的方法,把两种矛盾或对立的事物加以对照比较,从正反两方面进行说理,从而揭示事物的本质,使所阐述的事理更加深刻,更有说服力。

品味鉴赏

本文从心理学的本我、自我和超我的角度对人的内在和外在进行了描述。在心理动力论中,本我、自我和超我是由精神分析学家弗洛伊德之结构理论所提出的精神的三大部分。本我(id)代表思绪的原始程序——人最为原始的、属满足本能冲动的欲望,如饥饿、生气、性欲等。本我只遵循一个原则——享乐原则(pleasure principle),意为追求个体的生物性需求,如食物的饱足与性欲的满足,以及避免痛苦。自我(ego)是人格的心理组成部分。这里,现实原则暂时中止了快乐原则。由此,个体学会区分心灵中的思想与围绕着个体的外在世界的思想。自我在自身和其环境中进行调节。弗洛伊德认为自我是人格的执行者。超我(super-ego)是人格结构中的管制者,由完美原则支配,属于人格结构中的道德部分。在弗洛伊德的学说中,超我是父亲形象与文化规范的符号内化,由于对客体的冲突,超我倾向于站在"本我"的原始渴望的反对立场,而对"自我"带有侵略性。超我以道德心的形式运作,维持个体的道德感、回避禁忌。

美文感悟

Have You Seen the Tree?
你见过那棵树吗？

作者简介：

罗伯特・凯弗（Robert Kyff），作家，散文家。

My neighbor Mrs. Gargan first told me about it. "Have you seen that tree?" she asked as I was sitting in the back yard enjoying the October twilight.

"The one down at the corner," she explained. "It's a beautiful tree—all kinds of colors. Cars are stopping to look. You ought to see it."

I told her I would, but I soon forgot about the tree. Three days later, I was jogging down the street, my mind swimming with petty worries, when a **splash**[1] of bright orange caught my eye. For an instant, I thought someone's house had caught fire. Then I remember the tree.

As I approached it, I slowed to a walk. There was nothing remarkable about the shape of the tree, a medium-sized maple. But Mrs. Gargan had been right about its colors. Like the messy whirl of an artist's palette, the tree blazed a bright crimson on its lower branches, burned with vivid

---

注释　1. **splash** [splæʃ] *n.* 溅，飞溅

yellows and oranges in its center, and **simmered**² to deep burgundy at its top. Through these fiery colors **cascaded**³ thin **rivulets**⁴ of pale-green leaves and blotches of deep-green leaves, as yet untouched by autumn.

Edging closer—like a pilgrim approaching a shrine—I noticed several bare branches near the top, their black twigs scratching the air like claws. The leaves they had shed lay like a scarlet carpet around the trunk.

With its varied nations of color, this tree seemed to become a globe, embracing its broad branches all seasons and continents: the spring and summer of the Southern Hemisphere in the light and dark greens, the autumn and winter of the Northern in the blazing yellows and bare branches. The whole planet seemed **poised**⁵ on the pivot of this pastiche.

As I marveled at this all-encompassing beauty, I thought of Ralph Waldo Emerson's comments about the stars. If the constellations appeared only once in a thousand years, he observed in *Nature*, imaging what an exciting event it would be. But because they're up there every night, we barely give them a look.

I felt the same way about the tree. Because its majesty will last only a week, it should be especially precious to us. And I had almost missed it.

Once when Emily Dickenson's father noticed a brilliant display of northern lights in the sky over Massachusetts, he tolled a church bell to alert townspeople. That's what I felt like doing about the tree. I wanted to become a Paul Revere of autumn, awakening the countryside to its wonder.

I don't have a church bell or a horse, but as I walked home, I did ask each neighbor I passed the same simple but **momentous**⁶ question Mrs. Gargan had asked me: "Have you seen the tree?"

原文翻译

关于那棵树，最初是我的邻居嘉根太太告诉我的。那天，我坐在后院欣赏着10月的景色，嘉根太太过来问我："你见过那棵树吗？"

她接着说："就是那边下去拐角的一棵，五颜六色的，漂亮极了，好多车路过都停下来看，你该去看看才是。"

我对她说我会去看的，可转眼我就把这事全忘了。3天后，我在街上跑步，脑子里牵挂着几件扰人的小事，昏昏沉沉的。忽然，一片耀眼的橘红色跃入眼帘，一时间，我还以为是谁家的房子着火了呢，但我马上就想到了嘉根太太说的那棵树。

我朝着那棵树走去时，不由得渐渐放慢了脚步。这棵树的形状并没有什么特别之处，只是一棵不大不小的枫树。但嘉根太太说得不错，它的颜色确实奇特。整棵树就像画家手中五彩斑斓的调色板，树底部的枝丫

注释
2. **simmer** ['sɪmə] *vt.* 炖
3. **cascade** [kæs'keɪd] *vi.* 像瀑布般倾泻下来
4. **rivulet** ['rɪvjulɪt] *n.* 小河，小溪
5. **poise** [pɔɪz] *vt.* 使悬着，保持……姿势
6. **momentous** [məʊ'mentəs] *adj.* 重大的，重要

是鲜艳的梅红色，树的中部则燃烧着明快的鹅黄色和橘红色，再往上，到了树梢，枝条又缓缓地过渡成了绛红色。在这火样的色彩中，流淌着浅绿的叶子汇成的小溪，深绿的叶子则斑驳点缀其间，竟似至今未受过一点秋天的侵袭。

我慢慢走近这棵枫树，就像虔诚的朝圣者缓缓步向神殿。我发现靠近树梢的地方有几根光秃秃的枝丫，上面黑乎乎的小枝像鹰爪一般伸向天空。这些枯枝上落下的叶子一片猩红，像地毯似的铺在树干周围。

这颗枫树集各国颜色之大成，它展开宽大的枝丫，历数四季轮回，容纳着五湖四海，俨然是一个地球。深浅错落的绿叶，昭示着南半球的春夏，灿黄的花叶和光秃秃的枝丫勾勒出北半球的秋冬。整个星球似乎就是围绕这一时空的交集点和谐运转。

我不禁为这棵树无所不包的美惊叹不已。这时，我想起了著名的作家拉尔夫·沃尔多·爱默生有关星星的评论。他在《自然》一书中写道：倘若星座一千年才出现一次，那么，星座的出现该是一桩多么激动人心的事情；可正因为星座每夜都挂在天上，人们才很少去看上一眼。

对于眼前这棵树，我也有同感。这棵树此时的华美只能维持一个星期，所以它对于我们相当珍贵。可我竟差一点错过了。

有一次，当著名诗人艾米莉·迪金森的父亲偶然看见马萨诸塞州上空一道炫目的北极光时，他立刻跑到教堂鸣钟以告知所有市民。现在，对这棵树，我也产生了这种传诵它的冲动。我愿成为秋天忠诚的信使，让田园乡村每一个角落的人们都了解它的奇妙。

可我没有教堂的大钟，也没有快马，但我在回家路上每遇见一位邻居，就会去问他那个嘉根太太曾问过我的极其简单又极其重要的问题："你见过那棵树吗？"

文化点滴

Emily Dickenson

埃米莉·狄更生（1830—1886），美国诗人。诗风凝练，比喻尖新，常置格律以及语法于不顾。生前只发表过10首诗，默默无闻，死后近70年后开始得到文学界的认真关注，被现代派诗人追认为先驱。与同时代的惠特曼一同被奉为美国最伟大的诗人，后世对她的诗艺、恋爱生活、性取向多有揣测。

写作特点

本文在末尾设置了一个悬念：可我没有教堂的大钟，也没有快马，但我在回家路上每遇见一位邻居，就会去问他那个嘉根太太曾问过我的极其简单又极其重要的问题："你见过那棵树吗？" 悬念，是通过对剧情做悬而未决和结局难料的安排，以引起观众急欲知其结果的迫切期待心理的一种编剧技巧。

品味鉴赏

　　罗曼·罗兰曾经说过，生活中并不缺少美，而是缺少发现美的眼睛。的确，生活中美好的事物有很多，阳光、青草、鲜花，也有很多美好的情感，只是我们被现实的残酷和烦琐蒙蔽，心灵不得舒展，视线不够长远，以致对身边的美好熟视无睹。因此，生活需要我们有发现美的眼睛。欣赏美，是一件简单的事，但如果你对内在美丽的世界一无所知的话，你又如何看得见外在世界的美丽？抛开偏见和固执，抛开功名利禄，抛开心中的杂质，你将会感受到一种前所未有的美，因为美就藏在你的心中。找到心中的美，你将可以在每一个地方都找到美。

美文感悟

On Doors
论门

作者简介：

克里斯托弗·达灵顿·莫利（Christopher Darlington Morle，1890—1957），美国作家，是《星期六评论》（Saturday Review）的创办人和编辑。他是一个多产作家，许多作品是非常流行的小说，包括《车轮上的帕尔纳萨斯》（Parnassus on Wheels，1917）。他的小说《基蒂·福伊尔》（1939）是本畅销小说，根据小说拍成的电影曾获奥斯卡奖。

莫利的散文既轻松又刚健，文字高雅却又寓严肃于风趣之中。

The opening and closing of doors are the most significant actions of man's life. What a mystery lies in doors!

No man knows what awaits him when he opens a door, even the most familiar room, where the clock ticks and the hearth glows red at dusk, may **harbour**[1] surprises. The plumber may actually have called (while you were out) and fixed that leaking faucet. The cook may have had a **fit**[2] of the vapours and demanded her passports. The wise man opens his front door with humility and a spirit of acceptance.

Which one of us has not sat in some anteroom and watched the **inscrutable**[3] panels of a door that was full of meaning? Perhaps you were waiting to apply for a job; perhaps you had some "deal" you were ambitious to put over. You watched the confidential stenographer flit in and out, carelessly

---

注释
1. **harbour** ['hɑːbə] vt. 窝藏；怀有
2. **fit** [fɪt] n. 发作
3. **inscrutable** [ɪnˈskruːtəbl] adj. 高深莫测的；神秘的

turning that mystic portal which, to you, revolved on hinges of fate. And then the young woman said, "Mr. Cranberry will see you now." As you grasped the knob the thought flashed, "When I open this door again, what will have happened?"

There are many kinds of doors. Revolving doors for hotels, shops, and public buildings. These are typical of the brisk, **bustling**[4] ways of modern life. Can you imagine John Milton or William Penn skipping through a revolving door? Then there are the curious little slatteddoors that still swing outside denatured bar-rooms and extend only from shoulder to knee. There are trapdoors, sliding doors, double doors, stage doors, prison doors, glass doors. But the symbol and mystery of a door resides in its quality of **concealment**[5]. A glass door is not a door at all, but a window. The meaning of a door is to hide what lies inside; to keep the heart in suspense.

Also, there are many ways of opening doors. There is the cheery push of elbow with which the waiter **shoves**[6] open the kitchen door when he bears in your tray of supper. There is the suspicious and **tentative**[7] withdrawal of a door before the unhappy book agent or peddler. There is the **genteel**[8] and carefully modulated recession with which footmen swing wide the oaken barriers of the great. There is the sympathetic and awful silence of the dentist's maid who opens the door into the operating room, and, without speaking, implies that the doctor is ready for you. There is the brisk **cataclysmic**[9] opening of a door when the nurse comes in, very early in the morning—"It's a boy!"

Doors are the symbol of privacy, of **retreat**[10], of the mind's escape into blissful quietude or sad secret struggle. A room without doors is not a room, but a hallway. No matter where he is, a man can make himself at home behind a closed door. The mind works best behind closed doors. Men are not horses to be herded together. Dogs know the meaning and **anguish**[11] of doors. Have you ever noticed a puppy yearning at a shut portal? It is a symbol of human life.

The opening of doors is a mystic act: it has in it some flavour of the unknown, some sense of moving into a new moment, a new pattern of the human **rigmarole**[12]. It includes the highest glimpses of mortal gladness: reunions, reconciliations, the bliss of lovers long parted. Even in sadness, the opening of a door may bring relief: it changes and redistributes human forces. But the closing of doors is far more terrible. It is a confession of finality. Every door closed brings something to an end. And there are degrees of sadness in the closing of doors. A door slammedis a confession of weakness. A door gently shut is often the most tragic gesture in life. Every one knows the seizure of anguish that comes just after the closing of a door, when the loved one is still near, within sound of voice, and yet already far away.

The opening and closing of doors is a part of the stern fluency of life. Life will not stay still and let us alone. We are continually opening doors with hope, closing them with despair. Life lasts not much longer than a pipe of tobacco, and destiny knocks us out like the ashes.

注释

4. **bustling** ['bʌslɪŋ] *adj.* 忙乱的
5. **concealment** [kən'siːlmənt] *n.* 隐蔽
6. **shove** [ʃʌv] *vt.* 推
7. **tentative** ['tentətɪv] *adj.* 试探性的，尝试的
8. **genteel** [dʒen'tiːl] *adj.* 有教养的，文雅的
9. **cataclysmic** [kætə'klɪzmɪk] *adj.* 大变动的，剧烈的
10. **retreat** [rɪ'triːt] *n.* 静思，静修
11. **anguish** ['æŋgwɪʃ] *n.* 痛苦，苦恼
12. **rigmarole** ['rɪgmərəʊl] *n.* 冗长的废话

The closing of a door is **irrevocable**[13]. It snaps the pack-thread of the heart. It is no avail to reopen, to go back. Pinero spoke nonsense when he made Paula Tanqueray say, "The future is only the past entered through another gate." Alas, there is no other gate. When the door is shut, it is shut forever. There is no other entrance to that vanished pulse of time. "The moving finger writers, and having **writ**.[14]"

There is a certain kind of door-shutting that will come to us all. The kind of door-shutting that is done very quietly, with the sharp click of the latch to break the stillness. They will think then, one hopes, of our unfulfilled decencies rather than of our **pluperfect misdemeanours**[15]. Then they will go out and close the door.

原文翻译

开门和关门是人的生活中最有意思的行动，门内是怎样的神秘莫测啊！

一个人打开一扇门时，不知道等待着他的是什么。即使是最熟悉的房间，那里钟在嘀嗒作响，壁炉在暮色中闪着红光，也可能会藏有叫人吃惊的事情。管子工可能真的来过（在你外出时），修好了漏水的水龙头。厨师可能忧郁症发作，要求同意她离开。聪明的人总是带着谦恭和接受的态度打开前门。

我们中谁没有在某个接待室里坐过，眼睛盯着那扇含有各种可能的高深莫测的门板？也许你是在谋求职业，也许你有一项热切盼望能顺利做成的"交易"。你盯着那个机要速记员很快地进进出出，漫不经心地转动那扇神秘的门，而对你来说，它可是绕着命运的铰链在转动呢。后来，那个年轻的女子说："克雷伯里先生现在要见你。"当你握住门把手时，闪过一个想法："我再打开这扇门的时候，将会发生过什么事情？"

门有许多种类。旅馆、商店和公共大楼的旋转门。这些门代表着典型的活泼而忙碌的现代生活方式。你能想象约翰·弥尔顿或威廉·佩恩匆匆忙忙地走过一扇旋转门吗？还有那种开起来乒乓作响的古怪的小门，这种门只有从膝盖到肩那么高，仍在变质了的酒吧外面摆动。还有活板门、拉门、双折门、舞台门、监狱门、玻璃门等。不过一扇门的标志和神秘在于它的隐蔽性。玻璃门根本算不上是门，仅是一扇窗户而已。门的意义就在于把里面的东西隐藏起来，使你的心焦虑不安。

同样，开门也有许多种方式。有一种是用胳膊肘轻快地一推，侍者端着你的晚餐盘，打开厨房门时总是这样。有在愁苦的书籍代理商或小贩面前颇有戒心、犹犹豫豫地一点点地拉开后退的门。有随着有礼貌又小心地逐渐退出的男仆而敞开的大人物的栎木门。还有牙医女助手富于同情而悄然无声地打开的手术室的门，她一声不吭，暗示医生已经在等你了。另有一种，在清晨很早的时候，护士欢快而突然地打开门进来，嘴里喊着："是个男孩！"

门象征着隐私、静修、内心避入愉快的宁静或伤心的隐秘的斗争。一间没有门的房间不是房间，只是过道。不管在哪里，一个人待在一扇紧闭的门后面，就能使自己感到像在家里一样自在。在紧闭的门后面，人的思维作用发挥得最好。人不像马，得围在一起。狗懂得门的意义及门所能带来的苦恼。你有没有注意过一只小狗在一扇关闭的门前渴望不已？那是人类生活的象征。

开门是个神秘的动作：这里面包含有某种未知的情趣，某种进入新的时刻的感觉，一种人类烦琐手续的新形式。这包括对极大的快乐的显露：重聚、和解、久别重逢的恋人的狂喜。就是在悲伤时，开门也会给你带来宽慰：它改变并重新分配人的力量。但是，关门要可怕得多。那是声明结局。每一扇门关上都表示某件事情的结束。在关门中有不同程度的悲伤。砰的一声把门关上表明软弱。轻轻地关上门常常是生活中最悲剧

注释
13. irrevocable [ɪˈrevəkəbl] *adj.* 不能挽回的
14. writ （古）**write** 的过去式和过去分词
15. pluperfect misdemeanours 过去干过的不端行为。这两个单词都是古词，用在这里仿佛庄严实为幽默

性的举动。人人都知道，紧跟在关门后面袭来的是极度的痛苦，这时所爱的人虽仍在附近，听得见说话的声音，然而他已经远去了。

开门和关门是严峻的流水般生活的一部分。生活不会停止不动，撇下我们不顾。我们继续怀着希望开门，怀着绝望关门。生命持续的时间不超过一袋烟的工夫，命运最终像磕烟灰那样把我们击倒。

一扇门关上是不可挽回的。它"啪"地折断了心脏的血脉。重新打开、转回去是没有用的。平内罗让波拉·坦克瑞说："未来只是从另一扇门进入过去。"这是胡说八道。哎呀，没有其他的门。当门关上时，它永远就关上了。对那消失了的时间的搏动来说，没有其他入口。"运指儿写书，字儿落纸。"

我们每个人肯定都会碰到一种关门。这种关门关起来很轻，只有弹簧锁的咔嗒声会打破寂静。希望那时他们想到的是我们没有完成的正经事，而不要想到我们干过的不端行为。那样他们就会走出去，关上门。

文化点滴

John Milton

约翰·弥尔顿（1608—1674），英国诗人、政论家、民主斗士。弥尔顿是清教徒文学的代表，他的一生都在为资产阶级民主运动而奋斗，代表作《失乐园》，与《荷马史诗》和《神曲》并称为西方三大诗歌。

William Penn

威廉·佩恩（1621—1670），也翻译为威廉·宾，英国海军舰队司令、海军上将。青年时代即在海军服役，第一次英荷战争中任海军中将。1654年指挥前往西印度群岛的远征军，第二次英荷战争期间任舰队司令。

写作特点

There be a/the *adj. n.*/doing... There be +冠词+形容词+名词或动名词。第五段作者用了5个排比句来讲述开门的方式，句式工整，论述显得有条不紊。

There is the cheery push...

There is the suspicious and tentative withdrawal...

There is the genteel and carefully modulated recession...

There is the sympathetic and awful silence...

There is the brisk cataclysmic opening...

品味鉴赏

开门和关门是严峻的流水般生活的一部分。生活不会停止不动，撇下我们不顾。我们继续怀着希望开门，怀着绝望关门。生命持续的时间不超过一袋烟的工夫，命运最终像磕烟灰那样把我们击倒。

美文感悟

The Essay and the Essayist
散文和散文家

作者简介：

E.B.怀特（Edward Brooks White，1899—1985），美国当代最优秀的散文作家。曾长期为《纽约客》《哈泼斯》等杂志撰写专栏。1960年获全美文学艺术院金质奖章。著有散文集《天天都是星期六》（1934）、《一个人的肉》（1942）、《这儿就是纽约》（1949）、《拐角处倒数第二棵树》（1954）、《我罗盘上的方位》（1962）等。

The essayist is a self-liberated man, sustained by the childish belief that everything he thinks about, everything that happens to him, is of general interest. He is a fellow who thoroughly enjoys his work, just as people who take bird walks enjoy theirs. Each new **excursion**[1] of the essayist, each new "attempt", differs from the last and takes him into new country. This delights him. Only a person who is **congenitally**[2] self-centered has the **effrontery**[3] and the **stamina**[4] to write essays.

注释
1. **excursion** [ɪkˈskɜːʃən] *n.* 远足，游览
2. **congenitally** [kənˈdʒenɪtəlɪ] *adv.* 天生地，先天地
3. **effrontery** [ɪˈfrʌtərɪ] *n.* 厚颜无耻
4. **stamina** [ˈstæmɪnə] *n.* 毅力，持久力

There are as many kinds of essays as there are human attitudes or poses, as many essay flavors as there are Howard Johnson ice creams. The essayist arises in the morning and, if he has work to do, selects his garb from an unusually extensive wardrobe: he can pull on any sort of shirt, be any sort of person, according to his mood or his subject matter—philosopher, scold, jester, raconteur, confidant, pundit, devil's advocate), enthusiast. I like the essay, have always liked it, and even as a child was at

work, attempting to inflict my young thoughts and experiences on others by putting them on paper. I early broke into print in the pages of *St. Nicholas*. I tend still to fall back on the essay form (or lack of form) when an idea strikes me, but I am not fooled about the place of the essay in twentieth-century American letters—it stands a short distance down the line. The essayist, unlike the novelist, the poet, and the playwright, must be content in his self-imposed role of second-class citizen. A writer who has his sights trained on the Nobel Prize or other earthly triumphs had best write a novel, a poem, or a play, and leave the essayist to **ramble**[5] about, content with living a free life and enjoying the satisfactions of a somewhat undisciplined existence. (Dr. Johnson called the essay "an irregular, undigested piece"; this happy practitioner has no wish to quarrel with the good doctor's characterization.)

There is one thing the essayist cannot do, though—he cannot indulge himself in deceit or in concealment, for he will be found out in no time. Desmond Mac Carthy, in his introductory remarks to the 1928 E. P. Dutton & Company edition of *Montaigne*, observes that Montaigne "had the gift of natural **candour**[6]..." It is the basic ingredient. And even the essayist's escape from discipline is only a partial escape: the essay, although a relaxed form, imposesits own disciplines, raises its own problems, and these disciplines and problems soon become apparent and (we all hope) act as a **deterrent**[7] to anyone **wielding**[8] a pen merely because he entertains random thoughts or is in a happy or wandering mood.

I think some people find the essay the last resort of the egoist, a much too self-conscious and self-serving form for their taste; they feel that it is **presumptuous**[9] of a writer to assume that his little excursions or his small observations will interest the reader. There is some justice in their complaint. I have always been aware that I am by nature self-absorbed and egoistical; to write of myself to the extent I have done indicates a too great attention to my own life, not enough to the lives of others. I have worn many shirts, and not all of them have been a good fit. But when I am discouraged or **downcast**[10] I need only fling open the door of my closet, and there, hidden behind everything else, hangs the mantle of Michel de Montaigne, smelling slightly of **camphor**[11].

注释

5. **ramble** [ræmbl] *v.* 闲逛，漫游
6. **candour** ['kædə] *n.* 直率
7. **deterrent** [dɪ'terənt] *n.* 制止物，威慑力量
8. **wield** [wi:ld] *vt.* 行使，挥舞
9. **presumptuous** [prɪ'zʌmptjuəs] *adj.* 自以为是的；专横的
10. **downcast** ['daʊnkɑ:st] *adj.* 沮丧的；忧郁的
11. **camphor** ['kæmfə] *n.* 樟脑

原文翻译

散文家是一个自我解放的人,靠一种幼稚的信念支撑着,他总认为自己想到的一切,自己遭遇的一切,是大家都感兴趣的。他是一个充分欣赏自己工作的人,就像遛鸟的人欣赏他们的工作那样。散文家的每一次新的游览,每一次新的"尝试",都和前一次不同,而且总把他带进新的国度里去。这使他很快慰。只有生来以自我为中心的人才会厚颜无耻、持之以恒地去写散文。

散文种类之多,犹如人的姿态,而散文风格韵味之多则犹如霍华德·约翰逊的冰激凌。散文家清晨起来,倘若有工作得做,总从一批特别多样化的服装中挑选出他的外衣来:且不论他是哪一类人,他可以根据自己的心境或是题材披上任何种类的外衣——哲学家、爱骂人的人、诙谐的人、讲故事的人、知己朋友、学术权威、爱唱反调的人、热心人士。我爱好散文,一向爱好,孩提时就动手写文章,试图把我年轻的思想与经历写在纸上,强加给别人。我写的散文最早刊登在《圣尼古拉斯》杂志上。当我突然有了一个想法时,我还是倾向于采用散文这种形式(或者可以说是缺乏任何形式),不过我对于散文在20世纪美国文坛上的地位深信不疑——总的来说,散文地位偏低。散文家不像小说家、诗人和剧作家,他必须满足于自己强加于身上的二等公民的角色。一个目光瞄准诺贝尔奖或是世上其他荣誉的作家,最好写一篇小说,一首诗或一部戏剧,撇下散文家四处漫游,满足于一种自由自在的生活,享受着一种或多或少散漫生活的种种快事(约翰逊博士把散文称为"一篇不合常规的、未经整理的文字";我这个快乐的散文作者无意就那位好博士关于散文特性的描述进行指责)。

不过,有一件事是散文家所不能做的——他不能尽情欺骗或是隐瞒,因为那样一来,他很快就会被人发觉。德斯蒙德·麦卡锡在达顿公司1928年出版的《蒙田文集》的序言里说,蒙田"具有生性坦率的天赋……"这是基本要素。就连散文家摆脱法则的束缚也只是部分摆脱:散文虽然形式松散,却定有自己的法则,提出自己的问题。这些法则和问题不久就变得很明显,而且(我们全都希望)对任何一个仅仅因为自己浮想联翩或者因为心境快乐或胡思乱想而握起笔管来的人充当一种制约因素。

我想,有些人认为散文是利己主义者的最后一招,是符合他们口味的一种过于忸怩作态、过于自私自利的形式。他们觉得一个作家不要妄认为他的微不足道的旅行或是琐细的观察会引起读者的兴趣。他们的抱怨中倒也有相当的道理。我一贯知道,我生性是自我陶醉和利己的;把我自己写到这样的地步,表明我对自己的生活过分在意,而不太关心别人的生活。我穿过许多件衬衫,并不是所有的都很合身。不过遇到我心情沮丧或郁郁不快时,我只需要把衣橱的门一下拉开:那里藏在所有别的衣服后面,挂着米歇尔·德·蒙田的披风,微微地散发出樟脑的气息。

文化点滴

Howard Johnson
美国一家大众化的连锁旅店和餐馆,以创业人霍华德·约翰逊命名,并以销售的冰激凌品种繁多而闻名。

Dr. Johnson
塞缪尔·约翰逊(Samuel Johnson, 1709—1784),英国散文家、词典编纂家。

Desmond Mac Carthy
德斯蒙德·麦卡锡(1877—1952),英国文学评论家。作品有《肖像》《喜剧》《萧伯纳》等。

Montaigne
米歇尔·德·蒙田(Michel de Montaigne, 1533—1592),法国散文家、思想家。

写作特点

E.B.怀特,"其文风冷峻清丽,辛辣幽默,自成一格"。本文用词力求含蓄风趣。含蓄的语言耐人寻味;语言风趣,能使文章活泼,不觉呆板。

品味鉴赏

真诚,是一个散文家必须具有的生活和写作态度,这样才能准确地体验到生活的本质和真实,在作品当中体现出生活的本真,也是对读者的负责。

美文感悟

_____

_____

_____

_____

_____

Compting in a Flat World
无国界竞争

作者简介：

目前，全球化的大趋势已经势不可挡，仿佛是超越一切边界和界限的超限战。这是一个全球性的课题，谁也无法回避。本文作者托马斯·弗里德曼（Thomas Friedman，1953—）曾出版畅销书《世界是平的》。他认为，信息化时代为企业的全球化战略带来了种种可能与无尽的想象。但凡事总有其两面性，看似平坦的道路也暗藏了许多漩涡，要获得成功者，应适时地做出调整，抓住信息变革带来的契机，提升自身的全球竞争力。在本文中，托马斯·弗里德曼则就美国的年轻人如何在一个无国界竞争的环境下获得最好的成功提出了数项建议。

    A three-time Pulitzer Prize winner, Thomas Friedman has traveled hundreds of thousands of miles reporting the Middle East conflict, the end of the cold war, U.S. domestic politics and foreign policy, international economics, and the worldwide impact of the terrorist threat.

    Thomas Friedman was born on July 20, 1953. His family was of solid 1950s middle class. Friedman lived much of his early life in the shadow of his two older sisters. Their parents had high expectations for the children, and Thomas wasn't considered the brightest in the family. Even so, his intellectual curiosity was unusual among his friends.

He had a tight-knit group of friends. In the third grade, Friedman and his friend Greene were so **rowdy**[1] that their teacher promised they'd never be in the same class again. On Saturdays, the two would take the bus into downtown Minneapolis to eat at a cafeteria and go to a movie, generally a Western or a horror show. The horror films **fascinated**[2] Friedman.

It was in the tenth grade that Friedman became fascinated with the larger world. After high school, Friedman went to the University of Minnesota, where he began studying Arabic, an odd choice at the time. After he graduated from Oxford, Friedman threw himself into reporting.

In June 1989, he published *From Beirut to Jerusalem*, which was on the *New York Times* bestsellers list for nearly 12 months. *From Beirut to Jerusalem* has been published in more than 20 languages, including Japanese and Chinese, and is now used as a basic textbook on the Middle East in many high schools and universities.

His most recent book, *The World Is Flat*, jump-started a national debate over American competitiveness. The book itself has spent more than 60 weeks on the *New York Times* bestsellers list.

Friedman is on the road about a quarter of the time. He's recognized on the street in cities round the world. Such contacts, he says, are a source of **insight**[3] on how people feel in the places to which he travels.

He says, "I don't know whether I'm successful or not—depends on your **metric**[4]—but I'm sure having fun. Never had a bad day. Shame on me if I did."

I've been a journalist all my life. It's been a great ride. And what I thought I would talk with you about today is not the stories I've covered, but some of the lessons I accidentally learned along the way about getting through life.

Lesson NO.1 is a very simple piece of advice. It goes like this: Do what you love. The reason of that advice is, as I like to put it, the world is getting flat. The flatter the world gets, the more essential it is that you do what you love, because, all the boring, repetitive jobs are going to be automated or **outsourced**[5] in a flat world. The good jobs that will remain will be those that cannot be automated or outsourced, they will be the jobs that demand or encourage some uniquely human creative **flair**[6], passion and imagination. In other words, jobs that can only be done by people who love what they do. You see, when the world gets flat everyone should want to be untouchable.

Lesson NO.2: The second lesson I learned from journalism is that being a good listener is one of the great keys to life. The ability to be a good listener is one of the most under-appreciated talents a person or a country can have. People often ask me how I, an American Jew, have been able to operate in the Arab/Muslim world for 20 years, and my answer to them is always the same. The secret is to be a good listener. It has never failed me. You can get away with really disagreeing with people as long as you show them the respect of really listening to

注释

1. **rowdy** ['raʊdɪ] *adj.* 吵闹的
2. **fascinate** ['fæsɪneɪt] *vt.* 使着迷
3. **insight** ['ɪnsaɪt] *n.* 洞察力，见识
4. **metric** ['metrɪk] *n.* 度量，衡量标准
5. **outsource** ['aʊtˌsɔːs] *v.* 外部采办，外购
6. **flair** [fleə] *n.* 才能，本领

taking it into account when and if it makes sense. Indeed, the most important part of listening is that it is a sign of respect. It's not just what you hear by listening that is important. It is what you say by listening that is important. Never **underestimate**[7] how much people just want to feel that they have been heard, and once you have given them that chance they will hear you.

Lesson NO.3 is that the most enduring skill you can bring to the workplace is also one of the most important skills you always have to bring to reporting—and that is the ability to learn how to learn. That too is going to be really important if you want to be an untouchable, because jobs are going to change faster and faster in a flat world.

Lesson NO.4 is: Don't get carried away with the **Gadgets**[8]. I started as a reporter in Beirut working on an Adler **manual**[9] typewriter. I can tell you that the stories I wrote for the *New York Times* on that manual typewriter are still some of my favorites. Ladies and gentlemen, it is not about the skis. In this age of laptops and PDAs, the Internet and Google, mp3s and iPods, remember one thing: all these tools might make you smarter, but they sure won't make you smart, they might extend your reach, but they will never tell you what to say to your neighbor over the fence, or how to comfort a friend in need, or how to imagine a breakthrough in science or literature. You cannot download passion, imagination, **zest**[10] and creativity—all that stuff that will make you untouchable. You have to upload it, the old fashioned way, under the olive tree, with reading, writing and **arithmetic**[11], travel, study, reflection, museum visits and human **interaction**[12].

You can't bet your whole life on some destination. You've got to make the journey work too. And that is why I leave you with some wit and wisdom **attributed**[13] to Mark Twain: Always work like you don't need the money. Always fall in love like you've never been hurt. Always dance like nobody is watching. And always—always—live like it's heaven on earth.

原文翻译

三次获得普利策奖的托马斯·弗里德曼曾经远行千里，对中东冲突、"冷战"的结束、美国国内的政治和外交政策、国际经济学，以及全球范围内的恐怖威胁进行了报道。

托马斯·弗里德曼出生于1953年7月20日。他的家庭是20世纪50年代体面的中产阶级。弗里德曼大部分的童年时代都处于他两个姐姐的阴影之中。他们的父母对孩子期望非常高，而托马斯并非家中最聪明的孩子。即便如此，他充满智慧的好奇之心在他的朋友当中还是显得鹤立鸡群。

他有一群亲密无间的朋友。上三年级的时候，弗里德曼和他的朋友格林由于嬉闹过度，被老师警告说不让他们再待在一个班级中了。这两个小伙伴经常在星期六乘车到明尼阿波利斯市区，到自助餐厅去美餐一顿或者看一场电影（通常都是西部片或者恐怖片）。恐怖片往往会让弗里德曼深受吸引。

注释

7. underestimate [ˌʌndərˈestɪmeɪt] vt. 低估，看轻
8. gadget [ˈɡædʒɪt] n. 小器具，小玩意
9. manual [ˈmænjuəl] adj. 手工的，体力的
10. zest [zest] n. 热情，热心
11. arithmetic [əˈrɪθmətɪk] n. 算术，算法
12. interaction [ˌɪntərˈækʃən] n. 交互作用，交感
13. attribute [əˈtrɪbjuːt] v. 归结于

直到上十年级的时候，弗里德曼才对更多的外面世界产生兴趣。上完高中之后，弗里德曼进入了明尼苏达州大学，他选择学阿拉伯语，这在当时是个非常奇怪的选择。他从牛津大学毕业之后，弗里德曼投身到报道工作中去。

1989年6月，他出版了《从贝鲁特到耶路撒冷》，该书高居《纽约时报》畅销书排行榜长达将近12个月。《从贝鲁特到耶路撒冷》已经出版了20多种语言版本，其中包括日语和中文，并且现在被中东的许多高中和大学用作基础教材。

他最近的书《世界是平的》发动了一场关于美国竞争力的争辩。这本书高居《纽约时报》畅销书排行榜长达将近60个星期。

弗里德曼大约1/4的时间都花在路上。人们可以在全球各个城市的大街上遇到他。这样的接触，是了解他游访之处的人们内心想法的一大来源。

他说："我不知道我是否成功——这要看你衡量的标准是什么——但我确实过得非常开心。我从未度过糟糕的一天。如果我曾有过，必定引以为耻。"

我一直都是一名记者。这是一种伟大的旅行。我今天要给你们讲的并不是我曾经报道过的故事，而是我在途中偶然得到的关于生活的教益。

教导一是一条很简单的忠告。这条忠告是：做你所喜爱的。我作此忠告的理由是——我喜欢这样说——世界变得扁平了。世界越扁平，做自己所喜爱的事就越有必要。因为，在一个扁平的世界里，所有的令人厌烦的重复性的工作将会被自动化完成或通过外部采购来完成。剩余的好工作将是那些不能被自动化或通过外部采购来完成的，这些工作的完成需要高超的创造性才能、激情和想象，或者能激发这些才能、激情和想象。换句话说，这些工作只能由热爱他们的人来完成。你知道，当世界变得扁平时，每个人都成为不可或缺的。

教导二：我从新闻业学到的第二条经验是——善于倾听是生活的关键之一。善于倾听的能力，是一个人或一个国家能拥有的最未受到充分赏识的才能。人们常常问我——个美籍犹太人——是怎么能够在阿拉伯/伊斯兰世界工作20年，而我给他们的回答一直都是一样的，这个秘密就是做一个善于倾听的人。这从来没有让我失望过。只要你很尊重他们——真正去倾听他们一定要讲的内容，重视他们所讲的有意义的东西——就可以消除因意见相左而引起的不快。事实上，倾听最重要的就是它是一种尊重的标志，重要的不仅仅是你在听的过程中听到了什么，而在于你听的行为是重要的。永远不要低估人们是多么想要感到别人在倾听他的讲话，而且，一旦你给了他们那样的机会，他们将会听从你。

教导三：你能带到工作场所的最持久的、也是你一直在报告中不得不写进去的最重要的技能之一，那就是学会怎样学习的能力。这对于你想成为一个不可或缺的人也是很重要的。因为在一个扁平的世界里，工作将会转换得越来越快。

教导四：不要因为新技术而使自己变得可有可无。我在贝鲁特是用手动打字机工作而开始我的记者生涯的。我可以告诉你们，我用那台手动打字机为《纽约时报》写的报道仍是我最中意的部分。女士们、先生们，这不是滑雪板。在这个笔记本电脑和个人数字助理、网络和Google搜索、mp3和iPod的时代，请记住一点：所有的这些工具让你有可能变得更聪明，但是它们不会自动使你更聪明；它们可能会拓展你的触觉，但是它们永远不会告诉你该对篱笆另一边的邻居说什么，或者怎样安慰危难中的朋友，或者怎样在自然科学或文艺方面有所突破。你不可能下载热情、想象力、兴趣和创造力等这些使你不可替代的东西。你必须上载，用最老套的方法，在油橄榄树下，用阅读、书写、算术、旅行、研究、沉思、参观博物馆和与人群的互动——来进行上载。

你不能把你的全部生命寄托在某个终极目标上。在此期间你必须不断努力。这也是我为什么把马克·吐温的至理名言留给你们的原因。他的名言是这么说的：一直工作，好像你并不需要钱。一直恋爱，好像你从未受到过伤害。一直跳舞，好像没有人在注视你。一直生活——一直，好像你住在人间天堂。

文化点滴

Pulitzer Prize

普利策奖也称为普利策新闻奖。1917年根据美国报业巨头约瑟夫·普利策（Joseph Pulitzer）的遗愿设立，20世纪七八十年代已经发展成为美国新闻界的一项最高荣誉奖。现在，不断完善的评选制度已使普利策奖成为全球性的一个奖项。约翰·肯尼迪（John Kennedy, 1917—1963）是唯一获得这个奖项的美国总统。

写作特点

本文介绍了弗里德曼在做记者期间对生活的感悟和从中获得的四条教益：做你所喜爱的；善于倾听；学会怎样学习的能力；不要因为新技术而使自己变得可有可无。每条教益自成一段，思路清晰。

品味鉴赏

马克·吐温说过："一直工作，好像你并不需要钱。一直恋爱，好像你从未受到过伤害。一直跳舞，好像没有人在注视你。一直生活——一直，好像你住在人间天堂。"不论何时我们都要保持一个积极乐观的心态，做自己喜欢做的事情，学会倾听，学会学习的能力，提升自己的价值。

美文感悟

_____
_____
_____
_____

A Retrospect
回首往事

作者简介：

爱德华·吉本（Edward Gibbon, 1737—1794），英国历史学家，《罗马帝国衰亡史》作者。自幼好读书，但在气质上与学院派风气格格不入。在牛津呆过14个月，自认这是一生"最无聊最无益"的岁月。后赴瑞士学习法国文学和拉丁典籍。笃志史学，雅好文学，交结海内外文坛泰斗，加入约翰逊博士的文人俱乐部。1763—1765年周游欧洲，与伏尔泰、狄德罗等均有来往。发表的第一部著作是用法语写的《论文学研究》。历时近20个春秋完成不朽巨作《罗马帝国衰亡史》。该书组织细密，史料翔实，文笔优美，显示了作者史学和文学两方面的渊博知识。本文选自他的《吉本自传》。该书总结了他一生的学术历程，并详尽地描述了他发愤向上的苦学过程。

When I **contemplate**[1] the common lot of morality, I must acknowledge that I have drawn a high prize in the lottery life. The far greater part of the globe is overspread with **barbarism**[2] or slavery; in the civilized world the most numerous class is condemned to ignorance and poverty; and the double fortune of my birth in a free and enlightened country, in an honorable and wealthy family, is the lucky chance of a unit against millions. The general probability is about three to one that a new-born infant will not live to complete his fiftieth year. I have now passed that age, and may fairly estimate the present value of my existence in the three-fold division of mind, body, and estate.

注释
1. **contemplate** ['kɒntempleɪt] *v.* 凝视，沉思
2. **barbarism** [ˈbɑːbərɪzəm] *n.* 野蛮，未开化，原始

1. The first and indispensable requisite of happiness is a clear conscience, unsullied by the reproach or remembrance of any unworthy action.

—Hic murus aheneus esto,

Nil conscire sibe, nulla pallescere culpa.

I am endowed with a cheerful temper, a moderate sensibility, and a natural disposition to **repose**³ rather than to activity: some mischievous appetites and habits have perhaps been corrected by philosophy or time. The love of study, a passion which derives fresh vigor from enjoyment, supplies each day, each hour, with a perpetual source of independent and rational pleasure; and I am not sensible of any **decay**⁴ of the mental faculties. The original soil has been highly improved by cultivation; but it may be questioned whether some flowers of fancy, some grateful errors, have not been **eradicated**⁵ with the weeds of prejudice.

2. Since I have escaped from the long perils of my childhood, the serious advice of a physician has seldom been requisite. "The madness of superfluous health" I have never known, but my tender constitution has been **fortified**⁶ by time, and the inestimable gift of the sound and peaceful slumbers of infancy may be imputed both to the mind and body.

3. I have already described the merits of my society and situation; but these enjoyments would be tasteless or bitter if their possession were not assured by an annual and adequate supply. According to the scale of Switzerland I am a rich man; and I am indeed rich, since my income is superior to my expense, and my expense is equal to my wishes. My friend Lord Sheffield has kindly relieved me from the cares to which my taste and temper are most adverse: shall I add that, since the failure of my first wishes, I have never entertained any serious thoughts of a **matrimonial**⁷ connection?

I am disgusted with the affectation of men of letters, who complain that they have renounced a substance for a shadow, and that their fame (which sometimes is no insupportable weight) affords a poor compensation for envy, **censure**⁸, and persecution. My own experience, at least, has taught me a very different lesson: twenty happy years have been animated by the labor of my *History* and its success has given me a name, a rank, a character in the world to which I should not otherwise have been entitled. The freedom of my writings has indeed **provoked**⁹ an implacable tribe; but, as I was safe from the stings, I was soon accustomed to the buzzing of the hornets: my nerves are not tremblingly alive, and my literary temper is so happily framed that I am less sensible of pain than of pleasure. The rational pride of an author may be offended, rather than flattered, by vague **indiscriminate**¹⁰ praise; but he cannot, he should not, be indifferent to

注释

3. **repose** [rɪ'pəʊz] *vi.* 休息，依靠
4. **decay** [dɪ'keɪ] *n.* 腐朽，腐烂
5. **eradicate** [ɪ'rædɪkeɪt] *v.* 根除
6. **fortify** ['fɔːtɪfaɪ] *vt.* 设防于，增强(体力、结构等)；使坚强
7. **matrimonial** [ˌmætrɪ'məʊnɪəl] *adj.* 与婚姻有关的，根据结婚的惯例

8. **censure** ['senʃə] *n.* 责难
9. **provoke** [prə'vəʊk] *vt.* 激怒，挑拨，煽动
10. **indiscriminate** [ˌɪndɪ'skrɪmɪnət] *adj.* 不分青红皂白的，不加选择的

the fair testimonies of private and public esteem. Even his moral sympathy may be gratified by the idea that now, in the present hour, he is imparting some degree of amusement or knowledge to his friends in a distant land; that one day his mind will be familiar to the grandchildren of those who are yet unborn. I cannot boast of the friendship or favor of princes; the **patronage**[11] of English literature has long since been devolved on our booksellers, and the measure of their liberality is the least ambiguous test of our common success. Perhaps the golden **mediocrity**[12] of my fortune has contributed to fortify my application.

The present is a fleeting moment, the past is no more; and our prospect of futurity is dark and doubtful. This day may possibly be my last: but the laws of probability, so true in general, so **fallacious**[13] in particular, still allow about fifteen years. I shall soon enter into the period which, as the most agreeable of his long life, was selected by the judgment and experience of the sage Fontenelle. His choice is approved by the **eloquent**[14] historian of nature, who fixes our moral happiness to the mature season, in which our passions are supposed to be calmed, our duties fulfilled, our ambition satisfied, our fame and fortune established on a solid basis. In private conversation, that great and amiable man added the weight of his own experience; and this autumnal felicity might be exemplified in the lives of Voltaire, Hume, and many other men of letters. I am far more inclined to embrace than to dispute this comfortable **doctrine**[15]. I will not suppose any premature decay of the mind or body; but I must reluctantly observe that two causes, the abbreviation of time, and the failure of hope, will always tinge the evening of life with a browner shade.

原文翻译

在考察这芸芸众生的命运时，应当承认，我在问卜生命凶吉的时候所中的签要算得天独厚了。普天之下，绝大部分地方野蛮横行，奴役遍地；在开化地区，占人口绝大多数的阶级又注定愚昧贫困；而我降生在自由开明的国家，出身于富贵人家。这双重福分真是万里挑一，可遇而不可求。约莫有1/3的新生婴儿会活到五十来岁，这是大概的估计。如今我年过半百，不妨心平气和地估量一下目前个人的存在价值，谈谈精神、躯体、生活状况这三层内容。

第一，幸福的首要而又不可或缺的必备条件是问心无愧，不因任何不光彩的行止为人诟病或耿耿于怀而玷污良心。

"不怀罪愆的隐私，毫无令你面色发白的劣迹，
你的铜墙铁壁便拔地而起。"

快乐的性情，适度的敏感，喜静恶动的本性，这些都是与生俱来的：有些淘气的爱好和习性，或许由于知情达理或时光流逝而有所改正。好学，这种激情从乐趣中获得了勃勃生气，它朝朝夕夕时时刻刻带来一种源源不断的无所他求而又合乎理性的感受；我感觉不到精神功能的退化。这正如生荒的土地耕耘之后面貌大为改变；但是幻想的花朵，无伤大雅的过失，是否尚未被偏见的杂草所渐灭，恐怕这就令人产生疑问了。

注释
11. **patronage** ['pætrənɪdʒ] *n.* 保护人的身份；保护
12. **mediocrity** [ˌmiːdɪ'ɒkrɪti] *n.* 平常，平庸之才
13. **fallacious** [fə'leɪʃəs] *adj.* 谬误的，靠不住的，虚妄的
14. **eloquent** ['eləkwənt] *adj.* 雄辩的，有口才的
15. **doctrine** ['dɒktrɪn] *n.* 教条，学说

第二，我已经摆脱了孩提时代长期的险境，医生郑重其事的忠告多半是可有可无的了。"健康到发狂"我从未体验过，但岁月已增强了我柔弱的体质，婴儿阶段重组安宁的睡眠是无价之宝，我身心的状态可能都得之于此。

第三，上面我谈到了社会和境遇的有利条件，但是倘若拥有之后，每年并无足够的给养作为保证，那么这些享受就会变得毫无趣味或味同嚼蜡。根据瑞士的等级标准，我是一个富人，应该算是席丰履厚了，因为我的收入高于花费，而我花钱总是随心所欲。好友谢菲尔德勋爵又善意地帮我解决了不合我品味性情的烦恼：由于初衷未能如愿，我再也不曾认认真真地抱有缔结良缘的心思，这算不算多余的话呢？

看到文人墨客惺惺作态我便产生反感：他们自怨自艾弃实求虚，还说声誉（有时是名不副实）付出了几分代价，因为招致了嫉妒、苛评、纠缠。我亲身的经历至少使我懂得一个迥然不同的道理：撰著《罗马帝国衰亡史》的艰辛工作给过去20个幸福的春秋注入了活力，它的成功使我获得了人世间的名望、地位、身份，要不是这本书，我就没有资格得到这一切。著书立说中我畅所欲言，确实激怒了一班好事之徒；不过与我还算相安无事，没有遭人面刺，误议蜂起我不久也习以为常了：我的神经还不至于战战兢兢，我的文学性情形成得恰到好处，所以感受到的愉悦多于痛苦。含混其词不分高下的揶扬，可能会唐突作者不失理性的傲气，而不是令其感到溢美；但是他无法也不应当对人前人后评价的公正之词漠然置之。他甚至获得了道德满足感。因为他想到了现在，此时此刻，他正在给远方的友朋以一定的乐趣或知识；想到了有朝一日，那些尚未出世的子子孙孙，他都会成为他们的神交。我不敢自吹结交过王孙公子或他们对我优容有加；对于英国文学的护持早已转到了书本身上，衡量他们的手笔大小则是对我们共同成就最不过分的检验。我的运气当算中等，或许这一点促使我倍加勤奋。

现在只是俯仰之间，过去不复存在；我们对未来的展望一片黯然，充满疑团。今天可能便是我的末日：不过从概率规律来看，倘若天假以年，我还能活上15个年头；而泛泛而论的话，规律总是正确的，一到具体问题，规律又总是错误的。不久之后我就要走向另一个阶段，既有实力又有阅历的贤哲丰特奈尔视之为其漫长生命中无比欣慰的一段。他的抉择得到了那位出口成章的自然史家的许可，他把我们精神上的幸福安排在成熟的季节，这时我们的壮志已酬，我们的根基牢固，名利双收。在私下的交谈中，那位伟大和蔼的先哲补充了很有分量的现身说法；在伏尔泰、休谟和诸多文人的生命历程中，这份秋天里的福气都可引以为例。这种令人安慰的理论我倒真是乐于接受而无意提出异议。我不以为自己身心会未老先衰，担忧不得不说句心存不甘的话：时光渐短，心愿难遂，这两层原因会不断地给生命的黄昏抹上一团深深的阴影。

文化点滴

Voltaire

伏尔泰（1694—1778），法国启蒙思想家、文学家、哲学家。伏尔泰是18世纪法国资产阶级启蒙运动的旗手，被誉为"法兰西思想之王""法兰西最优秀的诗人""欧洲的良心"。

Hume

大卫·休谟（David Hume，1711—1776），苏格兰哲学家，出生在苏格兰的一个贵族家庭，曾经学过法律，并从事过商业活动。1734年，休谟第一次到法国，在法国，他开始研究哲学，并从事著述活动。1763年，休谟又去法国，担任英国驻法国使馆的秘书，代理过公使。1752—1761年，休谟曾进行过英国史的编撰工作。休谟的主要著作有：《人性论》（1739—1740）、《人类理解研究》（1748）、《道德原则研究》（1752）和《宗教的自然史》（1757）等。与约翰·洛克（John Locke）及乔治·贝克莱（George Berkeley）并称英国三大经验主义者。

写作特点

本文结构清晰明了,作者从三个层次,即精神、躯体和生活状况三个方面估量了自己的生存价值。

品味鉴赏

吉本出身贵族,从小体弱多病,但物质生活优裕。花20年写成的《罗马帝国衰亡史》为他带来了极大声誉。他认为,精神上的幸福,上帝安排在人的晚年是有道理的。因为人老了,七情六欲就平息了,人生的基本任务已经完成。人生的秋天就是收获,就是享受和煦的阳光。然而时光渐短,心愿难遂,这不得不算是抹在生命黄昏的一团阴影。吉本对生命是有点悲观的。其实有生就有死,心愿难遂,就要抓紧时间去实现。

美文感悟

The Goodness of Life
生命的美好

作者简介：

拉夫·马森是数字化时代的"牛仔"。在互联网"淘金热"中，他的成功展现了互联网作为一种潜在的大众媒体的魔力以及互联网上可以由任何人开掘的商机。拉夫·马森是一家网站《每日励志》（*The Daily Motivator*）的作者，他每天在该网站上写一篇文章，激励读者以积极的态度对待人生。

Many people are surprised to discover that I am a real person living in the present-day world. So many websites these days seem to be set up to hide the true identity of the people behind them, that folks assume I am some "made-up" person or some old guy who lived a few hundred years ago. In fact, I am pretty much a regular person with a yard to mow and a dog to walk.

As for me, I am in my early 50s and live in Texas with my wife of 25 years. We have two daughters.

Although it didn't start out that way, *The Daily Motivator* is now my full-time job. Back in 1995 I started writing the messages as part of another website. Within a few months, the response was so positive that *The Daily Motivator* took on a life of its own. After five years or so, subscription sales and book sales were providing a modest income, and since that time the website has grown to the point where I am able to devote all my working hours to it, which is a good thing, since it requires a good bit of time and I thoroughly enjoy it.

Since starting *The Daily Motivator* more than twelve years ago, I've been amazed at the tremendous positive response that it has received. People from all over the world, in all walks of life, have a sincere interest in living lives of meaning, caring, **dedication**[1] and fulfillment. I am extremely grateful that the technology of the Internet affords me the opportunity to share my work with so many people.

Beyond the website, I have several other things which keep me busy. I devote at least an hour each day to exercise. In the summer, I like to swim in our backyard pool. One of my favorite times to do this is just after sunset, when I can watch the stars come out while swimming. When the weather is cooler, I enjoy walking through our neighborhood and the greenbelt area that **adjoins**[2] our property. If the weather is rainy or cold and windy, I usually work out on a **recumbent**[3] exercise bicycle while listening to personal development audio programs.

We are very involved in our daughters' lives, though now that our older daughter is off at college, she's doing her own thing most of the time. Fortunately she gets home about once a month or so, which makes an ideal arrangement for all of us. Our younger daughter plays **lacrosse**[4] on her school's team, a sport that we previously knew nothing about, but we're learning quickly. It's a great game.

We enjoy traveling as a family, particularly to tropical beach locations. Closer to home, in the high-tech **mecca**[5] of Austin, there's something going on all the time: street festivals, live music, dining on every kind of **cuisine**[6] imaginable, sailing, water skiing and much more. Though there is much to be concerned about, there is far, far more for which to be thankful. Though life's goodness can at times be **overshadowed**[7], it is never **outweighed**[8].

For every single act that is senselessly destructive, there are thousands more small, quiet acts of love, kindness and compassion. For every person who seeks to hurt, there are many, many more who devote their lives to helping and to healing.

There is goodness to life that cannot be denied.

In the most **magnificent**[9] vistas and in the smallest details, look closely, for that goodness always comes shining through.

There is no limit to the goodness of life. It grows more abundant with each new encounter. The more you experience and appreciate the goodness of life, the more there is to be lived.

Even when the cold winds blow and the world seems to be covered in foggy shadows, the goodness of life lives on. Open your eyes, open your heart, and you will see that goodness is everywhere.

注释

1. dedication [ˌdedɪˈkeɪʃən] *n.* 贡献，奉献
2. adjoin [əˈdʒɔɪn] *v.* 邻接，毗连
3. recumbent [rɪˈkʌmbənt] *adj.* 靠着的，不活动的，休息的
4. lacrosse [ləˈkrɒs] *n.* 长曲棍球
5. mecca [ˈmekə] *n.* 众人渴望去的地方
6. cuisine [kwiːˈziːn] *n.* 烹饪，烹调风格
7. overshadow [ˌəʊvəˈʃædəʊ] *v.* 遮蔽，使失色
8. outweigh [aʊtˈweɪ] *v.* 在重量（或价值）上超过
9. magnificent [mægˈnɪfɪsnt] *adj.* 华丽的，高尚的

Though the goodness of life seems at times to suffer **setbacks**[10], it always endures. For in the darkest moment it becomes **vividly**[11] clear that life is a priceless treasure. So the goodness of life is made even stronger by the very things that would oppose it.

Time and time again when you feared it was gone forever you found that the goodness of life was really only a moment away. Around the next corner, inside every moment, the goodness of life is there to surprise and delight you.

Take a moment to let the goodness of life touch your spirit and calm your thoughts. Then, share your good fortune with another. For the goodness of life grows more and more magnificent each time it is given away.

Though the problems constantly scream for attention, and the conflicts appear to rage ever stronger, the goodness of life grows stronger still, quietly, peacefully, with more purpose and meaning than ever before.

原文翻译

许多人总是惊讶地发现我是生活在现实世界中的真人。由于现在很多网站都似乎会隐藏它们幕后的创作者的真实身份，人们也认为我是某个被"捏造"出来的人，或是某个生活在数百年前的老头。事实上，我是个非常普通的人，我平时也会在院子里割草和外出遛狗。

说到我，我的年纪是50岁刚出头，和结婚25年的妻子一起生活在得克萨斯州。我们有两个女儿。

虽然一开始不是这么计划的，但现在《每日励志》已经成为我的全职工作了。追溯至1995年，当时我开始为另外一个网站撰写一些短文。在数月之内，读者反应如此积极，于是《每日励志》展开了自己的生命之旅。差不多5年过去之后，订阅量和售书量为我提供了不错的收入，自此我得以将全部的工作时间投入到这个网站上来。这是好事，因为它要求很多的时间投入，而我也十分喜欢这份工作。

自从12年前开创《每日励志》以来，我一直对它已经收到的大量积极回应感到非常惊讶。来自世界各地各行各业的人们，都非常有兴趣过一种有意义、充满关怀和奉献并且充实的生活。我对互联网技术为我提供了一个与这么多人分享我工作成果的机会深表感激。

除了网站之外，我还忙于做一些其他的事情。每天我至少将一个小时用在锻炼上。夏天，我喜欢在我们后院的水池中游泳。我最喜欢游泳的时间之一是在日落之后，当我游泳的时候，我能看到星星自天际冒出来。天气比较冷的时候，我喜欢从我们的小区步行到邻接我们家的绿化带。如果遇上下雨天或者过度寒冷多风，我则往往会选择边踩着一辆固定不动的健身单车，一边聆听着关于个人发展方面的有声节目。

我们积极参与到我们的女儿的生活中去，虽然现在我们的大女儿离家去上大学，所以她大部分时间都会忙自己的事。幸运的是，她大约每月会回家一次，这对我们全家是一种理想的安排。我们的小女儿在她的校队中玩长曲棍球，我们此前对这项运动一无所知，但是现在我们正在迅速学习。这是一项很棒的运动。

我们喜欢全家外出旅行，尤其喜欢热带海滩地区。在我们家附近，是奥斯汀市的高科技圣地，那里的娱乐项目总是层出不穷：街道节日、现场音乐、吃任何可以想象出来的美食、航行、滑水，此外还有很多其他活动。

尽管有很多事让人忧虑，但相比而言，值得感激的事情要多得多。尽管生命的美好有时被蒙上阴影，但它却永远不会被埋没。

注释 10. setback ['setbæk] *n.* 挫折   11. vividly ['vɪvɪdlɪ] *adv.* 生动地、鲜明地

相对于每一个无谓的破坏行为而言，都有更多数以千计更为微小的，包含着爱、友善和同情的举动，静静地上演着。相对于每一个试图伤害他人的人而言，都有更多的人致力于帮助他人，治愈他人的创伤。

生命的美好不能否认。

在最为壮观的前景和最为琐碎的细节中，请仔细观察，因为美好的事物总是散发着耀眼的光芒闪亮登场。

生命的美好没有界限。每一次相遇都会使这美好变得越发丰富。你经历得越多，越能欣赏生命的美好，生命中的美好就会变得越多。即使当寒风袭来，整个世界似乎被雾气掩盖之时，生命的美好仍会存在。睁开你的双眼，打开你的心扉，你就会发现这份美好无处不在。

尽管生命的美好有时似乎遭受挫折，但它总会挺过来。因为，在最黑暗的时刻，有一点变得格外清晰，那就是，生命是无价的财富。因此，正是与生命的美好相对立的事物使其越发强大。

无数次地，当你担心这美好已经远离之时，你会发现生命的美好其实只与你相隔须臾。它就在下一个角落，存在于每个时刻之间，等着给你惊喜。

花些时间让生命的美好感动自己的灵魂，放松自己的思绪。然后，把你的幸运与他人分享。因为生命的美好会在每次给予之间变得越来越壮观。

尽管总是有问题让你去关注，冲突也似乎愈演愈烈，但生命的美好却总是静静地、平和地，带着比以前更强的意志和更多的价值，变得更加强大。

文化点滴

Texas

得克萨斯州，又称德克萨斯州、孤星之州，简称得州，是美国南方最大的一个州，也是全美第二大州，仅次于阿拉斯加州。州名来自于印第安Hasinai族中的Caddoan语"tejas"，意味着"朋友"或是"盟友"。西班牙的探险家在命名得州时，将这个本应该为人称的词误以为地名，就由此沿用下来。

品味鉴赏

对美丽的欣赏是一种高雅，向往美丽本身也是美丽。大自然给予我们无尽的美，人类自己创造了太多的美。美的环境，美的景致，一切美好的事物，通过我们的感官，给我们带来快乐的感受、恬静的心境和乐观的精神，会帮我们克服心理的压力，弥补心灵的创伤，排解心中的烦恼。善于发现美、学会欣赏美，会使生活变得更富有美感，更有意义，使我们的生命充满生机，人生更加丰富多彩。

美文感悟

_____
_____
_____

The Grief
悲怆

作者简介：

C.S.刘易斯（Clive Staples Lewis，1898—1963），是20世纪英国一位具有多方面天才的作家。他26岁即登牛津大学教席，被当代人誉为"最伟大的牛津人"。他是杰出的牛津剑桥大学文学史家和批评家，代表作包括《牛津英国文学史·16世纪卷》。他也是深受欢迎的科学幻想作家和儿童文学作家，代表作包括《太空》三部曲和《纳尼亚传奇》七部曲。本书选自作者的《卿卿如晤》，这是一篇悼亡手记，是刘易斯痛失爱妻之际，在那些"撕心裂肺、肝肠寸断的午夜"写下的文字。

No one ever told me that grief felt so like fear. I am not afraid, but the sensation is like being afraid. The same **fluttering**[1] in the stomach, the same restlessness, the yawning. I keep on swallowing.

At other times it feels like being mildly drunk, or **concussed**[2]. There is a sort of invisible blanket between the world and me. I find it hard to take in what anyone says. Or perhaps, hard to want to take it in. It is so uninteresting. Yet I want the others to be about me. I dread the moments when the house is empty. If only they would talk to one another and not to me.

注释
1. **flutter** [ˈflʌtə] vi. 悸动、烦扰
2. **concuss** [kənˈkʌs] vt. 使猛烈摇动，震动

There are moments, most unexpectedly, when something inside me tries to assure me that I don't really mind so much, not so very much, after all. Love is not the whole of a man's life. I was happy before I ever met H. I've plenty of what are called"resources". People get over these things. Come, I shan't do so badly. One is ashamed to listen to this voice but it seems for a little to be making out a good case. Then comes a sudden jab of red-hot memory — and all this "commonsense" **vanishes**[3] like an ant in the mouth of a furnace.

On the rebound one passes into tears and **pathos**[4]. Maudlin tears. I almost prefer the moments of agony. These are at least clean and honest. But the bath of self-pity, the **wallow**[5], the loathsome sticky-sweet pleasure of indulging it — that disgusts me. And even while I'm doing it I know it leads me to misrepresent H. herself. Give that mood its head and in a few minutes I shall have substituted for the real woman a mere doll to be **blubbered**[6] over. Thank God the memory of her is still too strong (will it always be too strong?) to let me get away with it.

For H. wasn't like that at all. Her mind was **lithe**[7] and quick and **muscular**[8] as a leopard. Passion, tenderness, and pain were all equally unable to disarm it. It scented the first whiff of cant or **slush**[9]; then sprang, and knocked you over before you knew what was happening. How many bubbles of mine she pricked! I soon learned not to talk rot to her unless I did it for the sheer pleasure — and there's another red-hot jab — of being exposed and laughed at. I was never less silly than as H.'s lover.

And no one ever told me about the laziness of grief. Except at my job — where the machine seems to run on much as usual — I loathe the slightest effort. Not only writing but even reading a letter is too much. Even shaving. What does it matter now whether my cheek is rough or smooth? They say an unhappy man wants distractions — something to take him out of himself. Only as a dog-tired man wants an extra blanket on a cold night; he'd rather lie there shivering than get up and find one. It's easy to see why the lonely become untidy, finally, dirty and disgusting.

Meanwhile, where is God? This is one of the most **disquieting**[10] symptoms. When you are happy, so happy that you have no sense of needing Him, so happy that you are tempted to feel His claims upon you as an interruption, if you remember yourself and turn to Him with gratitude and praise, you will be — or so it feels — welcomed with open arms. But go to Him when your need is desperate, when all other help is vain, and what do you find? A door slammed in your face, and a sound of bolting and double bolting on the inside. After that, silence. You may as well turn away. The longer you wait, the more emphatic the silence will become. There are no lights in the windows. It might be an empty house. Was it ever inhabited? It seemed so once. And that seeming was as strong as this. What can this mean? Why is He so present a commander in our time of

注释

3. vanish ['vænɪʃ] vi. 消失，突然不见
4. pathos ['peɪθɒs] n. 痛苦，感伤
5. wallow ['wɒləu] n. 沉迷，堕落
6. blubber ['blʌbə] v. 又哭又闹
7. lithe [laɪð] adj. 柔软的；轻快的
8. muscular ['mʌskjulə] adj. 肌肉的，强健的
9. slush [slʌʃ] n. 废话
10. disquieting [dɪs'kwaɪətɪŋ] adj. 令人不安的，令人忧虑的

prosperity and so very absent a help in time of trouble?

Not that I am (I think) in much danger of ceasing to believe in God. The real danger is of coming to believe such dreadful things about Him. The conclusion I dread is not "So there's no God after all," but "So this is what God's really like. Deceive yourself no longer."

Our elders submitted and said, "Thy will be done." How often had bitter resentment been **stifled**[11] through sheer terror and an act of love — yes, in every sense, an act — put on to hide the operation?

Of course it's easy enough to say that God seems absent at our greatest need because He "is absent — non-existent". But then why does He seem so present when, to put it quite frankly, we don't ask for Him?

One thing, however, marriage has done for me. I can never again believe that religion is manufactured out of our unconscious, starved desires and is a substitute for sex. For those few years H. and I feasted on love, every mode of it — solemn and merry, romantic and realistic, sometimes as dramatic as a thunderstorm, sometimes as comfortable and **unemphatic**[12] as putting on your soft slippers. No cranny of heart or body remained unsatisfied. If God were a substitute for love we ought to have lost all interest in Him. Who'd bother about substitutes when he has the thing itself? But that isn't what happens. We both knew we wanted something besides one another — quite a different kind of something, a quite different kind of want...

原文翻译

从未有人告诉我,这种悲恸犹如恐惧,二者何其相似! 我并不恐惧,但感觉上却似乎在恐惧着什么。胃里同样的翻江倒海,同样的坐立不安,只打哈欠,还不断地咽口水。

还有些时候,这种悲恸又如心有浅浅醉意,或脑受微微震荡的感觉,在我和世界之间,隔着某层看不见的帷幕,别人说什么,我都听不进去,或许,是不愿自己听进去,一切都是那么索然寡味。然而,我又希望有人在我身边,每当看见这房子空空如也,我总是不寒而栗,所以,最终还是有些人气,而他们又互相交谈,但是,别来同我说话。

又有些时候,多在意想不到的时候,内心有种声音试图向我证明:我其实并不真的这么在乎,起码并不是像现在这么强烈地在乎。毕竟,爱情不是一个男人生命的全部。在遇到妻子之前,我一直过得挺自得其乐的,现在也拥有许多所谓的"消遣"。人们不都是这么节哀顺变,并挺过来了么?那么,我又何必在这里斯人独憔悴?虽然,接受这种声音让我羞愧,但它听上去倒是很合理。然而就在此时,那些铁一般烙人的记忆,突然间刺痛心扉,于是,这一切刚培养起来的"合理感觉",又如炉口上的蚂蚁,立刻烟消云散,踪影全无。受此重创,眼泪不禁潸然而下,心中满是悲凄。多么可怜的眼泪啊! 我宁可选择痛苦,那至少是纯纯粹粹、实实在在的痛苦。而像现在这样一味沉浸在自怜中,咀嚼着那腻歪的快感,连我自己都讨厌自己。然而即便当我在自怨自艾中,我也明知这样实在愧对于妻。因为如果任这种情绪泛滥下去,不消片刻,我所哭泣哀悼的,便不再是一个真实的女人,而是一具虚设的木偶。不过感谢神,有关妻的记忆依然刻骨铭心,无

注释 11. **stifle** ['staɪfl] *vt.* 使窒息,抑制　　12. **unemphatic** [ˌʌnɪmˈfætɪk] *adj.* 不强调的,非着重的

法忘怀。但这记忆，会永远这般刻骨铭心下去吗？

因为，妻完全不是这样，她的心思像豹子一样灵巧敏锐、矫健有力。热情也好，温柔也好，伤痛也好，都不能使它缴械投降。你言语中一旦有伪饰的假话或无聊的废话，它能立刻嗅到，然后凌空一跃，在你还未来得及弄清到底发生了什么事情之前，向你扑来，让你人仰马翻。我那些夸夸其谈，被她一针见血地戳破的，不知有多少！我很快学会了不在她面前胡说八道，除非纯粹是为博一笑——享受那种被揭穿、被嘲笑的乐趣。唉，这又是一段烙心刺骨的回忆。自从做了妻的爱人，我再也含糊不了。

也从未有人告诉我，这种悲恸会使人变得懒散。现在做任何事情，哪怕仅需费吹灰之力，我都厌烦不已——倒是工作例外，因为工作只需头脑机械地照常运转即可——别说写封信，就连读封信我都嫌烦。甚至刮胡子也烦，我的脸是光滑还是粗糙，有什么紧要呢？据说，不快乐的男人需要找些事情来分分神、散散心，好从自我封闭中解脱出来。正像一个精疲力竭的男人，在寒冷的夜里，最需要加条毛毯暖身，可是，他宁可躺在那里瑟瑟发抖，也不愿意起身去找一条毛毯御寒。显而易见，这就是为何孤独的人最后都会变得肮脏邋遢，惹人生厌。

与此同时，神在哪里？这样的怀疑是丧偶所引出的最令人不安的并发症之一。当你很快乐，快乐到觉得根本不需要神，快乐到认为神对你的要求是多此一举，这时，你若反省自己，回转向他，献上感恩和赞美，他会伸开双臂欢迎你——或者说，你觉得他会如此接纳你。但是，当你迫切需要他，而所有其他的救助都山穷水尽无济于事时，你会发现什么呢？一扇当着你的面砰然关闭的门，从里头还传出上门栓——双重门栓——的声音。接着，是静寂。你还不如离开，因为，等待的时间越长，那静寂的气息就越深。窗子里没有灯光，可能是间空房子而已。里面曾经住过人吗？看似住过。这看似有人住过的感觉与这静寂无人的气息都同样的明显。这意味着什么？为何，当我们一帆风顺时，他俨然存在，指挥若定？可是，当我们四面楚歌时，他反而杳然无踪？

我想，我现在的问题并非不再相信神，而是我开始相信神也有可恐惧之处，这才是真正的危机所在。我所害怕的结论并非"正因如此，所以神并不存在"，而是"不要再欺骗自己了，这才是神的庐山真面目"。

老一辈的人会恭顺地说："愿你的旨意成全。"多少时候，心酸悲愤被彻底的恐惧和良善的行为（是的，从任何角度看，都是行为）抑制住了，并以此虚掩内心真正的感受。

当然，很容易下判断：当我们最需要神时，他却不临现，是因为，神根本就不在——不存在。但为何，坦白地说，当我们不需要神时，他却一直临现？

然而，还有一件事，就是婚姻带给我的体会。我再也不会相信：信仰是潜意识里欲望得不到满足所投射出来的产物，是性的替代品。在那些短暂的岁月，我和妻饱享过的盛筵——各种形态的爱情——庄严的、欢乐的、浪漫的、写实的。有时如暴风骤雨般一波三折，有时又像穿上柔软拖鞋那样平淡舒缓，身心细微处皆惬意无比。如果，神是爱情的替代品，我俩应不会对他产生兴趣。拥有了实物之后，谁还会需要这些替代品呢？然而，事实却并非如此。我俩都清楚，除了彼此之外，我们还需要别的东西——这是完全不同的某样东西，也是完全不同的某种需要……

文化点滴

C．S．刘易斯于1898年11月29日出生在爱尔兰的贝尔法斯特。他在1963年11月22日（就在肯尼迪遇刺的同一天）去世。除了哥哥沃伦，他没有其他兄弟姊妹，沃伦比他大3岁，也是他一生的挚友。C．S．刘易斯最早的记忆是"汗牛充栋的书"。在书房、厨房、衣帽间，甚至在卧室都有大量的书，而阁楼里的书摞起来都有他的肩膀那么高了。在沉闷的日子里，他常常花费很多时间来读书和玩一种虚构的游戏，游戏中有"穿着衣服的动物"和"浑身盔甲的骑士"。这些都成了他的第一部小说《博科森》里的角色，而创作这部小说时，他只有12岁。

C．S．刘易斯与乔伊·大卫德的婚姻在BBC和好莱坞版的《影子大地》中得到生动的演绎。好莱坞版的电影由安东尼·霍普金斯和黛布拉·温吉尔主演。影片中有很多失实之处，但道格拉斯·格莱舍姆——刘易斯的养子描述称，电影"在情感上是正确的"。当刘易斯和乔伊结合时，她已经患上了癌症，将不久于人世。然而，在进行了一次成功的摘除手术后，他们度过了两年的幸福时光，直到乔伊的癌症复发，并于1960年去世。

写作特点

本文采用了大量的心理描写。心理描写，是指对人物在一定的环境中的心理状态、精神面貌和内心活动进行的描写。心理描写是作文中表现人物性格品质的一种方法。最常用的是描写人物的内心独白，写出人物的所思所想，让人物一无遮掩地吐露自己的心声，说出他的欢乐和悲伤、矛盾和愁郁、忧虑和希望，使读者穿透人物外表，看到人物的内心世界。读者可以通过本文的心理描写了解到作者的丧妻之痛以及内心所经受的折磨和痛苦。

品味鉴赏

本文写于作者的妻子死亡之后。在文中，作者思考了在失落和迷惘中生命、死亡以及信仰这些根本问题。文中包含了作者在这一阶段简洁而真实的反思："只有痛苦才能带来真相，只有经历痛苦才能发现自我。"人是无法在快乐中成长的。快乐使人肤浅，我们在痛苦中成长，蜕变才会更了解人生。痛苦让人成长，是你进步的一次机会，一个挑战。别害怕痛苦的事情，它有另一面积极的作用。

美文感悟

The "Present"
今天是一份馈赠

Imagine life as a game in which you are juggling some five balls in the air. You name them—work, family, health, friends and spirit and you're keeping all of these in the air. You will soon understand that work is a rubber ball. If you drop it, it will bounce back.

But the other four balls—family, health, friends and spirit are made of glass. If you drop one of these they will be **irrevocably**[1] **scuffed**[2], marked, **nicked**[3], damaged or even shattered. They will never be the same. You must understand that and strive for balance in your life.

How?

Don't undermine your worth by comparing yourself with others. It is because we are different that each of us is special.

Don't set your goals by what other people **deem**[4] important. Only you know what is best for you.

Don't take for granted the things closest to your heart. Cling to them as you would your life, for without them, life is meaningless.

注释
1. **irrevocably** [ɪˈrevəkəbli] *adv.* 不能取消地，不能撤回地
2. **scuff** [skʌf] *v.* 磨损
3. **nick** [nɪk] *v.* 刻痕于
4. **deem** [di:m] *v.* 相信，认为

Don't let your life slip through your fingers by living in the past or for the future. By living your life one day at a time, you live ALL the days of your life.

Don't give up when you still have something to give. Nothing is really over until the moment you stop trying.

Don't be afraid to admit that you are less than perfect. It is this fragile thread that binds us to each together.

Don't be afraid to encounter risks. It is by taking chances that we learn how to be brave.

Don't shut love out of your life by saying it's impossible to find. The quickest way to receive love is to give; the fastest way to lose love is to hold it too tightly; and the best way to keep love is to give it wings.

Don't run through life so fast that you forget not only where you've been, but also where you are going.

Don't forget that a person's greatest emotional need is to feel appreciated.

Don't be afraid to learn. Knowledge is weightless, a treasure you can always carry easily.

Don't use time or words carelessly. Neither can be **retrieved**[5].

Life is not a race, but a journey to be **savored**[6] each step of the way.

Yesterday is History, Tomorrow is a Mystery and Today is a gift: that's why we call it—the Present.

原文翻译

设想人生是一场抛5个球的游戏。这5个球分别叫——工作、家庭、健康、朋友、精神，然后你把它们抛到空中。很快你就明白了，工作是一个橡皮球。如果你扔下它，它还会再弹回来。

而其他4个球——家庭、健康、朋友、精神，则是玻璃做的。如果你把它们其中一个扔开，它不可避免地就会颠着走开，留下印记，刻上伤痕，损坏，甚至全给毁了。它们再也复原不了。你一定要懂得努力平衡你的生活。

怎么做呢？

别处处拿自己和他人对比，低估了自己的价值。因为我们每个人都是与众不同而且独特的。

别按照他人认为重要的来设置你的目标。什么才是最好，只有你自己知道。

让你觉得很贴心的事物，别想成是当然。你要终其一生地去接近它们，因为没有了它们，生活只是空洞无意义。

别空对昨日或未来嗟叹而虚度了生命。过好每一个今天，你也就过好了一生。

只要你还愿意努力，就别轻谈放弃。不到你停止尝试的那一刻，就没有真正的结束。

别惧怕承认你并不完美。正是这根脆弱的线连紧了我们彼此。

别惧怕风险。正是这样的机会，让我们学习如何变得更加勇敢。

别说爱无从找寻，就把它拒在你的生活之外。得到爱的最快方式，就是给予；失去爱的最快方式，就是把它束缚得太紧；保持爱的最好办法，就是给它插上一双飞翔的翅膀。

注释
5. retrieve [rɪˈtriːv] v. 重新得到
6. savor [ˈseɪvə] v. 品味

别把生命挥洒得太快，那你会忘了过去的好光景，也忘了未来去向何方。

别忘了人在情感上的最大需要，就是被赏识的感觉。

别怕学习。知识没有重量，你可以永远把这块瑰宝轻松携带。

别虚度光阴，别言不由衷。这两者都是覆水难收。

生活不是比赛，但是旅程中的每一步都值得细细品味。

昨天已是历史，明天还是一个谜，今天则是一份礼物：那就是为什么我们把今天又称为馈赠。

文化点滴

在西方社会里，人们寻求个性化，提倡个人突出，追求个性的发展和个人价值的实现。个人主义是以美国为代表的西方文化的思想内核。美国人追求自我的意识较强，强调自我价值的体现，在尊重自己价值观的同时，不允许他人侵犯自己的权利。他们认为："只要努力，牛仔也能当总统。"因为他们知道，努力实现自我价值，就一定能取得成功。

写作特点

本文大量地使用了由"Don't …"构成的排比结构来说明一个人应该保持积极乐观的生活态度，珍惜今天。此处的排比达到了加强语势、条理分明的效果。排比的行文朗朗上口，有极强的说服力，增强了文章的表达效果和气势。

品味鉴赏

人生只有3天，昨天、今天和明天。昨天已成过去不堪回首，明天虚无缥缈，只有今天才属于自己。看人生成败，不在昨天，也不在明天，而在于是否把握住了今天，珍惜了今天才会有美好的明天。不会珍惜今天的人，既不会感怀昨天，也不会憧憬明天。乐观的人喜欢描述明天的美好憧憬，悲观的人总担心明天会发生什么不测，但生命的内涵只在于今天。人的生命是宝贵的，它是由一分一秒的时间堆积而成的，珍惜今天就是珍惜生命，荒废了今天就是荒废了生命。

美文感悟

60

If
假如

作者简介：

拉迪亚德·吉卜林（Rudyard Kipling，1865—1936），英国小说家、诗人，出生于印度孟买。父亲曾是孟买艺术学校教师，后任拉合尔艺术学校校长和博物馆馆长。吉卜林6岁时被送回英国受教育，17岁中学毕业返回印度，父亲为他在拉合尔找了份工作，担任拉合尔市《军民报》编辑。

If you can keep your head when all about you
Are losing theirs and blaming it on you,
If you can trust yourself when all men doubt you
But make allowance for their doubting too,
If you can wait and not be tired by waiting,
Or being lied about, don't deal in lies,
Or being hated, don't give way to hating,
And yet don't look too good, nor talk too wise:
If you can dream—and not make dreams your master,
If you can think—and not make thoughts your aim;
If you can meet with Triumph and Disaster
And treat those two **impostors**[1] just the same;

Chapter 6 灵魂思索

If you can bear to hear the truth you've spoken
Twisted by **knaves**[2] to make a trap for fools,
Or watch the things you gave your life to, broken,
And **stoop**[3] and build'em up with worn-out tools:
If you can make one **heap**[4] of all your winnings
And risk it all on one turn of pitch-and-toss,
And lose, and start again at your beginnings
And never breath a word about your loss;
If you can force your heart and nerve and **sinew**[5]
To serve your turn long after they are gone,
And so hold on when there is nothing in you
Except the Will which says to them: "Hold on!"
If you can talk with crowds and keep your virtue,
Or walk with kings—nor lose the common touch,
If neither **foes**[6] nor loving friends can hurt you;
If all men count with you, but none too much,
If you can fill the unforgiving minute
With sixty seconds' worth of distance run,
Yours is the Earth and everything that's in it,
And—which is more—you'll be a Man, my son!

原文翻译

如果当周围的人都失去理智却诿过于你，
你仍能保持清醒；
如果当所有的人对你心存怀疑，你仍能自信，
并也容许别人猜疑；
如果你能等待，而不厌倦；
被欺骗，而不还以欺心，
被嫉恨，而不嫉恨别人，
既不目空一切，也不夸夸其谈：
如果你有梦想——而不整天梦陷黄粱，
如果你能思考——而不只是胡思乱想，
如果你把胜利和灾难
这两种虚幻看作一样；

注释

1. impostor [ɪmˈpɒstə] *n.* 冒充者，骗子
2. knave [neɪv] *n.* 流氓
3. stoop [stuːp] *v.* 弯腰
4. heap [hiːp] *n.* 堆
5. sinew [ˈsɪnjuː] *n.* 精力，体力
6. foe [fəʊ] *n.* 敌人

如果你能忍受你说出的真相
被无赖变成诱骗傻瓜的网，
或看到你付出心血的东西被毁坏，
还能俯身用损坏的工具从头再来；
如果你能在用穷尽毕生所得的
孤注一掷的冒险失败后，
从零开始，
而绝口不提你的损失；
如果你能让你的心你的精力你的体格
在消沉很久后重新投入你的事业，
并在你一无所有，唯剩意志向它们命令"坚持！"时
依然继续下去；
如果你混迹于百姓而仍坚持你的美德，
与王者同行却不与世人隔绝；
如果你的敌人和你亲爱的朋友都再不能把你伤害，
如果所有的人都能依赖你却没有人期望过奢，
如果你能将无情的每一分钟，
填以等同于奔跑60秒的价值度过，
你的心便是宽广的大地，包容万物
而更重要的，我的孩子——你便是个成功的人！

文化点滴

成功者四项特质：

A—Adaptability

改变是必然的，学会适应改变，享受改变，甚至先去改变。

B—Brain Power

才智是基本条件，没有一定的聪明才智如何在现今社会立足？其实每个人的智商相差也不远，而且社会需要的不是异于常人的天才，而是可堪造就的人才。

C—Creativity

如果做的事情或做事方法10年如一日，那10年的工作经验等于一天的。每天要问自己："今天做的事还是跟昨天一样吗？"

C—Courage

有勇气才会有信心。勇于面对危机，承担风险。当然，心里也要想好应变的方案，也就是要具备第一项特质。

写作特点

此诗作大量地使用了由"If..."构成的排比结构来说明一个成功的人应达到的境界。利用两个或两个以上结构相同或相似的句子并排,达到一种加强语势的效果。用排比来说理,可收到条理分明的效果;用排比来抒情,节奏和谐,显得感情洋溢;用排比来叙事写景,能使层次清楚、描写细腻、形象生动。排比的行文朗朗上口,有极强的说服力,能增强文章的表达效果和气势。

品味鉴赏

如果我们相信美妙,未来就会过着美妙的日子;如果我们自行设限,转瞬间那些限制就在眼前。相信之后便会成真,如你所愿。成功者都是:不仅知道他所追求的,而且相信必能获得。热情和信念就如同汽油,推动你迈向卓越之境。没有信念的人就像一个没有灵魂的人,人的所有巨大的力量都是来源于他的信念。你只有拥有一定要成功的信念,你才会全力以赴;你只有拥有一定要健康的信念,你才会去坚持锻炼。没有信念的支撑,你是走不了多久的。

美文感悟

My Time and Space
时空于我

作者简介：

迈克·杜利（Mike Dooley），《秘密》影片和书籍中的心灵导师之一，美国著名演讲者和畅销书作家。2001年，他录制的音频节目《无限可能》创下了1500万的销量。2006年，他成为《秘密》纪录片中的导师，更奠定了他在心灵哲学殿堂的地位。2009年，他将《无限可能》改编成书，迅速荣登《纽约时报》畅销书榜，受到广大读者的追捧。

  I used to think everyone knew something that I didn't. They, like I, weren't aware of what it was, and they didn't seem to notice that I was without it, but to me the difference was painful. Life's "little things" seemed second nature to others, whereas I felt I had to fake that I knew what was going on. I felt **awkwardly**[1] different, which led to an overwhelming desire to question the things that most people seem to take for granted.

  For me, in the beginning, my search for answers generally centered around the issues of life, death, and the powers of the mind, but within these there were many other topics like time, space, heaven, hell, hypnosis, UFO's, ghost stories, ESP, the dream state, reincarnation, etc. I had arrived at several basic conclusions for each, but they were just **hunches**[2]. Without knowing how I knew,

---

注释

1. **awkwardly** [ˈɔːkwɜːdlɪ] *adv.* 笨拙地；无技巧地
2. **hunch** [hʌntʃ] *n.* 预感

for example, at the age of 12 or 13 I remember telling my mother that space and time couldn't really exist, and that neither could hell.

I didn't realize it at the time but my desire to "know" had put me on an inner path of understanding, or better my thinking was beginning to attract like thinking. As I walked this path the questions I **dwelled**[3] upon were somehow answered. I was never sure just when the answers had arrived. I only sensed, sometime after "illumination", that an intuitive knowing had been imparted when I wasn't paying close attention.

The first time I remember physically pursuing my fascinations with life's mysteries was at the age of 14. Hypnosis was an exciting and **bizarre**[4] affair I thought, so I checked some books out from my high school's library, and bought a few short "how to" ones of my own. In very little time I was successfully hypnotizing some of the younger neighborhood kids who looked to me with some authority, but it all became very boring when I ran out of ideas of what to say or do once my subjects had gone under.

Exploring hypnosis I **gleaned**[5] several breakthroughs. First, I saw the mind's influence over the body and its thoughts, and second, while rummaging in the school library I discovered *The Search for Bridey Murphy*, by Morey Bernstein. It blew my 9th grade mind. I couldn't understand why everyone didn't have a copy, or why the teachers and adults I knew hadn't heard of it. Surely, I thought, this was revolutionary material that should be studied and queried by the greatest minds of the world. But as far as I knew that hadn't happened since Bridey's publication in 1956. Nevertheless, the paranormal events and conditions described in Bridey made perfect sense to me, paralleling many of my own inner suspicions, and opening doors in my thinking that enabled me to ponder even greater questions.

Despite my early quest for hypnosis books, I've never been a "reader". Since attending college I've probably averaged only 1—2 new books a year. So it's ironic that over my life, several books, or authors, have helped define my own thoughts, and therefore my life, in the most profound ways.

With few exceptions, these books were introduced to me by my mother, who has always been an avid "reader" and who I've always been very close to. I was 15 when she gave me *The Inner Game of Tennis*, W. Timothy Gallwey and *Psycho-Cybernetics*, Maxwell Maltz. Both of which improved my game immeasurably, and further peaked my interest in the powers of the mind over our lives. I haven't read either since the year I carried them everywhere, but I recall that their gist was to **unleash**[6] the power of imagination so as to influence the course you'd like your game, or life, to take.

During my freshman year at the University of Florida, the pitch in my desire for "understanding" was its greatest, overshadowing everything else I did or thought. For the entire year I dwelled daily on the meaning of life, and the mystery of death, but to no visible avail. Then, out of nowhere, Mom sent another book, *The Silva Mind-Control Method*, by Jose Silva. Once again I was pondering the **untapped**[7] abilities of my mind, and felt a renewed excitement for the mysteries it contained. But before I had time to finish it another book arrived, the first in a series that

注释

3. dwell [dwel] *vi.* 居住；存在于；细想某事
4. bizarre [bɪ'zɑː] *adj.* 奇异的（指态度、容貌、款式等）
5. glean [gliːn] *vt.* 收集（资料）
6. unleash [ʌn'liːʃ] *vt.* 发动；解开……的皮带；解除……的束缚
7. untapped [ʌn'tæpt] *adj.* 未开发的；未使用的

illuminated the darkest corners of my mind. Written with a **clarity**[8] and depth unlike anything I'd ever read, it confirmed, without exception, my deepest feelings and intuitions about life. It put my abstract thoughts into words and filled the gaps in-between. As I finished each I felt that my almost desperate searching was coming to an end. My questions were either answered, or by then seemed at least, very answerable. These books contained the *Seth Material* as dictated by the late Jane Roberts.

Today it's through the pursuit of my goals and dreams that I learn my lessons and even greater secrets about life and myself.

My understandings have helped as much in other areas of my life from relationships to material possessions, and they continue to grow with their own momentum. I'm still a student, but also my own teacher, and in this journey I've begun to realize that as much as I enjoy thinking and living my thoughts, I enjoy sharing them too... and learning from others... which I expect, is at least part of the reason, that our paths have crossed here and now, you and I.

原文翻译

我曾以为，人人都知道一些我所不知道的事情。他们和我一样，不知道那是什么，他们没有注意到我的无知，而这其中的差别对于我来说痛苦不已。生命中的"小事情"对别人而言似乎是第二天性那么自然；反之，我却要装出一副自己也知道的模样。我笨拙地感受到不同，这引发了我无比的好奇心，去质疑别人看作理所应当的事情。

一开始，我要探求的答案主要是针对生命、死亡和意志力，可在这些其中，还有许多其他问题，比如时间、空间、天堂、地狱、催眠、不明飞行物、鬼故事、超感觉、梦境、转世等等。每个问题我都已有些基本结论了，不过都只是凭感觉罢了。不知道自己是怎么知道的，举个例子说，十二三岁时，我记得曾对妈妈说，时空并不存在，地狱也不存在。

那个时候我还无所意识，但求知的渴望让我在内心走上一条理解之路，或者说是让我的思想变得更善于思考。我走在这条道路上，思索的问题也慢慢找到了答案。我从不知晓这些答案是何时出现的，我只是感知到，有时是得到启发后，在不为我注意的时候，直觉上就这么知道了。

记忆中我第一次去探求生命的奥秘是在14岁的时候。我当时觉得催眠太刺激太古怪了，于是就去中学图书馆里找了些书来看，还买了好几本短篇的《教你如何做》。短短时间内，我成功地催眠了邻近的一些小孩，他们把我看作权威，可到后来这变得很无聊，我实在想不出把他们催眠后该说什么和做什么才好。

琢磨催眠倒是带给我几个重大突破。首先是我看到意识的力量对于身体和思想所起的作用；其次是，在学校图书馆里找书时，我发现了莫利·本斯坦因的著作《寻找布利迪·墨菲》。它在我九年级的心灵中一石激起千层浪。我都不明白为什么这本书不是人手一本，也不明白我认识的老师与大人们为什么从没听说过它。我肯定这书具有革命性的意义，全世界最伟大的人都该去读上一读。可据我所知，这本书在1956年出版后却备受冷落。不过书中描述的超自然事件与情景对我可是意义非凡，它与我心里的揣测不谋而合，并打开了我思维的大门，让我开始考虑更重大的问题。

除了早年去搜寻一些催眠书籍外，我并不是个用心的读者。上大学后我每年只平均看过一两本书。所以蛮讽刺的是，几本书（或者说几个作者）就定向了我的思维，从而把我的生活推向多彩多姿。

除抄取几本之外，这些书都是妈妈推荐给我看的，她可是一名孜孜不倦的读书人，我一直与她很亲近。当年我15岁，她给了我两本书：提莫西·高卫的《网球的心理游戏》和麦斯威尔·马尔兹的《心理控制论》。这两本

注释
8. clarity ['klærɪtɪ] *n.* 清楚，清晰；透明

书极大地提高了我的球艺，还更把我对意志力操控人生的这一理论兴趣拔升到最高点。当年我去哪都带上它们，之后就没怎么看过，可我记得书的要点是释放你的想象力，进而影响你比赛的发挥，或者人生道路的选择。

我在佛罗里达大学的第一年，正是最强烈想去渴知了解的时候，做的和想的其他事情相比其重要性反而次之。一整年，我成日都在思索生活的意义、死亡的奥秘这些看不见摸不着的问题。接着，正在这时，妈妈送来了另一本书：何塞·西瓦的《西瓦意识控制法》。我再次陷入对自己意识中不可汲取的能力的沉思中，并为其中蕴涵的神秘莫测感到新的兴奋。不过在我读完它前，另一本书到了，是一系列书当中的第一本照亮了我思想中最黑暗的角落。这本书和我看的其他书不一样，文笔清晰而具有深度，它毫无例外地印证了我对待生命的最深处感情与直觉。它把我最模糊不清的想法变成文字，填补了当中的空白沟壑。看完这两本书，我感到我一直以来竭尽心思的探求几近尾声。那时我的问题或者已经得到了解答，或者至少是有答案可寻的。这些书中包含了由已故的简·罗伯特口述写下的《塞思物质》。

今天，正是通过追逐自己的目标与理想，我明白了许多，甚至是与生命和自我有关的许多更重大的意义。

我的了解也对我生活中从人际关系到物质利益的其他方面有所裨益，而且这些都在继续不断地跨越高涨。目前我仍是个学生，但也是自己的老师，在这个旅程中，我已经认识到，我既乐于思考思索，也同样地乐于分享我的思考，并从他人那里汲取和学习。我相信，这也多少说明了为什么我们的人生道路此刻会在这里交界，你和我。

文化点滴

The Silva Mind-Control Method
西瓦意识控制法或西瓦心灵术是一套包含催眠、观想、冥想和自我暗示等范畴的一套技术，同时为一种放松的技巧。西瓦心灵术借由放松身心、减慢脑波频率、促进右脑的活动，进而产生正面的效果。

写作特点

本文大量地使用了举例论证。举例论证是议论文中的一种方法，列举确凿、充分，有代表性的事例证明论点。通过列举典型事例，具体有力地证明了中心论点，增强了说服力。

品味鉴赏

在这个信息化的世界里，读书是我们获取知识的必要途径之一。多读书可以拓宽我们的知识量，丰富我们的文学修养。我们的知识就像水库，大量的阅读使我们的水库能储存大量的知识，而我们在补充知识的同时，知识也在不停地往外泄漏。这时，如果我们停止读书，或者读的书少了，水库的水很快就会枯竭。只有不停地阅读，才能使自己的知识日见丰富。

美文感悟

If I Were a Boy Again
假如我又回到了童年

If I were a boy again, I would practice **perseverance**[1] more often, and never give up a thing because it was difficult or **inconvenient**[2]. If we want light, we must conquer darkness. Perseverance can sometimes equal genius in its results. "There are only two creatures," says a proverb, "who can **surmount**[3] the pyramids—the eagle and the snail."

If I were a boy again, I would school myself into a habit of attention; I would let nothing come between me and the subject in hand. I would remember that a good skater never tries to skate in two directions at once.

The habit of attention becomes part of our life, if we begin early enough. I often hear grown-up people say "I could not fix my attention on the sermon or book, although I wished to do so", and the reason is, the habit was not formed in youth.

If I were to live my life over again, I would pay more attention to the cultivation of the memory. I would strengthen that faculty by every possible means, and on every possible occasion. It takes a little hard work at first to remember things accurately; but memory soon helps itself, and gives very little trouble. It only needs early cultivation to become a power.

If I were a boy again, I would cultivate courage. "Nothing is so mild and gentle as courage, nothing so cruel and pitiless as cowardice," says a wise author.

We too often borrow trouble, and **anticipate**[4] that may never appear. "The fear of ill exceeds the ill we fear." Dangers will arise in any career, but presence of mind will often conquer the worst of them. Be prepared for any fate, and there is no harm to be feared.

If I were a boy again, I would look on the cheerful side. Life is very much like a mirror: if you

---

注释
1. perseverance [ˌpɜːsɪˈvɪərəns] *n.* 坚定不移
2. inconvenient [ˌɪnkənˈviːnjənt] *adj.* 不便的，有困难的
3. surmount [sɜːˈmaʊnt] *vt.* 战胜，在……顶上

smile upon it, it smiles back upon you; but if you **frown**[5] and look doubtful on it, you will get a similar look in return.

Inner sunshine warms not only the heart of the owner, but of all that come in contact with it. "Who shuts love out ,in turn shall be shut out from love."

If I were a boy again, I would school myself to say no more often. I might write pages on the importance of learning very early in life to gain that point where a young boy can stand erect, and decline doing an unworthy act because it is unworthy.

If I were a boy again, I would demand of myself more courtesy towards my companions and friends, and indeed towards strangers as well. The smallest courtesies along the rough roads of life are like the little birds that sing to us all winter long, and make that season of ice and snow more **endurable**[6].

Finally, instead of trying hard to be happy, as if that were the sole purpose of life, I would, if I were a boy again, I would still try harder to make others happy.

原文翻译

假如我又回到了童年，我做事要更有毅力，决不因为事情艰难或者麻烦而撒手不干。我们要光明，就得征服黑暗。毅力在效果上有时能同天才相比。俗话说："能登上金字塔的生物，只有两种——鹰和蜗牛。"

假如我又回到了童年，我就要养成专心致志的习惯；有事在手，就决不让任何东西令我分心。我要牢记：优秀的滑冰手从不试图同时滑向两个不同的方向。

如果及早养成这种专心致志的习惯，它将成为我们生命的一部分。我常听成年人说："虽然我希望能集中注意力听牧师讲道或读书，但往往做不到。"而原因就是年少时没有养成这种习惯。

假如我现在能重新开始我的生命，我就要更注意记忆力的培养。我要采取一切可能的办法，并且在一切可能的场合，增强记忆力。要正确无误地记住一些东西，在开始阶段的确要做出一番小小的努力；但要不了多久，记忆力本身就会起作用，使记忆成为轻而易举的事，只需及早培养，记忆自会成为一种才能。

假如我又回到了童年，我就要培养勇气。一位明智的作家曾说过："世上没有东西比勇气更温文尔雅，也没有东西比怯懦更残酷无情。"

我们常常过多地自寻烦恼，杞人忧天。"怕祸害比祸害本身更可怕。"凡事都有危险，但镇定沉着往往能克服最严重的危险。对一切祸福做好准备，那么就没有什么灾难可以害怕的了。

假如我又回到了童年，我就要事事乐观。生活犹如一面镜子：你朝它笑，它也朝你笑；如果你双眉紧锁，向它投以怀疑的目光，它也将还予你同样的目光。

内心的欢乐不仅温暖了欢乐者自己的心，也温暖了所有与之接触者的心。"谁拒爱于门外，也必将被爱拒之门外。"

假如我又回到了童年，我就要养成经常说"不"的习惯。一个少年要能挺得起腰，拒绝做不应该做的事，就因为这事不值得做。我可以写上好几页谈谈早年培养这一点的重要性。

假如我又回到了童年，我就要要求自己对伙伴和朋友更加礼貌，而且对陌生人也应如此。在坎坷的生活

注释　4. **anticipate** [æn'tɪsɪpeɪt] vt. 预期，期望　　6. **endurable** [ɪn'djʊəbl] adj. 可忍受的，能忍耐的
　　　5. **frown** [fraʊn] vi. 皱眉，蹙额；不赞成，反对

道路上，最细小的礼貌犹如在漫长的冬天为我们歌唱的小鸟，那歌声使冰天雪地的寒冬变得较易忍受。

最后，假如我又回到了童年，我不会力图为自己谋幸福，好像这就是人生唯一的目的；与之相反，我要更努力为他人谋幸福。

文化点滴

"There are only two creatures, who can surmount the pyramids—the eagle and the snail."（"能登上金字塔的生物，只有两种——鹰和蜗牛。"）这是一句埃及谚语。如果没有鹰的天赋，就做只老老实实、勤勤恳恳的蜗牛。鹰一旦失去了天赋，就会一落千丈。倘若做了蜗牛，即使爬不到塔顶，但只要实实在在地爬行，也不会一无所有。登上金字塔塔顶的鹰和蜗牛都是值得学习和标榜的。前者能抵制顺境里的迷惘，后者能克服逆境里的困难。

写作特点

本文大量地使用了"If…"这一排比的修辞手法。排比往往给人以一气呵成之感，节奏感强，增强语言气势，加强表达效果。排比多用于说理或抒情。用排比说理，可以把论点阐述得更严密，更透彻；用排比抒情，可以把情感抒发得淋漓尽致。此处运用排比，能充分地表达出作者对童年逝去的惋惜和对没有珍惜童年的大好时光而懊悔，并对如果能重返童年进行了无限的遐想。

品味鉴赏

这是一篇感人至深的文章，它告诉人们在年轻的时候奋斗和刻苦是多么的重要，而荒废时光换来的则是年老的追悔莫及。

美文感悟

The Death of Moth
飞蛾之死

作者简介：

弗吉尼亚·伍尔夫（Virginia Woolf, 1882—1941），英国女作家、评论家。父亲为著名的学者、编辑莱斯利·斯蒂芬。家学渊源，未受学堂教育却坐拥书城，多年通研古典文学，20出头便成为《泰晤士报·文学副刊》的撰稿人。

    Moths that fly by day are not properly to be called moths; they do not excite that pleasant sense of dark autumn nights and ivy-blossom which the commonest yellow underwing asleep in the shadow of the curtain never fails to rouse in us. They are hybrid creatures, neither gay like butterflies nor somber like their own species. Nevertheless the present specimen, with his narrow hay-coloured wings, fringed with a tassel of the same colour, seemed to be content with life. It was a pleasant morning, mid-September, mild, **benignant**[1], yet with a keener breath than that of the summer months. The plough was already scoring the field opposite the window, and where the share had been, the earth was pressed flat and gleamed with moisture. Such vigour came rolling in from the fields and the down beyond that it was difficult to keep the eyes strictly turned upon

注释　1. **benignant** [bɪˈnɪɡnənt] *adj.* 仁慈的，有益的，和蔼的

the book. The rooks too were keeping one of their annual festivities; soaring round the tree-tops until it looked as if a vast net with thousands of black knots in it has been cast up into the air; which, after a few moments sank slowly down upon the trees until every twig seemed to have a knot at the end of it. Then, suddenly, the net would be thrown into the air again in a wider circle this time, with the **utmost**[2] clamour and vociferation, as though to be thrown into the air and settle slowly down upon the tree-tops were a tremendously exciting experience.

The same energy which **inspired**[3] the rooks, the ploughmen, the horses, and even, it seemed, the lean bare-backed downs, sent the moth **fluttering**[4] from side to side of his square of the window-pane. One could not help watching him. One was, indeed **conscious**[5] of a queer feeling of pity for him. The possibilities of pleasure seemed that morning so enormous and so various that to have only a moth's part in life, and a day moth's at that, appeared a hard fate, and his zest in enjoying his meagre opportunities to the full, **pathetic**[6]. He flew vigorously to one corner of his compartment, and, after waiting there a second, flew across to the other. What remained for him but to fly to a third corner and then to a fourth? That was all he could do, in spite of the size of the downs, the width of the sky, the far-off smoke of houses, and the romantic voice, now and then, of a steamer out at sea. What he could do he did. Watching him, it seemed as if a fibre, very thin but pure, of the enormous energy of the world had been thrust into his frail and **diminutive**[7] body. As often as he crossed the pane, I could fancy that a thread of vital light became visible. He was little or nothing but life.

Yet, because he was so small, and so simple a form of the energy that was rolling in at the open window and driving its way through so many narrow and **intricate**[8] corridors in my own brain and in those of other human beings, there was something marvelous as well as pathetic about him. It was as if someone had taken a tiny bead of pure life and decking it as lightly as possible with down and feathers, had set it dancing and zigzagging to show us the true nature of life. Thus displayed one could not get over the strangeness of it. One is apt to forget all about life, seeing it humped and bossed and **garnished**[9] and cumbered so that is has to move with the greatest circumspection and dignity. Again, the thought of all that life might have been—had been born in any other shape—caused one to view his simple activities with a kind of pity.

After a time, tried by his dancing apparently, he settled on the window ledge in the sun, and the queer spectacle being at an end, I forgot about him. Then, looking up, my eye was caught by him. He was trying to resume his dancing, but seemed either so stiff or so awkward that he could only flutter to the bottom of the window-pane; and when he tried to fly across it he failed. Being intent on other matters I watched these **futile**[10] attempts for a time without thinking, unconsciously waiting for him to resume his flight, as one waits for a machine, that has stopped momentarily,

注释

2. utmost [ˈʌtmənt] adj. 极度的，最远的
3. inspire [ɪnˈspaɪə] vt. 鼓舞，激发，激励
4. flutter [ˈflʌtə] vt. 拍翅，鼓翼
5. conscious [ˈkɒnʃəs] adj. 有意识的，有知觉的
6. pathetic [pəˈθetɪk] adj. 可怜的，悲惨的
7. diminutive [dɪˈmɪnjutɪv] adj. 小的，小型的
8. intricate [ˈɪntrɪkɪt] adj. 复杂的，错综的，难以理解的
9. garnish [ˈɡɑːnɪʃ] v. 装饰
10. futile [ˈfjuːtaɪl] adj. 琐细的；无用的，无效果的

to start again without considering the reason for its failure. After perhaps a seventh attempt he slipped from the wooden ledge and fell, fluttering his wings, on to his back on the window-sill. The helplessness of his attitude roused me. It flashed upon me that he was in difficulties; he could no longer raise himself; his legs struggled vainly. But, as I stretched out a pencil, meaning to help him to right himself, it came over me that the failure and awkwardness were the approach of death. I laid the pencil down again.

The legs **agitate**[11] themselves once more. I looked as if for the enemy against which he struggled. I looked out of doors. What had happened there? Presumably it was midday, and work in the fields had stopped. Stillness and quiet had replaced the previous animation. The birds had taken themselves off to feed in the brooks. The horses stood still. Yet the power was there all the same, massed outside indifferent, impersonal, not attending to anything in particular. Somehow it was opposed to the little hay-coloured moth. It was useless to try to do anything. One could only watch the extraordinary efforts made by those tiny legs against an oncoming doom which could, had it chosen, have submerged an entire city, not merely a city, but masses of human beings; nothing, I knew, had any chance against death. Nevertheless after a pause of exhaustion the legs fluttered again. It was superb this last protest, and so **frantic**[12] that he succeeded at last in righting himself. One's sympathies, of course, were all on the side of life. Also, when there was nobody to care or to know, this gigantic effort on the part of an insignificant little moth, against a power of such magnitude, to retain what no one else valued or desired to keep, moved one strangely. Again, somehow, one saw life, a pure bead. I lifted the pencil again, useless though I knew it to be. But even as I did so, the unmistakable tokens of death showed themselves. The body relaxed, and instantly grew stiff. The struggle was over. The insignificant little creature now knew death. As I looked at the dead moth, this minute wayside triumph of so great a force over so mean an **antagonist**[13] filled me with wonder. Just as life had been strange a few minutes before, so death was now as strange. The moth having righted himself now lay most decently and uncomplainingly composed. O yes, he seemed to say, death is stronger than I am.

原文翻译

白昼出没的飞蛾，准确地说，不叫飞蛾；它们激发不起关于沉沉秋夜和青藤小花的欣快意念，而藏在帷幕幽暗处沉睡的最普通的"翼底黄"飞蛾却总会唤醒这样的联想。"翼底黄"是杂交的产物，既不像蝴蝶一般色彩鲜艳，也不像飞蛾类那样全身昏暗。尽管如此，眼前这只蛾子，窄窄的双翼显现着枯灰色。翼梢缀有同样颜色的一圈流苏，看上去似乎活得心满意足。这是一个令人神清气爽的早晨。时届9月中旬，气温舒适宜人，而吹过来的风已比夏季清凉。窗户对面，犁耕已经开始。犁铧过处，泥土被翻了起来，显得湿漉漉又乌油油。从田野以及更远处的丘陵，一股勃勃生机扑面而来，使双眼难以完全专注于书本。还有那些白嘴鸦，

注释
11. **agitate** ['ædʒɪteɪt] v. 搅动，摇动，煽动
12. **frantic** ['fræntɪk] adj. 狂乱的，疯狂的
13. **antagonist** [æn'tæɡənɪst] n. 敌手，对手

飞蛾之死

像是正在欢庆某一次年会，绕着树梢盘旋，远远望去仿佛有一张缀有万千黑点的大网撒开在空中。过了一会，大网慢慢降下，直到林中的每一处枝头落满黑点。随后，大网突然再次撒向天空，这一回，画出的圆弧更大，同时伴以不绝于耳的队队鸦噪，似乎一会儿急急腾空而去，一会儿徐徐栖落枝头，乃是极富刺激性的活动。

一种活力激励着白嘴鸦、掌犁农夫和辕马，影响所及甚至连贫瘠的秃丘也透出了生气。正是这种活力撩拨着飞蛾鼓翅，从正方形窗玻璃的一侧移动到另一侧。你无法不去注视它；你甚至对它产生了一种莫名的怜悯。这天早晨，生命的乐趣表现得淋漓尽致又丰富多样。相比之下，作为一只飞蛾浮生在世，而且是只有一天生命的飞蛾，真是命运不济。虽则机遇不堪，飞蛾却仍在尽情享受，看到这种热情不禁引人唏嘘。它劲头儿十足地飞到窗格的一角，在那儿停了一秒钟之后，穿越窗面飞到另一角。除了飞到第三然后又是第四角，它还能做什么呢？这就是它能做的一切，虽然户外丘陵广袤，天空无际，远处的房屋炊烟缭绕，海上的轮船不时发出引人遐思的汽笛声。飞蛾能做到的事，它都做了。注视着它的时候，我觉得在它羸弱的小身体里，仿佛塞进了一缕纤细然而洗练的世间奇伟的活力。每当它飞越窗面，我总觉得有一丝生命之光亮起。飞蛾虽小，甚至微不足道，却也是生灵。

然而，正因为它微不足道，正因为它以简单的形式体现了从打开的窗户滚滚涌进并在我和其他人大脑错综复杂的狭缝中冲击而过的一种活力，飞蛾不但引人唏嘘，还同样令人惊叹，使人感到似乎有谁取来一颗晶莹的生命之珠，以尽可能轻盈的手法饰以茸羽之后，使其翩跃起舞，左右飞旋，从而向我们显示生命的真谛。这样展示在人们的面前，飞蛾使人无法不啧啧称奇，而在目睹飞蛾弓背凸现的模样同时，看它装扮着又像背负了重荷，因此动作既谨慎又滞重，人们不禁会全然忘记生命是怎么一回事。人们倒是会又一次想到，生命若以另一种不同于飞蛾的形态诞生将可能变成什么，而这种想法自会使人以某种怜悯的心情去观察飞蛾的简单动作。

过了一会，飞蛾像是飞累了，便在阳光下的窗沿上落停。飞舞的奇观已经结束，我便把它忘了。待我抬起头来，注意力又被它吸引了去，只见它在试图再次飞起，可是因为身体已太僵直，要不就是姿态别扭，而只能扑闪着翅膀，落到窗玻璃的底部。当它挣扎着往顶部飞时，它已力不从心了。因为我正专注于其他事情，所以只是心不在焉地看着飞蛾徒劳地扑腾。同时，无意识地等着它再一次飞起。犹如等着一台暂时停转的机器重新开动而不去探究停转的原因。也许扑腾了7次，飞蛾终于从木质窗沿滑下，抖动着双翅仰天掉在窗台上。它这种绝望无助的体位唤回了我的注意，我顿时意识到飞蛾陷入了困境，它的细腿一阵乱蹬，却全无结果，它再也无法把身体挺直。我手持一支铅笔朝它伸去，想帮它翻一个身，然而就在这时我认识到，扑腾失败和姿态别扭都是死之将至的表征。于是，我放下了铅笔。

细腿又抖动了一次。我像是为了寻找飞蛾与之搏斗的仇敌，便朝户外望去。那儿发生了什么？大概已是中午时分。田畴劳作业已停止。原先的奔忙已被静止所取代。鸟儿忙往小溪觅食，辕马立停。但是，那股力量依然聚集在那儿，一股冷漠超然、非人格化、不针对任何具体对象的力量。不知出于什么原因，与枯灰色的小飞蛾作对的，正是这股力量。试图抗拒这股力量，全然无用，我所能做的，唯有看着飞蛾软弱的细腿作出非凡的挣扎，抵拒那渐渐接近的毁灭伟力。毁灭伟力，只要它愿意，本可埋没整一座城池；除了城池，还可夺去千万人的生命。我知道，与死神搏斗，世间万物都无取胜的可能。虽说如此，因为筋疲力尽而小憩之后，细腿又抖动起来。这最后的抗争确属英勇超凡，而挣扎又是如此之狂暴，飞蛾竟然最终翻身成功了。当然，你定会赞同求生的一方。与此同时，在无人过问也无人知晓的情况下，这微不足道的小飞蛾为了维持既无他人重视又无他人意欲保存的生命，竟对如此巨大的伟力作出这样强悍的拼搏，这更使人受到异样的感动。不知怎的，我又一次见到了那晶莹的生命之珠。虽说意识到一切全是徒劳，我重又提起铅笔。然而正在这时，确凿无误的死亡症状出现了。蛾体先是松弛下来，旋即变得僵硬。搏斗告终，这微不足道的小生命死了。看着飞蛾的尸体，看着这股巨大的伟力把这么一个可怜巴巴的对手捎带着战胜，我心头充满了惊异感。几分钟之前，生命曾显得那样奇诡，如今死亡也是同样地奇诡。飞蛾端正了身体，安安静静躺在那儿，端庄而毫无怨尤。哦，是的，它好像在说，死神毕竟比我强大。

文化点滴

弗吉尼亚·伍尔夫，英国女作家、评论家。父亲为著名的学者、编辑莱斯利·斯蒂芬。家学渊源，未受学堂教育却坐拥书城，多年通研古典文学，20出头便成为《泰晤士报·文学副刊》的撰稿人。父亲去世后，移居伦敦布卢姆斯伯里区，交结文坛名流，往来于她的伦敦寓所的乃一代精英，如经济学家凯恩斯、小说家福斯特、诗圣艾略特及先锋派艺术家等。布卢姆斯伯里文社由此知名于世。其写作出于本能，小说创作上反对自然主义，多用"意识流"手法。散文以人物随笔和批评文字著称，女权主义思想强烈，见解卓越，感受真切，可谓出自灵性，别具一格。纵观伍尔夫的一生，作为一名独立的女性，宽松的生活圈子和志同道合的朋友们的支持令她可以不受约束，文思驰骋，但她深深感觉到广大妇女所面临的潜网，并试图在个人的程度上冲破这张潜网。虽然她为自己的追求付出了巨大的代价，但她的成就对当时普遍特定的"女人不会写作"的观点提出了有力的反驳，而她自身的经历也是妇女足以与男子抗衡的有力证明。

写作特点

《飞蛾之死》是伍尔夫的名作之一，文章通过对一只飞蛾从抗争到死亡的过程的描述来隐喻生命的渺小和奋斗的价值。文章的用词考究，问题严肃，阅读难度较大，需要一定的词汇量基础和语言储备才能完全读懂。通过这篇文章的阅读，要注意掌握一些常见的短语和句型。它们往往看似简单却容易导致理解偏差，从而影响到对文章的正确理解。下面列出一些在阅读中常见的、可能会影响理解的短语和句子。

anything but 根本不

nothing but 只不过是

all but 几乎，差一点，除……以外其余都是

but for 要不是

but that +从句，若不是……

only to+动词，结果是……

not so much...as... 与其说……不如说……

not so much as 连……都不（肯）

not nearly/by no means/far from 远不

to say nothing of, not to speak of, not to mention, let alone 更不用说

much less, still less 引导的词组或从句，表示一种追加的否定

no more...than... 和……一样都不……

more...than... 与其……不如……

no less than... 简直是，实在是

nothing less than 完全是，实在是

not that...but that... 不是……而是……

cannot...too... 再……也不过分，应该

other...than, other than 不同于，非，除了

the last person/thing, etc.+ to do sth... 最不可能的……

It is asserted that... 有人断言……

It is reported that... 据报道……

It is believed that... 人们/有人认为……

品味鉴赏

　　作者为我们描述了一只飞蛾的悲剧命运。在注定无法突围而出的舞台上，飞蛾用它全部的精神和勇气不断向外飞翔，又一次次被阻挡，最终迎接了自己死亡的命运。伍尔夫的笔调悲悯而热诚。就是这样一只微不足道的飞蛾，它在最后时刻，仍然在让自己的生命燃烧，不懈地追求着光明和希望。飞蛾小小的不屈灵魂和精神，加之伍尔夫饱满的热情，让这篇文章一直深受读者喜爱。更有人认为，伍尔夫通过《飞蛾之死》述说了自己的命运，这只飞蛾代她说出了她留给世间的遗言。

美文感悟

Human Happiness Is Sensuous
快乐是一种感觉

作者简介：

　　林语堂（1895—1976），福建龙溪（现福建漳州）人。1912年入上海圣约翰大学，毕业后在清华大学任教。1919年秋赴美哈佛大学文学系深造，1922年获文学硕士学位，同年转赴德国入莱比锡大学，专攻语言学。1923年获博士学位后回国，任北京大学教授、北京女子师范大学教务长和英文系主任。1935年后，在美国用英文创作《吾国与吾民》《京华烟云》《风声鹤唳》等文化著作和长篇小说。

　　1944年曾一度回国到重庆讲学。1945年赴新加坡筹建南洋大学，任校长。1966年定居台湾。1967年受聘为香港中文大学研究教授。1975年被推举为国际笔会副会长。1976年在香港逝世。

　　All human happiness is biological happiness. That is strictly scientific. At the risk of being misunderstood, I must make it clearer: all human happiness is **sensuous**[1] happiness. The spiritualists and materialists must forever misunderstand me, I am sure; the spiritualists and materialists must forever misunderstand each other, because they don't talk the same language, or mean by the same word different things. Are we, too, in this problem of securing happiness to be

注释　**1. sensuous** ['sensjuəs] *adj.* 感觉上的，给人美感的

deluded[2] by the spiritualists, and admit that true happiness is only happiness of the spirit? Let us admit at once and immediately proceed to qualify it by saying that the spirit is a condition of the perfect functioning of the endocrine glands.

Happiness for me is largely a matter of digestion. I have to take over under an American college president to insure my reputation and respectability when I say that happiness is largely a matter of the movement of the bowels. The American college president in question used to say with great wisdom in his address to each class of freshmen, "There are only two things I want you to keep in mind: read the *Bible* and keep your bowels open." What a wise, **genial**[3] old soul he was to have said that! If one's bowels move, one is happy, and if they don't move, one is unhappy. That is all there is in it.

Let us not lose ourselves in the abstract when we talk of happiness, but get down to facts and analyze for ourselves what are the truly happy moments of our life. In this world of ours, happiness is very often negative, the complete absence of sorrow or mortification or bodily ailment. But happiness can also be positive, and then we call it joy.

To me, for instance, the truly happy moments are: when I get up in the morning after a night of perfect sleep and sniff the morning air and there is an expansiveness in the lungs, when I feel inclined to **inhale**[4] deeply and there is a fine sensation of movement around the skin and muscles of the chest, and when therefore, I am fit for work; or when I hold a pipe in my hand and rest my legs on a chair, and the tobacco burns slowly and evenly; or when I am traveling on a summer day, my throat **parched**[5] with the thirst, and I see a beautiful clear spring, whose very sound makes me happy, and I take off my socks and shoes and dip my feet in the delightful, cool water; or when after a perfect dinner I **lounge**[6] in an armchair, when there is no one I hate to look at in the company and conversation rambles off at a light pace to an unknown destination, and I am spiritually and physically at peace with the world; or when on a summer afternoon I see black clouds gathering on the horizon and know for certain a July shower is coming in a quarter of an hour, but being ashamed to be seen going out into the rain without an umbrella, I hastily set out to meet the shower halfway across the fields and come home drenched through and through and tell my family that I was simply caught by the rain.

Just as it is impossible for me to say whether I love my children physically or spiritually when I hear their **chattering**[7] voices or when I see their plump legs, so I am totally unable to distinguish between the joys of the mind and the joys of the flesh. Does anybody ever love a woman spiritually without loving her physically? And is it so easy a matter for a man to analyze and separate the charms of the woman he loves—things like laughter, smiles, a way of tossing one's head, a certain attitude toward things?

---

2. delude [dɪˈluːd] *vt.* 迷惑，蛊惑

3. genial [ˈdʒiːnɪəl] *adj.* 亲切的

4. inhale [ɪnˈheɪl] *vt.* 吸入，吸气

5. parch [pɑːtʃ] *vt.* 烤，烤干，焦干

6. lounge [laʊndʒ] *vi.* 闲荡，懒洋洋地躺卧

7. chatter [ˈtʃætə] *vi.* 喋喋不休地谈话

And after all every girl feels happier when she is well dressed. There is a soul-uplifting quality about lipstick and rouge and a spiritual calm and poise that comes from the knowledge of being well-dressed, which is real and definite for the girl herself and of which the spiritualist has no inkling of an idea. Being made of this mortal flesh, the partition separating our flesh from our spirit is extremely thin, and the world of spirit, with its finest emotions and greatest appreciations of spiritual beauty, cannot be reached except with our senses. There is no such thing as morality and immorality in the sense of touch, of bearing and vision. There is a great probability that our loss of capacity for enjoying the positive joys of life is largely due to the decreased sensibility of our senses and our lack of full use of them.

原文翻译

所有人类的快乐都是生理上的快乐，这一观点是完全科学的。即便是冒着被人误解的危险，我也必须说得更清楚些：所有人类的快乐都是感观上的快乐。唯心论者会误解我，这点我能肯定。唯心论者和唯物论者必定永远彼此误解，因为他们无共同语言，抑或同词异解。在获得快乐的问题上，我们难道也要受唯心论者的蒙骗，承认真正的快乐仅仅是精神的快乐吗？让我们既承认一点，又即刻对此作出进一步的修正：精神是内分泌腺充分作用的一种状态。

快乐于我，在更大程度上是一个消化的问题。为了确保我的名声和责任，在我提出"快乐主要是肠运动的问题"这一观点时，我想借用一位美国大学校长的话。提及的这位美国校长惯常极富智慧地对每一班的新生说："我只希望你们能记住两件事情：诵读《圣经》和保持排便通畅。"言能及此，他真不愧是一位睿智而又亲切的长者！肠动，则人欢；肠止，则人颓。道理就在此。

在谈论快乐的时候，我们不能在抽象中迷失方向，而应认真地对待事实，自己分析到底什么才是生活中真正的快乐时光。在我们这个世界，快乐经常以否定形式出现，如彻底的无忧、无辱、无羞。但快乐也能以肯定的形式出现，我们称之为欢乐。

以我为例，真正的快乐时光有：一夜酣睡之后晨起，用力呼吸清晨的空气，感受到肺部在扩张，当我想深呼吸时，胸部周围的皮肤和肌肉舒展的感觉让人惬意，因此，此刻适宜于工作；或者，当我手持烟斗，脚搁在椅子上，让烟草缓慢而又均匀地燃烧；或者，当我在夏日旅游，正口干舌燥之时，突然见到一泓美丽而又清澈的泉水，叮咚之时，令人喜悦，我便脱下鞋袜，把双脚浸入那欢快清凉的水中；或者，当美食一餐之后，我懒洋洋地躺在扶手椅子里，没有看不顺眼的人在旁，一通轻松自由、漫无目标的神聊，让我的身心和世界平静交融；或者，在一个夏日午后，看见天际正在集聚乌云，确定一场7月的阵雨片刻将至，不好意思被人发现没有带雨伞就往外奔，我急忙出发到田野对面的半道上去迎接阵雨，回家时浑身湿透，还骗家人说，正巧路遇大雨。

就像听见孩子们叽叽喳喳的声音，看见他们圆滚滚的小腿时，我不可能说清楚，到底是爱他们的肉体还是精神一样，我也完全不能区分精神的愉快和肉体的愉快。有没有这样的人，他喜欢一个女人的精神，而不喜欢她的身体？让一个男人分析并说出他所爱的那个女人的魅力——诸如一颦一笑、举手投足或处事态度，会是一件容易的事情吗？

每一个女孩子毕竟都会因穿着漂亮而格外快乐。口红和胭脂有令人提神的功能，知道自己穿着体面能令人心境平和，这对女孩子来讲，是真实无疑的，而唯心论者对此却毫无所知。作为凡人，我们的精神和肉体仅一纸之隔，精神世界、最纤细的情感、对精神美的最伟大的赏识，假如没有我们的感知，是不可能达到的。触觉、仪态和视觉，诸如此类，与精神上的道德或不道德毫不相干。我们之所以失却欣赏生活真实欢乐的能力，在很大程度上，是因为我们感观钝化和未能对其充分利用所致。

文化点滴

spiritualist

唯心论者信奉唯心主义（idealism，即唯心论，又译作理念论），是哲学中与思想、心灵、语言及事物等彼此之间关系的讨论及看法。马克思主义认为，唯心主义是哲学两大基本派别之一，是与唯物主义对立的理论体系。在哲学基本问题上主张精神、意识第一性，物质第二性，即物质依赖意识而存在，物质是意识的产物的哲学派别。

materialis

唯物论者信奉唯物主义，唯物主义是哲学里关于本体论的一种基本观点。它与唯心主义相反，认为在意识与物质之间，物质决定意识，意识是客观世界在人脑中的反映。也就是说"物质第一性、精神第二性，世界的本原是物质，精神是物质的产物和反映"。

写作特点

本文在第四段使用了由多个"when..."引导的排比的修辞手法。排比的修辞手法，给人以一气呵成的感觉，增强语言气势，用排比抒情能够把情感抒发得淋漓尽致。此处运用排比能充分地表达出什么时候是作者本人真正的快乐时光。

品味鉴赏

生活，就像是一场规模盛大的假面舞会，而我们都戴着伪善的面具示人。点头、微笑、转身，流着眼泪跌跌撞撞，戴着躯壳寻找灵魂。都说，我不是真正的快乐，那么，什么时候才会拥有真正的快乐？童年的快乐是无瑕的，也是难忘的。学生时代的友情纯真、朴素，也是快乐的一部分。爱情的甜蜜，无以替代，但是其代价也是每个成熟的人所经历过的伤痛。所以，一生中最快乐的时光是内心如镜的时候。当残酷的现实压力围绕在身边的时候，没有很深的修行，是很难体会真正的快乐的。真正的快乐，是来自内心的、来自于对自己今生所遇到的一切油然而生的一种满足之感。

美文感悟

Chapter 7

生活艺术

生活不一定是要有多么伟大的理想或者成为多么伟大的人，生活也可以是简单的。但是，简单生活不是要节衣缩食或者过一种毫无诱惑力的生活；相反，是要拥有更加富裕、有趣、充实、长久而健康的生活。生命逝去越多，我们就越应该精选自己的生活，不要徒劳地让生活变得复杂。给自己的生命留出空间吧！简化生活，净化心灵，提高生活的品质。我们想成为什么样的人、过怎样的生活，必须有清晰、正确、合理的构想。

A Treatise on Good Manners and Good Breeding
论礼貌与教养

作者简介：

乔纳森·斯威夫特（Jonathan Swift，1667—1745），英国讽刺作家和散文家。遗腹子，出生于都柏林。曾当过退休外交家、散文家威廉·坦普尔（Sir William Temple）的私人秘书。经典传世之作《格列佛游记》（*Gulliver's Travels*）已经被译成了多国语言。

Good manners are the art of making those people easy with whom we converse.

Whoever makes the fewest persons uneasy is the best bred in the company.

As the best law is founded upon reason, so are the best manners. And as some lawyers have introduced unreasonable things into common law, so likewise many teachers have introduced **absurd**[1] things into common good manners.

One principal point of this art is to suit our behaviour to the three several degrees of men, our superiors, our equals, and those below us.

For instance, to press either of the two former to eat or drink is a breach of manners; but a farmer or a tradesman must be thus treated, or else it will be difficult to persuade them that they are welcome.

---

1. **absurd** [əb'sɜːd] *adj.* 荒谬的，可笑的

Pride, ill nature, and want of sense, are the three great sources of ill manners; without some one of these **defects**², no man will behave himself ill for want of experience; or of what, in the language of fools, is called knowing the world.

I defy anyone to assign an incident wherein reason will not direct us what we are to say or do in company, if we are not misled by pride or ill nature.

Therefore, I insist that good sense is the principal foundation of good manners; but because the former is a gift which very few among mankind are possessed of, therefore all the civilized nations of the world have agreed upon fixing some rules for common behaviour, best suited to their general customs, or fancies, as a kind of artificial good sense, to supply the defects of reason. Without which the gentlemanly part of dunces would be perpetually at cuffs, as they seldom fail when they happen to be drunk, or engaged in **squabbles**³ about women or play. And, God be thanked, there hardly happens a **duel**⁴ in a year, which may not be **imputed**⁵ to one of those three motives. Upon which account, I should be exceedingly sorry to find the legislature make any new laws against the practice of dueling; because the methods are easy and many for a wise man to avoid a quarrel with honour, or engage in it with **innocence**⁶. And I can discover no political evil in suffering bullies, sharpers, and rakes, to rid the world of each other by a method of their own; where the law hath not been able to find an expedient.

As the common forms of good manners were intended for regulating the conduct of those who have weak understandings; so they have been corrupted by the persons for whose use they were **contrived**⁷. For these people have fallen into a needless and endless way of multiplying ceremonies, which have been extremely troublesome to those who practise them, and insupportable to everybody else: insomuch that wise men are often more uneasy at the over **civility**⁸ of these refiners, than they could possibly be in the conversations of peasants or mechanics.

The **impertinencies**⁹ of this ceremonial behaviour are nowhere better seen than at those tables where ladies preside, who value themselves upon account of their good breeding; where a man must reckon upon passing an hour without doing any one thing he has a mind to; unless he will be so hardly to break through all the settled **decorum**¹⁰ of the family. She determines what he loves best, and how much he shall eat; and if the master of the house happens to be of the same **disposition**¹¹, he proceeds in the same tyrannical manner to prescribe in the drinking part: at the same time, you are under the necessity of answering a thousand apologies for your entertainment. And although a good deal of this humour is pretty well worn off among many people of the best fashion, yet too much of it still remains, especially in the country; where an honest gentleman assured me, that having been kept four days, against his will, at a

注释

2. **defect** ['di:fekt] *n.* 过失，缺点
3. **squabble** ['skwɒbl] *n.* 争论
4. **duel** ['dju:l] *n.* 决斗
5. **imputed** [ɪmpʊt] *vt.* 归咎于，归因于
6. **innocence** ['ɪnəsəns] *n.* 无知，愚笨
7. **contrive** [kən'traɪv] *v.* 设计，创制
8. **civility** [sɪ'vɪlɪtɪ] *n.* 礼貌
9. **impertinency** [ɪm'pɔ:tɪnəs] *n.* 无礼，不合理
10. **decorum** [dɪ'kɔ:rəm] *n.* 礼仪，礼节
11. **disposition** [dɪspə'zɪʃən] *n.* 性情；脾气

friend's house, with all the circumstances of hiding his boots, locking up the stable, and other contrivances of the like the house to the moment he left it, any one thing, wherein his inclination[12] was not directly contradicted; as if the whole family had entered into a combination to torment him.

原文翻译

礼貌就是使与我们交谈的人安然处之的一种艺术。

在一群人中，谁越不让人感到局促不安，谁就越有教养。

最公正的法律是建立在理智之上的；同样，最好的行为举止也是建立在理智之上的。有的律师把没有道理的东西引进了习惯法；同样，许多教师把荒唐可笑的东西引进了日常的礼貌之中。

礼貌艺术的一大要素是以适当的行为举止来对待三种不同层次的人，即我们的长者、我们的同辈和低于我们这一层次的人。

例如，强迫前两种层次的人吃菜喝酒是失礼的，但是农夫或者商贩就应这样对待，否则就会很难让他们相信他们是受欢迎的。

骄傲自大、性情乖僻、缺乏理性是失礼的三大根源。如果能根除这些弊病，没有人会因为缺乏经验，或者，如某些愚人所说，因为谙于世故而有失礼貌的。

因此，我坚持认为理性是礼貌所需的最重要的基础。但是，由于人类之中很少有人具备理性这种天赋才能，所以世界上所有的文明国度都同意制定最能适合他们风俗或想象的规范行为举止的规章制度，作为一种人为的理性以弥补理智的缺乏。没有这种人为的理性，愚蠢的人之中举止尚属文雅的那部分人便会无休止地挥拳相向，他们在喝得酩酊大醉时，或者在大声谈论女人和玩乐时总是这样的。并且谢天谢地，每年之中发生的决斗几乎无一不可归咎于上述三个原因中的一个。由于这一缘故，我将对立法机构制定任何旨在禁止决斗行为的新法律深表遗憾；因为明智的人可以有许多简捷的办法避免体面的决斗或无知的搏杀。并且在法律尚无有效对策的地方，容忍恃强凌弱、诈骗者和浪荡子自己采取方法来相互铲除，以求清理世界——我看不出这样做有什么政治祸害。

制定良好行为的规范形式，是为了指导调整知识肤浅的人的举止；然而，这些规范形式又恰恰为这些规范形式的制定对象所破坏。因为这些人已习惯于无必要和无休止地增加种种繁文缛节，这些繁文缛节使遵守执行的人无所适从，使所有别的人不敢赞同。现在情况已经到了这样的地步，明智的人对这些谨小慎微的人的过分客套感到更加局促不安，倒不如与农夫商贩的交谈更为轻松自如。

这种繁文缛节、虚礼矫饰到处可见，但是，在那些以良好教养自居的女士所张罗的款待客人的餐桌上尤为荒谬。在那里，一个男子必须甘心枯坐一个钟头而无所事事，除非他铁了心敢打破这家的全部成规礼仪。这位女主人决定男人应该最喜爱吃什么和吃多少。如果这家的男主人也是同样的禀性，他便会在饮酒时刻同样专横地发号施令。与此同时，你不得不成百上千次应答他们的种种道歉，叫你无法消受。尽管在风尚高雅的许多人之间，这种可笑的习气已经大为削弱，但是尤其是在乡间，它的流弊仍广。我曾听到一位诚实的先生说，他曾4天被硬留在乡间友人的家里，终日忙于藏匿靴子、锁上马厩之类矫揉造作的礼节，结果简直想不出，从他来时到他去日的全部逗留时间内，没有任何一件不违背他本意的事，仿佛是朋友的全家人都结成一伙来折磨他。

注释　12. inclination [ɪnklɪ'neɪʃən] *n*. 意愿，爱好

文化点滴

legislature

立法机构是现代社会中负责制定法律的机构，一般由当地公民按人口比例组成，通常称为国会、立法院或议会，但亦有使用不同名称。立法部门除了制定法律外，通常亦负责审批政府（行政部门）的公共开支要求、监督政府运作、同意司法首长的任命等。在议会制中，行政部门亦是由立法部门产生，向立法部门负责。在总统制中，行政首长并不由立法部门产生，而是分开选举。但不论在何种制度中，由于立法部门掌握了公共财政的大权，可以说是最根本的权力来源。立法机构的决策方式是按照少数服从多数的原则进行集体决策，为此各国都设有一套自己的仪式和议事程序。

good manners, civility

礼貌和教养对于装饰人类或其他一切优良品质和天资，都是必不可少的。礼貌不用花钱，却能赢得一切。礼貌使有礼貌的人喜悦，也使那些受人以礼貌相待的人们喜悦。人的潜意识里可能都渴求别人的尊重和赞赏，于是产生了礼貌。礼貌可能是人类文明史上最伟大的发明，它可以帮我们解决很多很多的问题。

写作特点

本文作者旨在善意规劝，阐明了礼貌是为了便于人际交往，但物极必反，不可矫揉造作。文章中作者用了举例的方法来阐明自己的观点。例如：For instance, to press either of the two former to eat or drink is…，…when they happen to be drunk, or engaged in squabbles（争论）about women or play等。利用举例法，不但能够更明确地阐明作者的见解，还可以起到贴近人们生活、把道理化繁为简的效果。

品味鉴赏

礼仪就是一种敬人、律己的行为规范，是表现对他人尊重和理解的过程与手段。从个人修养的角度来看，礼仪是一个人内在修养和素质的外在体现；从交际的角度来看，礼仪是人际交往中适用的一种艺术、一种交际方式或方法，是人际交往中约定俗成的对人表示尊重、友好的习惯做法；从传播的角度来看，礼仪是人际交往中相互沟通的技巧。任何一个文明的社会、文明的民族都会十分注重礼仪。我国就是一个历史悠久的礼仪之邦。

美文感悟

Change Your Bad Habits to Good
改掉坏毛病，养成好习惯

作者简介：

罗伯特·爱泼斯坦（Robert Epstein, 1953—），美国国际大学研究员，人类行为学专家，《今日心理学》（*Psychology Today*）杂志主编和该网络电台主持人，伊诺金国际公司董事长兼执行总裁。著作有《为训练者准备的压力控制与放松活动》、《新编今日心理学》、《为训练者准备的创造力游戏》、《认知、创造力和行为：论文集》等。

At the University of California, my students and I surveyed more than 2,000 years of self-change techniques—perhaps most of the major self-change methods that have ever been proposed by religious leaders, philosophers, psychologists and psychiatrists. We also reviewed the scientific research literature on self-change, a topic that behavioral scientists began to explore in earnest in the 1960s.

Here is what we found: Of the hundreds of self-change techniques that have been suggested over the centuries, perhaps only a dozen are distinctly different. Many have now been subjected to scientific study, meaning that researchers have tried to see which ones work best.

Three deserve special mention: they're powerful, simple and easy to learn. What's more, individuals who have made successful changes in their lives—changes in eating habits, exercise **regimens**[1], career paths, coping strategies, and so on—often relied on one or more of these

---

注释
1. **regimen** ['redʒɪmən] *n.* 养生法

methods.

Modify Your Environment

People who have never tried this are **astounded**[2] by the enormous effect it often has. One of my students got herself bicycling every day simply by putting her bicycle in her doorway before she left for school. When she returned home, that was the first thing she saw, and that's all she needed to start pedaling away. I've known several people who have overcome nail-biting simply by buying 50 nail files and distributing them everywhere: in their pockets, their desks and their bedrooms. With a nail file always within reach, they tended to groom rather than bite.

My children have used this simple technique many times. Justin, my 17-year-old, often places small **fluorescent**[3] reminder notes at eye level on the inside of the frame of his bedroom door. A recent one read "Remember to shampoo the dog on Saturday or Dad will kill you". (Here he was using exaggeration to good effect.)

The power of rearranging one's space has been well demonstrated in studies since it was first reported in the 1960s. Psychologist Israel Goldiamond of the University of Chicago taught this technique to patients with a variety of personal problems. For example, a young woman who had difficulty studying made dramatic strides when she got a better desk lamp and moved her desk away from her bed.

Psychologist Richard Stuart, who **ultimately**[4] became a director at Weight Watchers International, showed in the 1960s that overweight women could lose pounds by modifying both their eating behavior and "**stimulus**[5] environment"—for example, eating from smaller plates and confining all food to the kitchen. To change yourself, change your world.

Monitor Your Behavior

I've been reading research studies on self-monitoring for 20 years, and I've conducted some myself. To be honest, I still don't fully understand why this technique works, but it does, and remarkably well for most people. The fact is, if you monitor what you do, you'll probably do better.

Weigh yourself regularly and you may well start to lose weight. Keep a record of what you eat and you'll probably start eating more wisely.

Use gizmos. If you say "you know" too much, wear a golf counter on your wrist, and press the button whenever you catch yourself saying "you know". I'll bet you say it less frequently in just a few days. If a wrist counter is embarrassing, then make a small **tear**[6] in a piece of paper in your pocket each time you say "you know". The result is the same: you become more aware of what you're doing, and that makes you perform better.

If techniques like this sound silly, keep in mind that the power of self-monitoring has been demonstrated by a variety of research conducted over the last four decades. In a study I

注释

2. **astounded** [əˈstaʊndɪd] adj. 感到惊讶的
3. **fluorescent** [flʊəˈresənt] adj. 荧光的
4. **ultimately** [ˈʌltɪmətlɪ] adv. 最后；终于
5. **stimulus** [ˈstɪmjʊləs] n. 刺激物
6. **tear** [teə] n. 裂口；撕破的地方

published in 1978 with Claire Goss, for example, we taught a **disruptive**[7] fifth-grade boy to rate his own classroom behavior twice a day. He simply checked off a score for himself, indicating how well-behaved he had been in the morning or afternoon. With his awareness increased, he stayed in his seat more than usual, completed more assignments and rarely got in trouble.

A similar study by Canadian researchers Thomas McKenzie and Brent Rushall showed that teenagers arrived more promptly at a swim practice when they were given an attendance sheet to record their arrival times. Working with emotionally disturbed children, Sonya Carr of Southeastern Louisiana University and Rebecca Punzo, a New Orleans teacher reported that self-monitoring improves academic performance in reading, mathematics and spelling. Recent research even demonstrated that students will compose better stories given a simple checklist that includes elements of good writing. Dozens of studies have similar results, all **spurred**[8] by **heightening**[9] our awareness of our behavior.

Make Commitments

When you make a commitment to another person, you establish what psychologists call a contingency of reinforcement; you've automatically arranged for a reward if you **comply**[10] and a punishment if you don't. It puts some pressure on you, and that's often just what you need.

For instance, if you want to exercise more, arrange to do it with a friend. If you don't show up, your friend will get angry, and that may be just the ticket to keeping you punctual. Decades of research have demonstrated the power of this strategy. For example, in 1994 Dana Putnam and other researchers at the Virginia Polytechnic Institute and State University showed that patients who made written commitments were far more likely to take prescribed medicine than patients who hadn't. Mary Lou Kau and Joel Fischer of the University of Hawaii reported a case of a woman who got herself to jog regularly by setting up a simple arrangement with her husband: he paid her quarters and took her out on weekends whenever she met her jogging goals.

There's good news here for all of us. We can meet many of the demands and overcome many of the challenges of life with simple skills—straightforward practices that anyone can master and that don't require **willpower**[11]—in other words, with skill, not will.

原文翻译

在加利福尼亚大学，我和我的学生调查了两千多年来人们用来改变自我的技巧——也许主要方法中的大部分都是由宗教领袖、哲学家、心理学家和精神病专家提出的。我们还回顾了有关改变自我的科学研究文献。早在20世纪60年代，改变自我就是行为科学家开始认真探索的课题。

我们的发现结果如下：在几个世纪以来人们提出的几百种改变自我的方法中，也许仅有十来种与其他方法截然不同。许多方法至今一直是科学研究的对象，这意味着研究人员一直试图探明其中最有效的方法。

注释

7. disruptive [dɪsˈrʌptɪv] adj. 引起混乱的
8. spur [spɜː] v. 激励；鞭策
9. heighten [ˈhaɪtən] vt. 增加；提高
10. comply [kəmˈplaɪ] vi. 遵守
11. willpower [ˈwɪlpaʊə] n. 意志力，毅力

有三种方法值得特别提及：它们效力强大而又简单易学。此外，那些已成功改变了其人生道路的人们，也常常是依靠这些方法中的一种或多种来改变其饮食习惯、养生之道、事业方向和处世策略等等。

改善周边环境

从未尝试改善环境的人通常会对其所产生的显著效果感到惊奇不已。我的一个学生为了促使自己每天骑车锻炼，采取了离家上学前将自行车放在门道里的简单方法。这样一回家，她首先看见的就是那辆车，而所需做的就是骑上自行车锻炼去。我认识几个人，他们为了改掉咬指甲的坏习惯而买了50把指甲锉并把它们分放到各处：口袋里，书桌上，卧室里。由于指甲锉总能伸手可及，他们就会去修指甲，而不是啃指甲了。我的孩子们多次运用过这样的简单技巧。我17岁的儿子贾斯汀经常把小小的荧光纸记事便条放在他卧室门框内侧齐眼高的位置。前不久的一张上写道："记得星期六给狗洗澡，否则爸爸会杀了你的。"（为了达到良好效果，他这里用的是夸张手法。）

重新布置自己的空间具有很大的影响力，该观点首次提出于20世纪60年代，在诸多研究中已得到充分证明。当时，芝加哥大学的心理学家伊斯雷尔·戈戴蒙德将这一技巧传授给那些为形形色色的私人问题所困扰的病人。就拿一位年轻女士来说吧，她在学习上困难重重，自从换了一个好点儿的台灯并把书桌搬离床边后，她在学习上就取得了长足进步。心理学家理查德·斯图尔特最终当上了国际体重观察员组织的总监，他在20世纪60年代曾指出：体重过重的妇女可以通过纠正饮食习惯和改变"刺激食欲的环境"的方法来减肥——例如，用小一点的盘子吃饭和把食物全都集中放在厨房里。要改变自我就必须改变你周围的世界。

监督自身行为

20年来我一直在阅读有关自我监督的研究报告，而且自己也做过一些研究。老实说，我仍未完全弄懂为何自我监督这种方法行之有效，但它确实有效，而且对多数人都效果显著。实际上，只要你常留意自己的所作所为，很可能就会表现得更完美。

经常称一称体重，你或许就会真的开始减肥。记录下自己每天的饮食，你可能就会更为明智地选择用餐。

试着用一些小把戏吧。如果你总是把"you know"挂在嘴边，就在手腕上戴个高尔夫计数器，每当意识到自己说一次"you know"时就按一下计数键。我敢打赌，过不了几天，你就不会那么频繁地说它了。倘若嫌戴腕部计数器令人难堪，那么就在每说一次"you know"时口袋里的一张纸弄破一个小洞。其结果是一样的：你会变得更留意自己的行为，因而也就表现更佳。

如果说这样的方法听起来颇为荒唐，请记住：自我监督的力量已在40年来所进行的各种研究中得到了证实。我和克莱尔·戈斯于1978年发表的一篇研究报告中就有一个实例。我们教一个爱捣乱的五年级小男孩每天对自己的课堂表现作两次等级评定。他只是简单地给自己打个分数，以表明自己上午或下午表现得如何好。随着自我检测意识的增强，他比平常更能待在座位上，完成的作业也更多了，而且很少再惹麻烦了。

加拿大研究人员托马斯·麦肯其和布伦特·拉希尔所做的一项类似研究表明，在青少年拿到出勤单记录出勤时间后，他们会更加及时地赶到，参加游泳训练。东南路易斯安那大学的索尼娅·卡尔和新奥尔良教师丽贝卡·庞佐在研究过情绪失常儿童后发表报告称，自我监督能改善这些孩子在阅读、数学和拼写方面的学习表现，学生只要得到一张含有优秀写作要素的简单清单，就能写出更好的故事来。大量研究都取得了类似的结果，而且都是通过加强自我行为意识而得出的。

许下诺言

当你向别人许诺时，你就形成了心理学家所说的"后效强化"这么一种情况。一旦实现承诺，你自然早已准备好得到嘉奖；如果食言，面临的就是惩罚。这将给你带来压力，而通常这也正是你所需要的。

比方说，如果你想加强锻炼，那么就安排和朋友一起锻炼吧。假如你到时没露面，你的朋友就会生气，这或许正是督促你守时的一种手段。几十年的研究已证实了这一措施的效力。例如，在1994年，弗吉尼亚理工学院和州立大学的达纳·帕特南等研究人员证明，作出书面承诺的病人远比未作书面保证的病人更能按医嘱服药。夏威夷大学玛莉·卢·考和乔尔·费希尔报告过一位妇女的案例，这位女士使自己坚持慢跑锻炼的方法就是和丈夫达成了一项简短的协议——无论何时，只要她实现了慢跑目标，丈夫都给她一些零钱，并在周末陪她出去玩。

对我们大家来说这都是好消息。要满足生命中这诸多要求并克服众多挑战，我们只需运用简单技巧——而这些技巧是任何人都能掌握并且无需意志力的实战操作——换句话说，只用技巧，而非意志。

文化点滴

University of California（简称UC）

加利福尼亚大学，简称加州大学或加大。加州大学起源于1853年，建立在奥克兰的加利福尼亚学院。如今已发展成一所拥有10个校区并对加州发展影响深远的巨型大学系统。加州大学是美国最具影响力的公立大学之一，其伯克利校区（UC Berkeley）、戴维斯校区（UC Davis）、洛杉矶校区（UCLA）、圣巴巴拉校区（UC Santa Barbara）、圣迭戈校区（UC San Diego）和旧金山校区（UC San Francisco）（研究生）都是世界一流的学府。这些校区互为独立又紧密联系，共同组成了享誉全美乃至全世界的加州大学系统。

nail-biting

咬指甲癖的几种代表性病因学说：

（1）微量元素缺乏说。这一学说认为，咬指甲、啃手皮是因为孩子体内缺乏某种微量元素，如硒、钾、锌等，若补充了这些元素，孩子就自然停止了咬指甲等异常行为。

（2）人格类型说。按弗洛伊德的观点，他把人群分为三种人格模型：口唇型、肛门型、生殖型。咬指甲孩子多属于口唇型人格，这种人格类型的孩子易焦虑、依赖性强、喜嚼咬、有破坏欲。

（3）模仿说。有些学者认为，孩子咬指甲、啃手皮是互相模仿导致的，其理论依据是：在幼儿园，只要有一个儿童咬指甲，就会有许多小朋友跟着咬；家长咬指甲，子女大多也会模仿着咬。

（4）习惯成瘾说。这一学说认为，人类婴儿都有把手指放于口中吮吸的本能，该本能源自于寻找自我感觉和母亲乳头的替代物。由于这个动作能使婴幼儿获得某种安定感，所以这种感觉必然被深刻地记忆。一部分孩子虽进入青少年期，但若遇到紧张、焦虑、烦闷时，那种童年的记忆仍会被激发，又会情不自禁地将手指放于口中，久而久之，会形成习惯，再由习惯产生心理依赖，于是咬指甲等异常行为就这样发生了。

写作特点

本文先阐明结果，再提出方法，最后是总结。这种写作手法能够在文章的开始就抓住读者的好奇心理，写作手法深入浅出，使读者对文章脉络有清晰的认识，并且很容易从文章中学到新的知识，受到启发。

品味鉴赏

本文作者在对行为学进行认真研究的基础上，详细阐述了一个人只需运用简单技巧就可改变他的行为习惯的道理。要想开辟人生新道路，就试试这三个"M"：改善周边环境（Modify Your Environment）、监督自身行为（Modify Your Behavior）和许下诺言（Make Commitments）。

美文感悟

Take Your Home into Your Own Hands
亲手布置自己的家

作者简介：

伊夫林·沃（Evelyn Waugh，1903—1966），英国当代小说家。出身于伦敦出版商家庭。其讽刺小说，如《衰落与瓦解》（*Decline and Fall*，1928）和《邪恶的肉体》（*Vile Bodies*，1930），讽刺了上层社会。他的晚期作品，著名的《旧地重游》（*Brideshead Revisited*，1945）反映了他对罗马天主教的兴趣。

  I do not know who started the idea of "good taste". I strongly suspect that Dora had a younger brother who went to art classes at an evening **polytechnic**[1], and that it all began with him.

  Certainly no one worried much about it in the eighteenth century, when people who were rich enough put Cupids all over their ceilings, and built fireplaces in a style happily based on a combination of Greek, Chinese and French Gothic. Nor, I think, did it much concern our grandparents who went on **accumulating**[2] the grossest kinds of bric-a-brac in superb disregard of all that Mr. Ruskin was saying in his clever books. But quite lately, with the **advent**[3] of all the other worries which gave that hunted look to Mr. Strube's "*Little Man*", came the **plague**[4] of "good taste".

  One has only to look around today at the bleak little parlours of the suburbs and the still bleaker great drawing-rooms of Belgrave Square to see the havoc it has caused. Some terrific voice from

---

注释

1. **polytechnic** [ˌpɒlɪˈteknɪk] *n.* 工艺学校
2. **accumulate** [əˈkjuːmjuleɪt] *vi.* 积累、蓄积
3. **advent** [ˈædvənt] *n.* 出现、到来
4. **plague** [pleɪɡ] *n.* 麻烦、苦恼

behind the bar seems to have said "Time, gentlemen, please," and **forthwith**5 everyone began carrying away her dearest possessions to the lumber-room or sending them down to a very chilly reception in the servants' hall.

In some mysterious way, for which I strongly suspect my fellow journalists in the Home Pages are largely responsible, everybody seems to have been bullied into an **inferiority**6 complex about their own houses.

In Victorian times people were terrified of being thought poor, and starved themselves in order to clothe a second footman. Nowadays we are all desperately poor and quite boastful about it, but I have yet to find anyone but myself who still says with absolute **complacency**7, "I don't know much about art, but I do know what I like." I say that about three times a day and it always has the profoundly shocking effect that I hoped for.

Look around your own drawing-room. Where is the firescreen with the family coat-of-arms worked in coloured wools by your Aunt Agatha? And why is that horrible earthenware pot, which someone else's Aunt Agatha made in a suburb of Brighton, sitting so coldly on the mantelpiece? And do you really find it comfortable to read by that triangular lamp shade which throws all the light on the ceiling? And where is the stuffed parrot?

Have you made all these changes because you really like them or because someone has been at you about "good taste"?

It may be that you really do like them, but it seems odd that Colonel Brown's wife who disagrees with you about politics and religion and how to bring up her daughters should see eye to eye with you on this point. And the vicar's drawing-room is exactly like yours, although you could never bear the vicar; and so is the doctor's wife's, who, they say, drinks far more than is good for her, and wears such extraordinary hats.

If by some odd coincidence you really do heartily agree with your neighbour's taste in house decoration, well and good; but if she likes to fill her window with arts-and-crafts pottery bowls of crocuses, and you like aspidistras till it looks like a **conservatory**8, and if you like Benares brass pots, put them in those, and if you like bamboo stands, put them on them. By all means hide the tiger's head which your Uncle George shot in India, if it keeps you awake at night, but if you like it, don't be bullied into putting it away by Mrs. Brown who lives next door. March round with your umbrella and tell her that her hunting prints and Straffordshire pottery are "middle class" or "bad taste".

And if you see sarcastic glances being cast on the family photograph album or the cup you won at the cycling **gymkhana**9 or at the **tinted**10 photograph of the Acropolis or the Landseer gravings, just you say very decisively, "I don't know much about art, but I do know what I like"; then they will see that they are beaten, and Mrs. Brown will say to the vicar's wife that it is so sad that you have no taste, and the vicar's wife will say to the doctor's wife that it really only shows what sort of people you are, but all three will envy you at heart and even perhaps, one by one, bring out from the attics a few of the things they really like.

注释

5. **forthwith** [fɔː'θ'wiːð] *adv.* 立刻

6. **inferiority** [ɪn,fɪərɪ'ɒrɪtɪ] *n.* 下等、劣等

7. **complacency** [kəm'pleɪsənsɪ] *n.* 自鸣得意

8. **conservatory** [kən'sɜːvətərɪ] *n.* 温室

9. **gymkhana** [dʒɪm'kɑːnə] *n.* 比赛

10. **tinted** ['tɪntɪd] *adj.* 带色彩的

原文翻译

我不知道是谁首先提出"高尚的情趣"这个概念的。我非常怀疑多拉有一个在工艺专科夜校上美术课的弟弟,而且怀疑这一概念是始于他的。

当然,在18世纪对此谁也不会有多大担心,因为那些够富的人们在自家的天花板上布满了丘比特的像,建造壁炉,其式样巧妙地把希腊、中国和法国哥特风格结合在一起。我认为我们的祖父辈对这一概念也无多大关心,因为他们继续积攒各种最粗劣的小摆设,完全不顾罗斯金先生在他睿智的论著里所说的一切。但是,近来随着施特鲁布先生画的《小男人》挂着一脸疲惫不堪的倦容的所有其他令人忧虑的事情的出现,"高尚的情趣"这一烦扰也接踵而来。

今天,我们只要环顾市郊的那些乏味的客厅和贝尔格索夫广场更乏味的宽敞的起居室,就能看到它引起的混乱。在餐柜后面,一个可怕的声音似乎说了声"请注意,时间到了,先生们"。接着大家立即开始把她最宝贵的财产带到杂物间或把它们送到佣人的饭厅,在那里受到非常冷淡的接待。

大家好像不可思议地被吓唬得对自己的家感到自卑,我非常怀疑我们家庭版的记者同仁们对此负有很大的责任。

在维多利亚时代,人们害怕被别人认为自己是穷人,因而宁可饿肚皮也要再雇一个男仆。现在,我们大家都穷得要命,并以此为荣。但是,除了我自己,我还得找到一个人,他仍旧沾沾自喜地说:"我对艺术懂得不多,但我知道我喜欢什么。"我每天这么说3次,且总是能产生我所希望的极其令人震惊的效果。

环顾一下你自己的起居室,饰有你的阿加莎姨妈用彩色毛线编织的家徽的挡火隔板现在在哪里?为什么那个难看的陶罐现在正孤零零地放在壁炉架上?它是别人的阿加莎姨妈在布赖顿市郊制造的。你真的觉得在把所有的光线射到天花板的三角形灯罩旁看书很舒适吗?那个鹦鹉标本又在哪里?

你做了这些改变是因为你真的喜欢这些改变,还是因为有人一直缠着你大谈"高尚的情趣"呢?

可能你真的确实喜欢这些变化,但是似乎很奇怪,布朗上校的妻子在这一点上竟然同你的看法完全一致,虽然她在政治、宗教和怎样教养她的女儿方面与你意见完全相左。教区牧师的起居室与你的完全一样,虽然你以前根本忍受不了他。医生妻子的起居室也和你的完全一样,人们说她酒喝得太过量了,还戴着这样别致的帽子。

如果由于某种奇怪的巧合,你确实真心实意同意你邻居在装饰房屋方面的情趣,那你就同意吧。但是,如果她喜欢在她的窗户塞满种着红花的手工艺陶碗,而你则更喜欢蜘蛛抱蛋花,那就在你房屋里放满蜘蛛抱蛋花,直到你的房屋看上去像一个暖房;如果你喜欢贝拿勒斯铜花盆,就把这些花放在里面;如果你喜欢竹架子,那就把这些花放在竹架上。如果你的乔治舅舅在印度射死的老虎头使你夜不能眠,那就千万把它藏起来;但是,如果你喜欢它,那就不要由于住在隔壁的布朗太太的胁迫而把它藏起来。打着伞毅然走到她家,对她说她的狩猎图和斯特拉福德郡的陶器都是"劣等货"或者"品位低级"。

如果你看到家庭照相簿,或者你在自行车比赛获得的奖杯,或者雅典卫城的着色照片,或者兰西尔的雕刻遭到讥讽的冷眼,你就非常坚定地说:"我对艺术懂得不多,但我知道我喜欢什么。"然后,他们将会知道他们占了下风。布朗太太会对教区牧师的妻子说你没有审美感太可悲了;教区牧师的妻子会对医生的妻子说这确实显示出你是哪种人。但是,这三位都会在心底里嫉妒你,或许她们甚至会一个接一个从阁楼里拿出几件她们真正喜欢的东西来。

文化点滴

Cupids

丘比特一直被人们喻为爱情的象征，相传他是一个顽皮的、身上长着翅膀的小神，他的箭一旦插入青年男女的心上，便会使他们深深相爱。在古希腊神话中，他是爱与美的女神阿芙罗狄忒与战神阿瑞斯的小儿子。

Gothic

哥特式包含多种意思，主要有：在建筑上，哥特式建筑如大教堂（Cathedral），其最大的特色就是高大的梁柱和尖拱形的天花板与结构；在文学上，歌特式是用以形容那些以黑暗寂寞地点（如荒废城堡）为背景的奇异冒险故事；歌特式也代表一种字体相当华丽的印刷或书写风格。哥特式艺术指12—16世纪欧洲出现的以建筑为主的艺术，包括雕塑、绘画和工艺美术。哥特式艺术是夸张的、不对称的、奇特的、轻盈的、复杂的和多装饰的，以频繁使用纵向延伸的线条为其一大特征。表现在建筑上，就有尖拱券、小尖塔、垛墙、飞扶壁和彩色玻璃镶嵌等典型元素。

写作特点

本文采取了对比的手法。例如：One has only to look around today at the bleak little parlours of the suburbs and the still bleaker great drawing-rooms of Belgrave Square to see the havoc it has caused. Some terrific voice from behind the bar seems to have said "Time, gentlemen, please," and forthwith everyone began carrying away her dearest possessions to the lumber-room or sending them down to a very chilly reception in the servants' hall. 对比手法的运用，有利于充分显示事物的矛盾，突出被表现事物的本质特征，加强文章的艺术效果和感染力。

品味鉴赏

本文作者针对都市生活中追求所谓高雅趣味的风气，发表了一番议论。他主张大家可以根据各自的喜好并用自己的双手去装饰自己的居室，而不要附庸风雅，千篇一律。

美文感悟

The Art of Living Simply
平淡生活的艺术

作者简介：

理查德·罗尔（Richard Roll, 1943—）。

We paddled down Maine's Saco River that September afternoon, five couples in canoes, basking in the summer's last golden sunlight. Gazing deer, fluttering their white tails, watched our flotilla pass. That evening we pitched tents, broiled steaks and **sprawled**[1] around the campfire, staring sleepily at the stars. One man, strumming his guitar, sang an old Shaker song: "'Tis the gift to be simple. 'Tis the gift to be free."

Our idyll ended, of course, and we drove back to the world of loan payments, jobs and clogged washing machines. "'Tis the gift to be simple," I found myself humming at odd moments, "'Tis the gift to be free." How I longed for that simplicity. But where could I find it?

"Our life is **frittered**[2] away by detail. Simplify, simplify." That dictum of Henry David Thoreau's echoing from the days of steamboats and ox-drawn plows, had long hunted me. Yet Thoreau

注释
1. **sprawl** [sprɔːl] *vi.* 不规则地伸展；蔓延
2. **fritter** ['frɪtə] *vt.* 浪费；细切；剁碎

himself was able to spend only two years in the cabin he built beside Walden Pond. And Henry—wifeless, childless, jobless—never had to tussle with such details as variable-rate mortgages.

My life attracted detail, as if my motto were: "Complicate, complicate." And I've found I'm not alone. But one day my thinking about simplicity turned upside down.

I was visiting a physicist in his office tower jutting from his Illinois farmlands. We looked through his window at the laboratory's miles—around particle accelerator, an immense circle in the **prairie**[3] far below. "It's a kind of time machine," he said, explaining that the accelerator enables physicists to study conditions like those shortly after Creation's first moment. The universe was simpler then, he noted, a mere dot comprising perhaps only one kind of force and one kind of particle. Now it has many kinds of forces, scores of different particles, and contains everything from stars and galaxies to dandelions, elephants and the poems of Keats.

Complexity, I began to see from that tower, is part of God's plan.

Deep down, we sense that we speak, **disparagingly**[4], of a "simpleton". Nobody wants to be guilty of "simplistic" thinking.

But blinding ourselves to complexity can be dangerous. Once I bought a home. I liked its setting so much I unconsciously avoided probing into its possible defects. After it was mine, I found it needed **insulation**[5], roofing, a new heating system, new windows, a new **septic**[6] system—everything. That old house became an albatross, costing far more than I could afford, the cost in stress was even higher, I had refused to look at the complexities.

Even ordinary finances are rarely simple—what does your insurance policy actually cover? Yet, economics are simplicity itself compared with moral questions.

One afternoon when I was ten, I found myself the leader of an after-school gaggle of boys. I had to divert them quickly, I knew, or my career as leader would be brief. And then I saw Joe.

Joe was an Eiffel Tower of a kid, an incipient giant. His family had emigrated from Europe, and he had a faint accent.

"Let's get him!" I said.

My little troop of Goths swarmed upon Joe. Somebody snatched his hat and we played catch with it. Joe ran home, and I took his hat as a **trophy**[7].

That night, our doorbell rang. Joe's father, a worried-looking farmer with a thick accent, asked for Joe's hat. I returned it sheepishly, "Please don't upset Joe," he said earnestly, "He has asthma. When he has an attack, it is hard for him to get better."

I felt a lead softball in my chest. The next evening I walked to Joe's house. He was in the garden, tilling the soil; he watched me warily as I walked up. I asked if I could help. "Okay," he said. After that I went often to help him and we became best friends.

I had taken a step toward adulthood. Inside myself I had seen possibilities, like a tangle of

注释
3. **prairie** ['preərɪ] *n.* 大草原，牧场
4. **disparagingly** [dɪ'spærɪdʒɪŋlɪ] *adv.* 以轻视的态度，蔑视地
5. **insulation** [ɪnsju'leɪʃən] *n.* 隔绝；隔离，孤立
6. **septic** ['septɪk] *n.* 腐烂物
7. **trophy** ['trəʊfɪ] *n.* 战利品，奖品

wires. This red wire was the possibility for evil, which requires no more than ignoring another's pain. And here was the white wire of sympathy. I could have a hand in connecting all those wires—it was a matter of the decisions I made. I had discovered complexity, and found in it an opportunity to choose, to grow. Its price is responsibility.

Perhaps, that is one reason we yearn for the simple life. In a way, we want to be children, to let somebody else carry the awkward backpack of responsibility.

We are like wheat, here on earth to ripen. We ripen intellectually by letting in as much of the universe's complexity as we can. Morally we ripen by making our choices. And we ripen spiritually by opening our eyes to Creation's endless detail.

One afternoon I picked up a fallen leaf from the sugar maple in our yard. Up close it was yellow, with splashes of red. At arm's length it was orange. Its color depended on how I looked at it.

I knew a little about how this leaf had spent its life, transforming sunlight and carbon dioxide into nutrients, and I knew that we animals breathe that oxygen that such plants emit, while they thrive upon the carbon dioxide we **exhale**[8]. And I knew that each cell of the leaf has a nucleus containing a chemical—DNA—upon which is inscribed all the instructions for making and operating a sugar maple. Scientists know far more about this than I. But even their knowledge extends only a short way into the sea of complexity that is a sugar maple.

I'm beginning to understand, I think, what simplicity means. It does not mean blinding ourselves to the world's stunning complexity or avoiding the choices that ripen us. By "simplify, simplify", Thoreau meant simplifying ourselves.

To accomplish this, we can:

Focus on deeper things. The simple life is not necessarily living in a cabin, cultivating beans. It is refusing to let our lives be "frittered away by detail". A professor taught me a secret for focusing: Turn off the TV and read great books. They open doors in your brain.

Undertake life's journey one step at a time. I once met a young couple both blind since birth. They had a three-year-old daughter and an infant, both fully sighted. For those parents, everything was complex: bathing the baby, monitoring their daughter, mowing the lawn. Yet, they were full of smiles and laughter. I asked the mother how she kept track of their lively daughter. "I tie little bells on her shoes," she said with a laugh.

"What will you do when the infant walks too?" I asked.

She smiled. "Everything is so complicated that I don't try to solve a problem until I have to. I take one thing at a time!"

Pare down your desires. English novelist and playwright Jerome Klapka caught the spirit of that enterprise when he wrote, "Let your boat of life be light, packed only with what you need—a

---

8. **exhale** [ɪksˈheɪl] vi. 呼气，发出

homely home and simple pleasures, one or two friends, worth the name, someone to love and someone to love you, a cat, a dog and a pipe too, enough to eat and enough to wear and a little more than enough to drink, for thirst is a dangerous thing."

Not long ago I flew home to see my father in the hospital. He has a disease that nibbles away the mind. I was a snarl of worries. Treatments? Nursing homes? Finances?

He was crouched in a wheelchair, a **shriveled**[9], whitened **remnant**[10] of the father I had known. As I stood there, hurt and confused, he looked up and saw me. And then I saw something unexpected and wonderful in his eyes: recognition and love. It welled up and filled his eyes with tears. And mine.

That afternoon, my father came back from wherever his illness had taken him. He joked and laughed, once again the man I had known. And then he tired, and we put him to bed. The next day, he did not remember I had come. And the next night he died.

Every death is a door opening on Creation's mystery. The door opens, but we see only darkness. In that awful moment, we realize how vast the universe is, complexity upon complexity, beyond us. But that is true gift of simplicity: to accept the world's infinite complication, to accept bewilderment.

And then, especially, we can savor simple things. A face we love, perhaps, eyes brimming with love.

It is the simplest of things. But it is more than enough.

原文翻译

那个9月的下午，我们5对夫妇泛舟于缅因州的萨科河上，沐浴着夏日最后一缕金色阳光。正在吃草的小鹿摇动着白色的尾巴，看着我们的船驶过。那晚，我们搭起了帐篷，烤了牛排，围着篝火懒散地躺着，睡眼惺忪地望着星空。其中一人弹拨着吉他，唱起了一首古老的震教徒的歌曲："这是使你平淡的礼物，这是使你自由的礼物。"

我们田园式的漫游结束了，当然，我们又回到支付贷款、工作以及塞满了衣服的洗衣机的世界中来。"这是使你平淡的礼物，"我发现自己偶尔哼起来。"这是使你自由的礼物。"我是多么向往那种平淡啊，但我能在哪儿找到它呢？

"我们的生活都被琐事浪费掉了。简单化，简单化。"这是亨利·大卫·梭罗的名言。这句从蒸汽机船和牛拉犁的时代就回响着的名言萦绕在我耳边很长一段时间了。而梭罗本人也只是在瓦尔登湖畔自己造的小屋里度过了两年时光。而亨利无妻、无子、无工作——他不必为利率不同的抵押这类事情伤脑筋。

我的生活"吸引"着琐碎，好像我的座右铭是"复杂化，复杂化"。并且我发现并不是我一个人这样。可是有一天，我有关简单化的思考整个翻了个个儿。

那时我正在访问一位物理学家，他的办公室是一座耸立在伊利诺伊农场的塔楼。透过窗户我们看到在下面很远的草场上的一个巨大的圆形物——那是实验室的回转几英里的粒子急加速器。"它是一种计时器。"

注释 9. shrivel [ʃrɪvəl] vi. 起皱纹，枯萎   10. remnant ['remnənt] n. 呼气，剩余

他解释道，加速器使物理学家能够研究创世纪之后的那一瞬间的情况。那时的宇宙要简单得多，他解释说，可能只由一种力和一种微粒组成的一个小点。现在有很多的力，很多种微粒，并且包含各种东西：从恒星星系到蒲公英，从大象到济慈的诗歌。

我从那个塔楼上开始认识到复杂化是上帝的计划的一部分。

内心深处，我们感觉到这一点，我们轻蔑地谈到头脑简单的傻瓜。没有人愿意被认为是头脑简单。

但我们无视复杂化却是危险的。一次，我买了一所房子。我非常喜欢它的环境，所以不自觉地避免探究它可能有的缺陷。它终于为我所有之后，我却发现，它需要隔热，需要覆顶，需要一个新的供热系统，需要新窗户，需要新的污水处理系统——需要一切。那老房子成了一个累赘。在它上面的花费远非我所能负担，而我精神上的付出却更高，这一切只因我无视复杂化。

甚至一项普通的支付都不会是简单的——你须考虑，你的保险单上到底包括哪些项目？然而与道德问题相比，经济问题还算是简单的。

我十岁时的一天下午，发觉自己成为一群放学后的孩子们的头。我必须尽快使他们高兴起来，否则，我这个头目就当不长。正在这时，我看到了乔。

对于他的年龄而言，乔是一个少年巨人。他全家是从欧洲移民过来的，他有着轻微的口音。

"咱们抓住他！"我说。

我的小队野蛮人马团团围住了乔。有人抢走了他的帽子，我们就用它来玩游戏。乔跑回了家，我就把他的帽子当了战利品。

那天晚上，我家的门铃响了。乔的父亲，一个面带愁容、说话口音很重的农民，来向我要乔的帽子，我局促不安地还给了他。"请不要为难乔，"他真诚地说，"他有气喘病。如果他喘起来，要恢复是很困难的。"

我感到心情沉重，胸口像有块铅。第二天晚上，我走到乔的家，他正在花园里翻土。我走近的时候，他警惕地看着我。我问是否可以帮他的忙。"好吧。"他说。从那以后，我经常去帮他，我们成为很要好的朋友。

（就这样）我向成人迈进了一步。省视自身，我看到了各种前景，就像一团缠结的金属丝。这条红线是邪恶的前景，它无视别人的痛苦，这条白线是体谅别人的。我可以参与联结所有的线——这只是我作出怎样的决定的问题。我已发现了复杂，发现它是一个选择，是一个成长的机会，它的代价就是责任心。也许，那是我们渴望平淡生活的一个理由。在某种程度上，我们想做小孩，让其他人担负那种难以承受的责任感。

我们就像小麦，生长在土地上等待着成熟。通过尽可能多地吸收宇宙的复杂性使我们智力上成熟，通过各种选择使我们道德上成熟，通过睁开眼睛看到创世纪的无尽的琐碎使我们心灵上成熟。

一天下午，我在院子里捡起了一片枫叶，近看它是黄色的，带有一道道红色，而从离开眼睛一臂长的地方看，它是橘黄色的。它的颜色取决于我如何看它。

我对这片树叶如何度过它的一生，如何把阳光和二氧化碳转化为有机物了解一些，也知道我们和其他动物吸入植物所释放出的氧气，同时植物吸收我们呼出的二氧化碳而得以成长。我还知道，这片树叶的每一个细胞中都有一个包含了化学物质DNA的核，它上面记载着让枫树成长和运动的指令。科学家对此知道的远比我多，但即使他们也只不过对一棵枫树这一复杂的认识之海扩展了一小步。

我想开始理解简单意味着什么。它并不是意味着让我们无视世界的缤纷复杂，或拒绝作出使我们成熟的选择。"简单化，简单化。"梭罗的意思是简化我们自身。

要做到这一点，我们必须：

关注深层次的东西。平淡的生活并不是必须住在木屋里，种植豌豆。它只不过是不让我们的生命由于琐屑之事而浪费掉。一位教授曾教给我集中思想的秘诀：关掉电视，阅读伟大的著作。它们会开启你的智慧之门。

在人生之旅中，一次只迈一步。我曾遇到一对天生失明的夫妇，他们有一个3岁的女儿和一个婴儿，两个孩子都视力完好。对这样的父母来说，每一件事情都是复杂的：给婴儿洗澡，了解女儿的行踪，修剪草坪。可是，他们的生活却充满了欢笑。我问做妈妈的如何知道活泼的女儿的行踪。"我在她的鞋上系上小铃铛。"她笑着说道。

"等婴儿也会走路的时候你该怎么办？"我问道。

她笑了："每件事情都是如此复杂，问题未来之前，我是不会考虑解决它的。我每次只做一件事情！"

降低我们的欲望。英格兰小说家和剧作家杰罗姆·克拉卜克抓住了问题的实质。他写道："让你的生命之舟轻装前行，只载着你必需的东西——一个朴素的家和单纯的乐趣，一两个名副其实的朋友，你爱的人和爱你的人，一只猫，一只狗，一个烟斗，足够的食品、足够的衣物以及富余的饮品，因为口渴是一件危险的事情。"

不久前，我飞回家看望我住院的父亲，他患的是一种吞噬脑细胞的病。我满脑子焦虑不安：治疗？疗养所？费用？

他无精打采地萎缩在轮椅里——我所熟识的父亲只剩下一个枯萎而苍白的残躯。我心痛而迷惑地站在那儿，他抬起头看到了我。那时，我看到他的眼睛里闪现出意想不到的东西：认识，还有爱。泪水涌出并充满了他的双眼。而我也是热泪盈眶。

那天下午，我的父亲从病魔的折磨中清醒过来。他有说有笑，再度回复我所熟悉的样子。后来他累了，我们把他扶上床。第二天，他记不起我曾来过，当夜，他过世了。

每个人的死亡都是按照创世纪的神秘指示打开的一扇门。门开了，我们只看到黑暗。在这样一个黑暗恐怖的时刻，我们意识到宇宙有多么浩瀚，超出我们认知范围之外有无数的复杂体。但那正是对简单的真正领悟：接受世界的无限复杂，接受困惑。

于是，我们就更能够品味平淡的事物，我们所爱的面孔，也许还有充满爱的眼睛。

文化点滴

Shaker

震教徒又称为震教教友会教徒，属于基督再现信徒联合会，是贵格会在美国的分支，1774年由安·李（Ann Lee, 1736—1784）在美国建立。现已基本消亡。震教徒的赞美诗、灵歌、舞蹈等祈祷音乐非常著名，有着大量的相关整理和研究。这些音乐往往在一名震教徒突发宗教灵感的时候产生，并在震教徒集会上演唱或演奏。震教徒会在这种集会上集体震颤身体，也同样是由某一名震教徒开头，然后迅速波及所有的人。震教徒的音乐采用独特的记谱法，近似于美国海滨地区的原始方法。歌词有英文，也有黑人及印第安人语言，或者没有任何意义的词汇。

Henry David Thoreau

19世纪美国最具有世界影响力的作家、哲学家。他的祖先是法国人，从古恩西岛迁到美国来，他是他的家族里最后一个男性后嗣。他的个性偶尔也显示由这种血统上得到的特性，很卓越地与一种非常强烈的撒克逊天才混合在一起。梭罗的主要作品有著名散文集《瓦尔登湖》和论文《论公民的不服从权利》（又译为《消极抵抗》《论公民的不服从》）。

写作特点

　　本文是一篇散文。它意境深邃，注重表现作者的生活感受，抒情性强，情感真挚。作者借助想象与联想，由此及彼，由浅入深，由实而虚的依次写来，可以融情于景、寄情于事、寓情于物、托物言志，表达作者的真情实感，实现物我的统一，展现出更深远的思想，使读者领会更深的道理。

品味鉴赏

　　"采菊东篱下，悠然见南山。"这样朴素的生活态度，恬淡的人生品味，只能在那些阅历过世间沧桑的人身上才能找到。同样的，这种平淡中寻找幸福、平凡中感受人生的观念，也不仅仅存在于中国的古人身上。本篇文章描述的正是这样一种人生态度："平淡生活的态度，平淡生活的艺术。"文章指出：在成长中，在发展中，人才能逐渐成熟起来，才能品味到平淡的真谛，追求到一种平淡又趣味盎然的生活。

美文感悟

How Should One Read a Book?

书应该怎么读？

作者简介：

弗吉尼亚·伍尔夫（Virginia Woolf，1882—1941），英国近代小说家、文学批评家和散文家，她的突出贡献在于创建了"意识流"（stream of consciousness）小说。她的散文也体现了新的写作手法，语言本身简单之极，但含蓄蕴藉，而且充溢着微妙的诗情，耐人寻味。

It is simple enough to say that since books have classes—fiction, biography, poetry—we should separate them and take from each what it is right that each should give us. Yet few people ask from books what books can give us. Most commonly we come to books with blurred and divided minds, asking of fiction that it shall be true, of poetry that it shall be false, of biography that it shall be flattering, of history that it shall enforce our own prejudices. If we could banish[1] all such preconceptions when we read, that would be admirable beginning. Do not dictate to your author; try to become him. Be his fellow-worker and accomplice. If you hang back, and reserve and criticize at first, you are preventing yourself from getting the fullest possible value

注释
1. **banish** ['bænɪʃ] *vt.* 消除，驱逐

from what you read. But if you open your mind as widely as possible, then signs and hints of almost **imperceptible**[2] fineness, from the twist and turn of the first sentences, will bring you into the presence of a human being unlike any other, **steep**[3] yourself in this, acquaint yourself with this, and soon you will find that your author is giving you, or attempting to give you, something far more definite. The thirty-two chapters of a novel—if we consider how to read a novel first—are an attempt to make something as formed and controlled as a building: but words are more **impalpable**[4] than bricks; reading is a longer and more complicated process than seeing. Perhaps the quickest way to understand the elements of what a novelist is doing is not to read, but to write; to make your own experiment with the dangers and difficulties of words. Recall, then, some event that has left a distinct impression on you—how at the corner of the street, perhaps, you passed two people talking. A tree shook; an electric light danced; the tone of the talk was comic, but also tragic; a whole vision, an entire conception, seemed contained in that moment.

But when you attempt to reconstruct it in words, you will find that it breaks into a thousand conflicting impressions. Some must be **subdued**[5]; others emphasized; in the process you will lose, probably, all grasp upon the emotion itself. Then turn from your blurred and littered pages to the opening pages of some great novelist—Defoe, Jane Austen, Hardy. Now you will be better able to appreciate their mastery. It is not merely that we are in the presence of a different person—Defoe, Jane Austen, or Thomas Hardy—but we are living in a different world. Here, in *Robinson Crusoe*, we are **trudging**[6] a plain high road; one thing happens after another; the fact and the order of the fact is enough. But if the open air and adventure mean everything to Defoe they mean nothing to Jane Austen. Hers is the drawing-room, and people talking, and by the many mirrors of their talk revealing their characters. And if, when we have accustomed ourselves to the drawing-room and its reflections, we turn to Hardy, we are once more spun around. The moors are round us and the stars are above our heads. The other side of the mind is now exposed—the dark side that comes uppermost in solitude, not the light side that shows in company. Our relations are not towards people, but towards Nature and destiny. Yet different as these worlds are, each is consistent with itself. The maker of each is careful to observe the laws of his own perspective, and however great a strain they may put upon us they will never confuse us, as lesser writer so frequently do, by introducing two different kinds of reality into the same book. Thus to go from one great novelist to another—from Jane Austen to Hardy, from Peacock to Trollope, from Scott to Meredith—is to be **wrenched**[7] and uprooted; to be thrown this way and

注释
2. imperceptible [ɪmpə'septɪbl] *adj.* 觉察不到的，感觉不到的
3. steep [stiːp] *vi.* 沉浸
4. impalpable [ɪm'pælpəbl] *adj.* 感触不到的，难解的
5. subdue [səb'djuː] *vi.* 减弱
6. trudge [trʌdʒ] *vt.* 跋涉
7. wrench [rentʃ] *vt.* 猛扭、曲解

then that. To read a novel is a difficult and complex art. You must be capable not only of great finesse of perception, but of great boldness of imagination if you are going to make use of all that the novelist—the great artist—gives you.

原文翻译

　　书既然有小说、传记、诗歌之分，我们就应对其区别对待，从各类书中汲取它能够给予我们的东西。这话说起来很简单，然而很少有人向书索取它能给我们的东西。多数情形下，我们怀着模糊而又杂乱的想法拿起书来，要求小说是真实的，诗歌是虚假的，传记要吹捧，史书能巩固我们自己的偏见。读书时如能抛开这些成见，便是很好的开端。不要对作者发号施令，而要尽力与他融为一体，和他共同创作，共同策划。如果你从一开始就置身其外，而且百般挑剔，那你就无法从书中获得最大的益处。反之，如果你完全敞开心扉，那么，书中精细入微的寓意和暗示便会把你从开头的那些迂回绕转的句子中带出来，把你带到一个最独特的人物面前，使自己沉浸其中。你很快就会发现，作者展示给你的或想要展示给你的是一些非常明确的东西。我们先来谈谈如何读小说吧。一部长篇小说分成32章，是作者的匠心独运，目的是要将小说内容建构得如同一座错落有致、布局合理的大厦。可是词语不像砖块那样可以触摸；而阅读是比观看更费时、更复杂的过程。要了解作家创作过程中的各种体会，也许最有效的途径不是读，而是写；通过写亲自体验一下文字中所包含的艰难困苦。回想一件仍令你记忆犹新的事吧。比方说，你在街道的拐角处遇到两个人正在谈话。当时树影婆娑，灯光摇曳，谈话的调子亦喜亦悲；那一瞬间似乎包含了一种完整的意境和一个全面的构思。

　　然而，当你打算用文字来重现这一场景时，你脑海中的印象却变得千头万绪，七零八落。有些必须淡化，有些则应加以突出。在此过程中你可能对整个意境都把握不住了。那么，还是把你那些写得杂乱无章的一页页书稿搁到一边，翻开某位小说大师的佳作，如笛福、简·奥斯汀或哈代的作品来，看看他们是如何开篇的吧。这时你就能更深刻地领略大师们的技巧了。我们不单单见到不同的人物——笛福、简·奥斯汀或托马斯·哈代，而且被带到了不同的世界里。阅读《鲁滨逊漂流记》时，我们仿佛跋涉在平原大道上；事件一个接一个地发生；只考虑故事和故事情节的安排就足够了。如果说旷野和历险对笛福来说是一切的话，那么对简·奥斯汀便毫无意义了。她的世界是客厅和客厅中闲聊的人们。这些人的言谈像一面面镜子，反映出他们各自的性格特征。当我们熟悉了奥斯汀的客厅及其反映出来的事物以后再去读哈代的作品，又得进入另一个世界。在我们的周围是茫茫荒野，头顶上是一片星空。此时，不是聚会时显示出来的轻松愉快，而是心灵的另一面——孤独时最容易产生的忧郁阴沉的一面被暴露无遗。和我们具有关系的不是人，而是自然与命运。虽然这些世界截然不同，它们自身却浑然一体。每一个世界的创造者都小心遵循自己观察事物的法则，不管他们的作品读起来如何费力，却不会像蹩脚作家那样，把完全不同的两种现实塞进一部作品中，使我们感到困惑不解。因此，读完一位伟大作家的小说再去读另一位的——从简·奥斯汀到哈代，从皮科克到特罗洛普，从司各特到麦勒迪斯，我们就好像树木一样被猛力扭动，连根拔起，然后抛来抛去。读小说是一门困难而又复杂的艺术。如果你想充分享用小说作者——伟大的艺术家——给予你的一切，你不仅要具备高度的感知能力，还必须有大胆的想象力。

文化点滴

Robinson Crusoe

《鲁滨逊漂流记》于1719年4月25日出版，是英国作家丹尼尔·笛福的代表作。这部小说一问世既风靡全球又历久不衰，在世界各地拥有一代又一代的读者。小说从初版至今，已出了几百版，几乎译成了世界上所有各种文字。据说，除了《圣经》之外，《鲁滨逊漂流记》是再版最多的一本书。该书被誉为英国文学史上的第一部长篇小说，成了世界文学宝库中一部不朽的名著。该书故事情节引人入胜，叙事语言通俗易懂，是一部雅俗共赏的好作品。《鲁滨逊漂流记》中关于鲁滨逊在荒岛上经历的描写是全书的精华。作者把鲁滨逊描绘成充满劳动热情的人。他凭着自己顽强不息的劳动与大自然做斗争，表现出惊人的毅力。《鲁滨逊漂流记》是一部成功的现实主义小说。作者用生动逼真的细节把虚构的情景描写得使人如同身临其境，使故事具有强烈的真实感。作品语言朴素生动，文字明白易懂。虽然艺术上并不十分成熟，但它对英国小说的发展起了积极的作用，小说主人公鲁滨逊也因此成为欧洲文学史上一个著名的文学形象。

写作特点

本文作者谈了怎样读书，读者想充分享用小说作者——伟大的艺术家——给予你的一切，你不仅要具备高度的感知能力，还必须有大胆的想象力。为了突出这一主题，作者用了非常流畅、平滑的句子予以解释说明：Thus to go from one great novelist to another—from Jane Austen to Hardy, from Peacock to Trollope, from Scott to Meredith—is to be wrenched and uprooted; to be thrown this way and then that. To read a novel is a difficult and complex art. 这种排比句给人一种气势磅礴、行文紧凑的感觉。作者在这里把文章的主旨推向了高潮，给读者一种豁然开朗的感觉；同时又使读者为文章的内容深深吸引，久久回味，为作者高超的写作水平所折服。

品味鉴赏

这篇散文是弗吉尼亚·伍尔夫总结自己的读书经验，规劝世人应以什么样的态度、读什么样的书，字里行间充满了对读书的热爱。

美文感悟

_____
_____
_____
_____

How to Grow Old?
如何慢慢变老？

作者简介：

伯特兰·阿瑟·威廉·罗素（Bertrand Arthur William Russell，1872—1970），是20世纪最有影响力的哲学家、数学家和逻辑学家之一，同时也是活跃的政治活动家，并致力于哲学的大众化、普及化。

Psychologically there are two dangers to be guarded against in old age. One of these is **undue**[1] absorption in the past. It does not do to live in memories, in regrets for the good old days, or in sadness about friends who are dead. One's thoughts must be directed to the future, and to things about which there is something to be done. This is not always easy; one's own past is a gradually increasing weight. It is easy to think to oneself that one's emotions used to be more vivid than they are, and one's mind more keen. If this is true it should be forgotten, and if it is forgotten it will probably not be true.

注释　1. **undue** [ʌnˈdjuː] *adj.* 不适当的

The other thing to be avoided is **clinging**² to youth in the hope of sucking vigour from its vitality. When your children are grown up they want to live their own lives, and if you continue to be as interested in them as you were when they were young, you are likely to become a burden to them, unless they are unusually **callous**³. I do not mean that one should be without interest in them, but one's interest should be contemplative and, if possible, philanthropic, but not

unduly emotional. Animals become indifferent to their young as soon as their young can look after themselves, but human beings, owing to the length of infancy, find this difficult.

I think that a successful old age is easiest for those who have strong impersonal interests **involving**⁴ appropriate activities. It is in this sphere that long experience is really fruitful, and it is in this sphere that the wisdom born of experience can be exercised without being **oppressive**⁵. It is no use telling grown-up children not to make mistakes, both because they will not believe you, and because mistakes are an **essential**⁶ part of education. But if you are one of those who are incapable of impersonal interests, you may find that your life will be empty unless you concern yourself with your children and grandchildren. In that case you must realise that while you can still **render**⁷ them material services, such as making them an allowance or knitting them jumpers, you must not expect that they will enjoy your company.

Some old people are oppressed by the fear of death. In the young there is a **justification**⁸ for this feeling. Young men who have reason to fear that they will be killed in battle may justifiably feel bitter in the thought that they have been cheated of the best things that life has to offer. But in an old man who has known human joys and sorrows, and has achieved whatever work it was in him to do, the fear of death is somewhat **abject**⁹ and ignoble.

The best way to overcome it—so at least it seems to me—is to make your interests gradually wider and more impersonal, until bit by bit the walls of the ego **recede**¹⁰, and your life becomes increasingly merged in the universal life. An individual human existence should be like a river—small at first, narrowly contained within its banks, and rushing passionately past rocks and over waterfalls. Gradually the river grows wider, the banks recede, the waters flow more quietly, and in the end, without any visible break, they become merged in the sea, and painlessly lose their individual being. The man who, in old age, can see his life in this way, will not suffer from the fear of death, since the things he cares for will continue. And if, with the decay of vitality, weariness increases, the thought of rest will not be unwelcome. I should wish to die while still at work, knowing that others will carry on what I can no longer do and content in the thought that what was possible has been done.

注释

2. **cling** [klɪŋ] *vi.* 坚持，墨守
3. **callous** ['kæləs] *adj.* 无情的，冷淡的；起老茧的
4. **involve** [ɪn'vɒlv] *vt.* 包括，使陷于
5. **oppressive** [ə'presɪv] *adj.* 压制性的，压迫的
6. **essential** [ɪ'senʃəl] *adj.* 本质的，实质的，基本的
7. **render** ['rendə] *vt.* 呈递，归还
8. **justification** [dʒʌstɪfɪ'keɪʃən] *n.* 理由，辩护，释罪
9. **abject** ['æbdʒekt] *adj.* 卑鄙的，可怜的
10. **recede** [rɪ'siːd] *v.* 后退

原文翻译

从心理上说，老年时期要防止两种危险。其一是过分沉湎于过去。生活于回忆之中，为以往的好时光而抱憾，或因朋友作古而悲伤，这些皆无济于事。人的思想必须朝着未来，朝着还可以有所作为的方面。这并非总是容易做到；因为一个人的过去是一份不断加重的负担。人们容易认为自己的感情，过去比现在充沛，自己的思想，过去比现在敏锐。如果这是事实，就应该忘掉它。如果它被忘掉，那它也许将不成其为事实。

另一件要避免的事是紧拽着年轻人，希望从他们的生机中汲取活力。当你的孩子们已经长大，他们就要过他们自己的生活，如果你还是像他们小时候那样对他们关心备至，你就可能成为他们的包袱，除非他们特别麻木不仁。我不是说对他们应该不闻不问，但是你所给予的关心应当是理性的、解囊相助的（如果可能的话），而非过于感情冲动。动物在自己的后代一旦能够生活自理时，便不再给予关怀；但是人类，由于幼年时期太长，很难做到这一点。

我想一个人能做到对合适的活动兴趣盎然、不计较个人得失，那么，他就极易享有成功的晚年，因为长期积累的经验在此可以结出累累硕果，而由经验产生的在此时既有用武之地，而又不至于咄咄逼人。告诉已经成人的孩子不要犯错误是没有益处的，因为他们不会相信你，同时也因为犯错误是接受教育的不可少的一环。但假如你做不到不计个人得失，那么，不将心放在儿孙身上，你便会觉得生活空虚无望。假使如此，你必须明白：虽然你还能给他们物质上的帮助，诸如给点补贴或织几件毛衣，但你千万不要指望他们会喜欢和你在一起。

有些老人为死的恐惧所困扰。如果年轻人有这种恐惧，那倒无可厚非。年轻人有理由害怕战死沙场；当他们想到被骗走了生命所能给予的美好生活，他们有理由愤愤不平。但对于一个备尝人生甘苦、业已完成该做的一切的老人来说，怕死就有点不大可取了。

克服这种恐惧的最好方法是——至少在我看来如此——使你的兴趣逐渐扩大，越来越超出个人之外，最终你的自我之墙将一点一点地后退，你的生命将越来越和人类的生命之墙融合在一起。一个人的一生应该像一条河——起初很小，被两岸紧紧束缚，猛烈地冲向岩石和瀑布。逐渐地它变宽了，两岸后退了，河水静静地流淌。到最后，不经过任何可见的停留，就和大海汇合在一起，毫无痛苦地失去它自身的存在。一个在老年能这样看待生活的人，将不会感到死的恐惧，因为他所关心的事物将继续下去。如果由于生命力的衰退，倦意日增，安息的想法也许不无可喜之处。我希望我能死于工作之时，并且临终时能知道别人将继续做我不能再做的工作，同时能为自己已完成力所能及的一切而心满意足。

文化点滴

伯特兰·阿瑟·威廉·罗素（Bertrand Arthur William Russell）是20世纪最有影响力的哲学家、数学家和逻辑学家之一，同时也是活跃的政治活动家，并致力于哲学的大众化、普及化。无数人将罗素视为这个时代的先知；与此同时，罗素的许多政治立场却又是十分有争议性的。他出生于1872年正值巅峰的大英帝国，逝于1970年，此时的英国已经历两次世界大战的摧残，帝国已经土崩瓦解。1950年，罗素获得诺贝尔文学奖，"以表彰其多样且重要的作品，持续不断地追求人道主义理想和思想自由"。

写作特点

　　文章的难度适中，阅读起来不会太吃力，有的句子结构比较复杂，有的段落还很拗口，比如下面这个例子：

　　Scientists look for patterns in nature-patterns to help us understand our universe and shape our environment. Thousands of materials have been synthesized and studied by materials researchers, who see again and again that atomic architecture dictates physical properties. If you want a strong fiber, use chains of carbon atoms. If you want a flexible electrical conductor, stick with metals. If you want a tough electrical insulator, find a ceramic. We can use our understanding to design atom and new materials.

　　这段文章是由3个"If"引导的句子组成。对这个句组进行层次分析，我们会发现，"If"引导的句子所举的例子都是用来说明atomic architecture dictates physical properties的，层次感非常强烈。对于这样写作特点的作品，我们在阅读时速度不可能是均衡的。要成为一名具有超强阅读能力的高手，要学会在限定的时间内完成阅读内容。依据句组进行阅读或适当地省略部分内容，将是阅读的捷径之一。

品味鉴赏

　　《如何慢慢变老》论述了老年人对待生命和生活的正确态度。

美文感悟

The Two Roads
两条路

作者简介：

约翰·鲁斯金（John Ruskin）是英国作家、评论家和艺术家。

It was New Year's night. An aged man was standing at a window. He raised his **mournful**[1] eyes towards the deep blue sky, where the stars were floating like white lilies on the surface of a clear calm lake. Then he cast them on the earth, where few more hopeless people than himself now moved towards their certain goal—the tomb. He had already passed sixty of the stages leading to it, and he had brought from his journey nothing but errors and **remorse**[2]. Now his health was poor, his mind **vacant**[3], his heart sorrowful, and his old age short of comforts.

The days of his youth appeared like dreams before him, and he recalled the serious moment when his father placed him at the entrance of the two roads—one leading to a peaceful, sunny place, covered with flowers, fruits and resounding with soft, sweet songs; the other leading to a deep, dark cave, which was endless, where poison flowed instead of water and where devils and

注释
1. **mournful** [ˈmɔːnfʊl] *adj.* 悲哀的
2. **remorse** [rɪˈmɔːs] *n.* 懊悔，自责
3. **vacant** [ˈveɪkənt] *adj.* 空的，头脑空虚的

poisonous snakes hissed and **crawled**⁴.

He saw the lights flowing away in the darkness. These were the days of his wasted life; he saw a star fall from the sky and disappear, and this was the symbol of himself. His remorse, which was like a sharp arrow, struck deeply into his heart. Then he remembered his friends in his childhood, who entered life together with him. But they had made their way to success and were now honored and happy on this New Year's night.

The clock in the high church tower struck and the sound made him remember his parents' early love for him. They had taught him and prayed to God for his good. But he chose the wrong way. With shame and grief he dared no longer to look towards that heaven where his father lived. His darkened eyes were full of tears, and with a despairing effort, he burst out a cry: "Come back, my early days! Come back!"

And his youth did return, for all this was only a dream, which he had on New Year's night. He was still young though his faults were real; he had not yet entered the deep, dark cave, and he was still free to walk on the road which leads to the peaceful and sunny land.

Those who still **linger**⁵ on the entrance of life, hesitating to choose the bright road, remember that when years are passed and your feet stumble on the dark mountains, you will cry bitterly, but in vain. "O youth, return! Oh give me back my early days!"

原文翻译

这是新年的夜晚。一位老人站在窗边，忧伤的双眼眺望着深蓝的天空。空中的繁星犹如飘浮在清澈如镜的湖面上的朵朵百合。他慢慢将目光投向地面，此刻，没有什么人比他还绝望，迈向他最终的归宿——坟墓。他已走过通向坟墓的60级台阶，除了错误和悔恨，他一无所获。现在，他体弱多病，精神空虚，心哀神伤，人到晚年无慰藉。

年轻岁月，如梦般展现在他面前。老人想起父亲把他带到岔路口的那个庄严时刻——一条路通向安宁、快乐的世界，鲜花遍布，果实丰硕，甜美轻柔的歌声在空中回荡；另一条路则通向幽深黑暗、没有尽头的洞穴，洞内流淌着的不是水而是毒液，群魔乱舞，毒蛇嘶嘶爬动。

他仰望星空，痛苦地大喊："啊，青春，回来吧！啊，父亲，再一次带我到人生的岔路口吧，我会选一条更好的道路。"但是，他的父亲和青春岁月都已经一去不复返了。

他看到亮色在黑暗中流逝，就像他挥霍掉的往昔；他看到一颗流星自天边坠落，消失不见，就像是他的化身。无尽的悔恨，像一支利箭，深刺心间。他又记起和自己一同迈入人生之途的儿时玩伴。但他们已功成名就，在这个新年之夜，备受尊崇，幸福快乐。

注释　4. **crawl** [krɔːl] *vi.* 爬行，徐徐行进　　5. **linger** ['lɪŋɡə] *v.* 逗留，闲荡，拖延

高高的教堂钟楼传来敲钟声，这声音使他记起父母早年对他的疼爱。他们教育他，为他祈祷。然而，他却选择了错误的道路。羞愧和悲哀令他再也没有勇气仰望父亲所在的天堂。黯淡的双眼噙满了泪水，他绝望地嘶声大呼："回来吧，我的往昔！回来吧！"

他的青春真的回来了，但所有这些只是一个梦，一个他在新年之夜所做的梦。他仍然年轻，虽然他犯的错误是真实的；他尚未走入那幽深黑暗的洞穴，还有自由选择通向安宁、快乐的道路。

仍在人生路口徘徊、仍在为是否应当选择光明坦途而犹豫不决的人们啊，请记住：当青春不再、当你的双脚在黑暗的山岭间跌绊时，你会痛苦地呼喊："啊，青春，回来吧！啊，还给我往昔吧！"此时，一切已是徒劳。

文化点滴

Heaven

宗教意义上的美好世界，跟"地狱"相对。基督教《圣经》中，Heaven指的是神的国或天国中具体的一个地方，认罪悔改、遵守神诫命的人死后可以去的地方。

写作特点

这是一篇感怀青春易逝、激励人在年轻时就努力奋斗的散文。作者的思绪从现实转移到对过去的想念，再转移到现实。这样的写法深深地吸引了读者，使读者跟着作者的思绪不断转移；最终，在突出了文章中心思想的同时，对读者产生了巨大的教育意义。

品味鉴赏

这篇散文借两条道路比拟两种截然不同的生活态度，也象征着人生道路上不同的选择。每个人的生活中都有无数种选择的可能性，每一次选择都是一个机会，可以帮助你走向成功或者万劫不复。选择安逸的生活，则生命注定要平庸；而选择奋斗不息的艰难道路，最终将通向人生的辉煌大道。

美文感悟

The Lesson of a Tree
一棵树的启示

作者简介：

沃尔特·惠特曼（Walt Whitman, 1819—1892），美国诗人。生于美国长岛一个海滨小村庄。父亲当时是个无地的农民。惠特曼5岁那年全家迁移到布鲁克林，父亲在那儿做木工，承建房屋，惠特曼在那儿开始上小学。1841年以后，他又回到了纽约，开始当印刷工人，不久就改当记者，并开始写作。几年以后，他成了一家较有名望的报纸《鹫鹰报》的主笔，不断撰写反对奴隶制、反对雇主剥削的论文和短评。由于内战时辛劳过度，惠特曼于1873年患半身不遂症，在病榻上熬过了近20年。1892年3月26日，惠特曼在卡姆登病逝。

    I should not take either the biggest or the most **picturesque**[1] tree to illustrate it. Here is one of my favorites now before me, a fine yellow poplar, quite straight, perhaps 90 feet high, and four thick at the butt. How strong, vital, enduring! How **dumbly**[2] eloquent! What suggestions of imperturbability and being, as against the human trait of mere seeming. Then the qualities, almost emotional, palpably artistic, heroic, of a tree; so innocent and harmless, yet so **savage**[3]. It is, yet says nothing. How it rebukes by its tough and equable serenity all weathers, this gusty-tempered little whiffet, man, that runs indoors at a mite of rain or snow. Science (or rather half-

注释
1. **picturesque** [ˌpɪktʃəˈresk] adj. 独特的；生动的；别致的；图画般的
2. **dumbly** [ˈdʌmlɪ] adv. 默默地；无言地
3. **savage** [ˈsævɪdʒ] adj. 野蛮的；残酷的；狂怒的；荒凉的

way science) scoffs at **reminiscence**[4] of dryad and **hamadryad**[5], and of trees speaking. But, if they don't, they do as well as most speaking, writing, poetry, sermons—or rather they do a great deal better. I should say indeed that those old dryad-reminiscences are quite as true as any, and profounder than most reminiscences we get. ("Cut this out," as the quack mediciners say, "and keep by you.") Go and sit in a grove or woods, with one or more of those voiceless companions, and read the foregoing, and think.

One lesson from **affiliating**[6] a tree—perhaps the greatest moral lesson anyhow from earth, rocks, animals, is that same lesson of inherency, of what is, without the least regard to what the looker on (the critic) supposes or says, or whether he likes or dislikes. What worse—what more general malady **pervades**[7] each and all of us, our literature, education, attitude toward each other (even toward ourselves), than a morbid trouble about seems(generally temporarily seems too), and no trouble at all, or hardly any, about the sane, slow-growing, **perennial**[8], real parts of character, books, friendship, marriage—humanity's invisible foundations and hold-together.

原文翻译

　　我不会选那最大最独特的树来描绘。在我面前，有我最喜欢的一棵树，那是一颗美丽的黄杨树，它很直，可能有90英尺那么高，最粗的地方直径达4英尺。它是如此的强壮！如此的富有生命力！如此挺拔在风雨中！又是如此的无言而善谕！它所启示的泰然自若与生存本质与人生浮华的表象形成了如此鲜明的对比。可以说，一棵树也是有感情的，它富有生动的艺术性质，它也是英勇无畏的。它是如此天真，不会伤害任何东西，它又是那么原始粗野。它无言地存在着，用自己坚强而平和的宁静有力地斥责了风雨雷电以及人类——这个一碰到风吹草动就躲到屋子里的没用的小东西。科学（或者更准确地说是半懂不懂的科学）对有关树精、树仙和会说话的数等现象嗤之以鼻。然而，即使树木不会说话，它们却与大多数的语言、文字、诗歌、训诫一样善谕，甚至比它们有过之而无不及。我敢断定那些古老的有关树精的联想是非常真实的，甚至比我们的大多数理想都更为深刻。（"把它砍下来"，骗人的游医这么说，"然后保存在你身边。"）请到树丛中或林地间坐下来，与无言的树木做伴，然后再把前面的那些话读一读、想一想。

　　人们从一棵树那里得到的启示——或者说大地、岩石以及动物赋予人们的最大道德教义，就是它们对于生存的内在本质的提示与观望者（或批评者）的推测和述说完全无关，与他的喜好与憎恶完全无关。一种疾患在我们每个人和我们大家的心间充斥着，渗透于我们的文学、教育、彼此对待（甚至自我对待）的态度之中，这便是对表面现象的喋喋不休，而对于人物、书籍、友谊、婚姻之合理的、逐渐增强的、经常存在的真实，亦即人类无形的本质和基础不予过问或几乎不加过问。还有什么疾患比这更糟糕、更普遍吗？

注释

4. reminiscence [ˌremɪˈnɪsns] *n.* 回忆；怀旧；引起联想的相似事物
5. hamadryad [ˌhæməˈdraɪəd] *n.* 树神
6. affiliate [əˈfɪlieɪt] *vt.* 使附属；接纳；使紧密联系
7. pervade [pəˈveɪd] *vt.* 遍及；弥漫
8. perennial [pəˈreniəl] *adj.* 多年生的；常年的；四季不断的；常在的；反复的

文化点滴

Dryad

树妖（森林女神）是半神人赛纳留斯的女儿，这些顽皮好动的生物非常类似半人马（她们被诅咒的表亲，但她们的体形更适合在森林中居住。她们反应敏捷，并且和森林中的其他生物和睦相处。

Literature

文学是指以语言文字为工具，形象化地反映客观现实、表现作家心灵世界的艺术，包括诗歌、散文、小说、剧本、寓言、童话等，是文化的重要表现形式，以不同的形式（称作体裁）表现内心情感和再现一定时期和一定地域的社会生活。

写作特点

本文运用了对比的写作手法。对比是写作中的一种常用的手法，它通常将不同事物或同一事物的不同的两面列举出来，加以对照，突出矛盾双方最本质特征，使形象更加鲜明，起到相辅相成的艺术效果。本文对比的主要效果是烘托突出了黄杨树的卓越品质。例如：How dumbly eloquent! ...so innocent and harmless, yet so savage.

品味鉴赏

本文共两段话，第一段主要描写了作者喜爱的黄杨树的卓越品质。第二段突出了人们从树身上所得到的启示——生存的内在本质的提示与观望者（或批评者）的推测和述说完全无关，与他的喜好与憎恶完全无关。其目的要让读者尊重事实，不要被表面现象所迷惑，同时要更加坚定对真理的肯定。

美文感悟

The Joys of Writing
写作的乐趣

作者简介：

温斯顿·丘吉尔（Winston Churchill, 1874－1965），英国传记作家、历史学家、政治家。生于牛津附近的布莱尼姆宫。1893年考入桑德斯特陆军军官学校，1895年以少尉军衔编入皇家第四骑兵团。1945年，在反法西斯胜利前夕，因保守党在大选中失败，丘吉尔失去首相职位。其后，他用6年时间完成了6卷《第二次世界大战回忆录》。1951年，保守党在选举中获胜，丘吉尔77岁高龄再次出任首相。1955年因年事高，辞职退休，专心撰写《英语民族史》。1965年1月因脑溢血辞世。

The fortunate people in the world—the only really fortunate people in the world—in my mind, are those whose work is also their pleasure. The class is not a large one, not nearly so large as it is often represented to be, and authors are perhaps one of the most important elements in its composition. They enjoy in this respect at least a real harmony of life. To my mind, to be able to make your work your pleasure is the one class distinction in the world worth striving for, and I do not wonder that others are inclined to envy those happy human beings who find their livelihood in the gay effusions of their fancy—to whom every hour of labour is an hour of enjoyment—to whom repose—however necessary—is a tiresome interlude, and even a holiday is almost **deprivation**[1].

注释　1. **deprivation** [ˌdeprɪˈveɪʃən] *n.* 剥夺

Whether a man writes well or ill, has much to say or little, if he cares about writing at all, he will appreciate the pleasures of composition. To sit at one table on a sunny morning, with four clear hours of uninterruptible security, plenty of nice white paper, and a Squeezer pen, that is true happiness. The complete absorption of the mind upon an agreeable occupation, what more is there than that to desire? What does it matter what happens outside? The House of Commons may do what it likes, and so may the

House of Lords. The heathen may rage furiously in every part of the globe. The bottom may be knocked clean out of the American market. Consols may fall and **suffragettes**[2] may rise. Never mind, for four hours, at any rate, we will withdraw ourselves from a common ill-governed, and disorderly world, and with the key of fancy unlock that cupboard where all the good things of the infinite are put away.

And speaking of freedom, is not the author free, as few men are free. Is he not secure, as fewmen are secure? The tools of his industry are so common and so cheap that they have almost **ceased**[3] to have commercial value. He needs no **bulky**[4] pile of raw material, no elaborate apparatus, no service of men or animals. He is dependent for his occupation upon no one but himself, and nothing outside him that matters. He is the sovereign of an empire, self-supporting, self-contained. No one can **sequestrate**[5] his estates. No one can deprive him of his stock in trade; no one can force him to exercise his faculty against his will; no one can prevent him exercising it as he chooses. The pen is the great liberator of men and nations. No chains can bind, no poverty can choke, no tariff can restrict the free play of his mind, and even the Times Book Club can only exert a moderately depressing influence upon his rewards. Whether his work is good or bad, so long as he does his best he is happy. I often fortify myself amid the uncertainties and vexations of political life by believing that I possess a line of retreat into a peaceful and **fertile**[6] country where no rascal can pursue and where one need never be dull or idle or even wholly without power. It is then, indeed, that I feel devoutly thankful to have been born fond of writing. It is then, indeed, that I feel grateful to all the brave and generous spirits who, in every age and in every land, have fought to establish the now unquestioned freedom of the pen.

And what a noble medium the English language is. It is not possible to write a page without experiencing positive pleasure at the richness and variety, the flexibility and the profoundness of our mother-tongue. If an English writer cannot say what he has to say in English, and in simple English, depend upon it, it is probably not worth saying. What a pity it is that English is not more generally studied. I am not going to attack classical education. No one who has the slightest pretension to literary tastes can be insensible to the attraction of Greece and Rome. But I confess our present educational system excites in my mind grave misgivings. I cannot believe that a system is good, or even reasonable, which thrusts upon **reluctant**[7] and uncomprehending

注释

2. **suffragette** [sʌfrə'dʒet] *n.* 妇女参政权论者
3. **cease** [siːs] *v.* 停止，终了
4. **bulky** ['bʌlkɪ] *adj.* 大的，体积大的
5. **sequestrate** [sɪ'kwestreɪt] *vt.* 扣押，没收
6. **fertile** ['fɜːtaɪl] *adj.* 肥沃的，富饶的
7. **reluctant** [rɪ'lʌktənt] *adj.* 不顾的，勉强的，难得到的

multitudes treasures which can only be appreciated by the privileged and gifted few. To the vast majority of boys who attend our public schools a classical education is from beginning to end one long useless, meaningless rigmarole. If I am told that classes are the best preparation for the study of English, I reply that by far the greater number of students finish their education while this preparatory stage is still incomplete and without deriving any of the benefits which are promised as its result.

And even of those who, without being great scholars, attain a certain general acquaintance with the ancient writers, can it really be said that they have also obtained the mastery of English. How many young gentlemen there are from the universities and public schools who can turn a Latin verse with a facility which would make the old Romans squirm in their tombs. How few there are who can construct a few good sentences, or still less a few good paragraphs of plain, correct and straight forward English. Now, I am a great admirer of the Greeks, although, of course, I have to depend upon what others tell me about them, and I would like to see our educationists imitate in one respect, at least, the Greek example. How is it that the Greeks made their language the most graceful and **compendious**[8] mode of expression ever known among men. Did they spend all their time studying the languages which had preceded theirs? Did they explore with tireless persistency the ancient root dialects of the vanished world? Not at all. They studied Greek. They studied their own language. They loved it, they cherished it, they **adorned**[9] it, they expanded it, and that is why it survives a model and delight to all posterity. Surely we, whose mother-tongue has already won for itself such an unequalled empire over the modern world, can learn this lesson at least from the ancient Greeks and bestow a little care and some proportion of the years of education to the study of a language which is perhaps to play a predominant part in the future progress of mankind.

Let us remember the author can always do his best. There is no excuse for him. The great cricketer may be out of form. The general may on the day of decisive battle have a bad toothache or a bad army. The admiral may be seasick—as a sufferer I reflect with satisfaction upon that **contingency**[10]. Caruso may be **afflicted**[11] with catarrh or Hackenschmidt with influenza. As for an orator, it is not enough for him to be able to think well and truly. He must think quickly. Speed is vital to him. Spontaneity is more than ever the hallmark of good speaking. All these varied forces of activity require from the performer the command of the best that is in him at a particular moment which may be fixed by circumstances utterly beyond his control. It is not so with the author. He need never appear in public until he is ready. He can always realise the best that is in him. He is not dependent upon his best moment in any one day. He may group together the best moments of twenty days. There is no excuse for him if he does not do his best. Great is his opportunity; great also his responsibility. Someone—I forget who—has said: "Words are the only things which last for ever. "That is, to my mind, always a wonderful thought. The most durable structures raised in stone by the strength of man, the mightiest monuments of his power, crumble

注释
8. **compendious** [kəm'pendɪəs] *adj.* 扼要的，简明的
9. **adorn** [ə'dɔːn] *vt.* 装饰，增加……的重要性或吸引力
10. **contingency** [kən'tɪndʒənsɪ] *n.* 偶然，可能性
11. **afflict** [ə'flɪkt] *vt.* 使痛苦，折磨

into dust, while the words spoken with fleeting breath, the passing expression of the unstable fancies of his mind, endure not as echoes of the past, not as mere archaeological curiosities or **venerable**[12] relics, but with a force and life as new and strong, and sometimes far stronger than when they were first spoken, and leaping across the gulf of three thousand years, they light the world for us today.

原文翻译

  在我看来，世上幸运的人——世上唯一真正幸运的人，是那些以工作为乐的人。这个阶层的人并不多，还没有人们常说的那样多。也许，作家是其中最重要的组成部分之一。就幸运而言，他们至少享受着生活中真正的和谐美。依我看，能使工作成为乐趣，是世人值得为之奋斗的一种崇高的荣誉；而且，我毫不怀疑别人会羡慕这些幸福的人，因为他们在快乐地喷涌的幻想中找到了生计，对他们来说，每劳动一小时，就是享受一小时，而休息——无论多么有必要——是令人讨厌的插曲，甚至度假也几乎成了一种损失。无论写得好坏，写成多少，只要在意，就可尝到谋篇布局的乐趣。在一个阳光明媚的早晨，临桌而坐，整整4个小时不受打扰，有足够数量的雪白稿纸，还有一支"挤压式"妙笔——那才叫真正的幸福。全心全意地投入一项令人愉快的职业——此愿足矣！外面发生什么事又有何妨？下院想干什么就干什么吧，上院也可如此。异教徒可以在全球各地大发作。美国市场可以彻底崩溃。证券可以下跌。女权运动可以兴起。没有关系，不管怎么说，我们有4个小时可以躲开这俗气的、治理不善的、杂乱无章的世界，并且用想象这把钥匙，去开启藏有大千世界一切宝物的小橱。

  说到自由，既然自由自在的人为数不多，难道作家还不算自由？既然获得安全感的人并不多，难道作家还不算安全？作家作业的工具极为平常，极为便宜，几乎不再有商业价值。他不需要成堆的原材料，不需要精密仪器，不需要有人效犬马之劳。他的职业不靠任何人，只靠自己；除了他自己以外，任何事都无关紧要。他就是一国之君，既自给，又自立。任何人都不能没收他的资产，任何人都不能剥夺他的从业资本，任何人都不能强迫他违心地施展才华，任何人都不能阻止他按自己的选择发挥天赋。他的笔就是人类和各民族的大救星。他的思想在自由驰骋，任何锁链束缚不住，任何贫困阻挡不住，任何关税限制不住，甚至"泰晤士"图书俱乐部也只能有节制地对他的收获泼一点冷水。无论作品是好是糟，只要已经尽力而为，他就会感到欢快。在变幻无常、扑朔迷离的政坛活动中，我每每以此信念自励：我有一条通向安逸富饶之地的退路，在那里，任何无赖都不能追踪，我永远不必垂头丧气或无可事事，即便没有一丁点权力。确实，在那时，我才为自己生来就爱好写作而真诚地感到欣慰不已；在那时，我才对各个时代、各个国家所有勇敢而慷慨的人充满感激之情，因为他们为确立如今无可争议的写作自由进行了斗争。

  英语是多么崇高的工具！我们每写下一页，都不可能不对祖国语言的丰富多彩、灵巧精深产生一种实实在在的喜悦。如果一位英国作家不能用英语、不能用简单的英语说出他必须说的话，请诸位相信，那句话也许就不值得说。英语没有更广泛地得到学习是何等的憾事！我不是要攻击古典教育。凡自命对文学有一丁点鉴赏力的人，都不可能对希腊罗马的吸引力无动于衷。但我承认，我国目前的教育制度却使我忧心忡忡。我无法相信这个制度是好的，甚至是合理的，因为它把唯有少数特权人物和天才人物才能欣赏的东西，一股脑儿摆在很不情愿又很不理解的人民大众面前。对公立学校的广大学童来说，古典教育从头至尾都是一些冗长的、毫无用处和毫无意义的废话。如果有人告诉我，古典课程是学习英语的最好准备，那我就回答说，迄今为止，大批学生已完成了学业，而这个准备阶段却仍然很不完善，未能收到它所保证的任何好处。

注释　12. venerable ['venərəbl] *adj.* 庄严的，值得尊敬的

即使那些无缘成为大学者、但对古代作家有所了解的人，难道可以说他们已经掌握了英语吗？究竟有多少从大学和公学毕业的年轻绅士，能够娴熟地写下一段拉丁诗文，使坟墓中的古罗马人闻之动情？能写出几行佳句的人何其少也！更不要说能用简单的、正确的和练达的英语写出几个精彩段落的人了。不过，我倒是极为仰慕古希腊人——当然我得仰仗别人把他们的情况告诉我——我想见到我们的教育专家至少能在一个方面效法古希腊人。古希腊人是如何使自己的语言成为人类迄今所知最典雅、最简练的表达方式的呢？他们花毕生时间学习希腊语以前的语言了吗？他们无休无止地坚持探索已消失的世界的原始方言了吗？根本没有！他们只学习希腊语。他们学习自己的语言。他们热爱它，珍惜它，点缀它，发展它，因此，它才能延续下来，成为所有后代人的楷模和乐趣。毫无疑问，对我们来说，既然英语已经为自己在现代世界赢得了如此无与伦比的疆域，我们至少能从古希腊人那里学到一条道理，在数年教育中稍微操点心并拨出一些时间，去学习一种也许将在人类未来进步中起到主导作用的语言。

让我们都记住，作家永远可以尽最大的努力，他没有任何借口不这样做。板球巨星也许会状态不佳。将军在决战之日也许会牙疼，或者他的部队很糟糕。舰队司令也许会晕船——我作为晕船者满意地想到了那种意外。卡鲁索也许会得黏膜炎，哈肯施米特也许会得流感。至于一位演说家，想得好和想得正确是不够的，他还需想得快。速度至关重要，随机应变越来越成为优秀演说家的标志。所有上述活动都需要行动者在一个特定的时刻倾其所能，而这一时刻也许决定于他完全无法控制的种种事态。作家的情况不一样。不到万事俱备，他永远不必出场，他永远可以发挥最大的能力。他并不依赖于自己在某一天的最佳一刻，他可以把20天的最佳时刻加起来。他没有理由不尽最大的努力。他的机会很多，他的责任也很重。某人说过——我忘了此君是谁——"话语乃唯一持久不灭之物"。依我看，这永远是绝妙的思想。人类力量的最伟大的杰作，即人类用石块垒起的无比坚固的大厦，也会夷为废墟，而那脱口而出的话语，那思绪起伏转瞬即逝的表达却延续了下来，但它不是过去的回响，不是纯粹的建筑奇迹或神圣的遗址，它力量依旧，生命依旧，有时候远比初说时更坚强有力，它越过了3000年时光的峡谷，为今天的我们照亮了世界。

文化点滴

heathen

异教徒。对于基督徒来说，异教徒指不信仰基督徒的宗教信徒，专指犹太人和穆斯林；伊斯兰教中引用"异教徒"一词为"卡菲尔"。异教徒一词含有贬义。

cricket

板球，又名木球，一向给人称颂为"绅士的游戏"（gentleman's game），是一项崇尚体育精神（sportsmanship）和"公平比赛"（fairplay）的运动。板球起源于英国，盛行于英国、澳大利亚、新西兰、印度、孟加拉、尼泊尔等国家。据说早在13世纪，英王爱德华一世就曾在英格兰东南部的肯特参加过类似板球的运动。板球被誉为贵族运动，亨利八世称板球为"国王的运动"。直至今日，板球仍被看成中产阶级的运动。虽然出身高贵，英国正在采取措施，普及板球运动。过去近20年来，澳大利亚一直是板球运动的霸主。

写作特点

　　这是一篇杂文，它具有战斗性与愉悦性的和谐统一。它具有战斗性，对于"有害的事物""立刻给予反响或抗争"，是"感应的神经""攻守的手足"；它又有愉悦性，它使读者在笑声中愉快地和那些旧事物告别，获得美的精神享受。愉悦性伴随战斗性而生。例如，在倒数第二段的这些句子：And even of those who, without being great scholars, attain a certain general acquaintance with the ancient writers, can it really be said that they have also obtained the mastery of English. How many young gentlemen there are from the universities and public schools who can turn a Latin verse with a facility which would make the old Romans squirm in their tombs. How few there are who can construct a few good sentences, or still less a few good paragraphs of plain, correct and straight forward English. 我们都可以感受到这样的特点。

品味鉴赏

　　《写作的乐趣》是丘吉尔的一篇杂文，文章秉承了丘吉尔的一贯文风：观点深刻、独到，词汇量大。如同丘吉尔的其他作品一样，本文阅读起来也比较困难，尤其是把握其核心思想时。通常，我们要看文章的开篇部分和结尾部分。开篇部分通常指出了文章的主要话题乃至全文的中心思想，而收尾部分又进一步概括、总结或者分析了文章的中心思想。

美文感悟

Dream Big
远大理想

I don't remember anymore—it must have been during high school. Someone said, "Have a dream. And dream big! It won't cost you extra to dream a big dream."

Yes, like every aspiring young student, I had a dream. In fact, I had a lot of dreams — visions of a future I wanted for myself, and things I wanted to have, everything that I knew would make me happy.

First of all, I dreamed about a life partner—a soul mate who would take care of me, love me with all his heart, and accept the love and care I offer him in return. He would be my "knight in shining **armor**[1]", my pillar when I need someone to lean on, my cushion to catch me when I fall, and my inspiration each waking moment of the day. I dreamed of a partner who would hold my hand and share all my dreams and aspirations.

Then I dreamed about a worthwhile career—where I can learn about as many things as I can. I wanted a job which not only **compensated**[2] me for my hard work, but which gave me fulfillment, pride in my achievements, and the opportunity to make a difference in other people's lives.

I also dreamed about a life of adventure and excitement—to compete in sports, engage in outdoor activities that challenge the limitations of the body and spirit, travel to distant places, taste **exotic**[3] foods, meet interesting individuals, and explore the wonders of the earth.

And finally, I dreamed about growing old in comfort—with my lifelong partner, in a country house by a river, where I can sit on a porch to watch the sunset, listen to the rustle of leaves, and reminisce about how all my dreams came true.

Oh, I must've been sixteen then, when dreams were so easy to draw up, from a clean **slate**[4] of

注释　**1. armor** [ˈɑːmə] *n.* 装甲

innocence and naive.

As the years rolled on, I found myself having to deal with the **harshness**5 of the real world. Major crossroads and decisions brought me pain before they enlightened me with valuable lessons. So much of the growing years were trial and error, and I almost felt **resigned**6 to live a life not the least bit anything like what I had elaborately pictured in my younger years.

I was almost forty when I finally decided that it was time to take control of my life. I had to stop allowing myself to blindly drift **downstream**7. I had to stick my head out of the water, get a visual fix on the riverbank, and swim ashore, no matter how difficult it seemed. It was time to act, to make my dreams come true. It wasn't too late.

I knew that if I didn't do something extremely **drastic**8, I will sadly let the years go by, and watch my dreams fade away. And sometime in the future, I will regret not having had the courage to take that vital leap to get to where I really wanted to go.

So, at forty, I looked back at what I originally had as my teenage dreams. Do I still want those dreams to come true? Are they still the dreams I want to pursue and be willing to pay the price for? Maybe the reason they weren't coming true was because I wasn't willing to pay the price. Big dreams have big trade-offs—should I risk it?

This time I wrote them down—not as dreams but as goals. I made commitments to myself and I recorded my progress. In less than five years, I had "all my ducks in a row".

My dream of adventure and excitement has seen initial fulfillment in my trips overseas and my involvement with a mountaineering group. I traveled to four countries and peaked seven mountain climbing sites within a span of four years.

My worthwhile career? You're reading it right now. Becoming a full-time **freelance**9 writer was a leap of faith. But as a writer I am able to research and learn as much as I can about anything I want to. I find fulfillment in sharing what I know, and in knowing that what I share can make a difference in a reader's life. And I even get paid for being proud of myself!

My soul mate? Even I couldn't believe it, but yes, I have found him. Last year I had to uproot, leave an old life, and cross an ocean, to join him. But like I said, I needed to be willing to pay the price, and to me, that is the very high value of this particular one-in-a-million dream-come-true!

So, there is just one dream left to go after—that country house in the mountains, next to a river. I have a clear picture of the house in my mind's eye. That's all we need to make a dream come true—a clear picture and the willingness to pay the price.

Who knows, maybe within the next five years (or after I print my first bestseller?), I will be a lot closer to sitting on that **porch**10, watching the sunset, listening to the rustle of leaves, and reminiscing about how all my teenage dreams finally came true.

It's never too late to dream. And yes, dreams do come true. I know.

注释

2. **compensate** ['kɒmpenseɪt] v. 补偿
3. **exotic** [ɪɡ'zɒtɪk] adj. 异国情调的
4. **slate** [sleɪt] n. 石板，石片
5. **harshness** ['hɑːnɪs] n. 严肃，粗糙的事物
6. **resigned** [rɪ'zaɪnd] adj. 顺从的
7. **downstream** ['daʊnstriːm] adv. 下游
8. **drastic** ['dræstɪk] adj. 激烈的
9. **freelance** [friː'lɑːns] n. 自由作家

原文翻译

记不清是什么时候了——一定是中学吧，有人说过："要有理想，而且要树立远大理想。远大的理想不会让你付出更多代价的！"

是啊，和每个雄心勃勃的年轻学生一样，我曾有过梦想。实际上，我有过很多梦想——理想中的各种未来蓝图，想要得到的东西，还有那些我知道能让我快乐的一切。

首先，我想找到生活的伴侣——一个情投意合的人，他会照顾我，用心地爱我，也接纳我回应的爱与关怀。他是我的"穿着锃亮盔甲的骑士"，在我需要依靠的时候他会是我的支柱，当我摔倒的时候他会是一张软垫，每天醒来的时候他是我的灵感。我多想有一个伴侣，他握着我的手，与我志相同，道相合。

其次我梦想做一番有价值的事业——从中我能学到许许多多东西。这份理想中的工作不仅要劳有所值，还要能给我带来满足感，成就感，并提供改变他人生活的机会。

我还梦想拥有冒险刺激的人生——进行体育竞赛，参加挑战身体与精神极限的户外活动，到遥远的地方旅行，品尝异国风味的食品，邂逅有趣的人，探索地球的奇妙。

最后，我梦想有个安逸的晚年——和我一生的爱人一起，住在河边的一套房子里，我要坐在前廊处观看落日，聆听树叶沙沙的响声，回想着我的一切梦想都是怎么慢慢实现。

哦，那时候我才16岁吧，纯真犹如一块干净的石板，梦想的描画是那么简单。

随着年龄变大，我发现自己不得不面对严峻的现实生活。人生大转弯与重大决策总先带来痛苦，然后才予以我宝贵经验的启迪。在很长的成长岁月中，尝试了又尝试，错了还错，生活磨平了我的棱角，这几乎与我从前精心设想过的生活是丝毫不同的。

到了差不多40岁，我终于打定主意，是时候整顿一下我的生活了。不能再漫无边际地飘荡。我要浮出水面，望准河岸，朝岸边游过去，不管那边看似有多艰险。是时候行动起来，实现我的梦想了。时机尚未太晚。

我知道，如果我再不抓紧奋起，我只会以悲伤度日，看着梦想熄灭。而到未来的某个时候，我会懊悔不曾有勇气迈出这重要的一步，走向我理想的彼岸。

所以，正值40岁的时候，我回顾我青少年时期的最初梦想。我现在还希望实现那些梦想吗？我还想继续追逐这些梦想，并心甘情愿为之付出代价吗？也许，它们不曾实现，是因为我不曾情愿付出代价。远大梦想必然牺牲巨大——我该冒这个险吗？

这一回，我把它们写了下来——不再是梦想，而是作为目标。我自我约束并记录下自己的进展。不到5年，我已然有了一系列的收获。

到国外的旅行和参加登山小组，初步地满足了我对冒险和刺激的梦想。我去过四个国家，四年之内攀登了7座高山的顶峰。

我有价值的事业呢？你现在正看着呢。成为一个全职的自由作者需要很大的信心迈出这一步。但是身为写手，我能去研究与学习一切自己想了解的东西。分享知识，而且明白这些分享会如何改变读者的人生，这些给予我满足感。再说，我为自己而骄傲，还有薪酬来犒劳！

人生伴侣呢？尽管我自己也难以置信，不过是的，我已经找到他了。去年我重新定位，告别了旧的生活，越过重洋，去和他在一起。可正如我所说的，我必须是心甘情愿地付出这个代价的，对我而言，那有多重要啊，这个梦想本只有一百万分之一的实现几率呢！

那么，还剩下最后一个梦想要去实现了——依山傍河的乡村屋子。我脑子里很清楚地勾画出房屋的模样。想实现梦想，我们需要的就只是一幅清晰的构想图和愿意付出代价的决心。

谁知道呢，也许下一个5年里（或者在我的第一本畅销书印出来后？），我就离这个梦想更近了些：坐

注释　**10. porch** [pɔːtʃ] *n.* 门廊

在前廊处观看落日，聆听树叶沙沙的响声，回想我一切的梦想怎么慢慢成真。

梦想，永远不会太迟。而且，真的，梦想确实可以实现。我知道。

文化点滴

knight in shining armor

白马王子是出现在一些童话故事里的一种定型角色。通常，这位王子出现并解救落难少女，最为典型的就是把她从邪恶的魔法中释放出来。很多传统民间故事里的英雄人物都会被赋予白马王子的名字，其中包括《白雪公主》和《灰姑娘》。这些角色一般都很英俊并且十分浪漫。白马王子也用于指代少女或年轻的女人在梦想中遇到的英俊、富有、能干的男士。

写作特点

本文运用了first of all, then, also, finally等连接词连接段落。这些词是在连接句子、段落中常用的，也是最容易记住的。这体现了作者朴实无华的文风，也正像一个16岁孩子的文笔那么稚嫩、简单。

品味鉴赏

本文主要描述了作者的远大理想。首先是中学时代，作为一名学生，在内心深处懵懵懂懂的理想愿望，尔后等到作者40岁的时候，重新整顿一下生活，不能"漫无边际地飘荡"，要向着自己的梦想行动了。人都是有理想、有梦想的。如果只是理想，只是做梦，虽然美好但是永难实现。只有不断地向着自己的目标前进，理想、梦想才能实现。而这也是人生存的意义所在。心有所梦，身有所动。

美文感悟

_____

_____

_____

_____

_____

Are We Having Fun Yet?

我们快乐吗?

作者简介:

Marie T.Russell（玛丽T.罗素），是Inner Self杂志的创办人（创办于1985年）。她还制作并主持每周一次的南佛罗里达州的电台广播和Inner Power节目。此节目的主题专注于如自尊、个人成长和福祉等。

We were all taught the work ethic: "Work (and suffer) till you die, or if you're lucky retire. We have responsibilities to fulfill. We have to be serious, work hard, rise in our career, make lots of money, and make earning money and advancing in our career a priority."

I wish to change that programming in my life. I know that when I do the things I enjoy doing, things work out better for me. I know that when I do something against my will, against my heart, it doesn't work out well. I know that stressing myself out to try to get a job done usually takes twice as long as taking time out and doing that same task at some other time in a relaxed manner.

We can change the **criteria**[1] by which we decide what to do in our lives. Instead of: "Will it bring in lots of money or advance my career?" We need to ask ourselves, "Will I enjoy doing this? Will this be fun? Am I looking forward to getting started on this?"

If you can't answer "yes" to these questions, then quite possibly this is not the task for you! If it is something that must be done, i.e. taxes, dishes, etc., the solution is to find someone else to do them for you. There are some people who will enjoy and love to do what you prefer not to do. Really!

We are all very different and different things appeal to each one of us. Just because someone else enjoys a particular thing does not mean that you must. We can trust what I call the "fun **index**[2]" to assist us in knowing if a particular action is the one for us. We can break away from the rule of thumb that judges things by whether they bring money or career advancement. We can change that to making our decisions based on whether an action will bring us pleasure and personal satisfaction. Does the work you do leave you feeling proud and pleased with yourself? Are you following the voice of "should" or the one of "want to"? I find myself struggling over a task and it ends up **dragging**[3] itself out. Have you noticed that the things that you dislike doing are the ones that seem to take forever to get done? As for the opposite viewpoint, well as the saying goes "Time flies when you're having fun!"

Learning to go against that old programming and trusting the "fun index" is an **ongoing**[4] project. Every small step is, at the same time, a big leap. Each step will move you away from dissatisfaction with your life and closer to self-love, self-acceptance, self-esteem and joy in your everyday existence.

Anytime you ignore that inner prompting, you accumulate self-loathing and disappointment in your being. Your inner child once again feels let down and unimportant. Each let-down **reinforce**[5] the inner child's belief that everybody else's wishes are more important than its own. Once again its desires are relegated to the lowest priority on the list.

Yet, it's YOUR life! Ask yourself what steps YOU want to take! Listen to the voice within which will tell you what would really make you feel fulfilled and satisfied. You ARE the boss of your life! After all, it's yours, isn't it?

注释

1. criteria [kraɪˈtɪərɪə] n. 标准，条件
2. index [ˈɪndeks] n. 指标；指数；索引；指针
3. drag [dræg] vt. 拖累；拖拉；缓慢而吃力地行进
4. ongoing [ˈɒngəʊɪŋ] adj. 不间断的，进行的；前进的
5. reinforce [riːɪnˈfɔːs] vt. 加强，加固；强化；补充

Chapter 7 生活艺术

原文翻译

这样的工作理念曾被灌输给我们:"生命不休,工作(痛苦)不止。或者,除非你是已经幸运地退休了。履行这个理念是我们的责任。我们必须一丝不苟、勤勤勉勉、出人头地、拼命赚钱,把赚钱和晋升当成职业生涯中的首要点。"

我希望改变我人生的这个程序。我知道,当作自己感兴趣的事情时,结果就越变越好。我知道,违背自己的心意行事,结果只能差强人意。我知道背负着压力去完成的一项工作,要比别的时候以轻松姿态去作业,花多两倍的时间。

一生中要做什么,我们可以改变决策的标准。别问自己:"这会有助于我赚大钱还是晋升?"与此相反,我们要问的是:"我会喜欢做这件事吗?会乐在其中吗?我盼望着它的开始吗?"

如果你不是肯定地给出这些问题的答案,那么很可能这个任务并不适合你!如果是不得不做的事情,譬如交税、洗碗等,解决的办法是找别人替你来做。总有人喜欢做你不感兴趣的事情。真的。

人各有不同,每个人感兴趣的东西也不同。一些人喜欢某些东西,不代表你也非要喜欢不可。我们在评定某个特定的行为是否适当时,可以借助和信任我称为"快乐指数"的标码进行衡量。破除"赚钱"和"晋升"第一的拇指定律,转而把决策建立在行动是否能给我们带来欢乐与个人满足感的基础上。你的工作能让你感到骄傲以及自得其乐吗?你追随的声音是"我应该做"还是"我想要做"?

我自己正熬着一个工作任务,结果给拖沓得不能再拖沓。你是否注意过呢,一份你不喜欢的工作看似要花无限长的时间去完成?反过来,正如谚语所说的:"走得最快的总是快乐的时刻!"

打破旧有程序并信任"快乐指数"要坚持做下去。每一个小进步同时也代表着一个大飞跃。每一步都带离生活中的不满,推动你走进一个自爱自尊、自我包容和快乐喜悦的生活,它日日复新。

不管是什么时候,只要你忽视了内心的鼓舞斗志,人生就积攒下了自怨自艾和悲伤失望。你内心的孩子便会再一次沉陷于消沉与不被重视的情绪里。每多一次消沉,内心的孩子就多一层这样的成见:任何人的愿望都比他的来得更重要。于是他把自己的愿望更往下压得不能再低。

是的,这是你的人生!问问自己你要怎样过!倾听来自内心的声音,它会告诉你什么会让你充满成就感和满足感。你才是你生命的主宰!毕竟,生命只属于你,不是吗?

文化点滴

fun index

快乐感是一种心理体验,它既是对生活的客观条件和所处状态的一种事实判断,又是对于生活的主观意义和满足程度的一种价值判断。它表现为在生活满意度基础上产生的一种积极的心理体验。而快乐指数,就是衡量这种感受具体程度的主观指标数值。

the rule of thumb

拇指规则又译为大拇指规则,又叫经验法则,是一种可用于许多情况的、简单的、经验性的、探索性的但不是很准确的原则。

写作特点

本文运用了大量的排比句式，或相似结构的句式，在第二、三、四、五段中均有所体现。排比是一种修辞手法，利用3个或3个以上意义相关或相近、结构相同或相似、语气相同的词组（主谓/动宾）或句子并排，达到一种加强语势的效果。它可使文章的节奏感加强，条理性更好，更利于表达强烈的感情。它使内容集中，增强气势；叙事透辟，条分缕析；节奏鲜明，长于抒情。

品味鉴赏

本文作者希望改变"生命不休，工作不止"的工作状态，进而探讨了"一生中要做什么"这个伟大的议题。人的一生忙忙碌碌，每个人都有自己的理想和自己的"快乐指数"。那么，一定要守住"快乐指数"，坚持下去。就像文章最后一段所说："是的，这是你的人生！问问自己你要怎样过！倾听来自内心的声音，它会告诉你什么会让你充满成就感和满足感。你才是你生命的主宰！毕竟，生命只属于你，不是吗？"

美文感悟

_____
_____
_____
_____
_____

Chapter 8

成功凯歌

冯友兰先生谈到过人生成功的三种因素：才能、努力和机会。他认为有三种类型的成功：一是学问方面的成功。有所发明或创作，如大文学家、大艺术家、大科学家等等。二是事业方面的成功。如大政治家、大军事家、大事业家等等。三是道德方面的成功。在道德上成为完人，如古之所谓圣贤。这三种成功也就是古人所说的三不朽——立德（道德成功）、立功（事业成功）和立言（学问成功）。

Be an Expert in Your Field
成为本领域的专家

作者简介：

博恩·崔西（Brian Tracy），当今世界上个人职业发展领域最成功的演说家和咨询家之一，在成功学、潜能开发、销售策略及个人实力发挥等各方面均有不小建树。他每年在美国国内和国外的听众人数达到45万人之多。另外，他还为500多家公司提供咨询服务，其中包括IBM、美国麦道公司、安达信公司、百万圆桌会等等。博恩·崔西还是畅销书作家，著述颇丰，作品包括《吃掉那只青蛙》《涡轮战略》《成为百万富翁的21个秘窍》《创建你的未来》《关键点》等。

In our economic system, your income will be determined by three factors. First, what you do, second, how well you do it, and third, the difficulty of replacing you. One of the qualities of top people is that at a certain point in their careers, they decided to commit to excellence. They decided to be the best at what they do. They decided to pay any price, make any sacrifice, and invest any amount of time necessary to become very very good in their chosen fields. And as a result of this decision, they pulled away from the pack of average performers, and moved themselves upwards in the income category where today they earn three, four, five and ten times as much as their peers. When I started my sales career many years ago, someone told me about "80-20 rule" as it applied into sales. He said that 20% of the sales people made 80% of the money. Well this means that, 80% of the sales people only made 20% of the money and they have to divide it amongst themselves.

At that point many years ago, I decided that I would prefer to be a member of the top 20% rather than the bottom 80%. This decision changed my life for ever. Because I had come from a difficult childhood, received below average grades in school, I grew up with a poor self-image and a low level of self-confidence. It never occurred to me that I could be good at anything. If ever I attempted something and did it well, I immediately **dismiss**[1] it as an accident or a lucky break. For years I saw myself as an average or below average performer in any job I worked at.

Then one day, I had a sudden flash of insight. I realized that everybody who is in the top 10% of their field started in the bottom 10%, everybody who is doing well today was once doing poorly, everybody who is at the front of buffet line of life started at the back of the line, and even more importantly, it dawned on me that whatever others had done within reason, I could do as well. And this turns out to be true for just about everyone. No one is better than you and no one is smarter than you. People are just better or smarter in different areas. In addition, all business skills are learnable, people who are doing better in some areas of business have learned the essential skills in **combination**[2] with other skills before you have. If you're not achieving what others are achieving, it simply means that you have just not learned those skills yet. Here is another **breakthrough**[3] for me. You can learn anything you need to learn, to achieve any goal you can set for yourself. There are no limits on what you can accomplish except the limits you can place on your own mind and imagination. If you decided to become excellent to join the top 10% of people in your field, there is nothing on earth that can stop you from getting there except yourself.

Will it be easy? Of course not. I don't use the word "easy" in this program. Everything worthwhile takes a long time and a lot of work to accomplish. But it is possible if you want it badly enough and if you are willing to work long enough and it is worth every bit of the efforts by which you get there. Les Brown, the motivational speaker, says, to achieve something that you never achieved before, you must become someone that you have never been before. Wolfgang von Goethe, a German philosopher, said, to have more, you must first be more. Once you decide to become one of the best people in your field, the only question you ask is, "How do I achieve it?"

The very fact that hundreds of thousands or even millions of people have gone from the bottom to the top in every field is ample proof that you can do it as well. Many of these people, if not most of them, may not even have the natural talents and abilities that you have. In most areas of life, it's more hard work and **dedication**[4] than natural ability and talent that leads to excellence in great success.

In an analysis for the members of *Forbes* 400, the 400 richest men and women in America, **conducted**[5] a couple of years ago, they found that a person who dropped out of high school and who made it into the *Forbes* 400, was worth on average $333 million more than those who had

注释

1. **dismiss** [dɪsˈmɪs] *vt.* 不再考虑
2. **combination** [ˌkɒmbɪˈneɪʃən] *n.* 结合(体)、联合(体)
3. **breakthrough** [ˈbreɪkθruː] *n.* 突破,突破性进展,重要的新发现
4. **dedication** [ˌdedɪˈkeɪʃən] *n.* 奉献
5. **conduct** [kɒnˈdʌkt] *vt.* 管理;指挥

completed college or university. The reason I mention this, is because many people feel that they didn't get good grades in school, they are **permanently**[6] limited in what they can accomplish later on in life. Nothing could be further from the truth. Some of the most wealthy and successful men and women in America, and throughout the world, did poorly in school. Remember the question "How do you eat an elephant?" and the answer was one bite at a time. This is the same way that you become absolutely excellent at what you do. You move to the top, one step, one skill, one small improvement at a time.

原文翻译

在我们的市场体系中，个人的收入取决于三个因素。首先，你所从事的行业；其次，你的业绩如何；最后，你被取代的难度。顶尖人物所具备的特性之一，便是他们能够在其职业生涯的某个契合点决心做到优秀。他们决心在所从事的领域中做到最好。他们决心付出任何代价，做出任何牺牲，投入任何的时间以使得自己在所选择的领域中卓尔不群。其结果是，他们从平庸的工作者中胜出，使自己上升到一定的薪金层次，即他们的收入是常人的3倍、4倍、5倍甚至10倍。回顾我所从事的销售领域，多年以前，曾经有人对我提起销售领域的"80-20规则"。他说，20%的销售人员挣到80%的钱，也就是说，80%的销售人员只能挣到20%的钱，而且这些钱还要在他们中间进行再分配。

多年前听到这话的那一时刻，我就暗下决心，争取做20%中的一员，而不是80%中的一分子。这个决定也从此永远改变了我的生活。因为我少年时代不太顺心，我的学业成绩平平。在成长的过程中，我总是自惭形秽，缺乏信心。我从来没有想过我会把什么事情做好。即便是我偶尔做过什么不赖的业绩，我也会自我否认地认为不过是碰巧或运气好罢了。在很多年里，我一直认为自己在工作领域中表现平平甚至是中等偏下。

突然有一天，我幡然醒悟，意识到10%处于顶尖领域的人实际上可能是来自最底层的那10%的人们，所有现在表现突出的人都有可能是曾经表现糟糕的，现今处于领先地位的人曾经可能是落后者。更重要的是，我突然意识到，别人在合理范围内能够做到的事情，我也能做到。对于任何人来说都是如此。别人并不比你强，也并不比你聪明。每个人都有自己擅长的领域。同时，所有的商业技巧都是能够学到的，那些在某个业务领域表现突出的人不过是比你先掌握了要领和其他的技巧。如果你还没有取得他人已有的成就，只能说明你还没有学会那些技巧。此外，我还得到另一个启示：你会学到所有你应该学的东西，你能达到所有为自己所设定的目标。你的成就将会是无限的，而有限的只是你的思维或想象。如果你决心成为本领域中表现最突出的那10%的人物，除了你自己，没有任何事物能成为你达到目的的樊篱。

实现目标很容易吗？当然不是，在这里，我并没有使用"容易"一词。任何一件值得做的事情都需要大量的时间和精力。但是，如果你充满渴望，如果你准备长期致力于此，你的每一份付出便是值得的。莱斯·布朗，一个鼓舞人心的演说家，曾经说道，要想达到你从未达到的目标，你必须尝试从未有过的改变。德国哲学家沃夫冈·冯·歌德曾说过，要想获得更多，你首先应该有更多技能。一旦你下定决心，想成为本领域中的佼佼者，你唯一需要问自己的是："我如何去实现此目标？"

在各行各业，成千上万，甚至是数以百万的人从最底层脱颖而出的成功范例足以说明你也可以成功。他们中有许多人——即使不是大多数——甚至比不上你的天资和能力。在生活中的许多场合，是努力和决心，而不是天资和聪颖能使一个人取得巨大的成功。

几年前，在对美国最富有的《福布斯》排行榜最富有的400人的分析中，人们发现，在入围《福布斯》财富榜的400人中，其中中学辍学的人比那些大学毕业的人平均多挣333万美元。我之所以提及此事，只是想说明，很多人因为认为他们上学时成绩不佳，使得他们未来的成就受到限制。没有什么比事实更有说服力。美国最富有的男士和女士，甚至是世界范围内最富有的人士，都曾经在学校表现平平。还记得那个经典的问

注释 6. permanently ['pəumentlı] *adv.* 永久地；持久地

题"怎么才能把大象吞掉"吗?答案是"一口一口地吃"。这和你在自己领域里如何获得成功是一个道理。你要向着成功,一步一个脚印,一步一个收获,一点点不断积累每一个小小的成就。

文化点滴

Forbes

《福布斯》是美国一本世界知名的商业杂志,由苏格兰人B.C.福布斯于1917年创办。杂志宗旨是"创业精神、创富工具"。《福布斯》也有发行《福布斯》亚洲版、《福布斯》生活和《福布斯》女性杂志。另外,《福布斯》也出版10种不同语言的刊本,分别是中国、克罗地亚、印度、印度尼西亚、以色列、韩国、波兰、罗马尼亚、俄罗斯和土耳其。《福布斯》亚洲杂志所发行的10种版本遍布在世界各地,有将近600万读者。《福布斯》着重于描写企业精英的思维方式,秉承"以人为本"的理念,倡导"企业家精神"。《福布斯》被誉为"美国经济的晴雨表"。

写作特点

本文在说明的过程中使用了倍数、数字。为了说明事物的情况或事理,有时光从道理上讲,人们不太理解,这就需要举些既通俗易懂又有代表性的例子来加以说明。数字能使所要说明的事物具体化,以便读者理解。让数字来说明问题,能使说明更准确,也使说明更具说服力,让人信服。

品味鉴赏

读到这篇文章,尤其是看到莱斯·布朗,那个鼓舞人心的演说家,就想跟大家分享一个他的故事。美国当代最著名的作家、演讲家莱斯·布朗,如今的演讲酬金是每小时2万美元。当有人问起他成功的秘诀时,他指了指左耳上的一个厚茧,语重心长地说:"我初涉演讲界时,一没名气,二没资历,更缺乏个人魅力和经验。可我决心要在这个行业里干出点儿名堂来,不达目的决不罢休。于是,我一天到晚给人打电话,求教演讲技能,联系演讲业务。成名初期,我每天至少打100多个电话,请求别人给我机会到他们那里去演讲……这个老茧是我获得成功的见证和记录,值几百万美元啊。"

每个成功者都有其成功的理由和原因,以及为此而做出的努力和付出的代价。向往成功的人们,你有如此的厚茧么?

美文感悟

_____
_____
_____

The Challenge to Succeed
通往成功的挑战

作者简介：

吉姆·罗恩（Jim Rohn，1930—2009），国际知名的商业思想家、美国吉姆·罗恩培训机构创办人。吉姆·罗恩还是世界成功学大师安东尼·罗宾的启蒙老师。他是当今最受欢迎的企业界领袖之一，经常为顶级的销售组织和管理团体开办培训课程，其中包括众多的世界500强公司，并常受邀到全球各大企业去演讲。曾荣获1985年全美演讲协会CPAE奖。

It is a challenge to succeed. If it were not, I'm sure more people would be successful, but for every person who is enjoying the fruit from the tree of success, a thousand are examining the roots. They are trying to figure it all out. They are **mystified**[1] and **perplexed**[2] by what seems to be some strange, complex and **elusive**[3] secret that must be found if ever success is to be enjoyed.

While most people spend most of their lives struggling to earn a living, a much smaller number seem to have everything going their way. Instead of just earning a living, the smaller group is busily engaged in designing and enjoying a fortune. Everything just seems to work out

---

注释
1. **mystify** ['mɪstɪfaɪ] *v.* 使神秘化；蒙蔽，迷惑
2. **perplexed** [pəplekst] *adj.* 困惑的
3. **elusive** [ɪ'lju:sɪv] *adj.* 躲避的

for them, while the much larger group sits in awe at how life can be so unfair, complicated and unjust.

"I am a nice person," the man says to himself. "How come this other guy is happy and prosperous, and I'm always struggling?" He asks himself, "I am a good husband, a good father and a good worker. How come nothing seems to work out for me? Life just isn't fair. I'm even smarter and willing to work harder than some of these other people who just seem to have everything going their way," he says as he slumps into the sofa to watch another evening of television.

But you see you've got to be more than a good person and a good worker. You've got to become a good planner and a good dreamer. You've got to see the future finished in advance. You've got to put in the long hours and put up with the setbacks and the disappointments. You've got to learn to enjoy the process of disciplines and of putting yourself through the paces of doing the uncomfortable until it becomes comfortable. You've got to be prepared and willing to attack the challenges if you want the success because challenges are part of success.

Now that may sound like a full menu of activities, but let me assure you that the process of going from average to fortune isn't really all that difficult. Thinking about it is the difficult part. Anticipating all the effort and the changes and the disciplines is far worse in the mind than in reality. I can promise you that the challenges you'll meet on the road to success are far less difficult to deal with than the struggles and the disappointments that come from being average. Confronting and overcoming challenges is an **exhilarating**[4] experience. It does something to feed the soul and the mind. It makes you more than you were before. It strengthens the mental muscles and enables you to become better prepared for the next challenge.

Now let's assume that you are one of those who is willing to tackle the challenges that you really do want to know about the process of going from average to fortune, and you are determined to make the journey so that you can experience the rewards. What do you do? Where do you start? What are the changes you have to make and disciplines you have to master? These are the questions I often hear from those who want to do well but aren't. And it is in response to the many inquiries I receive from those who want to enjoy the good life, that I have taken the time to prepare this library of ideas and insights that we now call the challenge to succeed.

Actually I didn't really prepare this program that you are about to listen to. It evolved. It is evolving from the very best concept that I've managed to assemble all over the years. As I've traveled the world teaching ideas that count to people who care. It isn't the complex, mystical techniques that will require you to undergo some strange form of mental transformation. It is merely a set of basic principles that will get you started on the journey that can be life changing. I've learned over the years that about half dozen things make about 80% of the difference in how your life turns out. And this program will address those simple but necessary basics that will start for you what I like to call the miracle process. All you've got to do is listen and absorb the ideas

注释　4. exhilarating [ɪɡˈzɪləreɪtɪŋ] *adj.* 使人兴奋的

that I'll share with you. Then when you've got the ideas, your new appetite for success, and your new confidence in yourself will start you on that unique journey. It's a journey that will lead you along the path that you always want to travel but could never find, amid the amaze of highway to feel **capacity**[5] by those who are hopelessly lost and **confused**[6].

The hours that we will spend together examining these special insights, will start a whole new process for you. And if you will start to apply these ideas we will share, I can promise you that your life will never be the same again. You don't ever have to remain how and what you are after today except by your own choice. The seeds of high achievements are about to be placed in the soil of your mind, then with the magic of your own activity, the practice of these basic ideas will start the growing process. Soon you will enjoy the full harvest of rewards that comes from applying these simple basics. The challenges to success will go into full retreat. As you begin to see just how simple success really is, and you will be fascinated by the result you will soon begin to enjoy. I want to congratulate you for making this investment in yourself. We live in an age when so many tend to spend more money on the outside of their head than they do on the inside. That usually leads to **tragic**[7] consequences with our lives sleeping by without any real or lasting progress being made.

To have more, we must first become more. And to become more, we must begin the process of working harder on ourselves than we do anything else. Here's one of the more valuable discoveries I've made on the subject of going from average to fortune. The achievement of success is found not just in the gathering of new knowledge, the **acquisition**[8] of new skills or in the accumulation of new experiences. It is also in the discovery of new emotions. It's how we feel about what we know that makes the biggest difference in how our lives turn out. How we feel about the chances we have and the choices we have determines the intensity of our efforts, whether we try or don't try, join or don't join, believe or don't believe. So as you listen to the information in the Challenge To Succeed seminar, I'd like for you to discover some strong feelings about your life and about what you want to do with that life. You probably have much of the knowledge and a lot of experience, and perhaps most of the skills that it takes to become successful. What you may be lacking in are the strong feelings about what you want and what you want to do. You may be one of those who have become so involved in the process of earning a living, that you've forgotten about the choices and the chances you have for designing your own life.

So let the message that follows touch you. Let it help you discover the feeling that will make you take a second look at your life and where you head it. After all, you've only got one life at least on this planet, so why not make it an adventure in achievement? Why not discover what all you can do and what all you can have? Why not discover how many others you can help and in the process how that will help you? Now let's get started in a journey of ideas and insights, that might very well be life-changing for you. Let's take a close look at the challenge to succeed and what that might mean to your better future.

---

5. capacity [kə'pæsɪtɪ] *n.* 容量；才能，能力
6. confuse [kən'fjuːz] *vt.* 使困惑，把……弄糊涂；混淆
7. tragic ['trædʒɪk] *adj.* 悲惨的，可悲的
8. acquisition [ˌækwɪ'zɪʃən] *n.* 取得，获得，习得

原文翻译

　　成功需要历经挑战，如若不然，我相信更多的人会成功。但是对于每一个正在品尝成功果实的人，有数以千计的人们正在探究其成功之源，并试图找出所有的成功秘诀。正是由于人们对于成功的渴求，才使得人们对看似奇特复杂的成功的秘诀感到困惑和好奇。

　　当芸芸大众终其一生艰难谋生时，只有很少的一部分人似乎一帆风顺。对于这一部分少数人，他们并不只是在谋生，而是在忙于筹划和享受财富。当大多数人都敬畏于生活是如此不平等、如此之复杂、如此不公时，少数人的一切事物却如其所愿地进展着。

　　人们抱怨道："我是个好人，为什么别人又快活又有钱，而我却一天到晚挣扎度日？"也有人问道："我是一个好丈夫，好父亲，好员工，为什么我事事不顺，生活真是太不公正了。我比那帮人更聪明，更勤奋，他们好运连连，万事皆顺，而我却一直不如意。"他们一边抱怨，一边却又一屁股坐在沙发里整个晚上地看着电视。

　　你要知道，你不仅需要做一个好人，一个好员工，你还应该是一个好的计划者，好的梦想家。你需要预知未来，你需要长期奋斗，还需要忍受挫折和失望。你还需要严格自律，你得学会忍受不适直到将其变得舒适。如果你要获得成功，你必须有所准备，愿意迎接挑战。因为挑战是成功的必不可少的组成部分。

　　看起来似乎需要作出各种努力，实际上，我可以向你保证，从平常到财富的过程并没有那么困难。困难的是去思考如何达到这一目的。头脑中对于一切努力、一切变化或一切训练的预想远比现实要可怕得多。我能担保，你在通往成功道路上所遇到的挑战远比你碌碌无为时的挣扎和失望简单许多。面对挑战、克服挑战是一个令人兴奋的过程，是一个历练灵魂和思想的过程。它能使你拥有更多原先未曾拥有的东西。它使你心智更加坚强，使你能更好地为着下一个挑战做好准备。

　　现在，假设你是个愿意接受挑战的人，你真心想探寻如何从平庸变得富有，你决定接受这一挑战之旅以便能品尝到回报的喜悦。你该如何去做？你该从何入手？你应该历经怎样的改变、拥有何种的修养？这些问题我经常从那些渴求成功却未能如愿的人那里听到。对于那些渴望享受美好生活的人们所提出的问题，我的回答是，我已经花了大量时间来准备这些我们今天称之为"通往成功的挑战"的想法和启示。

　　实际上我并没有刻意为你们将要听到的这个演讲做出准备，这些观点是自然而然地形成的，它是从这些年里我所积累下来的观点中自然而然地形成的。当我周游世界、讲授这些对于那些真正感兴趣的人来说起作用的理念。这并不是一些复杂的、神秘的技巧，也不需要你经历多么奇特的变革。这只是一些基本的原则，他们会使得你开始一个改变终身的历程。这么多年的经历使我明白，很少的一些事情能使你的生活产生80%以上的不同。今天这个节目将会谈及那些非常简单但是必不可少的基本观点。它会使你开始一个被我称之为"奇迹"的过程。你们所需要做的便是仔细聆听，接受我与你们分享的这些想法。当你们接受了这些主意之后，你们对成功的渴求和你们对自身的信心，将会使你们走上一个奇特的旅程。这个旅程将会引领你走向你盼望已久却从未寻到的路径。就宛如在公路上，拥有那些绝望的迷路者和困惑者所不曾拥有的能力。

　　我们聚在一起来探寻这些特殊人生体验的几个小时，将会给你开始一个全新的旅程。一旦你开始运用我们今天一起分享的这些观念，我敢保证你的人生会发生根本的改变。除非你刻意坚持，我相信你将不会再像从前那样行事。成功的种子将会种植到你的头脑中去，这些想法将会在你的头脑中慢慢成长，不久你就会收获因为运用这些想法而产生的丰厚回报。到那时，通往成功的挑战将不会存在。当你开始发现成功原来如此简单，你也就会感到你将要享受的结果是如此神奇。祝贺你，祝贺你对自己进行的这个智力投资。在我们生活的这个年代里，人们对头脑之外的投资花费太多，而很少顾及大脑里边的智力投资，这往往导致悲惨的结果，我们的生命沉沉睡去，而不曾留下任何真正、持久的进步。

　　想拥有更多，首先，你便需要在更多方面有所成就；想在更多方面有所成就，我们需要艰苦努力开始重塑自身，而不是去做一些其他的事情。谈到如何从平庸走向财富，以下是我这些年里非常有价值的发现之一，成功的收获不仅体现在新知识、新技巧的获得和新经验的积累上，它还体现在新情感的发现上。对于我们所知道的知识，我们如何感受，这才是使得我们生活全然不同的关键所在，对于我们所拥有的机会以及我们所作出的决定如何感受，决定着我们付出多大的努力，不管我们尝试与否，参与与否，相信与否。因此，当你今天再次聆听这些关于成功的挑战这一论坛，我希望你挖掘出你内心关于你的人生以及关于你想如何谋划人生的强烈感受。也许你知识渊博、经验丰富，也许还拥有通向成功所必需的技巧。但是，你所缺乏的，正是这些对于你所需和所愿的一些强烈感情。你也许是芸芸众生中忙于谋生的一员，你也许因此而忘掉你所拥有的人生筹划的选择和机会。

因此，就让下面的这些信息来感染你，在你回顾你的人生经历、在你思索如何前进时，就让这些信息来帮助你发现这些感受。毕竟，至少在这个星球上，我们只有一次生命，为什么不把它当作一次充满收获的冒险之旅呢？为什么不去尝试探寻你能做些什么，你能拥有些什么？为什么不去探寻你能帮助多少人，并在帮助他们的过程中，你将有何收获？现在，就让我们开始这一思想和启示之旅，这一旅途对你来说，将是改变一生的。让我们仔细考量通往成功将要遇到的挑战，同时了解这些挑战对于成就美好未来的意义。

文化点滴

discipline
培养高尚的品质和正确的待人处世的态度，求取学识品德之充实完美。古代儒家多指按照其学科的要求培养完善的人格，使言行合乎规矩。

investment in yourself
用于智力开发，使人们获得科学知识和技能的费用，主要包括各级各类学校的教育经费、教育事业的基本建设费用以及受教育者支付的学杂费用等。它是一种对经济发展有重要作用的投资，有时也指家庭用于子女智力开发的费用。这里是指对自己的"开发"。

写作特点

本文运用了举例子的写作方法，例如文章的第三、六段等。举例子，是通过列举有代表性的、恰当的事例来说明事物特征的说明方法。为了说明事物的情况或事理有时光从道理上讲，人们不太理解，这就需要举些既通俗易懂又有代表性的例子来加以说明，使欲描写的事物更清晰。

品味鉴赏

如果你要获得成功，你必须有所准备，愿意迎接挑战。因为挑战是成功的必不可少的组成部分。这看起来似乎需要作出各种努力，实际上，最困难的是去思考如何达到这一目的。头脑中对于一切努力、一切变化或一切训练的预想远比现实要可怕得多。

美文感悟

Secrets to Be Ten Great Geniuses
伟大天才的秘密

作者简介：

托尼·亚历山德拉博士（Dr. Tony Alessandra），美国著名的市场策划和应用行为学家，市场策略和建立终身客户关系领域内的研究权威，被誉为"美国最令人震撼的演讲家"。从一名普通的销售员到一位极具影响力的营销专家，30多年间托尼积累了极为丰富的销售实战经验，并给诸多跻身世界一百强的著名公司做过销售培训，如GE、IBM、AT&T等。迄今为止，托尼共出版了14部著作，如《魅力》《白金法则》《管理人的艺术》《非操纵性销售》等，并被翻译成17种语言，广泛流传于世界各地，其中有的长期雄踞《时代周刊》畅销书榜之首，有的被指定为美国多家商学院和保险公司的培训教材。

(1) Why You See Yourself not as a Genius

Recently, a story in the *New York Times* described the typical day in the life of a rather a typical college student. She is a senior, studying physics, biology and mathematics, and she gets straight As in all her courses. This is impressive of course, but it's a description that I could apply to a lot of bright, motivated students across the country. The difference is that this college senior is only 13 years old. She started reading when she was 8 months old, and by age 5 she had finished the entire reading curriculum at her school. In second grade, she was taking 8th grade math. By 4th grade, her teachers felt they could no longer **accommodate**[1] her special needs. Her parents couldn't find a university that would accept such a young student. So she took a year off which she spent reading and earning a black belt in Karate. The next year at age 10, she began college. She reads at a rate of between 70 and 100 pages an hour depending on the material. She also plays the clarinet at the level of a professional musician.

Does it sound like you at the age of 13? Certainly not me. Do you find it easy to identify with this young woman? May be not. But I think you should agree that she is definitely a **prodigy**[2] and perhaps a genius, that's certainly a word that already has been applied to her many times already. Although you may not see yourself in the league, you probably remember kids from your school years who are much more advanced than average. For this program, those are very important memories. Because when those memories were created, you began to see yourself as something other than a genius. That was when you decided that certain other people were smarter than you. They learn faster, they did their homework without a single mistake. And maybe you weren't wrong about those things, except that you drew the wrong conclusion, you **generalize**[3] the rather broad lesson from a very narrow set of experiences. You confused with what might be called giftedness with what deserves to be called genius.

(2) Type of Genius

Paul MacCready, as a writer and an inventor, who has carefully studied genius and the ways people understand that concept. MacCready has evolved several categories on what genius seems to mean. And these can be very useful, as a starting point, for defining what genius really is. In the first category are what Paul MacCready calls and what everyone agrees on what genius is. These people are the great icons of civilization, including Einstein, Leonardo da Vinci, Shakespeare, Mike Angelo. Is there anybody who believes Einstein was't a genius? I don't think so. So this category is for the geniuses who are elected by **unanimous**[4] consent. These are many of the things people who were mentioned in my own informal research. We'll have much more to say about them in this section and throughout the program. In fact, most of our models said the various genius categories will be drawn from this group.

The MacCready second category is the officially **designated**[5] geniuses. These are people who have won Nobel Prizes, or other highly-respected awards. Whether or not we understand what they've accomplished, we think of them as geniuses based on their **recognition**[6] by people who are supposed to know one when they see one.

注释

1. **accommodate** [ə'kɒmədeɪt] vt. 容纳；向……提供住处的
2. **prodigy** ['prɒdɪdʒɪ] n. 奇才，天才（尤指神童）
3. **generalize** ['dʒenərəlaɪz] v. 概括，归纳，推断
4. **unanimous** [juː'nænɪməs] adj. 全体一致的，一致同意
5. **designate** ['dezɪgneɪt] vt. 指派，委任；标出，把……定名为
6. **recognition** [ˌrekəg'nɪʃən] n. 识别；确认

A third category includes people who haven't yet gained national or international pr**ominence**[7], but who have done something so remarkable that they seem to be in a different realm from ordinary morals. Some of these are the prodigies, young people I've mentioned in the earlier session— students who have won national science contests or gotten perfect scores on standardized tests. Often they are not the best in the day-to-day conduct at school in business, but they have some special gifts that eventually reveal themselves. Quite often, these people are underachievers who struggle with shyness and low self–esteem. Their surprising success, it's surprising only because they deliberately try to stay in the background.

I think you can see how each of these three categories seems quite **legitimate**[8], but it's the fourth one that's really most important for this program. And you maybe surprised to learn that the fourth category questions or even completely refutes the other three, because the fourth category includes everybody. It's based on the idea that we all have the potential for achievements that are wrongly considered possible for only a few. And there's plenty of evidence for this. After all, the physical and mental challenges of learning to walk and talk are more difficult than anything we face later in life—yet the vast majority of human beings meet these challenges successfully. True, it's been argued that these primary skills are hardwired into our genetic makeup. But there are many things that the genetic argument can't account for. In the 17th and 18th centuries, for example, it was simply expected that every member of the educated class would be able to read and speak several different languages, be able to write poetry, play a musical instrument, and know much of the Bible by heart. Furthermore, all of these skills would be performed at a very high level and at very early ages. In other words, thousands of people routinely displayed the abilities that today would be considered truly amazing—and perhaps even evidence of genius. But in those days what we call genius was just the fulfillment of society's expectations.

When we speak of everybody being a genius in this sense, it doesn't mean everyone has to get 800 on the SATs or have an IQ of 150 or above. It doesn't mean everybody can play the violin or create beautiful oil paintings. Those are other ways of looking at the concept of genius. But right now let's go back to the origin of the word itself. A researcher by the name of Thomas Armstrong has done some excellent work on this. He points out that the word genius is closely related to the word genesis, which comes from Greek and Latin words meaning "beget", "be born", or "come into being." It's also related to the word genial, meaning "festive" or "jovial." In the Middle East, the term has been linked to the word jinni, or genie, the magical power that lays dormant and hidden in Aladdin's lamp until a secret method released it.

Combining all these roots leads to a very powerful and beautiful definition of genius. It means "giving birth to your joy." In this sense, genius is a word for an individual's hidden potential. It also

---

7. prominence ['prɒmɪnəns] *adj.* 突出的，杰出的　　**8. legitimate** [lɪ'dʒɪtɪmɪt] *adj.* 合情合理的；合法的

includes the process of discovering that potential and transforming it into action. But the first step is belief, the first step is certainty that you have greater capabilities than you thought, not only do you have those capabilities, you also have a responsibility to develop them and put them into use.

原文翻译

1. 你为什么不把自己看作是天才

最近，《纽约时报》上的一则故事描述了一个典型大学生的具有代表性的一天。她是一位大四的学生，学习科目主要包括物理、生物和数学。她的所有课程成绩全部为A。这的确令人感到印象深刻，但是这样的说辞似乎适用全国范围内所有的聪明爱学的学生。这篇报道的不同之处在于，这个学生只有13岁。在她8个月大的时候，她就已经开始阅读，到了5岁时，她已经完成了所在学校的所有阅读课程。二年级的时候，她在上八年级的数学。到了四年级的时候，她的老师觉得他们再也不能满足她对学习的特殊需要了。但是，那时她父母却无法找到一所大学愿意接收如此低龄的学生，她不得不休学一年，在家读书，并且还获得了空手道黑带。第二年，她10岁的时候，开始了大学生活。她的阅读速度按照材料的难易，大约是每小时70～100页。她还能以专业水平演奏竖笛。

这听起来和你13岁的时候一样吗？反正和我的完全不一样。你觉得和这样的女孩子产生共鸣容易吗？可能不容易。但我觉得至少你会认为她的确是一个奇才，或者说是天才，我相信这个词已经被多次用在她身上。虽然你可能从未认为自己是这个类型的人物，但你一定记得学生时代那些远比一般孩子聪明的同学。在今天这个培训项目里，这些是非常重要的记忆。因为当你们形成这些记忆的时候，你并没有把自己归属于天才的行列。在此时，你断定有一些人比你更聪明，他们学得更快，他们的作业没有一点错误。你说的这些都没有错，错的是你的结论。你从自己很有限的经历中归纳出一个相当广泛的结论。你混淆了那些可能被称为有天赋的人和应该被叫作天才的人。

2. 天才的类型

保罗·麦克格雷，一位作家和发明家，曾仔细地研究了天才以及人们对此概念的理解。麦克格雷把天才这一概念分成了几个不同的种类。他的分类起了一个抛砖引玉的作用，对于我们理解什么是真正的天才起到了很多作用。第一类是麦克格雷称为的而且人人都认可的所谓天才，他们是人类文明史上的代表人物，包括爱因斯坦、达·芬奇，莎士比亚，麦可·安奇洛等。有没有人否认爱因斯坦是天才？我想没有。所以这类天才是毫无争议并得到大家公认的人。这些也是我在自己的非正式研究里提到的那类人。我们会在今后的节目中更多地谈论这类人。事实上，我们所谓的偶像大部分属于这一类。

麦克格雷划分的第二类天才是得到官方认可的天才。这些人曾获得诺贝尔或其他颇受推崇的奖项。不管我们是否了解他们所取得的成就，我们都认为他们是天才，因为他们得到了那些我们认为有资格认可天才的人的承认。

第三类天才指的是那些尚未取得国内外瞩目的人，他们做了一些非同寻常的事情，使得他们完全不同于凡夫俗子。他们中的有些人是我在前面提到的那些青年才俊，有些是在国家级科学竞赛里获奖的人，有些是在标准化考试里得到完美成绩的人。通常，他们并不是那些在学校或商业领域表现最为突出的人，但是他们的特殊天赋最终使他们脱颖而出。这些人通常性格内向，胆小害羞，自尊心不强。他们的成功令人惊奇，之所以令人惊奇，是因为他们有意使自己显得默默无闻。

大家一定都认为这三类天才是当之无愧的。但是，正是这第四类天才对于我们今天这个培训项目来说，才是真正最重要的。你可能会惊奇地发现第四类天才的定义可能是对前三类天才定义的质疑或驳斥，因为第四类天才包括每个人。这类定义是基于一种观念，即认为我们每个人都有获得成功的潜力，而这种潜力常常被错误地认为只有少数人才拥有。这种常人天才的说法在很多方面都可以得到证实。毕竟，学习走路和说话所面临的生理和心理上的挑战比我们在以后生活中遇到的任何事都更严峻，然而，大部分人都成功地战胜了这些挑战。不可否认，有人会辩驳说这些基本技能完全是由于我们的基因所决定的，但是还是有许多事情我们的基因参数是解释不了的。比如，在17、18世纪，几乎所有受过教育的阶层都能阅读和使用几门语言，他们能做诗，会乐器，还能记住《圣经》里的大部分内容。而且，所有这些技能都达到了很高的水平，并且在年纪轻轻的时候就具备了。换句话说，那时常人的日常技能在今天看来则是不可思议的——甚至被认为是天才的有力证据。但是，在那个年代，被我们今天称之为天才的不过只是达到了社会的平均水平罢了。我们所说的人人皆为天才，并不意味着人人都要在SAT考试中得800分或每个人的智商都达到150或以上，也并不意味着每个人都要会拉小提琴或能画出漂亮的油画。那些是看待天才这个概念的其他方式。现在让我们来回顾一下"天才"这一词的词源。学者托马斯·阿姆斯特朗对此作了一番深入的研究。他指出，"天才"这个词和"起源"这个来自希腊拉丁语的词联系很紧密。该词的意思是"得到""出生"或"形成"。它同样和"欢快的"一词有关联，意思是"节日""高兴"。在中东，这个词还和"精灵""杰尼"相关，指的是埋藏在阿拉丁神灯里的神奇力量，只能通过秘密的方法才能使它得以释放。

把"天才"一词所有词源结合起来，我们就会给"天才"下一个令人信服的优美定义。它的意思是"产生你的快乐"。在这个概念下，"天才"是一个用以描述人们潜能的词。它还包括发现潜能并把它转换成行动的过程。但是，信念是第一步要拥有的。人们首先要确信自己拥有比自己想象的更大的能力，同时人们还有责任去发挥潜力，运用潜力。

文化点滴

The New York Times

《纽约时报》有时简称为《时报》（*The Times*），是一份在美国纽约出版的日报，在全世界发行，有相当的影响力，美国高级报纸、严肃刊物的代表，长期以来拥有良好的公信力和权威性。由于其风格古典严肃，它有时也被戏称为"灰色女士"（The Gray Lady）。它最初的名字是《纽约每日时报》（*The New—York Daily Times*），创始人是亨利·贾维斯·雷蒙德和乔治·琼斯。

Karate

空手道亦称空手，是发源于琉球王国（今琉球群岛）的一种格斗技术（类似我国的武术）。关于空手道的起源众说纷纭，目前最为学术界所认同的一种说法是，空手道的前身是古代琉球的武术"琉球手"或"手"，融合了传入的中国武术后，被琉球人尊称为"唐手"；后来又受了日本武道的影响，成为现代的"空手道"。1994年日本广岛第十二届亚运会，空手道首次成为正式比赛项目。空手道比赛场地一般为8×8米。比赛项目有套路赛（型）和格斗赛（组手）两种。在格斗比赛中，一方有效进攻导致对手瞬时丧失战斗能力或重心明显移动为得分标准。

black belt in Karate

腰带的颜色代表着跆拳道练习者的水平。从低到高依次为白带（10级）、白黄带（9级）、黄带（8级）、黄绿带（7级）、绿带（6级）、绿蓝带（5级）、蓝带（4级）、蓝红带（3级）、红带（2级）、红黑带（1级或一品、二品、三品）、黑带（一段至九段）。黑带代表练习者经过长期艰苦的磨炼，其技术动作与思想修为均已相当成熟。黑带也象征跆拳道不受黑暗与恐惧的影响。

SATs

SAT（全称Scholastic Assessment Test，俗称美国高考），中文名称为学术能力评估测试。由美国大学委员会（College Board）主办，SAT成绩是世界各国高中生申请美国名校学习机会及奖学金的重要参考值。

写作特点

本文在第二部分"天才的类型"中运用了分类列举的写作方法。该方法是按描述对象的不同类别或不同方面等顺序来写的。因此写作时不一定要交代观察点，也不一定要按时间或空间的顺序来描写。

品味鉴赏

给"天才"下一个令人信服的优美定义，它的意思就是"产生你的快乐"。在这个概念下，"天才"是一个用以描述人们潜能的词。它还包括发现潜能并把它转换成行动的过程。但是，信念是第一步要拥有的。人们首先要确信自己拥有比自己想象的更大的能力；同时，人们还有责任去发挥潜力、运用潜力，才能成为"天才"，取得成功。

美文感悟

The Greatest Salesman in the World
世界上最伟大的推销员

作者简介：

奥格·曼狄诺（Auger Mandinuo，1924—1996），是当今世界上最能激发起读者阅读热情和自学精神的作家。他的18部作品被译成18种语言，销量超过3000万册。 他既是世界上最具激励效应的畅销书作家，还是世界上最受追捧的演讲家之一。这位极具影响力的作家与您分享获得成功和财富的最大秘诀。

Today I begin a new life.

Today I shed my old skin which hath, too long, suffered the **bruises**[1] of failure and the wounds of mediocrity.

Today I am born anew and my birthplace is a vineyard where there is fruit for all.

Today I will pluck grapes of wisdom from the tallest and fullest vines in the vineyard,for these were planted by the wisest of my profession who have come before me, generation upon generation.

Today I will savor the taste of grapes from these vines and verily I will swallow the seed of success buried in each and new life will sprout within me.

The career I have chosen is **laden**[2] with opportunity yet it is **fraught**[3] with heartbreak and

注释
1. bruise [bru:z] n. 瘀伤，擦伤
2. laden ['leɪdn] adj. 装满的，负载的；苦恼的
3. fraught [frɔ:t] adj. 充满……的

despair and the bodies of those who have failed, were they piled one atop another, would cast a shadow down upon all the pyramids of the earth.

Yet I will not fail, as the others, for in my hands I now hold the charts which will guide through **perilous**[4] waters to shores which only yesterday seemed but a dream.

Failure no longer will be my payment for struggle. Just as nature made no provision for my body to tolerate pain neither has it made any provision for my life to suffer failure. Failure, like pain, is alien to my life. In the past I accepted it as I accepted pain. Now I **reject**[5] it and I am prepared for wisdom and principles which will guide me out of the shadows into the sunlight of wealth, position, and happiness far beyond my most **extravagant**[6] dreams until even the golden apples in the Garden of Hesperides will seem no more than my just reward.

Time teaches all things to him who lives forever but I have not the luxury of eternity. Yet within my **allotted**[7] time I must practice the art of patience for nature acts never in haste. To create the olive, king of all trees, a hundred years is required. An onion plant is old in nine weeks. I have lived as an onion plant. It has not pleased me. Now I wouldst become the greatest of olive trees and, in truth, the greatest of salesman.

And how will this be accomplished? For I have neither the knowledge nor the experience to achieve the greatness and already I have stumbled in ignorance and fallen into pools of self-pity. The answer is simple. I will commence my journey unencumbered with either the weight of unnecessary knowledge or the handicap of meaningless experience. Nature already has supplied me with knowledge and instinct far greater than any beast in the forest and the value of experience is overrated, usually by old men who nod wisely and speak stupidly.

In truth, experience teaches thoroughly yet her course of instruction devours men's years so the value of her lessons **diminishes**[8] with the time necessary to acquire her special wisdom. The end finds it wasted on dead men. Furthermore, experience is comparable to fashion; an action that proved successful today will be unworkable and impractical tomorrow.

Only principles endure and these I now possess, for the laws that will lead me to greatness are contained in the words of these scrolls. What they will teach me is more to prevent failure than to gain success, for what is success other than a state of mind? Which two, among a thousand wise men, will define success in the same words; yet failure is always described but one way. Failure is man's inability to reach his goals in life, whatever they may be.

In truth, the only difference between those who have failed and those who have succeeded lies in the difference of their habits. Good habits are the key to all success. Bad habits are the

---

注释

4. **perilous** ['perɪləs] *adj.* 危险的
5. **reject** [rɪ'dʒekt] *vt.* 拒绝，抵制
6. **extravagant** [ɪks'trævəgənt] *adj.* 奢侈的，浪费的；放纵的
7. **allot** [ə'lɒt] *vt.* 分配，分派
8. **diminish** [dɪ'mɪnɪʃ] *v.* 使减少，使变小
9. **impulse** ['ɪmpʌls] *n.* 推动，刺激，冲动

unlocked door to failure. Thus, the first law I will obey, which precedeth all others is —I will form good habits and become their slave.

As a child I was slave to my **impulses**[9]; now I am slave to my habits, as are all grown men. I have surrendered my free will to the years of accumulated habits and the past deeds of my life have already marked out a path which threatens to imprison my future. My actions are ruled by appetite, passion, prejudice, greed, love, fear, environment, habit, and the worst of these tyrants is habit. Therefore, if I must be a slave to habit let me be a slave to good habits. My bad habits must be destroyed and new furrows prepared for good seed. I will form good habits and become their slave.

原文翻译

今天，我开始新的生活。

今天，我爬出满是失败创伤的老茧。

今天，我重新来到这个世上，我出生在葡萄园中，园内的葡萄任人享用。

今天，我要从最高最密的藤上摘下智慧的果实，这葡萄藤是好几代前的智者种下的。

今天，我要品尝葡萄的美味，还要吞下每一粒成功的种子，让新生命在我心里萌芽。

我选择的道路充满机遇，也有辛酸与绝望。失败的同伴数不胜数，叠在一起，比金字塔还高。

然而，我不会像他们一样失败，因为我手中持有航海图，可以领我越过汹涌的大海，抵达梦中的彼岸。

失败不再是我奋斗的代价。它和痛苦都将从我的生命中消失。失败和我，就像水火一样，互不相容。我不再像过去一样接受它们。我要在智慧的指引下，走出失败的阴影，步入富足、健康、快乐的乐园，这些都超出了我以往的梦想。

我要是能长生不老，就可以学到一切，但我不能永生，所以，在有限的人生里，我必须学会忍耐的艺术，因为大自然的行为一向是从容不迫的。造物主创造树中之王橄榄树需要100年的时间，而洋葱经过短短的9个星期就会枯老。我不留恋从前那种洋葱式的生活，我要成为万树之王——橄榄树，成为现实生活中最伟大的推销员。

怎么可能？我既没有渊博的知识，又没有丰富的经验，况且，我曾一度跌入愚昧与自怜的深渊。答案很简单：我不会让所谓的知识或者经验妨碍我的行程。造物主已经赐予我足够的知识和本能，这份天赋是其他生物望尘莫及的。经验的价值往往被高估了，人老的时候开口讲的多是糊涂话。

说实在的，经验确实能教给我们很多东西，只是这需要花费太长的时间。等到人们获得智慧的时候，其价值已随着时间的消逝而减少了。结果往往是这样，经验丰富了，人也余生无多。经验和时尚有关，适合某一时代的行为，并不意味着在今天仍然行得通。

只有原则是持久的，而我现在正拥有了这些原则。这些可以指引我走向成功的原则全写在这几张羊皮卷里。它教我如何避免失败，而不只是获得成功，因为成功更是一种精神状态。人们对于成功的定义，见仁见智，而失败却往往只有一种解释：失败就是一个人没能达到他的人生目标，不论这些目标是什么。

事实上，成功与失败的最大分别，来自不同的习惯。好习惯是开启成功的钥匙，坏习惯则是一扇向失败敞开的门。因此，我首先要做的便是养成良好的习惯，全心全意去践行。

小时候，我常会感情用事，长大成人了，我要用良好的习惯代替一时的冲动。我的自由意志屈服于多年养成的恶习，它们威胁着我的前途。我的行为受到品味、情感、偏见、欲望、爱、恐惧、环境和习惯的影响，其中最厉害的就是习惯。因此，如果我必须受习惯支配的话，那就让我受好习惯的支配。那些坏习惯必须戒除，我要在新的田地里播种好的种子。我要养成良好的习惯，全心全意去践行。

文化点滴

the pyramids

一般的金字塔基座为正三角形或正方形,也可能是其他的正多边形,侧面由多个三角形或梯形的面相接而成,顶部面积非常小,甚至呈尖顶状,像一个金字,而且基本上都是角锥形物体,且通常是四棱锥。古代金字塔大部分是用石块堆积而成,层级越高使用材料越少,这样可以有效抵挡自然灾害。

olive

橄榄树,别名齐墩果,木樨科,属亚热带常绿乔木,耐旱、耐寒,是生长能力很强的长寿树种。全世界橄榄树的栽培品种有500余种。橄榄枝叶茂密,可作为庭荫树、行道树、观果树和油料经济林栽培。树皮粗糙,老时深纵裂,小枝四棱形。叶近革质,对生,窄卵状披针形,表面暗绿色,叶背密生灰白色鳞片,中脉在两面隆起,侧脉不甚明显。圆锥花序,花白色,芳香。核果近球形,黑色、光亮。花期4-5月,果熟期10-12月。

写作特点

《世界上最伟大的推销员》是奥格·曼迪诺的经典励志畅销书。本篇所选的是该书中所提到的"羊皮卷"之第一卷。本文语言风格独特,文字难度适中,但也有一些不太常见的单词和短语出现。这篇文章有很多励志口号,涉及很多方面,所以读懂其中心含义不很容易。在遇到这种情况时,我们可以注意一下文中核心词汇之间的逻辑关系,并通过这些关系来推测和判断作者的中心思想。

品味鉴赏

《世界上最伟大的推销员》记载了一则感人肺腑的传奇故事。一个名叫海菲的牧童,从他的主人那里幸运地得到10道神秘的羊皮卷,遵循卷中的原则,他执着创业,最终成为一名伟大的推销员,并建立起了一座浩大的商业王国……这是一本在全世界范围内影响巨大的书,适合任何阶层的人士自我激励。它振奋人心,激励斗志,改变了许多人的命运……本书一经问世,英文版销量当年突破100万,迅即被译成18种文字,每年销量有增无减。本章精选其中的励志名言,它们都可以作为激励自己的座右铭。

美文感悟

The Strenuous Life
勤奋的生活

作者简介：

西奥多·罗斯福（Theodore Roosevelt, 1858—1919），共和党人，美国总统，毕业于哈佛大学。曾组织志愿骑兵团参加美西战争，1900年任副总统，次年迈金利总统遇刺身亡，继任总统，时年42岁。任期内推出多项改革，以"改革家"面貌治国，对外则实行"大棒"政策。本文是1899年4月10日发表于芝加哥的一次著名演说节录。19世纪末期，美国贪图享乐之风盛行，罗斯福特意对共和党俱乐部成员发表了《勤奋的生活》这一演说，旨在遏制当时的腐败之风。

In speaking to you men of the greatest city of the West, men of the State which gave to the country Lincoln and Grant, men who preeminently and distinctly **embody**[1] all that is most American in the American character, I wish to **preach**[2] not the doctrine of **ignoble**[3] ease but the doctrine of the strenuous life; the life of toil and effort; of labor and strife; to preach that highest form of success which comes not to the man who desires mere easy peace but to the man who does not shrink from danger, from hardship, or from bitter toil, and who out of these wins the splendid ultimate triumph.

注释
1. **embody** [ɪmˈbɒdɪ] vt. 具体表达，使具体化，包含
2. **preach** [priːtʃ] v. 鼓吹
3. **ignoble** [ɪɡˈnəʊbl] adj. 不光彩的

The timid man, the lazy man, the man who disturbs his country, the overcivilized man, who has lost the great fighting, masterful virtues, the ignorant man and the man of dull mind, whose soul is incapable of feeling the mighty lift that thrills "stern men with empires in their brains"—all these, of course, shrink from seeing the nation undertake its new duties; shrink from seeing us build a navy and army adequate to our needs; shrink from seeing us do  our share of the world's work by bringing order out of chaos in the great, fair tropic islands from which the valor of our soldiers and sailors has driven the Spanish flag. These are the men who fear the **strenuous**4 life, who fear the only national life which is really worth leading. They believe in that cloistered life which saps the hardy virtues in a nation, as it saps them in the individual; or else are wedded to that base spirit of gain and greed which recognizes in commercialism the be-all and end-all of national life, instead of realizing that, though an indispensable element, it is after all but one of the many elements that go to make up true national greatness. No country can long endure if its foundations are not laid deep in the material prosperity which comes from hard unsparing effort in the fields of industrial activity; but neither was any nation ever yet truly great if it relied upon material prosperity alone. All honor must be paid to the architects of our material prosperity; to the great captains of industry who have built our factories and our rail roads; to the strong men who toil for wealth with brain or hand; for great is the debt of the nation to these and their kind. But our debt is yet greater to the men whose highest type is to be found in a statesman like Lincoln, a soldier like Grant. They showed by their lives that they recognized the law of work, the law of **strife**5; they **toiled**6 to win a competence for themselves and those dependent upon them; but they recognized that there were yet other and even loftier duties— duties to the nation and duties to the race.

I preach to you, then, my countrymen, that our country calls not for the life of ease, but for the life of strenuous endeavor. The twentieth century looms before us big with the fate of many nations. If we stand idly by, if we seek merely swollen, slothful ease, and ignoble peace, if we **shrink**7 from the hard contests where men must win at hazard of their lives and at the risk of all they hold dear, then the bolder and stronger peoples will pass us by and will win for themselves the domination of the world. Let us therefore boldly face the life of strife, resolute to do our duty well and manfully; resolute to **uphold**8 righteousness by deed and by word; resolute to be both honest and brave, to serve high ideals, yet to use practical methods. Above all, let us shrink from no strife, moral or physical, within or without the nation, provided we are certain that the strife is justified; for it is only through strife, through hard and dangerous endeavor, that we shall ultimately win the goal of true national greatness.

注释	4. **strenuous** ['strenjuəs] *adj.* 奋发的，艰辛的	7. **shrink** [ʃrɪŋk] *v.* 收缩，退缩；回避
	5. **strife** [straɪf] *n.* 斗争，冲突，竞争	8. **uphold** [ʌp'həʊld] *vt.* 支持，赞成
	6. **toil** [tɔɪl] *vi.* 苦干，跋涉	

Chapter 8 成功凯歌

原文翻译

在向你们——西部最大的城市的公民,为国家培育了林肯和格兰特的国家的公民,最能体现美国精神的公民——讲话时,我想谈的不是贪图安逸的人生哲学,而是向你们宣讲勤奋生活论——即过勤奋苦干的生活,过忙碌奋斗的生活。我想说,成功的最高境界不属于满足安逸的人们,而是属于那些在艰难险阻面前从不畏惧终获辉煌的人们。

凡怯懦、懒惰、不相信祖国的人,不像刚毅有抱负的人那样——总之,当看到国家有新的责任要承担,当看到祖国正在建立足以应付需要的陆海军,当看到英勇的士兵和水手在美丽的热带岛屿上驱逐西班牙势力,承担起应尽的世界责任,恢复当地秩序——当看到这一切时,所有这些人都退缩了。就是这样一些人,他们害怕过勤奋的生活,害怕过真正值得过的国民的生活。他们相信与世隔绝的生活,任由这种生活在侵蚀他们个人吃苦耐劳品德的同时,也侵蚀一个民族的吃苦耐劳精神。若不然,他们就沉迷于唯利是图、贪得无厌的卑污泥潭而不能自拔,认为国家应一切以商业利益为根本。但他们却不明白,商业利益固然是不可或缺的因素之一。诚然,如果一个国家不是扎根于其工业活动领域的艰苦努力所带来的繁荣的物质基础之中,那么这个国家也不可能长久地生存下去。但是,如果仅仅依赖于物质财富,任何国家也永远不会成为伟大的国家。我们应该向那些创造了物质财富的人们致敬,向那些创建了工厂和铁路的实业巨头们致敬,向那些用勤劳和智慧换取财富的强者们致敬,国家很感激他们以及像他们一样的人。但是,我们更感激另外一些人,他们的最佳楷模就是林肯那样的政治家和格兰特那样的军人。他们的生活轨迹表明,他们清楚工作和斗争的法则,他们含辛茹苦,使自己和依赖他们生活的人们过上了富足的生活,但他们懂得还有更崇高的责任——对国家和民族的责任。

所以同胞们,我要讲的是,我们的国家要求我们不能好逸恶劳,而只能过刻苦勤奋的生活。迫在眉睫的20世纪将决定许多国家的命运。假如我们只是一味地袖手旁观,贪图享乐,苟且偷安;假如我们面临激烈的竞争考验时,不是冒着牺牲个人生命和失去亲人的危险去赢得胜利,而是落荒而逃的话,那么,更勇敢坚强的民族就会超过我们,得以统领世界。因此,让我们勇敢地面对充满斗争考验的生活,下定决心卓越而果断地履行我们的职责;下定决心无论在语言还是在行动上都坚持正义;下定决心诚实勇敢地以切实可行的方法为崇高的理想服务。最重要的是,无论是精神还是物质的斗争,无论是国内还是国外的斗争,只要我们确定正义在手,我们就决不能逃避退缩。因为只有通过斗争,通过艰苦和充满危险的努力,我们才能最终达到目标——成为真正伟大的国家。

文化点滴

Lincoln

亚伯拉罕·林肯(Abraham Lincoln,1809—1865),美国政治家,第16任总统(1861年3月4日—1865年4月15日),也是首位共和党总统。在其总统任期内,美国爆发了内战,史称南北战争。林肯击败了南方分离势力,废除了奴隶制度,维护了国家的统一。但就在内战结束后不久,林肯不幸遇刺身亡。2006年,亚伯拉罕·林肯被美国的权威期刊《大西洋月刊》评为影响美国的100位人物第1名。最新版5美元纸币正面就是亚伯拉罕·林肯的头像。

Grant

尤里西斯·辛普森·格兰特(Ulysses Simpson Grant,1822—1885),美国军事家、陆军上将和第18任总统。他是美国历史上第一位从西点军校毕业的总统。在美国南北战争后期任联邦军总司令,屡建奇功。

但能征善战并不等于善于理政，格兰特的平平政绩与他的赫赫战功成为明显对照。特别是在第二次总统任期内，他对南方奴隶主妥协让步以及对贪污腐化的属员采取姑息纵容态度，引起了选民的普遍不满。格兰特卸职后曾周游世界，并想在政治上东山再起，但未能如愿。晚年经商失败，抑郁病逝。

写作特点

本文的写作特点是主题、主旨句突出。主旨句是文章的灵魂，而主题句（topic sentence）则是文章主旨最直接的载体。找到了主题句，即大体把握了文章的重要内容，而文章的其余部分则都是对文章主题的解释、展开、论证和进一步深化等。掌握主旨，直奔主题，略过庞杂，自可节约您宝贵的时间。按一般的英文写作习惯，主题句通常会在文章的开头。

品味鉴赏

本文是美国总统西奥多·罗斯福1899年4月10日发表于芝加哥的一次著名演说节录，的一篇演讲稿，其中的内容主要是激励美国人勤奋进取，不要满足于现有成果。作为一篇正式的演讲稿，《勤奋的生活》用词、造句等都很严肃。19世纪末期，美国贪图享乐之风盛行，罗斯福特意对共和党俱乐部成员发表了《勤奋的生活》这一演说，旨在遏制当时的腐败之风。我们的国家要求我们不能好逸恶劳，而只能过刻苦勤奋的生活。

美文感悟

ELDORADO
黄金国

作者简介：

罗伯特·路易斯·史蒂文森（Rabert Louis Stevenson，1850—1894），英国新浪漫主义小说家兼小品文作家，生于爱丁堡，毕业于爱丁堡大学法律系，但他最大的志向是在文学方面。他的第一部散文著作《内陆航行》于1878年出版。他一生为肺病所困扰，周游各地养病，期间发表了大量短篇小说和游记。主要作品有《金银岛》《化身博士》等。他的作品中的很多故事都被改编成电影，受到全世界儿童的广泛喜爱。他作品情节奇妙浪漫，文笔优美雅致。本篇标题为西班牙文，意思是"黄金之国"，指的是人类梦想中的乐土和家园，揭示出只有通过不断的努力，才能挖掘幸福人生的奥妙，只有坚持奋斗才能获得成功。

It seems as if a great deal were attainable in a world where there are so many marriages and decisive battles, and where we all, at certain hours of the day, and with great gusto and despatch, stow a portion of **victuals**[1] finally and irretrievably into the bag which contains us. And it would seem also, on a hasty view, that the attainment of as much as possible was the one goal of man's **contentious**[2] life. And yet, as regards the spirit, this is but a **semblance**[3]. We live in an ascending scale when we live happily, one thing leading to another in an endless series. There is always a new horizon for onward-looking men, and although we dwell on a small planet, immersed in petty business and not enduring beyond a brief period of years, we are so

---

注释
1. **victual** ['vɪtl] *n.* 食物
2. **contentious** [kən'tenʃəs] *adj.* 好争吵的、争论的、有异议的
3. **semblance** ['sembləns] *n.* 外表，伪装

constituted that our hopes are inaccessible, like stars, and the term of hoping is prolonged until the term of life. To be truly happy is a question of how we begin and not of how we end, of what we want and not of what we have. An aspiration is a joy for ever, a possession as solid as a landed estate, a fortune which we can never exhaust and which gives us year by year a revenue of pleasurable activity. To have many of these is to be spiritually rich.

Life is only a very dull and ill-directed theatre unless we have some interests in the piece; and to those who have neither art nor science, the world is a mere arrangement of colours, or a rough footway where they may very well break their shins. It is in virtue of his own desires and curiosities that any man continues to exist with even patience, that he is charmed by the look of things and people, and that he wakens every morning with a renewed appetite for work and pleasure. Desire and curiosity are the two eyes through which he sees the world in the most enchanted colours: it is they that make women beautiful or fossils interesting; and the man may **squander**[4] his estate and come to beggary, but if he keeps these two amulets he is still rich in the possibilities of pleasure. Suppose he could take one meal so compact and comprehensive that he should never hunger any more; suppose him, at a glance, to take in all the features of the world and allay the desire for knowledge; suppose him to do the like in any province of experience—would not that man be in a poor way for amusement ever after?

One who goes touring on foot with a single volume in his knapsack reads with **circumspection**[5], pausing often to reflect, and often laying the book down to **contemplate**[6] the landscape or the prints in the inn parlour; for he fears to come to an end of his entertainment, and be left companionless on the last stages of his journey. A young fellow recently finished the works of Thomas Carlyle, winding up, if we remember aright, with the ten note-books upon Frederick the Great. "What!" cried the young fellow, in **consternation**[7], "is there no more Carlyle? Am I left to the daily papers?" A more celebrated instance is that of Alexander, who wept bitterly because he had no more worlds to subdue. And when Gibbon had finished the *DECLINE AND FALL*, he had only a few moments of joy; and it was with a "sober melancholy" that he parted from his labours.

Happily we all shoot at the moon with ineffectual arrows; our hopes are set on inaccessible El Dorado; we come to an end of nothing here below. Interests are only **plucked**[8] up to sow themselves again, like mustard. You would think, when the child was born, there would be an end to trouble; and yet it is only the beginning of fresh anxieties; and when you have seen it

注释
4. **squander** ['skwɒndə] v. 浪费，挥霍
5. **circumspection** [ˌsɜːkəm'speʃən] n. 细心，慎重
6. **contemplate** ['kɒntempleɪt] v. 凝视；沉思；预期，企图
7. **consternation** [ˌkɒnstə'neɪʃən] n. 惊愕，恐怖，惊慌失措
8. **pluck** [plʌk] vt. 鼓起勇气等

through its teething and its education, and at last its marriage, alas! It is only to have new fears, new **quivering**⁹ sensibilities, with every day; and the health of your children's children grows as touching a concern as that of your own.

Again, when you have married your wife, you would think you were got upon a hill top, and might begin to go downward by an easy slope. But you have only ended courting to begin marriage. Falling in love and winning love are often difficult tasks to overbearing and rebellious spirits; but to keep in love is also a business of some importance, to which both man and wife must bring kindness and goodwill. The true love story commences at the altar, when there lies before the married pair a most beautiful contest of wisdom and generosity, and a life-long struggle towards an unattainable ideal. Unattainable? Ay, surely unattainable, from the very fact that they are two instead of one.

"Of making books there is no end," complained the Preacher; and did not perceive how highly he was praising letters as an occupation. There is no end, indeed, to making books or experiments, or to travel, or to gathering wealth. Problem gives rise to problem. We may study for ever, and we are never as learned as we would. We have never made a statue worthy of our dreams. And when we have discovered a continent, or crossed a chain of mountains, it is only to find another ocean or another plain upon the further side. In the infinite universe there is room for our swiftest diligence and to spare. It is not like the works of Carlyle, which can be read to an end. Even in a corner of it, in a private park, or in the neighbourhood of a single hamlet, the weather and the seasons keep so deftly changing that although we walk there for a lifetime there will be always something new to startle and delight us.

There is only one wish realisable on the earth; only one thing that can be perfectly attained: Death. And from a variety of circumstances we have no one to tell us whether it be worth attaining.

A strange picture we make on our way to our chimaeras, ceaselessly marching, grudging ourselves the time for rest; **indefatigable**¹⁰, adventurous pioneers. It is true that we shall never reach the goal; it is even more than probable that there is no such place; and if we lived for centuries and were **endowed**¹¹ with the powers of a god, we should find ourselves not much nearer what we wanted at the end. O toiling hands of mortals! O unwearied feet, travelling yet know not whither! Soon, soon, it seems to you, you must come forth on some **conspicuous**¹² hilltop, and but a little way further, against the setting sun, descry the spires of El Dorado. Little do you know your own blessedness; for to travel hopefully is a better thing than to arrive, and the true success is to labour.

注释
9. quiver ['kwɪvə] vt. 颤抖，振动，使颤动
10. indefatigable [ˌɪndɪ'fætɪɡəbl] adj. 不知疲倦的
11. endow [ɪn'daʊ] v. 捐赠；赋予
12. conspicuous [kən'spɪljuəs] adj. 显著的

原文翻译

这个世界上，可以得到的东西似乎很多：婚姻和决战数不胜数；每天到了某个时候，我们都津津有味地、急急忙忙地把一份食物无可挽回地装进我们藏身的皮囊。匆匆看来，尽量多得仿佛就是纷争的人生的唯一目标。但是，就精神而言，这不过是一种假象。生活幸福了，我们就像处在上升的阶梯，一级连一级，无穷无尽。向前看的人，眼前总有一番新天地；尽管我们居住在一个小行星上，整天埋头于琐事，寿命只有短短的几十年，但我们生来就怀有星辰一样高不可及的愿望，生命不息，向往不止。真正的幸福是个怎样开始而不是怎样结束的问题，是个想要什么而不是得到什么的问题。渴望是一种永久的快乐，一份像地产一样实在的财产，一笔取之不尽、年年增益、教我们快乐生活的财富。渴望多，精神上就富有。对于那些既不懂艺术又不懂科学的人，世界只是各种颜色的组合，或只是一条不平的小路，很可能让他们扭断小腿。正是靠着自己的愿望和好奇，一个人才坦然而有耐心地生存下来，迷恋人物、事物的外表，每天早上醒来时又想工作和娱乐。愿望和好奇是他观看这个色彩迷人世界的两只眼睛：因为它们，女人才变得美丽，化石才变得有趣。这个人可能挥霍财产沦为乞丐，但如果能保持住这两道护身符，他仍然拥有许多潜在的快乐。假如他一顿饭吃得很紧凑，什么都吃到了，永远不饿；假如他一眼看清世间万象，平息了求知的欲望；假如他在任何领域都做到这样——那么这个人不就从此难得到乐趣了吗？

一个徒步旅行的人，随身只带了一本书，他会精心研读，不时思考一下，还会合上书本凝视风景或者玩赏小酒馆雅间中的画；他害怕书读完了，乐趣也随之消失，剩下的旅程将寂寞而无以慰藉。最近，一个年轻人拜读完托马斯·卡莱尔的著作。如果我没记错的话，他把有关腓特列大帝的笔记整整做了10本。"什么？"这个年轻人惊讶地叫道："卡莱尔的书都看完了？那我只能天天看报纸了？"最典型的例子是亚历山大，因为已无国家供他征服，他号啕大哭。吉本写完《罗马帝国衰亡史》时也只兴奋了一时；他带着一种"清醒而又悲凉的心情"与以往的劳动成果辞别。

我们快快乐乐地把无用的箭射向月亮；我们的愿望寄托在不可企及的黄金国；我们在世上什么也没有做完。兴趣收起来只是为了再撒下去，像芥菜一样。孩子生了，你会以为麻烦结束了；然而这只是新的麻烦的开始；你看着他长了牙，上了学，最后结了婚，唉！也不过是每天都有新的忧虑，新的感情的震颤；你的孩子的孩子的健康逐渐像你自己的健康一样让你担心。

再有，你和妻子结了婚，认为就到了山顶，可以开始轻轻松松地下坡了。但是求爱的结束仅仅是婚姻的开始。对于傲慢不逊的人，恋爱和赢得爱情通常是困难的事；但维持爱情也是一件相当重要的事，丈夫和妻子都必须现出善良的友好。真正的爱情故事从圣坛开始，摆在夫妻二人面前的是一场智慧和慷慨的极其美丽的较量，他人要为一个不可实现的理想奋斗终生。不可实现？啊，当然是不可实现，因为他们不是一个人而是两个人。

传道者哀叹"著书无止境"，却没有观察到它已经高度评价了作家这一职业。确实，世界上有很多是无止境的，例如著书立说、旅行、试验、获取财富等。一个问题会引发另一个问题。我们必须活到老学到老，我们学习永远得不到满足。我们从未雕刻出符合我们梦想的塑像。我们发现一个新大陆，翻过一座山脉时，总会看到远方还有未曾涉足的海洋和大陆。宇宙浩渺，不像卡莱尔的著作可以读完。即使在其一角，一个私人花园，一个农庄附近，尽管在那里生活一辈子，天气和季节的无常变化也令我们有常看常新的感觉。世界上只有一种愿望可以实现，也仅有一种事物绝对能得到，那就是死亡。死的方式很多，但没有人知道是否能死得其所。

当我们不作休息，不停地走向幻想时，一副奇异的画面展现出来：不知疲倦、勇于冒险的先锋。是的，我们永远不会达到目标，甚至目的地根本就不存在。即使活上几百年，具有神的力量，我们也会觉得没有接近目标多少。啊，辛苦的双手！啊，不知疲倦的双脚，并不知道走向何方！你总觉得，一定能登上某个光辉的山顶；在夕阳下，看到不远的前方黄金国那尖尖的塔。你是处于幸福当中却没有察觉；奋斗胜过得到；真正的成功就是奋斗。

文化点滴

Alexander

亚历山大大帝（Alexander the Great，公元前356—前323年），古代马其顿国王，亚历山大帝国皇帝，世界古代史上著名的军事家和政治家。他足智多谋，在担任马其顿国王的短短13年中，以其雄才大略，东征西讨，先是确立了在全希腊的统治地位，后又灭亡了波斯帝国；在横跨欧、亚的辽阔土地上，建立起了一个西起希腊、马其顿，东到印度河流域，南临尼罗河第一瀑布，北至药杀水的以巴比伦为首都的庞大帝国；创下了前无古人的辉煌业绩，促进了东西方文化的交流和经济的发展，对人类社会的进展产生了重大的影响。

DECLINE AND FALL

《罗马帝国衰亡史》(*The History of The Decline and Fall of the Roman Empire*) 是英国历史学家爱德华·吉本（Edward Gibbon, 1737—1794）的一部巨著，被认为是第一部"现代"历史著作，共有6卷，分期出版。第一卷出版于1776年，第二、三卷出版于1781年，第四、五、六卷出版于1788年。该著作包括罗马帝国的全部历史。英国18世纪史家爱德华·吉本，于游历罗马城废墟时发思古幽情，遂穷毕生之力，勾勒罗马帝国衰亡的历史。其著作上起罗马帝国早期两安东尼朝的黄金时期，直到东罗马帝国毁于异族之手，凡此1000多年的风云变幻，无不尽收笔下，精彩生动，充满洞见，堪称如椽巨笔。

写作特点

本篇是罗伯特·路易斯·史蒂文森的一篇散文。这篇作品情节奇妙浪漫，文笔优美雅致。本篇标题为西班牙文，意思是"黄金之国"，指的是人类梦想中的乐土和家园。这篇文章具有其他散文的共同特点，即"形散而神不散"。本篇的中心主题就是只有通过不断的努力，才能挖掘幸福人生的奥妙，只有坚持奋斗才能获得成功。

品味鉴赏

《黄金国》是史蒂文森为数不多的几篇散文之一。文章赞赏奋斗，提倡辛勤工作，指出只要你努力工作，奋斗不止，你就能到达梦想中的黄金之国。文章的结构非常严谨，语篇特点突出，用词较难，阅读难度较大。

美文感悟

A Ball to Go Around
滚球

作者简介：

罗伯特·G.奥尔曼（Robert G.Allman）是位盲人，他在运动、法律及体育广播电台三个不同的领域都获得了极大的成功。他幼时就读于美国费城奥弗布鲁克盲人学校，并在该校学会了摔跤，在宾夕法尼亚大学学习期间，曾在50多场摔跤比赛中获胜。由于热爱运动，他一度任电台体育节目广播员。他认为盲人不应该只从盲人身上寻求安慰，而应该"走出家门与世人接触"。

I lost my eyesight when I was four years old by falling off a box car in a freight yard in Atlantic City and landing on my head. Now I am thirty-two. I can **vaguely**[1] remember the brightness of sunshine and what color red is. It would be wonderful to see again, but a **calamity**[2] can do strange things to people. It occurred to me the other day that I might not have come to love life as I do if I hadn't been blind. I believe I love life now. I am not so sure that I would have believed in it so deeply, otherwise. I don't mean that I would prefer to go without my eyes. I simply mean that the loss of them made me appreciate the more what I had left.

Life, I believe, asks a continuous series of adjustments to reality. The more readily a person is able to make these adjustments, the more meaningful his own private world becomes. The

---

注释 1. **vaguely** [ˈveɪgli] *adv.* 含糊地；暧昧地；茫然地   2. **calamity** [kəˈlæmɪti] *n.* 灾难；不幸事件

adjustment is never easy. I was **bewildered**³ and afraid. But I was lucky. My parents and my teachers saw something in me—a potential to live, you might call it—which I didn't see, and they made me want to fight it out with blindness.

The hardest lesson I had to learn was to believe in myself. That was basic. If I hadn't been able to do that, I would have **collapsed**⁴ and become a chair rocker on the front porch for the rest of my life. When I say belief in myself I am not talking about simply the kind of self-confidence that helps me down an unfamiliar staircase alone. That is part of it. But I mean something bigger than that: an assurance that I am, despite imperfections, a real, positive person; that somewhere in the sweeping, **intricate**⁵ pattern of people there is a special place where I can make myself fit.

It took me years to discover and strengthen this assurance. I had to start with the most elementary things. Once a man gave me an indoor baseball. I thought he was mocking me and I was hurt. "I can't use this." I said. "Take it with you," he urged me, "and roll it around." The words stuck in my head. "Roll it around!" By rolling the ball I could hear where it went. This gave me an idea how to achieve a goal I had thought impossible: playing baseball. At Philadelphia's Overbrook School for the Blind I invented a successful variation of baseball. We called it ground ball.

All my life I have set ahead of me a series of goals and then tried to reach them, one at a time. I had to learn my limitations. It was no good to try for something I knew at the start was wildly out of reach because that only invited the bitterness of failure. I would fail sometimes anyway but on the average I made progress.

原文翻译

4岁那年，我在大西洋城，从货场的一辆棚车上摔下来，头先着地，于是双目失明。现在我已经32岁了，我能模糊地记起灿烂的阳光和鲜艳的红色。能恢复视力固然好，但一场灾难也可以对人产生奇妙的作用。有一天，我突然想到，倘若我不是盲人，我可能不会像现在这样热爱生活。现在，我相信生活，但我不能肯定，如果我是明眼人，会不会像现在这样深深地相信生活。我并不是说我宁愿失去视力，我的意思是由于视力的丧失使我更加珍惜自己其他方面的能力。

我认为，生活要求人们不断地自我调整以适应现实。人越能及时地调整自己，他的个人世界便越有意义。调整是件很困难的事。我一度感到茫然、恐惧，但我是很幸运的。我的父母和老师在我身上发现了某种东西——可以称之为"活下去的潜力"——虽然我自己并没有发现。他们激励我与失明拼搏到底。

我不得不学会的最艰难的一课就是相信我自己，这一点是最基本的。如果做不到这一点，我可能会精神崩溃，只能坐在前门廊的摇椅中度过人生。我相信自己并不仅仅指支持我独自走下陌生楼梯的那种自信。那只是自信的一部分。我指的范围更大：那就是坚信自己虽然有缺陷，却是一个真正有进取心的人；坚信在芸芸众生错综复杂的格局当中，一定有一个特殊的位置供我立足。

我花了很多年才树立起并不断加强这一信念，这必须从最简单的事情做起。有一次，一个人送给我一个

注释
3. **bewildered** [bɪˈwɪldəd] *adj.* 困惑的
4. **collapse** [kəˈlæps] *vi.* 倒塌；瓦解；暴跌
5. **intricate** [ˈɪntrɪkət] *adj.* 复杂的；错综的，缠结的

室内玩的棒球，我想他在嘲笑我，感觉受到了伤害。"我不能玩这个东西。"我说，"你拿着。"他竭力劝我说："你可以在地上滚。"他的话深深地印在我的脑海里。"在地上滚！"滚动的球可以使我听见它朝哪个方向滚动。我马上联想到一个我曾认为不可能做到的事情：打棒球。在费城的奥弗布鲁克盲人学校，我成功发明了一种很受欢迎的棒球游戏，我们称它为地面球。

我给自己的一生树立了一系列目标，然后一次一个、竭尽全力地去实现它们。我必须知道自己的局限。如果一开始就知道某个目标根本不可能实现却硬要去做，那不会带来任何益处，因为它只会带来失败的苦果。我有时也会失败，但一般来说我总会取得进步。

文化点滴

box car
棚车是有侧墙、端墙、地板和车顶，在侧墙上开有滑门和通风窗的铁路货车，用以装运贵重和怕日晒雨淋的货物。有的在车内安装火炉、烟囱、床板等，必要时可以运送人员和牲畜。

baseball
棒球运动是一种以棒打球为主要特点，集体性、对抗性很强的球类运动项目。它在国际上开展得较为广泛，影响较大，被誉为"竞技与智慧的结合"。棒球在美国、日本尤为盛行，被称为"国球"。棒球比赛法定比赛人数最少为9人，与其近似的运动项目为垒球。棒球球员分为攻、守两方，利用球棒和手套，在一个扇形的棒球场里进行比赛。比赛中，两队交替进攻：当进攻球员成功跑回本垒，就可得1分。9局中得分最高的一队就胜出。

写作特点

本文在写作中既有记叙又有议论，我们称之为夹叙夹议。它的特点是叙事和议论穿插进行，写法上灵活多变，作者可以自由自在地表情达意。本篇文章叙事连贯，议论自然。"叙"是"议"的基础，"议"是"叙"的深化。叙述是为议论服务的，它和议论有机地结合在一起，表达作者的思想和观点；议是叙述点睛之笔，议论恰到好处，使文章的主题得到升华，使读者更能理解和品味出文章的主旨来。

品味鉴赏

人类是社会性群体高级动物，需要不断地自我调整以适应现实。一个人越能及时地调整自己，他的个人世界便越有意义。然而，调整却是件不容易的事。如果一个人从一开始就知道某个目标根本不可能实现却硬要去做，那不会带来任何益处，除非善于调整自己的心态、做法等，否则必然品尝失败带来的苦果。

美文感悟

Contemplation on Success
如何心想事成之苦思冥想篇

In many of our life's **endeavors**[1] we say, "Oh well, I tried", and take our failure as "a lesson to be learned". Too often, we conclude that the lesson is, "I better not try that again". Perhaps the real lesson is that we didn't really try. Maybe we only made a **halfhearted**[2] attempt and life gave us back exactly what we gave to it.

Think of some examples in your past where the results were not what you wanted, or said you wanted. Did you give it all you had? Now think of some times when you did give it all you had. Just for fun. How about when you were a teenager and wanted the family car for a special date, or when you were working to a deadline and knew you had to have the job done. In such cases don't we keep pushing until we get what we want?

When we give our full effort, we stop "trying", and we start doing it. Our words change, reflecting our thoughts. We don't stop at the first **obstacle**[3]; we don't accept the first "no"; we make the time that's necessary; we apply all the resources we have, and we start being truly creative. We are being truly alive. The life energy begins zooming through us. This is what we call the "rush of commitment". Success is then assured. Miracles happen!

Commitment means no matter what. When we commit to a relationship, we stop wondering if

注释　　1. **endeavor** [ɪd'devə] n. 努力　　　　　　2. **halfhearted** [hɑːfhɑːtɪd] a. 不认真的，不热心的

someone else out there might make an even better partner for us. If we commit to a career, we give it our best, and waste no time trying with other possibilities. The feeling of commitment doesn't come naturally. We have to develop it, and earn it.

The moment one commits oneself, then Providence moves too. All sorts of things occur to help one that would never have otherwise occurred. A whole stream of events; all manner of **unforeseen**[4] incidents, and chance meetings, and material assistance come forth which no one could have dreamt would appear.

I have learned a deep respect for one of Goethe's **couplets**[5]:

"Whatever you can do, or dream you can, begin it.

Boldness has genius and power and magic in it."

Commitment does not, however, require that we stand firm and **inflexible**[6] even when our heart tells us that a situation isn't working over time. To keep commitment from becoming blind stubbornness, apply the following two principles to your life:

1) If a situation doesn't work, first do everything to make it work; this may mean exploring new options and choices rather than **passively**[7] tolerating the situation or merely escaping.

2) If, after giving it your BEST effort for a reasonable time (ranging from an hour to a decade or more, depending upon the context) the situation still doesn't work, then leave it with full confidence that you've done the right thing.

And for those of you who enjoy poetry:

I would love to kiss you

—the price of kissing is your life

Now my loving is running toward my life shouting

—what a bargain, let's buy it!

(Rumi)

What this means is that your life will and must change when you want to "kiss", or embrace a new endeavor. Are you willing to give it your best?

原文翻译

我们在一生的许多次努力中对自己说："噢，就这样吧，我已经尝试过了"，然后把失败看成"必修一课"。太多次了，我们把教训总结为"我最好别再去试"。或许真正的教训是，我们并没有真正去尝试；或许我们的尝试太过三心二意，生活回赠我们的正恰如其分。

注释

3. **obstacle** ['ɒbstəkl] *n.* 障碍
4. **unforeseen** [ˌʌnfɔː'siːn] *adj.* 不可预见的
5. **couplet** ['kʌplɪt] *n.* 相连；长度相同并押韵的两行诗
6. **inflexible** [ɪn'fleksɪbl] *adj.* 不屈不挠的，顽固的
7. **passively** ['pæsɪvlɪ] *adv.* 被动地，顺从地

回想一下过去一些不如意的事。你全力付出了吗？现在再来想你曾全力付出过的例子。就当作好玩吧。年少时想要家里最好的车去赴一个特别的约会？赶截止日期而你不得不完成的工作？在这些例子中，我们难道不是一直奋斗直到如愿以偿吗？

当我们全身心投入的时候，我们已经脱离"尝试"了，我们开始行动。我们说的话有所改变，这也反映着我们思想的变化；我们不会一遇障碍则停止不前；我们不甘心接受第一个"不"字；我们挤出需要的时间；我们运用出一切可用的资源，我们开始发挥真正的创造能力；我们真正变成生龙活虎。生命力开始穿透我们。这就是所称的"承诺张力"。这样的成功就有了保证，奇迹才能出现！

承诺的含义是无论何种情形。当我们承诺一段关系，就不再考虑是否还有其他人作为我们的伴侣更好；当承诺一份事业，我们就全力投入，决不浪费任何时间去试探别的可能。承诺的感觉不会是与生俱来的。我们得让它成长、成熟。

从你开始承诺的一刻起，深谋远虑的目光也随之而来。一切事情应运而生，推动着原本不可能的事情的发生。一整串的大事，所有预见不到的意外事情，机遇汇集，物质援助——这些都从梦想变成了现实。

歌德有两句话被我奉为箴言：

"无论你能做什么，或者梦想你能做什么，开始行动吧。

大胆行事中也不乏天才、力量和魔力。"

但是，承诺并不要求我们磐石不移地僵持，哪怕心知肚明情况不会假以时间而好转。为了避免让承诺变成盲目顽固，你在生活中要遵照以下两点：

第一，如果情况没有起色，首先要努力改善；这或多或少意味着尝试新方法、做出新选择，而不只是一味消极地忍受糟糕的情况或者逃之夭夭。

第二，如果经过一段合理时间（根据情形，可能是1小时到10年，长短不等），你全力以赴地努力过了，情况还是没有起色，那么就把它放到一边去，并深信自己这么做是正确的决定。喜欢诗歌的人请看这个：

我想要吻你

——用你的一生来奖励这个吻

我的爱人跑进我的人生，大喊着

——多划算啊，就这么样吧！

　　　　　（鲁米）

这当中意思是说，当你想要"吻"，或者想做一番新的努力时，你的人生即将并且一定会有所改变。而你愿意全力以赴地去为之奋斗吗？

文化点滴

Goethe

约翰·沃尔夫冈·冯·歌德，出生于德国法兰克福。作为诗人、自然科学家、文艺理论家和政治人物，歌德是魏玛的古典主义最著名的代表；而作为诗歌、戏剧和散文作品的创作者，他是最伟大的德国作家之一，也是世界文学领域一个出类拔萃的光辉人物。

Rumi

鲁米出生于1207年9月30日。他自幼受父亲的教育和熏陶，在伊斯兰教神学、哲学和文学等方面打下坚实的功底。父亲去世后，鲁米在1231年继承父业，成为一名伊斯兰教的学者。　将他引入神秘主义之门的人是一个名叫大不里士的沙姆士（Shamsi of Tabriz）的苦修僧人。与沙姆士在1244年的相遇，使鲁米发生了巨大的转变。　用鲁米自己的话来说："我从人类身上看到了从前认为只有在真主身上才有的东西。"他开始成为一位神秘主义诗人。鲁米把他的抒情诗集命名为《沙姆士·大不里士诗歌集》。这部诗集收录了3230首抒情诗，共计35000诗行。诗中运用隐喻、暗示和象征等艺术手法，通过对"心上人"、"朋友"的思念、爱恋和追求，表达修道者对真主的虔诚和信仰，阐发了"人神合一"的苏菲之道。 8年之后，沙姆士去世。为了纪念这位挚友，鲁米创立了苏菲派莫拉维教派，即西方所熟知的"旋转的苦修僧"（Whirling Dervishes）。鲁米通过诗歌、音乐和旋转舞将苏菲们引向对真主的爱、最终进入与真主合一的境界。 鲁米在生命的最后13年中，创作了诗歌巨作——叙事诗集《玛斯那维》（Mathnawi），共6卷，51000千余行。这是应他最喜欢的学生胡珊·切利毕（Husam al-Din Chalabi）的要求而写的。在这部鸿篇巨制中，鲁米将苏菲教义以诗歌的形式传达出来，更易于苏菲们的理解和记忆。整部诗集都是由鲁米口述、胡珊听写而成。《玛斯那维》被誉为"波斯语的《古兰经》"。诗集取材广泛，内容异常丰富，以寓言、传奇和故事的形式传了神秘的苏菲教派的哲学和宗教思想，被誉为"知识的海洋"。 此外，鲁米还有《讲道集》和《书信集》等著述传世。 鲁米在波斯文学史上享有极高的声誉，他与菲尔多西、萨迪、哈菲兹齐名，有"诗坛四柱"之称。集诗人和神秘主义者于一身的鲁米，受到过诸如黑格尔、柯勒律支、歌德、伦勃朗、教皇约翰二十二世等人的赞誉。

写作特点

本文最大的特点就是运用了引用的写作手法。引用了鲁米的诗词，突出表现了作者的思想。这也是引用这种写作手法经常可以起到的作用。借用名人的话，帮助自己表达出观点、看法，能够起到说服读者的作用，而本文无疑又是一个成功的典范。

品味鉴赏

本作者奉为箴言的歌德的两句话：

"无论你能做什么，或者梦想你能做什么，开始行动吧。

大胆行事中也不乏天才、力量和魔力。"

正如作者所说：如果情况没有起色，首先要努力改善；如果经过一段合理时间，你全力以赴地努力过了，情况还是没有起色，那么就把它放到一边去，并深信自己这么做是正确的决定。

决心、坚定的意志和毅力诚然可贵；然而，在我们决不轻言放弃的同时，也要客观辩证地看待事物的发展变化，而不要呆板地消极地忍受糟糕的情况。

美文感悟

Self-surpassing
自我超越

作者简介:

弗里德里希·威廉·尼采（Friedrich Wilhelm Nietzsche，1844—1900），19世纪德国哲学家。尼采的主要影响力在于哲学及其相关领域，其中特别值得一提的是存在主义和后现代主义。尼采被称为"虚无主义之父"，他的哲学文章和诗作对同时代的人颇有影响。他的作品很复杂，所以他的理论常常被惨遭误解。

"Will to Truth" do **ye**[1] call it, ye wisest ones, that which impelleth you and maketh you ardent? Will for the thinkableness of all being: thus do I call your will!

All being would ye MAKE thinkable: for ye doubt with good reason whether it be already thinkable.

But it shall accommodate and bend itself to you! So willeth your will.

Smooth shall it become and subject to the spirit, as its mirror and reflection.

That is your entire will, ye wisest ones, as a Will to Power; and even when ye speak of good and evil, and of estimates of value.

Ye would still create a world before which ye can bow the knee: such is your ultimate hope and **ecstasy**[2].

注释　1. **ye** [ji:] *pron.* 【古语】你，你们　　2. **ecstasy** ['ekstəsɪ] *n.* 入迷

The ignorant, to be sure, the people—they are like a river on which a boat floateth along: and in the boat sit the estimates of value, **solemn**[3] and **disguised**[4].

Your will and your valuations have ye put on the river of becoming; it betrayeth unto me an old Will to Power, what is believed by the people as good and evil.

It was ye, ye wisest ones, who put such guests in this boat, and gave them **pomp**[5] and proud names—ye and your ruling Will!

Onward the river now carrieth your boat: it MUST carry it. A small matter if the rough wave foameth and angrily resisteth its keel!

It is not the river that is your danger and the end of your good and evil, ye wisest ones: but that Will itself, the Will to Power— the unexhausted, procreating life-will.

But that ye may understand my gospel of good and evil, for that purpose will I tell you my gospel of life, and of the nature of all living things.

The living thing did I follow; I walked in the broadest and narrowest paths to learn its nature.

With a hundred-faced mirror did I catch its glance when its mouth was shut, so that its eye might speak unto me. And its eye spake unto me.

But wherever I found living things, there heard I also the language of obedience. All living things are obeying things.

And this I heard secondly: Whatever cannot obey itself, is commanded. Such is the nature of living things.

This, however, is the third thing which I heard—namely, that commanding is more difficult than obeying. And not only because the commander beareth the burden of all obeyers, and because this burden readily crusheth him:—

An attempt and a risk seemed all commanding unto me; and whenever it commandeth, the living thing risketh itself thereby.

Yea, even when it commandeth itself, then also must it atone for its commanding. Of its own law must it become the judge and avenger and victim.

How **doth**[6] this happen! so did I ask myself. What persuadeth the living thing to obey, and command, and even be obedient in commanding?

Hearken[7] now unto my word, ye wisest ones! Test it seriously, whether I have crept into the heart of life itself, and into the roots of its heart!

Wherever I found a living thing, there found I Will to Power; and even in the will of the servant found I the will to be master.

That to the stronger the weaker shall serve—thereto persuadeth he his will who would be master over a still weaker one. That delight alone he is unwilling to forego.

And as the lesser surrendereth himself to the greater that he may have delight and power over the least of all, so doth even the greatest surrender himself, and staketh—life, for the sake of power.

It is the surrender of the greatest to run risk and danger, and play dice for death.

---

3. **solemn** ['sɒləm] adj. 庄严的，隆重的，严肃的
4. **disguised** [dɪs'gaɪzd] adj. 假装的，伪装的
5. **pomp** [pɒmp] n. 夸耀
6. **doth** [dʌθ] v. （古）do的第三人称单数，现在式
7. **hearken** ['hɑːkən] vi. 倾听

And where there is sacrifice and service and love-glances, there also is the will to be master.

By byways doth the weaker then slink into the fortress, and into the heart of the mightier one—and there stealeth power.

And this secret spake Life herself unto me. "Behold," said she, "I am that WHICH MUST EVER SURPASS ITSELF.

To be sure, ye call it will to procreation, or impulse towards a goal, towards the higher, remoter, more **manifold**[8]: but all that is one and the same secret.

Rather would I **succumb**[9] than **disown**[10] this one thing; and **verily**[11], where there is succumbing and leaf-falling, lo, there doth Life sacrifice itself—for power!

That I have to struggle, and becoming, purpose, and cross-purpose—ah, he who divineth my will, divineth well also on what CROOKED paths it hath to tread!

Whatever I create, and however much I love it,—soon must I be adverse to it, and to my love: so willeth my will.

And even thou, discerning one, art only a path and footstep of my will: verily, my Will to Power walketh even on the feet of thy Will to Truth!

He certainly did not hit the truth who shot at it the formula: 'Will to existence': that will—doth not exist!

For what is not, cannot will; that, however, which is in existence—how could it still strive for existence!

Only where there is life, is there also will: not, however, Will to Life, but—so teach I thee—Will to Power!

Much is reckoned higher than life itself by the living one; but out of the very reckoning speaketh—the Will to Power!" —

Thus did Life once teach me: and thereby, ye wisest ones, do I solve you the riddle of your hearts.

Verily, I say unto you: good and evil which would be everlasting —it doth not exist! Of its own accord must it ever surpass itself anew.

With your values and formulae of good and evil, ye exercise power, ye valuing ones: and that is your secret love, and the sparkling, trembling, and overflowing of your souls.

But a stronger power groweth out of your values, and a new surpassing: by it breaketh egg and egg-shell.

And he who hath to be a creator in good and evil—verily, he hath first to be a destroyer, and break values into pieces.

Thus doth the greatest evil pertain to the greatest good: that, however, is the creating good. —Let us SPEAK **thereof**[12], ye wisest ones, even though it be bad.

To be silent is worse; all suppressed truths become poisonous.

And let everything break up which—can break up by our truths! Many a house is still to be built!

Thus Spake Zarathustra.

注释

8. **manifold** [ˈmænɪfəʊld] *adj.* 多种形式的，多方面的
9. **succumb** [səˈkʌm] *vi.* 屈服，屈从，死
10. **disown** [dɪsˈəʊn] *vt.* 否认
11. **verily** [ˈverɪlɪ] *adv.* 真正地，肯定地
12. **thereof** [ðeərˈɒv] *adv.* 有关这，从此

原文翻译

大智者，你们称推动你们、燃烧你们的是"求真之意志"吗？

我却称你们那意志为理解一切之意志！

你们想使存在的一切成为可理解的：因为你们很有理由地怀疑着：这一切早就可以理解了。

但是，存在的一切都得屈服于你们！你们的意志要如是。

它应当恭敬而服从着精神，如精神之镜子与形象。

大智者啊，这是你们整个的意志，你们的权力意志；便是你们谈说善恶和判断价值的时候也是如此。

你们想创造一个你们可以对着下跪的世界：这是你们最后的希望与最后的陶醉。

不错，愚昧者，民众——像一条推送着小船的河：在这小船里，价值之判断戴着面具庄严地坐着。

你们曾把你们的意志与价值放在演变之河里浮着；在民众认为是善与恶的东西里，我看出一个老的权力意志。

啊，大智者，你们把这样的客人放在小船上，而用奢侈的装饰品与骄傲的名称打扮了他们——你们和你们的统治的意志！

现在这条河推送着你们的小船前进：这河必须载着它。被冲破的波浪尽管白沫四溅地怒抗着船底，那有什么重要呢！

大智者，你们的危险和你们的善恶之终结不是这条河，而是你们的意志，权力意志——不竭的创造性的生命意志。

但是，为使你们了解的我善恶之说教，我先把我的关于生命之说教与生物本性之说教告诉你们。

我曾因为考察生物之本性，而在大大小小的路上跟随它们，追逐它们。

我在百面的镜里，捉住了生命之目光，使它不开口的时候，眼睛可以向我说话。而它的眼睛确曾说话。

无论我在哪里发现了生物，我便听到关于服从的话，一切生物必得服从。

而这是第二件事：不解服从自己的人，便受别人的命令。这是生物的本性。

而我听到的第三件事是：去命令难于去服从。不仅因为命令者捆着一切服从者之重负，而且因为这重负会轻易压扁他：——

而且我看出一切命令是尝试与冒险；当生物发出命令的时候，他便冒着生命之危险。

是的，即当他命令自己的时候，他也得赋予这命令以代价。他必得成为自己的法律之法官、报复者与牺牲品。

这是为何缘故呢？我曾自问。使生物服从、发令，甚至在命令的同时也服从的是什么呢？

大智者啊，倾听我的话罢！严格地考察：我是否已经进到生命的核心里，直达了它的深处！

无论何地我找到生物，我便找到权力意志；即便在服从者之意志里，我也找到了做主人的意志。

弱者之意志说服了弱者，使他为强者执役；同时这意志也想成为更弱者的主人。这是他不愿被剥夺的唯一快乐。

弱者屈服于强者，以取得统治更弱者的快乐：同样地，强者屈服于他的权力意志，而为权力冒着生命的危险。

冒险与生命之孤注实则是强者之屈服。

牺牲、服务与爱之眼波存在的地方，便也是想做主人的意志之所在。

弱者取暗道潜入强者之堡寨和心里——也可盗去权力。

生命自己曾向我说出这秘密。"看罢，"它说，"我是必得常常超越自己的。"

不错，你们称这个为创造的意志，或是达到目的的、往较高较远较复杂去的冲动；但都一样的，同一个秘密。

我宁死去，也不愿放弃这唯一之物；真的，只要有没落和树叶飞坠的地方，便有为权力而牺牲的生命！

我必得成为争斗、演变、目的和目的之反面：唉，谁猜出了我的意志，必也猜出了它遵循着的弯曲的途径！

无论我创造的是什么，而我又如何地喜爱它，——我不久便成为它的对手与我的爱之对手：我的意志要我如是。

便是你这求知者，只是我的意志之小路与足迹：真的，我的权力意志也跟在你的求真之意志的后面！

谁谈说着"求存之意志"，便是不曾找到真理：那意志——是没有的！

因为不存在的不能有意志。但是，已存在的何能还追求着存在呢！

只是生命所在的地方，即有意志：但是这意志不是求生之意志，——我郑重地告诉你——而是权力意志！

许多东西是被生物视为高于生命的，这种定位就是权力意志的作用！

这是生命曾经给我的教训：啊，大智者，我用这教训解透了你们心里的谜。

真的，我告诉你们：不灭的长存的善与恶——那是不存在的！依着它们的本性，善与恶必得常常超越自己。

你们这些评价者，用你们的价值标准与善恶程式施行你们的权力：那正是你们的秘密的爱与你们灵魂之光明、战栗与泛滥。

但是从你们的价值体系里，长出一个更强的权力，于是有一个新的超越：它破壳而出。

真的，谁不得不创造善恶，便不得不先破坏，先打碎价值。

所以，最大的恶也是最大的善的一部分：但是这是创造性的善。——让我们谈论这个罢，大智者啊，虽然不太合适。

沉默是更不好的，受压制的真理将变成毒药。

真理可以打碎的东西就让它破碎罢！——须建的房屋多着呢！

——《查拉图斯特拉如是说》。

文化点滴

Thus Spake Zarathustra

《查拉图斯特拉如是说》是德国著名哲学家、诗人尼采最成熟的作品。尼采假托古波斯琐罗亚德教创始人查拉斯图拉修行多年后下降人世传经布道的传奇故事，阐述了作者激越高迈的哲学思想，用如诗如歌的语言，道出了作者对人生、痛苦、欢乐、期许的深邃体悟。正是在本书中，尼采提出了诸如"上帝死了""超人"等对后世思想界和社会影响深远的思想。

写作特点

　　本文运用了大量的比喻手法。比喻就是打比方，即抓住两种不同性质的事物的相似点，用一事物喻另一事物。比喻一般由三部分组成，即本体（被比喻的事物）、喻体（作比方的事物）和比喻词（比喻关系的标志）。构成比喻的关键：甲和乙必须是本质不同的事物，甲乙之间必须有相似点，否则不能成立。本文中的比喻生动形象地写出了大智者和愚昧的民众之间的关系，化深奥为浅显，十分具有说服力。

品味鉴赏

　　尼采一直强调人类的自我超越。在他看来："人存在的意义便是超人，即自乌云（人类）中迸射出来的雷电！"人类存在的终极意义便是超越自己，成为超人。尼采的《查拉图斯特拉如是说》采用不多见的散文诗体，在世界哲学史和诗歌史上均占有独特的不朽地位。但是，由于内容复杂，尼采的学说常常受到误解和歪曲。德国纳粹分子曾把他的学说肆意曲解为法西斯的理论支柱。所以，只有深入理解了尼采的精神实质，才能真正理解他的怪论。

　　尼采是一位伟大的唯心主义哲学家，本文谈论的善与恶是哲学中永恒的辩证话题。如果说善就是善，恶就是恶；爱就是爱，恨就是恨。这是没有错的，而恶就是善，恨就是爱；恨是爱不足，恶是善不足，这种观点就需要我们辩证地看待。其实哲学中这样的辩证话题还有很多，我们看待事物一定不能只看其一，不看其二，要统筹考虑，用最周全的办法去解决现实生活中的难题。

美文感悟

Five Forms of Wealth
财富的五个表现形式

作者简介：

罗宾·夏玛（Robin Sharma），全美领导学与自我超越领域的首席权威，也是北美洲最令人振奋与刺激思想的知名演说家，他拥有3部全美畅销书，包括《出售法拉利的和尚》（*The Monk Who Sold His Ferrari*）及续集《出售法拉利的和尚中的领导智慧》（*Leadership Wisdom—The Monk Who Sold His Ferrari*），还有潜能激发的经典之作《大生活》（*Mega Living*）。

Hi, it's Robin Sharma, welcome to this podcast called "The Five Forms of Wealth". You know so many of us fall into this **trap**[1] of judging our wealth in economic terms, in other word, in terms of how much money we have in our bank account, and we look at people or maybe hear about people in our community, or people we watch on TV, we will say that they're worth this amount in terms of their work and we are not in this level and then we actually make ourselves feel like that we are not successful. Oh, here is the big idea, I believe that the amount of money in your bank account is only one method, a way to measure wealth in particular, there are many forms of wealth. You know, there are a lot of people I worked with, as a coach, a success coach, an **executive**[2]

注释　1. **trap** [træp] *n.* 陷阱；困境　　　　2. **executive** [ɪɡˈzekjutɪv] *n.* 主管，行政部门

coach, who have economic abundance, a very high level of economic abundance, they've hundreds of millions of dollars in their bank account, and yet they're not happy, they don't have such a sense of connection with other human beings, so what I am trying to say is economic abundance is only one form of wealth, and there are many people who are rich, and yet they are not what I would call wealthy because they don't have all the five of the forms of wealth.

So here is the idea, there are five forms of wealth, and having each of those will make you a truly wealthy or successful person. The first form of wealth, is Economic Abundance, is having money. I think money is important, it makes life easier, it gives you freedom.

The second form of wealth, is what I call Relational Wealth. We have a deep need as human beings for community and a sense of **belongings**[3]. If you have lots of money, but you are not connected with human beings, you don't have great relationships, you don't know your family, you have no friends, I don't think you're wealthy, you might be rich. So the second form of wealth is relational wealth—strong relationships.

The third form of wealth is Health. If you have your good health, you are wealthy in so many ways. There are so many people suffering from illness, they don't experience wellness, so it is important to put your health No. 1 and take care of the temple which is your body.

The fourth point, the fourth form of wealth is Adventure. I believe in life in so many ways, life is all about having adventure, so it's important to have fun. There are a lot of people who have a lot of money, but who don't have fun. They don't have that childlike sense of wonder, they don't enjoy living in the moment, they don't know how to play. So they forgot the child that lives within them. One psychologist said "Adults are nothing more than **deteriorated**[4] children". And I find it is a form of wealth when you connect with this childlike spirit to make what you have lost.

And then the fifth form of wealth is **Contribution**[5] and Impact. A lot of people have a lot of money, but they don't have a sense of meaning, they don't have a sense that they are making a difference. And one of the highest of all human hungers is this hunger to know that we are not working to plan it in vain, that the world in some way, no matter how small way, is better because we agree to plan it. So I think it's really important to find true wealth in your life to work out all five of these forms of wealth in concern.

Now, Let me give you some simple **tactics**[6] to help you work out each of these five forms of wealth. No. 1, Economic Wealth, work with a financial coach; No.2 , come up with a game plan, another tactic around this economic wealth is to save 10% of what you earn. Some tools for tackling with the second form of wealth is what I call Relational Wealth. Put people first, that will help you build great relationships, spend time with people. (and) MTP, meet the people, face time is so important. Another idea is around Relational Wealth and build them around your life. Leave people better than you find them, some kind of awakening of two-day personal work transformation works out, called the "Awakening by Self-wakening", people from all around the world come to

---

3. **belongings** [bɪˈlɒŋɪŋz] n. 所有物，财产
4. **deteriorate** [dɪˈtɪərɪəreɪt] vi. 恶化，变坏
5. **contribution** [ˌkɒntrɪˈbjuːʃən] n. 贡献；促成作用
6. **tactics** [ˈtæktɪks] n. 策略；战术

learn how to break through their field and live a greatest life. I know a gentleman in the recent Awakening by Self-wakening, his name is John, and he came from Miami, he said my organizing principle in each day is pretty simple, it's to leave everyone I meet better than I found them. That's a great way to build Relational Wealth.

Another idea on that is to be the kindest person you know. Deal with the third form of wealth—health. Some ideas: exercise five times a week, eat ultra well because diet affects your health, of course. And really take care of the temple that is your body.

Some tactics around the fourth form of wealth—Adventure, have fun, make the time to dance in the park, make the time to listen to some great music, make the time to laugh. The human brain, according to the latest scientific research, the human brain creates novelty. So really, a great way to become happier is to challenge yourself through adventures. One of the things that I teach my coaching clients is that each week have a micro-adventure. So you don't know how to go down to the Bahamas or go parasailing or whatever it is. In your week, you can actually inject micro-adventures onto your schedule to increase the adventure level into your life. What is an example of the micro-adventure? It could be to try a new type of food if you've never tried Vietnamese food go and do that. You could be going to an **art gallery**[7] that you have never been to before. You could have lunch with the Yoga teacher, or a painter or someone with whom you have doing something you have never done. So that you can learn, and expand your horizons.

And some tactics for this fifth which is approximately the important forms of wealth—which is Contribution and Impact. Some ideas: No. 1: Do you impart to improve the world, do you impart to improve the community, do you impart to improve the organization that you are working for. Another idea—Volunteer. You know no matter what your problems are, I guarantee you there are people who are suffering from something that is even more serious, it makes me think that Persian proverb "I **curse**[8] the fact that I had no shoes on my feet until I saw a man who had no feet." So make sure that you focus on contribution and making the world a better place with the work that you do each day or what you do each day. It makes me think of my dad's comment, "When you were born, you cried while the world rejoiced." He said, "Son, make sure you live a life in such a way that when you die, the world cries while you **rejoice**.[9]" Or as Mark Twin once said, "Live your life in such a way that when you die, even the undertaker has tears in his eyes."

OK, those are the five forms of wealth: Economic Wealth; Relational Wealth; Health Wealth; Adventure and finally, the fifth form of wealth: Contribution and Impact. Work on each form of those five and you will truly get to a place, not only wealth—true wealth, but great happiness.

注释

7. **gallery** ['gælərɪ] *n.* 画廊、美术馆

8. **curse** [kɜːs] *v.* 咒骂、诅咒

9. **rejoice** [rɪ'dʒɔɪs] *vi.* 感到高兴、充满喜悦

原文翻译

大家好，我是罗宾·夏玛，欢迎各位参加今天这个关于"财富的五个表现形式"的播客。大家知道，很多人都陷入这个怪圈，即仅仅从经济角度来评判财富；也就是说，根据他人银行户头上的存款来判断财富。看看周围的一些人，或者从他人口中听说，或者从电视中看到，我们会说他们如此勤奋，因此理所当然应该富有，实际上我们在试图说明自己不是成功人士。现在，我想说出自己的这个大观点，我认为银行账户里的存款数只是一种评判财富的独特方法和途径，实际上，财富有很多表现形式。作为一个教练，一个研究成功之道的教练，一个执行教练，我曾经在工作中遇到很多人，他们拥有巨大的财富，其数目非常之巨，他们银行账户上的存款多达数百万美金。但是，他们并不幸福，他们缺乏和他人之间交流的概念。因此，我想说的是，经济层面的富有只是财富的一个表现形式，有很多有钱人，但是我却不会将其称为富人，那是因为他们并没有拥有全部的五种表现形式的财富。

这就是我的观点，财富有五个表现形式，只有拥有其中每一个表现层面，你才会变得富有和成功。财富的第一个表现形式，便是经济上的富有，也就是拥有足够的金钱。我认为金钱的确很重要，它能使生活更加舒适安逸，它能使你拥有足够的自由。

财富的第二个表现形式，我把它称为关系财富。作为人类，我们非常需要群体感和归属感。如果你非常有钱，但是却从不与他人交往，你没有很好的人际关系，对你的家人都不了解，并且没有朋友。如果是这样，我认为你并不富有，也许你只能被称为有钱人。因此，财富的第二个表现形式是丰富的关系网——即拥有很强大的社交圈。

财富的第三个表现形式是健康。如果你拥有健康的身体，那么可以说你在很多方面都很富有。很多人饱受疾病折磨，甚至没有清醒的神智，因此应该把身体健康放在第一位，时刻关注你的身体这座庙宇。

第四点，财富的第四个表现形式是冒险。我用各种方法来阐释生活，生活就是充满了种种冒险，因此重要的是要有生活的乐趣。很多有钱人并没有找到生活的乐趣。他们没有孩子般的好奇心，他们不会享受当下的生活，也不知道如何去自娱自乐。因此，他们忘记了他们心中的童趣。一个心理学家曾经说道："成年人不过是变坏了的孩子。"当你以这种孩子般的精神去找寻你失去的一些事物时，我认为这是财富的一种表现形式。

财富的第五个表现形式是奉献和影响。很多有钱人，却没有生活的意义，并没有感觉与他人有何不同。在所有人类的渴求中，最需要解决的是我们要知道，我们并不是徒劳地在努力改变着世界，这个世界将会由于我们的努力而变得更好，不管这种变化多么细微。我认为，去寻找人们一生中真正的财富，使得财富的这五个表现形式都得以实现是至关重要的。

现在，我要告诉大家一些技巧，使财富的这些表现形式逐一成为现实。首先，经济财富，找一个财务教练来帮助你；其次，制订活动计划。此外，围绕经济财富这一层面给大家另外一个建议，即把自己收入的10%积攒下来。谈到财富的第二个表现形式，即我所谓的关系财富，要先人后己，这样才能帮助你建立完美的关系网络，多花时间和他人沟通，我们将其称为MTP，就是说多和他人当面沟通，面对面的交谈时间颇为重要。关于丰富的关系，把周围的人建成一个有力的关系网。我还想谈及另外一个观点，即同周围的人和平相处远比可以去找寻关系网要好得多。有一个被称为"两天个人工作转变"的活动非常有效，来自世界各地的人聚集一堂，试图学会如何在自己的领域里有所突破，如何才能拥有伟大的人生。在最近的"个人反思活动"中，我结识了一位先生，名叫约翰，他来自迈阿密，他说我每天的管理方法颇为简单，这种方法就是让我碰到的每个人感觉他们比我所发现的更好。这是建立关系财富很重要的方法。

另一个诀窍就是成为一个尽可能善良的人。关于发展第三个形式的财富——健康，我的建议是每周锻炼5次；注重饮食，当然是因为饮食会影响健康。要真正关心自己的身体。

关于财富的第四种表现形式——冒险，要开心一些，花时间在公园里跳舞，抽空去欣赏美妙的音乐，找空笑一笑。根据最新的科学研究表明，人类的大脑惯于产生新奇的事物。因此，获得幸福的一个很好的途径，便是在冒险中挑战自我。我教给我那些受训客户的办法有：每周进行一次小的冒险。你不知道在去巴哈马群岛或做帆船运动时会发生什么，或者不管会有什么发生。在你的周计划中，实际上，你可以把这些小小的冒险安排到你的日程表中，从而提升你人生的冒险水平。能举一个小冒险的例子吗？比如去尝试一种新的食物。如果你从没有尝试过越南食物，就去试试吧。也可以是去参观一个你从未去过的艺术展。还可以是和你的瑜伽老师或画师或与你一起合作进行从未尝试过的事物的人士共进午餐。这样，你会学到一些知识，你会提高自己的水平层次。

关于第五点——也许是财富最重要的表现形式——奉献和影响。我想给出以下办法：第一，你是否为改善世界出过力？你是否为改善社区出过力？是否为自己曾经工作过的组织出过力？另一个想法——去担任志愿者。大家知道，不管你遇到什么样的难题，我敢保证还有人正在遭受着比你更大的不幸。我想起了那个波斯古谚："我抱怨我的脚上没有鞋可穿，却发现有人连脚都没有。"因此，一定要为世界作出贡献，使得这个世界变成一个你工作或者他能够每天工作的好地方。我还想起了我父亲曾经跟我说的话。他说道"当你出生的时候，你大声啼哭，而周围的人都为此欢呼。"父亲告诉我："儿子，你的一生应该这样度过：当你去世的时候，你含笑而去，而整个世界却悲痛无比。"或者如马克·吐温所说的："人的一生应该这样度过，当你去世的时候，就连殡葬业人员都眼泪汪汪。"

好，这就是财富的五个表现形式：经济财富、丰富的关系网、健康财富、冒险精神以及最后第五个表现层面——奉献和影响。为财富的这五个表现层面而努力工作，你一定会达到一种境界——不仅仅是富裕，实际的富有，而是最大的幸福。

文化点滴

Robin Sharma

罗宾·夏玛是夏玛领导学国际学社的创办人，该学社是受人推崇的训练公司，专门研究在快速变迁的时代中，如何开拓领导学及个人与组织团体的潜能表现，委托受训的单位包括《财富》500强企业、全国各主要协会和大型保健机构。拥有两个法律学位的罗宾·夏玛曾是一位杰出的诉讼律师，现今更是家喻户晓的媒体名人。罗宾·夏玛经常出现在世界各大媒体上，他参加过1000多场电视和电台节目的演讲，在全球颇受欢迎，被称为"心灵激励导师"。杰克·韦尔奇、比尔·克林顿、菲尔博士、迪帕克·乔普拉以及韦恩·戴尔等人经常聆听他的教诲，他用富有感召力和充满智慧的演讲，以及自己对生活的深刻感悟，改变了无数人的命运。

podcast

中文译名尚未统一，但最多的是将其翻译为"播客"。播客是Ipod+broadcasting的合成词。它是数字广播技术的一种，出现初期借助一个叫"iPodder"的软件与一些便携播放器相结合而实现。podcasting录制的是网络广播或类似的网络声讯节目，网友可将网上的广播节目下载到自己的iPod、MP3播放器或其他便携式数码声讯播放器中随身收听，不必端坐电脑前，也不必实时收听，享受随时随地的自由。更有意义的是，你还可以自己制作声音节目，并将其上传到网上与广大网友分享。

写作特点

本文层次严谨,脉络清晰,基本采用了一种"总—分—总"的写作模式。先是总说了财富有五种表现形式,然后分别对这五种表现形式予以说明,最后一段强调主题,并且得出自然而然的结论。这种写作模式比较容易把握,同时也是初学写作的学生最应该把握的一种写法。

品味鉴赏

财富的五个表现形式:经济财富、丰富的关系网、健康财富、冒险精神以及奉献和影响。真正富有的人是同时具备这五个表现形式的。而单独具有一两种,并不是完备"富有"的人。本文作者也正表达出这样的意思,即文章最后:为财富的这五个表现层面而努力工作,你一定会达到一种境界——不仅仅是富裕,实际的富有,而是最大的幸福。让我们牢记吧,为这些而努力奋斗就是在追求最大的幸福。

美文感悟